D1600263

Cromwell's major-generals

Godly government during the English Revolution

Christopher Durston

Manchester
University Press

Manchester and New York

distributed exclusively in the USA by Palgrave

Copyright © Christopher Durston 2001

The right of Christopher Durston to be identified as the author of this work has been asserted by him in accordance with the Copyright, Designs and Patents Act 1988.

Published by Manchester University Press
Oxford Road, Manchester M13 9NR, UK
and Room 400, 175 Fifth Avenue, New York, NY 10010, USA
http://www.manchesteruniversitypress.co.uk

Distributed exclusively in the USA by
Palgrave, 175 Fifth Avenue, New York, NY 10010, USA

Distributed exclusively in Canada by
UBC Press, University of British Columbia, 2029 West Mall,
Vancouver, BC, Canada V6T 1Z2

British Library Cataloguing-in-Publication Data
A catalogue record for this book is available from the British Library

Library of Congress Cataloging-in-Publication Data applied for

ISBN 0 7190 5187 8 *hardback*
ISBN 0 7190 6065 6 *paperback*

First published 2001

10 09 08 07 06 05 04 03 02 01   10 9 8 7 6 5 4 3 2 1

Typeset in Scala with Pastonchi display
by Koinonia Ltd, Manchester

Printed in Great Britain
by Bookcraft (Bath) Ltd, Midsomer Norton

FOR JOHN MORRILL
in thanks for a quarter of a century
of help and encouragement

'The search for facts, for places, names, influential events, important conversations and correspondences, political circumstances – all this amounts to nothing if you can't find the assumption your subject lives by.' (Anne Michaels, *Fugitive Pieces*)

'Religion can never be deemed a point of small consequence in civil government. But during this period it may be regarded as the great spring of men's actions and determinations.' (David Hume, *The History of Great Britain*)

'The roots of this Queen's Speech really belong with Cromwell's major-generals. There lies the root of the Government's puritanism. Are we talking about smoking, pistol shooting or country sports? If people enjoy it, ban it. ... In the short term, it is popular stuff. The British have always had a puritanical streak, and it is easy enough to appeal to it – for a while. I warn the Government that the British public's tolerance of puritanism runs out quite quickly.' (Andrew Rowe MP, House of Commons, 19 May 1997)

Contents

LIST OF MAPS AND TABLES—viii
ACKNOWLEDGEMENTS—ix
LIST OF ABBREVIATIONS—x

1 Introduction: background and historiography—1

2 The system: origins and construction—15

3 The men: backgrounds, careers and beliefs—38

4 The helpers: the commissioners for securing
the peace of the commonwealth—59

5 New local government and old local government—73

6 The decimation tax—97

7 Securing the peace of the commonwealth—127

8 The struggle for the godly nation—154

9 The major-generals and the 1656 election—187

10 Defeat at Westminster and fall from power—206

11 Conclusion—228

Postscript: The major-generals' later careers—234

SELECT BIBLIOGRAPHY—240
INDEX—251

List of maps and tables

Map 1   The major-generals' associations—30

Table 1   The major-generals' associations—31

Table 2   Numbers of parliamentary seats and exclusions
in the major-generals' associations—200

Acknowledgements

A number of distinguished historians have set out in the past to write a detailed history of the major-generals' experiment, only to abandon the attempt for a variety of reasons. Halfway into writing this book, I nearly became just one more scholar who had started the project and then shelved it. This has not proved an easy book to write and undoubtedly remains far from perfect. It would have been much less satisfactory but for the generous support and assistance I received from a considerable number of friends and colleagues. I should like to express my deep thanks to Barry Coward, Sue Doran, Peter Gaunt, Simon Healy, Clive Holmes, Ann Hughes, Sean Kelsey, John Morrill, Michael Questier, Henry Reece and Austin Woolrych, all of whom commented on sections of the text, and most of whom read the entire transcript of the book – sometimes more than once! Their comments and suggestions have proved invaluable and have saved me from numerous errors and misinterpretations. All remaining mistakes are, of course, entirely my own responsibility. Considerable thanks are also due to my colleagues in the History Programme at Strawberry Hill, for fostering what for some years now has proved a highly stimulating and supportive research environment.

I should like to acknowledge the generous financial support provided by the St Mary's Research Fund which allowed me two periods of research leave to work on the book as well as travel expenses to libraries and record offices. I should like also to express my gratitude to the staffs of the Bodleian Library, British Library, Public Record Office, Dr Williams's Library, and the county records offices in Bedfordshire, Buckinghamshire, Cheshire, Essex, Hampshire, Kent, Lancashire, Northamptonshire, Oxfordshire, Staffordshire, West Yorkshire, Wiltshire and Worcestershire. Thanks are also due to Ros Durston and Ruth Mellor for their help with the map. Some of the material in chapter 10 was included in my paper on the fall of the major-generals published in *English Historical Review* in 1998. I am grateful to the editors and the publisher, Oxford University Press, for permission to reproduce it here.

List of abbreviations

Abbott, *Writings and Speeches of Cromwell*   W. C. Abbott, *The Writings and Speeches of Oliver Cromwell* (4 vols, Cambridge, Mass., 1937–47)

Birch, *State Papers of John Thurloe*   Thomas Birch (ed.), *A Collection of the State Papers of John Thurloe Esq.* (7 vols, London, 1742)

BL   British Library, London

BL, E.   British Library London, Thomason Tracts Collection

Bod. Lib.   Bodleian Library, Oxford

DNB   *Dictionary of National Biography*

Firth and Rait, *Acts and Ordinances*   C. H. Firth and R. S. Rait (eds), *Acts and Ordinances of the Interregnum* (3 vols, London, 1911)

Gardiner, *Commonwealth and Protectorate*   Samuel Rawson Gardiner, *The History of the Commonwealth and Protectorate, 1649–1656* (4 vols, New York, 1965 edn)

HMC   Historic Manuscripts Commission

Macfarlane, *Diary of Ralph Josselin*   Alan Macfarlane (ed.), *The Diary of Ralph Josselin, 1616–1683* (London, 1976)

Morrill, Cheshire   J. S. Morrill, *Cheshire 1630–1660: County Government and Society during the English Revolution* (Oxford, 1974)

PRO   Public Record Office, Kew, London

Rutt, *Diary Of Thomas Burton*   J. T. Rutt (ed.), *The Diary of Thomas Burton Esq.* (4 vols, London, 1828)

Punctuation has been modernised in quotations. The year has been taken to begin on 1 January.

Chapter 1

—◆—

Introduction:
background and historiography

During the years from 1637 to 1655, the British Isles witnessed some of the most dramatic and destructive events in their entire history. In the late 1630s and early 1640s Charles I lost control of all three of his British kingdoms. In 1637 his Scottish subjects rose up in rebellion in protest at his attempt to impose a Laudian prayer book upon their church, and in 1640 a Scottish army invaded England and inflicted a humiliating military defeat upon Charles near Newcastle. In late 1641, the native Catholic population of Ulster launched a series of violent attacks upon the Protestant colonists who had been planted in their province over the previous thirty years. Within a couple of years their revolt had spread throughout Ireland and a provisional Catholic government had gained control of much of the island. At the end of 1640, the English MPs of the Long Parliament met at Westminster and over the ensuing eighteen months made strenuous efforts to resolve peacefully the serious political and religious differences with Charles which had accumulated over the course of his personal rule in the 1630s. Although a great deal of remedial legislation was enacted during 1641, ingrained mutual fear and distrust ultimately prevented any settlement and in 1642 the English parliament, too, resorted to arms.

The first civil war divided communities and families throughout England and inflicted considerable economic, social and psychological damage upon the nation. In the region of 80,000 soldiers were killed or injured in the numerous battles, sieges and sackings of the war, and a much greater number of civilians suffered from the food shortages, diseases and unprecedented financial demands which the armies brought in their wake. After parliament had emerged victorious in the summer of 1646, the following eighteen months witnessed a series of attempts by both the Long Parliament and the New Model Army to persuade the king to accept constitutional and religious concessions. Charles, however, eschewed all offers of a settlement and at the end of 1647 concluded instead a secret alliance with his Scottish subjects which led to a resumption of the conflict. This second civil war, which ended with another royalist defeat in the autumn of 1648, produced a considerable hardening of attitudes against Charles, and in its aftermath the New Model Army moved quickly to bring him to justice. After purging from parliament all the MPs they considered unsympathetic to their cause, the army leaders put Charles on trial at the beginning of 1649, found him guilty of committing high treason against his people, and executed him on 30 January.

In the wake of this momentous act of regicide, the New Model Army remained in effective control of the English state throughout the early 1650s. From February 1649 to April 1653, an executive council of state ruled in conjunction with the Rump of the Long Parliament, made up of those members whom the army had allowed to retain their seats in 1648. During 1650 and 1651, the army was preoccupied with the need to subdue Ireland and Scotland. Oliver Cromwell's ruthless crushing of Irish resistance in 1649 and 1650 was followed by the implementation of a policy of plantation and transportation which laid the foundations for the subsequent Protestant ascendancy in Ireland. Similarly, the defeats of the Scots at the battles of Dunbar and Worcester led to the English occupation of much of Scotland and its subsequent incorporation into the English state.

Once these campaigns had been successfully concluded at the end of 1651, the English army turned its attentions to persuading the Rump to introduce a number of constitutional, religious and legal reforms. When the MPs reacted slowly and unenthusiastically to this programme, the army increased the pressure upon them. In April 1653, its patience finally ran out and Cromwell forcibly dissolved the Rump, thereby removing the last vestige of legally constituted English government. The expulsion of the Rump was followed by the experiment of entrusting constitutional reform to the nominated members of Barebone's Parliament. This body, however, proved equally unpalatable to the army leadership, and at the end of 1653 the English republic was laid aside in favour of a more conservative protectorate, and the commander-in-chief of the army, Oliver Cromwell, was appointed head of state with the title Lord Protector.

The new protectoral constitution was laid out in the Instrument of Government, which established a system of mixed government, in which power was shared between the Lord Protector, a council and a parliament elected on a conservative, propertied franchise. The powers of the protector were substantial. He was appointed for life, with no provision for removal from office. All government documents ran in his name and he was the only source of public preferment or pardon. While he was expected to consult both his council and parliament, he had the final choice of the members of the former body and was only obliged to call the latter for five months every three years. He could delay and veto legislation and, probably because of an error in the drafting of the document, was given power over the army in the intervals between parliaments. He could also raise additional forces in the form of a reservist militia, although he was obliged to seek retrospective sanction for such troops when a parliament was called.

Over the course of 1654, Cromwell consulted his council on a regular basis and attended many of its sessions; in Peter Gaunt's phrase, he allowed it 'to play a substantial role in protectoral central government, handling the highest matters of State as well as the day-to-day mass of routine ... business'.[1] But, although the councillors were allowed to exercise real power in their own right, with the exception of John Lambert they lacked the necessary authority and independence seriously to challenge Cromwell and in reality rarely opposed his wishes. In contrast, when the first protectorate parliament met in September 1654, the MPs began by mounting a spirited attack on the Instrument of Government and later attempted to reduce both the size of the New Model Army and the taxation raised for its maintenance. The executive countered this threat first by forcing all those who wished to sit to sign a recognition of their suppport for the regime, and subsequently by dissolving it as soon as the five-month minimum period specified in the Instrument had elapsed. Thus, as Peter Gaunt has again commented, 'the overwhelming consensus of contemporary opinion that Cromwell towered over the protectorate and effectively controlled most aspects of central government is almost certainly correct in essence.'[2]

The real source of Cromwell's power at the beginning of 1655 remained, of course, the New Model Army. At the end of 1654, approximately 53,000 soldiers were under arms within the British Isles. Around 23,000 of these were serving in Ireland, nearly another 19,000 in Scotland, and the remaining 11,000 within England. Roughly 3,000 of those in England were stationed in London, while the remainder were dispersed among the thirty or so provincial garrisons situated mainly along the coast and on the Welsh and Scottish borders.[3] Some of the army's officers had been deeply disturbed by the establishment of the protectorate and during the course of 1654 a number had either been dismissed or resigned their commissions. Although Cromwell could not afford to take the loyalty of the remaining generals for granted, at the beginning of 1655 he continued to be regarded with enormous respect by both the high command and the rank and file soldiers, and the pre-eminent place in the army's affections he had enjoyed for more than a decade was not under serious threat.

In order to maintain such a large standing army, the protectoral government was forced to impose extremely heavy taxes upon the nation. At the beginning of 1655, the government was demanding £90,000 a month from the country under the direct assessment tax, as well as continuing to collect the hated excise tax. Unsurprisingly, these high levels of taxation were deeply unpopular and did nothing to endear the political nation either to Cromwell himself or to the army that sustained him. But even at this unprecedentedly high level, they nonetheless remained inadequate to meet the regime's expenses. By early 1655, the government was running at an annual deficit of around £700,000 and as a consequence was facing an acute and growing financial crisis.

One obvious way to address this problem was to reduce the size of the army, but Cromwell was very reluctant to take this step which he feared might leave him vulnerable to attack from his many external and internal enemies. His rule was fiercely opposed both by radical republicans and conservative royalists. Many religious and political radicals believed that, by accepting the position of Lord Protector, Cromwell had betrayed the 'good old cause' of republicanism, and erstwhile colleagues, such as John Bradshaw, Sir Arthur Haselrig and Edmund Ludlow, were by 1655 deeply hostile to the regime and regarded as a major security risk. Some of the radical religious sects were also causing the government concern. Groups of Fifth Monarchists were calling publicly for the violent overthrow of all secular authority as a prelude to the rule of the saints and the Second Coming of King Jesus, and members of the rapidly growing Quaker movement were refusing to recognise the legitimacy of the government and preaching a potentially explosive creed of social egalitarianism.

From the other end of the political spectrum, Cromwell's government also faced the implacable hostility of the exiled Stuart court and its thousands of supporters within England. Throughout the early 1650s, an active royalist underground had been attempting to destabilise the regime and, while its activities were closely monitored by the government's intelligence service, it continued to present a serious threat to the protectorate's survival. Many hundreds of other English royalists had declined to become actively involved in conspiracy and had remained quiescent during the early 1650s. In 1652 the Rump had passed an Act of Oblivion, offering those who had refrained from acting against the state since the battle of Worcester in September 1651 a pardon for their earlier treasons and felonies. But, while the opposition of most royalists to those who had deposed their king was passive rather than active, the great majority had nonetheless refused to become reconciled to the new regime. The fact that around 4,000 of them had had their lands sequestered and been forced to pay heavy composition fines during the late 1640s to regain them still rankled deeply. Further causes of complaint included the exempting from the Act of Oblivion of a number of named individuals and all those whose estates remained under sequestration or who were in prison under a parliamentary warrant, as well as the sale of the estates of around 750 royalists under acts passed by the Rump in 1651 and 1652. As a result of these and other grievances, the small band of active conspirators could rely on the tacit support and encouragement of the wider English royalist community, which continued to hope that Cromwell's regime might be toppled by an armed rising, the assassination of its head, or a mutiny by a republican section of the army.[4]

The political situation at the beginning of 1655 was, then, far from favourable for Cromwell and his advisers. Facing a deep and growing financial crisis, they had failed to persuade the MPs of the 1654 parliament that they should be given the fiscal and political backing that might have enabled them to begin the process of civilianising and legitimising their rule. As a result of the sterility of the parliament and the continuing hostility they faced from so many internal and external enemies, they did not feel sufficiently secure to distance themselves from the large and powerful army upon which their survival ultimately depended, but which was also deeply unpopular with the bulk of the population. The failure of the 1654 parliament to pursue the godly reformation whichwas so central to the aims of Cromwell's puritan regime was another major reason why the government was loath to break its ties with an army which was still firmly committed to the godly cause. The major-generals' experiment, which was launched in the autumn of 1655, was an attempt to square this particularly vicious political circle by enhancing the security of the regime and furthering godly reform, while at the same time reducing the overall burden of the large military establishment.

The rule of Cromwell's major-generals over the English provinces lasted for little more than a year. Appointed in the late autumn of 1655, the major-generals were active within their respective associations for at most ten months before they left for Westminster in September 1656 to take up their seats in the second protectorate parliament. Four months later in January 1657 they fell from power, following the voting down of a militia bill which they had hoped would provide them with the permanent revenue source upon which they could finance their continued rule. Despite the brevity of their period of power, however, many historians have argued that the episode was not only of great contemporary significance but also that it exerted a profound and lasting influence over later political developments and attitudes within England.

Over the course of the last three and a half centuries, successive gener-ations of commentators have overwhelmingly concluded that the rule of the major-generals was ill-conceived, unconstitutional, oppressive and deeply unpopular. The stark condemnation began when they were still in power. In the autumn of 1656, William Prynne denounced them in passionate terms, arguing that, unless they took steps to expiate their guilt, they would 'acquire the perpetual infamy of the most detestable perjury, treachery, hypocrisy, fraud, impiety, apotasy, tyranny, atheism that ever any Christian saint-like army and officer were guilty of in the eyes of God and men'.[5] Many subsequent scholars took their cue from Prynne and delivered similarly violent denunciations. In the 1820s, the Whig historian, Henry Hallam, labelled their rule as 'a despotism compared to which all the illegal practices of former kings ... appeared as dust', and a generation later the French writer and statesman, François Guizot, described it as 'one of those necessities inflicted by the justice of God, which reveal the innate viciousness of a government'.[6] In 1934 one of Cromwell's biographers, John Buchan, claimed that the the rule of the major-generals was 'the most intolerable experience England ever had', and three years later Alfred Wood, the historian of mid seventeenth-century Nottinghamshire, declared: 'it is at least certain that the rule of the sword and the rule of the saints ... were burnt into the minds of average, tolerant English-men as outrages which must never be permitted to occur again.'[7] Forty years later Ivan Roots claimed their period of rule was 'a monstrous apparition scaring the normal rulers of the countryside, who fancied they saw social as well as political and administrative revolution lurking in the dark shadows cast by musket and sword'.[8]

These and many other scholarly critics have attacked the major-generals on a number of linked but distinct grounds. Some writers have seen them principally as *parvenu* social upstarts, who were unused and unsuited to exercising authority and whose main preoccupation during their brief period of power was the vindictive persecution of their social betters. In his *A Detection of the Court and State of England*, published in 1694, the royalist writer, Roger Coke, labelled the major-generals an 'obscure company of mean fellows', who he claimed had 'lorded it over the nobility as well as gentry and clergy with an unheard of insolency'.[9] A few years later, the Tory historian, Laurence Echard, repeated the charge that they had 'lorded it over the nobility and gentry of the nation', adding that they had been 'imperious' in their dealings with Cromwell's aristocratic supporters.[10] In the mid nineteenth century, François Guizot commented dismissively during his discussion of their rule that 'persons of inferior quality ... are always ready to revel in the enjoyment of authority as of a rare and fleeting pleasure.'[11]

A second major strand of criticism has concentrated on the unashamedly military nature of their rule. In his *History of England* published in the 1870s, the German historian, Leopold von Ranke, created a nightmarish picture of England under the major-generals as a military state where 'every two miles troops were posted', where the roads were constantly watched by military patrols, and where 'day and night the soldiers were actively employed'.[12] In the mid 1950s Austin Woolrych argued that they had made 'much more im-mediate and irksome the "sword government" which was the most unpopular and easily criticised aspect of Cromwell's rule', and that as a result 'the experiment could only be hated'.[13] Several historians have claimed that the abiding legacy of the rule of the major-generals was the creation within all levels of English society of a deep hostility to the involvement of the army in politics. Godfrey Davies argued in the 1950s that, while their rule had been too shortlived to have a permanent effect on the morality of the English state, it had 'lasted long enough to leave behind it an abiding hatred of militarism'.[14] Not long after, Christopher Hill claimed that as a result of their actions subsequent generations of English people developed a negative conception of liberty within which 'freedom means being left alone'.[15] He later declared that they had 'left behind them in the memory of the ruling class a fixed hatred of standing armies that is one of the most important legacies of the revolutionary decades'.[16]

For some other historians the major-generals were above all else the agents of centralisation who were resented and opposed primarily because they represented a threat to long-established traditions of local autonomy and self-government. Paul Christianson, for example, declared in 1976 that their rule was 'the most stringent central invasion of local privileges and customs of the century', and a few years later Clive Holmes argued that they were 'the epitome of central interference in local government and their operations aroused very considerable antipathy'.[17] Yet another stream of criticism has emphasised the major-generals' adoption of the role of moral policemen and their spearheading of a determined campaign to bring about a godly reformation. One particularly influential scholar who saw this aspect of their work as the prime source of their unpopularity was Samuel Rawson Gardiner. In his *History of the Commonwealth and Protectorate*, published between 1897 and 1901, Gardiner argued that, if the major-generals had restricted themselves to security measures, 'posterity would have heard little of the illegality of their commissions', and went on to claim that 'it was as discouragers of vice and encouragers of virtue that they aroused the most virulent opposition.'[18]

The most common charge levelled against the major-generals by hostile scholars, however, has been that their administration was unrestrained, unconstitutional and fundamentally un-English. In 1656 William Prynne roundly denounced their 'exorbitant tyrannical proceedings', which he claimed involved the 'taxing, decimating, disofficing, disfranchising and sequestering all sorts of men in counties and corporations at their pleasure'.[19] After the Restoration, the antiquarian, William Dugdale, argued that they had 'not only exercised their authority in an arbitrary and unlimited manner, but at length grew so insolent that he [Cromwell] thought it not fit to continue them'.[20] In the 1740s, the leading light of the Scottish Enlightenment, David Hume, declared in his *History of Great Britain* that 'under cover of their powers which were sufficiently exorbitant, the major-generals exercised an authority still more arbitrary and acted as absolute masters of the property and persons of every subject.'[21] At the close of the nineteenth century, Charles Firth similarly claimed that their rule had been 'despotic' and had provoked widespread opposition even amongst the regime's strongest supporters.[22]

Drawing on his extensive knowledge of English medieval history, William Prynne had likened the major-generals' administration to that of Richard I's unpopular viceregent, William Longchamp, who 'had placed mercenary soldiers in every county to over awe and enslave the people'. As he himself pointed out, however, the analogy which was much more commonly employed by his contemporaries was the comparing of the major-generals with the 'bashaws and beglerbegs' who governed the subject nations of the Turkish Empire.[23] This eastern allusion was eagerly picked up by later writers and became a persistent *topos* of the historiography of the major-generals for well over a century. Between 1660 and 1800, the major-generals were repeatedly decried as 'Turkish bashaws' and their militia troops as 'bands of janissaries' by commentators from across the ideological spectrum, including the royalists, James Heath and Edward Hyde, the Tories, Laurence Echard and David Hume, and the republicans, Edmund Ludlow and Catherine Macaulay.[24] The dominant theme in the work of all these writers was that the powers enjoyed by the major-generals were vast, alien and arbitrary in nature and that, as David Hume put it, they were exercised 'not in the legal manner of European nations, but according to the maxims of eastern tyranny'.[25]

The decline of Turkish power during the nineteenth century drained this image of much of its power, and during the twentieth century hostile historians were forced to employ other negative reference points to condemn the major-generals' rule. During the 1940s, the editor of Cromwell's letters and speeches, Wilbur Cortez Abbott, described the episode as 'a military despotism such as England had never seen and never saw again', and went on to suggest that comparisons between the major-generals and 'Soviet commissars, Nazi gauleiters and Fascist secretaries' contained 'a certain hard core of truth'.[26] In his study of the royalist underground of the 1650s, published in 1960, David Underdown similarly hinted at parallels with Nazi Germany, declaring: 'not all the major-generals were blustering tyrants, but there were enough instances of ill-mannered abuse from men like Boteler and Packer for the regime to be remembered only for its overtones of jack-booted militarism.'[27]

One further negative theme to emerge in some more recent studies is the suggestion that the rule of the major-generals was a serious political miscalculation by Cromwell's government, which had greatly over-estimated its own insecurity and in reality had not needed to resort to such extreme measures to guarantee its survival. At the end of his brief study of the royalist uprisings of 1655, Austin Woolrych concluded that the appointment of the major-generals was 'a serious error' and that 'later events proved that Thurloe's intelligence system sufficed in itself, with the regular forces, to secure the Protectorate.'[28] Robert Ashton has similarly argued that the major-generals did more harm than good to Cromwell's government, in that they had brought about 'the alienation of far larger sections of the population than the royalist conspirators against whom they were principally directed'.[29]

Although, throughout the entire period from 1660 to the present, not one historian has been prepared to express enthusiastic and unreserved support for the major-generals, a number of scholars have detached themselves somewhat from the dominant chorus of disapproval and attempted to defend at least some aspects of their rule. The first writer seriously to question the orthodox denigration of the major-generals was the radical republican, William Godwin. Godwin's *History of the Commonwealth of England*, published in the 1820s, was based on his extensive study of a range of primary source material, including the order books of Cromwell's council and John Thurloe's state papers, and was by far the most balanced and authoritative study of mid seventeenth-century England to appear in the two centuries which followed the Restoration. While acknowledging that the major-generals had been extremely powerful, that it had been 'dangerous to slight their commands', and that their rule had contained 'the substance of tyranny', Godwin also argued that they had not only conducted themselves with 'exemplary diligence and zeal', but had also displayed 'equity' and 'great moderation' when carrying out their orders.[30]

Another nineteenth-century writer who stood out from his contemporaries by reserving judgement on the major-generals was the idiosyncratic but influential essayist, Thomas Carlyle. A devoted admirer of Oliver Cromwell, Carlyle was naturally inclined to think well of those who had worked so closely with his great hero. Reflecting on the major-generals in his edition of Cromwell's letters and speeches published in the 1840s, he declared in his own inimitable style that: 'the powers of these men are great: much need that they be just men and wise, men fearing God and hating covetousness – all turns on that! They will be supportable, nay welcome and beneficial if so. Insupportable enough if not so'. After outlining a set of precepts by which the major-generals should be judged and introducing the possibility that they might be found not only acceptable but admirable, Carlyle disappointingly failed to go on to pass judgement on them according to these moral criteria.[31]

A second Victorian writer who was prepared to argue that the major-generals' administration may have possessed some positive features was David Watson Rannie. Rannie's article, 'Cromwell's Major-Generals', which appeared in the newly founded *English Historical Review* in 1895, was the first specialist study of their rule to be published in England. On the basis of his detailed researches in Thurloe's state papers, he argued that, while their rule had been detested by the English royalist community and 'hated by the hetero-geneous mass of anti-Oliverians everywhere', the individual major-generals had nonetheless been 'high-minded and conscientious men, aware that their functions were novel and at many points lacking in legal definition, and eager, therefore, that these drawbacks should be met by tact and wisdom at headquarters'.[32] The major-generals also received some muted and qualified approval from several prominent twentieth-century historians. In the early 1960s, Christopher Hill described their rule as 'honest and efficient' and claimed that the idea that they had 'imposed gloomy godliness on a merrie nation' was a post-Restoration myth.[33] In 1973, Gerald Aylmer similarly argued that their image as 'military satraps' and 'kill-joy puritans' was inaccurate and should be abandoned.[34] Five years later, in a short paper on the religious motivation of the major-generals, Anthony Fletcher emphasised their desire to create a fairer and more just society, and declared that they 'never shrank from their task, despite the obstacles they encountered, because their vision of a better society and their belief in God's presence constantly sustained them'.[35]

During the last forty years a number of other historians have also distanced themselves from the stream of denigration of the major-generals on the grounds that, in practice, they did not possess anything approaching the exorbitant and unrestricted powers that earlier writers had assumed. The first historian to question seriously the received wisdom that the major-generals were all powerful agents of central government whom the local communities of provincial England were powerless to resist was Anthony Fletcher. In his study of early seventeenth-century Sussex, which appeared in 1975, he argued that puritan repression had been 'more a bogey than a reality' in that county, and that the divisive nature of the major-generals' administration had fre-quently been exaggerated.[36] In subsequent work, published in the mid 1980s, he claimed that 'as an administrative expedient, the intervention of the major-generals was a fiasco', and even went so far as to suggest that, as they had been unable to impose their will on the aristocratic and magnate gentry families who exercised real power within the English counties, it was inappropriate to describe their period of office as the rule of the major-generals, for in reality they 'never did rule'.[37]

Another historian who has recently claimed that earlier denunciations of the major-generals exaggerated their contemporary significance is Henry Reece. In his detailed study of the impact of the army in Interregnum England, Reece argued that the military was a constant feature in English life through-out the 1650s and that the major-generals' experiment was little more than 'a formalisation of the army's existing role in administration, a difference of degree rather than kind'. While accepting that the decimation tax was deeply resented, Reece questioned whether the major-generals were particularly dis-liked outside the royalist community, and suggested that they had acquired their 'infamous reputation' largely as a result of their opposition to the moves to make Cromwell king in 1657.[38]

Several other historians have taken their cue from Fletcher and Reece and downplayed both the importance and unpopularity of the major-generals. In 1982, Jean Mather claimed that 'despite their reputation, the Major-Generals were not primarily moral policemen', adding that 'in many ways they were not revolutionary; they worked with the justices of the peace, sheriffs, mayors, constables and town corporations; they did not supersede them.'[39] In 1990, Austin Woolrych substantially modified his earlier view of the major-generals, arguing that 'far from acting like satraps and bashaws' they had generally sought advice and operated within the law. He went on to argue that their period of rule was 'an untidy, improvised expedient', and that its influence on the subsequent development of local government was 'minimal'.[40] From his researches into military–civilian relations in mid seventeenth-century Hampshire, Andrew Coleby concluded that there was no clear evidence in that county of any widespread dislike of a military presence. In his view, by 1655 law-abiding soldiers had been 'accepted as part of the local scene' and earlier historians had been 'over-impressed with novel agencies, such as standing armies, major-generals and electoral agents'.[41] Ronald Hutton has similarly argued that, while there is no simple answer to the question of their popularity, their rule was probably 'no great trauma for the ruled', and Derek Hirst has commented that they were not particularly novel and should not be viewed as 'the high-point of early modern centralization'.[42] David Smith has claimed that their impact was 'limited', and Barry Coward that it was 'very slight indeed'.[43]

Over the three and half centuries which divide the major-generals from the present, then, a great many scholars have passed judgement on the nature and significance of their brief period of rule. While most have denigrated them as powerful and unprincipled local despots, a few have seen them as rather more high-minded than this, and some have suggested that many of their fellow historians have greatly exaggerated their contemporary impact and significance. The ensuing study will address many of the issues raised by this historiographical debate. It will investigate why and how the major-generals' experiment was launched, what sort of men were chosen as the new governors, and how they interacted with traditional local government. It will also consider the degree of success the major-generals achieved in the implementation of their objectives in the areas of taxation, security and godly reform, and how the provincial communities of Interregnum England reacted to their rule. It will attempt to judge whether, as many earlier historians have claimed, Cromwell's major-generals were the efficient, powerful and hated agents of a strong, centralising government; whether conversely, as others have argued more recently, they were the weak, bungling, harassed and largely ignored stooges of a discredited and declining regime; or whether in reality the truth lies somewhere in between these two conflicting views.

NOTES

1 Peter Gaunt, *Oliver Cromwell* (Oxford, 1996), p. 167.

2 *Ibid.*, p. 168.

3 H. M. Reece, 'The Military Presence in England, 1649–1660' (Unpub. D.Phil. thesis, University of Oxford, 1981), p. 287. See also, John Morrill, 'Postlude: Between War and Peace, 1651–1662', in John Kenyon and Jane Ohlmeyer (eds), *The Civil Wars: A Military History of England, Scotland and Ireland, 1638–1660* (Oxford, 1998), p. 307.

4 For more details, see Paul H. Hardacre, *The Royalists During the Puritan Revolution* (The Hague, 1956), pp. 93–105.

5 BL, E.892.3, William Prynne, *A Summary Collection of the Principal Fundamental Rights, Liberties, Proprieties of all English Freemen* ... (London, 1656), p. 35.

6 Henry Hallam, *The Constitutional History of England* (London, 1827), pp. 465–6; François Guizot, *The History of Oliver Cromwell and the English Revolution* (2 vols, London, 1854), vol. 2, p. 153.

7 John Buchan, *Oliver Cromwell* (London, 1934), p. 459; A. C. Wood, *Nottinghamshire in the Civil War* (Oxford, 1937), p. 170.

8 Ivan Roots, 'Swordsmen and Decimators: Cromwell's Major-Generals', in R. H. Parry (ed.), *The English Civil War and After, 1642–1658* (London, 1970), p. 79.

9 Roger Coke, *A Detection of the Court and State of England during the Last Four Reigns and Interregnum* (2 vols, London, 1694), vol. 2, p. 52.

10 Laurence Echard, *The History of England from the Beginning of the Reign of Charles I to the Restoration of King Charles the Second* (London, 1718), p. 778.

11 Guizot, *History of Oliver Cromwell*, vol. 2, p. 151.

12 Leopold von Ranke, *The History of England Principally in the Seventeenth Century* (6 vols, Oxford, 1875), vol. 3, pp. 144–5.

13 Austin Woolrych, *Penruddock's Rising, 1655* (London, 1955), p. 24.

14 Godfrey Davies, *The Early Stuarts, 1603–1660* (Oxford, 1952 edn), p. 178.

15 Christopher Hill, *The Century of Revolution 1603–1714* (Edinburgh, 1961), pp. 189–90.

16 Christopher Hill, *God's Englishman: Oliver Cromwell and the English Revolution* (London, 1970), p. 77.

17 Paul Christianson, 'The Causes of the English Revolution: a Reappraisal', *Journal of British Studies*, 15 (1976), 74; Clive Holmes, *Seventeenth Century Lincolnshire* (Lincoln, 1980), p. 214.

18 Gardiner, *Commonwealth and Protectorate*, vol. 4, p. 29.

19 William Prynne, *A Summary Collection*, pp. 34–5.

20 William Dugdale, *A Short View of the Late Troubles in England* (Oxford, 1681), p. 450.

21 David Hume, *The History of Great Britain from the Invasion of Julius Caesar to the Revolution of 1688* (4 vols, Montrose, 1766), vol. 4, pp. 511–12.

22 C. H. Firth, 'Cromwell and the Crown, part I', *English Historical Review*, 17 (1902), 430.

23 William Prynne, *A Summary Collection*, p. 34.

24 James Heath, *A Brief Chronicle of the Late Intestine War in the Three Kingdoms of England, Scotland and Ireland* (London, 1663), pp. 698–9; Edward Hyde, earl of Clarendon, *The History of the Rebellion and Civil Wars in England*, ed. W. Dunn Macray (6 vols, Oxford, 1888), vol. 6, pp. 16–17; Echard, *The History of England*, p. 778; Hume, *The History of Great Britain*, vol. 4, pp. 511–12; C. H. Firth (ed.), *The Memoirs of Edmund Ludlow* (2 vols, Oxford, 1894), vol. 1, pp. 406, 432; vol. 2, p. 3; Catherine Macaulay, *The History of England from the Accession of James I to the Election of the House of Hannover* (8 vols, London, 1763–83), vol. 5, pp. 158–9, 173, 206.

25 Hume, *The History of Great Britain*, vol. 4, pp. 511–12.

26 Abbott, *Writings and Speeches of Cromwell*, vol. 4, pp. 62, 373.

27 David Underdown, *Royalist Conspiracy in England 1649–1660* (New Haven, 1960), p. 169.

28 Woolrych, *Penruddock's Rising*, p. 24.

29 Robert Ashton, *Reformation and Revolution, 1558–1640* (London, 1984), p. 411.

30 William Godwin, *The History of the Commonwealth of England* (4 vols, London, 1828), vol. 4, pp. 229, 239, 241–2.

31 Thomas Carlyle, *The Letters and Speeches of Oliver Cromwell* (3 vols, London, 1846), vol. 3, pp. 147–8.

32 David Watson Rannie, 'Cromwell's Major-Generals', *English Historical Review*, 10 (1895), 500–2.

33 Hill, *Century of Revolution*, pp. 137, 172.

34 G. E. Aylmer, *The State's Servants: The Civil Service of the English Republic, 1649–1660* (London, 1973), p. 48.

35 Anthony Fletcher, 'The Religious Motivation of Cromwell's Major-Generals', in D. Baker (ed.), *Religious Motivation: Biographical and Social Problems for the Church Historian*, Studies in Church History, 15 (1978), 259–66.

36 A. J. Fletcher, *A County Community in Peace and War: Sussex 1600–1660* (London, 1975), p. 311.

37 Anthony Fletcher, *Reform in the Provinces: The Government of Stuart England* (New Haven and London, 1986), p. 357; Anthony Fletcher, 'Oliver Cromwell and the Localities: The Problem of Consent', in Colin Jones, Malyn Newitt and Stephen Roberts (eds), *Politics and People in Revolutionary England* (Oxford, 1986), p. 203.

38 Reece, 'Military Presence in England', pp. 201–10.

39 Jean Mather, 'The Moral Code of the English Civil War and Interregnum', *The Historian*, 44 (1982), 217, 220.

40 Austin Woolrych, 'The Cromwellian Protectorate: A Military Dictatorship?', *History*, 75 (1990), 219–24.

41 Andrew Coleby, 'Military–Civilian Relations on the Solent', *Historical Journal*, 29 (1986), 961; Andrew Coleby, *Central Government and the Localities: Hampshire 1649–1689* (Cambridge, 1987), pp. 125, 234.

42 Ronald Hutton, *The British Republic 1649–1660* (Basingstoke, 1990), pp. 84–5; Derek Hirst, *Authority and Conflict* (London, 1986), pp. 335–8.

43 David L. Smith, *A History of the Modern British Isles 1603–1707: The Double Crown* (Oxford, 1998), p. 189; Barry Coward, *Oliver Cromwell* (London, 1991), p. 163.

Chapter 2

The system:
origins and construction

In the years that followed the execution of Charles I in 1649, the rulers of Interregnum England remained acutely aware both of the constant and pressing need to defend their new republic against the threats to its survival posed by their internal and external enemies and of the fact that the main guarantor of the regime's security was the country's very large standing army. They also, however, knew very well that the costs of this army fell heavily upon the nation's taxpayers and did nothing to endear them to their rule. Throughout the early 1650s, therefore, they were forced to pursue simultaneously two contradictory objectives: the securing of the regime against its many enemies and the reduction of the huge financial burden of defence. The rule of the major-generals, which was instituted in the autumn of 1655 with the aim of reducing the size of the regular army and providing an alternative local security force at no cost to the great majority of the nation's taxpayers, was born out of Cromwell's compelling need to find a way out of the dilemma created by these apparently incompatible aspirations.

The first eighteen months of the protectorate witnessed a number of political developments, the combined effect of which was to push Cromwell's government toward an eventual decision to embark on the major-generals' experiment. Principal amongst these were its intense disappointment at what it saw as the failure of the first protectorate parliament; the ineffective but alarming royalist insurrection of March 1655; the growing problem of government finance, which by the summer of 1655 had reached crisis proportions; and the fiasco of the Western Design to the Caribbean.

Compared with its predecessor Barebone's Parliament, the first protectorate parliament, which met in September 1654, contained a more substantial number of representatives of the traditional governing elites of the English localities. When he addressed the MPs at the start of the parliament, Cromwell was optimistic that he would be able to work with them to legitimise and consolidate the new constitutional order established by the Instrument of Government the previous December. Any such hopes were very soon, however, dashed. The members immediately launched into a frontal assault on the Instrument, and after only a week Cromwell was forced to return to Westminster to forbid all further discussion of the fundamental principles underpinning the protectorate and to insist that all those who wished to continue sitting should sign a recognition of their support for the Instrument. Even after the government's fiercest critics had refused and withdrawn, the remaining MPs continued to debate the clauses of the Instrument at interminable length over the ensuing months, an approach which Cromwell and his advisers believed cast serious doubt on the legitimacy of the regime and encouraged their enemies in their efforts to destabilise it.

To make matters worse, a committee of the House chaired by the presbyterian Colonel Thomas Birch suggested that the financial support for the government should be restricted to just over £1 million, or only around half the sum that the government believed it needed to maintain the army and provide for the country's defence. Unsurprisingly, Birch's proposal found favour with members who were anxious to reduce the fiscal burden on their constituents and Cromwell was forced to agree to a reduction in the level of both the monthly assessment and the army establishment. That he considered these developments deeply unpalatable was made clear both in his discussions with the Birch committee and his speech at the early closure of the parliament in January 1655. He told the committee that he was opposed to a reduction in the size of the army because 'the numbers were but few, [and] the condition of the people such, as the major part, a great deal, are persons disaffected and engaged against us', adding that he preferred 'safety before any manner of charge'. In his closing speech, he repeated the argument that the imminent prospect of a royalist rising made it highly inadvisable to reduce the standing army and angrily declared that 'instead of peace and settlement, instead of mercy and truth being brought together ... weeds and nettles, briars and thorns have thriven under you, shadows, dissettlement and division, discontent and dissatisfaction, together with real dangers to the whole have been more multiplied within these five months of your sitting than in some years before.'[1] Cromwell's profound disillusionment with the parliament and his fear that it was intent on weakening his regime thus did much to propel him away from further attempts to cooperate with traditional local elites and encouraged him to see the army's ongoing involvement in politics as the only sure bulwark for his regime.

Just six weeks after the end of the parliament, the insurrection which Cromwell had warned the MPs about became a reality when the underground conspiring of the royalists culminated in an attempt to stage a series of coordinated armed insurrections in a number of locations throughout England. On the evening of 8 March 1655, a group of around eighty royalists gathered near Morpeth in Northumberland with the intention of surprising Newcastle; alarmed, however, by the accidental arrival of a body of foot soldiers marching south from Berwick, they abandoned their plan and quickly dispersed. The same evening, between 100 and 300 conspirators assembled on Hessay Moor, in the hope that the gates of nearby York would be opened for them by sympathisers in the city. When this did not happen, they too scattered in panic. At Rufford Abbey in Nottinghamshire, meanwhile, another 200 royalists gathered with the intention of riding north to rendezvous with the York conspirators, but on discovering that the authorities were aware of their plans they also threw away their weapons and fled. Another planned rising in Cheshire, which involved an attempt to seize Shrewsbury in Shropshire, failed to materialise at all. In the event, therefore, the much vaunted general royalist uprising proved a shambles; as Gardiner has commented: 'what really took place on the night of the 8th was the gathering of a few isolated bodies of enthusiasts whilst the great bulk of the Royalists, refusing to sacrifice life and property in so harebrained an adventure, remained quietly at home.'[2]

A few days later, however, another and potentially more serious rising occurred in the west country. The conspirators there had originally planned to attack Winchester on the 8th, but the idea had been dropped after the town's garrison was reinforced at the last minute. On the night of 11 March, several hundred cavalry led by John Penruddock rendezvoused instead at Clarendon Park in Wiltshire, and before dawn the next morning they rode into Salisbury and arrested the high sheriff of the county and the judges who were conducting the Wiltshire assizes sessions there. After proclaiming their support for Charles Stuart, they left Salisbury and rode westward through Blandford, Sherborne and Yeovil, in the hope that the royalists of Somerset and Dorset would come in to swell their numbers. Very few, however, joined them, and several days later a small force of government troops from the garrison at Exeter caught up with them at South Molton in Devon. After a short skirmish the royalists were defeated and their leaders captured. Penruddock and the other ringleaders were subsequently tried and executed for treason.[3] These events proved a major disappointment to both the most committed royalists within England and the exiled Stuart court on the continent. They were, nonetheless, to have a profound impact on subsequent political developments, for by considerably increasing the fears of Cromwell and his council for the safety of the regime and by forcing them to contemplate unprecedented security measures, they proved a major catalyst for the introduction of the rule of the major-generals six months later.

The government's intelligence services had informed Cromwell and his advisers in the early weeks of 1655 that a major royalist rising was imminent and they had moved quickly to strengthen their military defences. Aware that it might be necessary to dispatch most of its regular soldiers to deal with trouble in the provinces, the council decided to enhance the security of London by establishing a new militia for the capital. On 15 February it appointed new militia commissioners for London and ordered them to raise three new regiments of foot soldiers so that the city 'may not be left naked and exposed to the rage and will of wicked men in case we shall be necessitated to march with our army or the greatest part thereof into other parts of the nation'. Among the commissioners were the lord mayor, several of the city's aldermen and a number of army officers; the latter group included both Philip Skippon, who would later be appointed major-general for the capital, and John Barkstead, who was already serving as lieutenant of the Tower of London and who would subsequently act as major-general for Middlesex and Westminster.[4] Three weeks later, the commissioners were ordered to raise in addition 'a convenient number of horsemen such as are well affected and are willing to list themselves', and on 20 March the new militia numbering around 5,000 men was mustered in Finsbury Fields north of the city.[5] As additional security measures, in the weeks preceding the rising the council issued a proclamation banning all horse races throughout the country for six months and ordered the Middlesex justices of the peace to apprehend all idle and 'loose' people in the vicinity of the capital.[6]

On 12 March, the day Penruddock's royalists surprised Salisbury, Cromwell appointed his brother-in-law, John Desborough, major-general of the west and ordered him to take command of all the regular army units which were to be employed in the suppression of the rising. Two days later, the strengthening of the nation's militia forces, which was already well underway in London, was extended to a number of other areas where the danger was perceived to be most acute. New militia commissions were issued for Cambridgeshire and the Isle of Ely, Cheshire, Dorset, Durham, Essex, Hertfordshire, Huntingdonshire, Lancashire, Leicestershire, Monmouth, Northamptonshire, Rutland, Staffordshire, Suffolk, Yorkshire and South Wales, and also for the cities of Bristol, Chester and York.

The commissioners were instructed to raise and train new militia forces in their respective counties, recruiting to them men who were 'well affected' and 'fitt for war'. They were to use them to put down insurrections and invasions by the enemies of the state, whom they were authorised to 'kill and slay' if they resisted capture. They were also instructed to disarm papists, secure the weapons of those who had served in the earlier militias, and requisition arms and horses from the inhabitants of their areas 'with respect had unto the quantity of his or their estates, and with respect also to the ease of the peaceable and well affected people of this nation, that the charge and burden of these forces may be laid upon the malignant and disaffected party who have been the cause of this insurrection'.[7] The inclusion of this last instruction suggests that the risings had already led some members of Cromwell's government to conclude that those who remained persistent in their hostility towards the government should be required to bear a disproportionately large share of the costs of the state's defence. This was a principle which was to find its full expression later in the year in the decision to impose the decimation tax on the entire royalist community.

Although it was clear by mid March that the insurrection had failed and the immediate danger of widespread rebellion had passed, the government remained on its guard. On 24 March, Cromwell sent two letters to the commissioners of the new county militias. The first, which was dispatched to those in Buckinghamshire, Dorset, Hertfordshire, Lancashire, Oxfordshire, Somerset, Suffolk and Yorkshire, ordered them to proceed with the enlistment of troops and to remain vigilant to prevent further designs in their counties.[8] The second letter, directed to the commissioners in another fourteen shires where the security situation was considered more favourable, repeated the injunction to keep a careful watch on known royalists but also thanked them for their 'zeal and forwardness' and assured them that the readiness of the 'honest people' to appear against the conspirators had been a source of great encouragement to the government.[9] This second letter also made reference to several requests which the central government had received from militia commissioners that it should 'consider of waies how to find money to carry on this work', a remark which provides a further hint of how the events of the spring contributed to the subsequent decision to impose the decimation tax. The same day, a third letter was sent to the JPs throughout the country ordering them to keep watch for any strangers passing through their areas, to take action against loose and idle persons and to suppress all potentially dangerous assemblies.[10]

In the weeks following the abortive risings, the official government news-books reported them in great detail, losing no opportunity to stress the vital part which the government's puritan supporters had played in the suppression of the insurrection and how the outcome had proved a great encouragement to the godly element of the nation. A newsbook account of the raising of 500 horse in Leicestershire, for example, commented that 'it hath pleased God to make use of this design of the enemy to unite the hearts of all honest men.'[11] Another report from Gloucester declared that the royalists there had been resisted by 'honest men most of them of the congregational way or such as wish well to the same', with the help of local ministers 'whom the countrey doth indeed hate and call Independent'. It added that those 'tituled by the name Independent and Anabaptist and Presbyterian' had proved 'God's precious servants and the commonwealth's friend in time of need'.[12] The clear underlying message of these reports was that the nation remained fundamentally divided into irreconcilable groups of the ill and well affected and that, but for the support of the godly, the regime might not have survived the crisis of March 1655. The voicing of such sentiments in the official government mouthpieces may well indicate that the spring risings had reinforced the conviction of some of those around Cromwell that the best way to provide for the further security of the state was to take the godly minorities in the localities into a fuller partnership and work more closely with them to frustrate the designs of their enemies. It was just such a belief that underpinned the subsequent drive to establish close and cooperative relationships between the major-generals and the godly caucuses within their respective associations.

A third impulse behind the decision to embark on the rule of the major-generals was the government's decision in the summer of 1655 to deal with the extreme financial crisis it was facing by reducing the considerable and ongoing burden of a standing army of more than 50,000 men. In April 1655, a committee of army officers was asked by the government to consider how the expense of the army could be reduced without endangering the state's defences. After deliberating for some weeks, it recommended that the pay of the regular soldiers should be reduced and that a new reserve of horse militia should be raised as a replacement for some of the regular units. At the end of May, the council accepted this advice and proceeded to appoint the captains who would command these troops. Cromwell himself seems to have been heavily involved in the selection process, for the council secretary, John Thurloe, later told Henry Cromwell that his father had 'himself weighted every officer with all possible care and exactnes'.[13] On 1 June, the council dispatched instructions to these new officers, telling them to enlist troops who were 'well mounted for service and armed with one good sword and case of pistolls'. They were to be mustered four times a year and to be ready at forty-eight hours' notice to march anywhere in the country to put down rebellion. They would receive a retainer of £8 a year and be paid the standard daily rate of a regular soldier when on active service. This new militia which was raised over the next few weeks was made up of 6,520 men, divided up into sixty-four county troops of horse and an additional two troops of foot for the city of Norwich. Its annual salary bill was around £64,000.[14]

Having raised this new reservist force, in late July the council agreed to implement a substantial cut in the size of the regular army. Some of the army officers, however, were unhappy about the move. William Goffe, the major-general for Sussex, Hampshire and Berkshire, later reported to Thurloe that the officers of the Sussex militia had agreed with him that their newly raised force was 'a new quicksett hedge that will for a while need an old hedge about it'; he added: 'I hope His Highnes will be soe good a husband as not to take away the old one till the new be growne very substantiall.'[15] In the event, the proposed large cut was never actually carried out. The number of troops stationed in England did fall from around 11,000 in December 1654 to around 10,000 in October 1655, but it was not significantly reduced thereafter and by mid 1657 it had increased again to nearly 12,000.[16] The following year, John Thurloe commented in a letter to Henry Cromwell that after the raising of the new militia, 'things were so ordered that the standing force was not to be lessened thereby'.[17] While the meaning of this comment is far from clear, it does seem to confirm that, perhaps as a result of the reservations of Goffe and some of his fellow officers, at some point the government reversed its decision of July 1655 and decided not to proceed with the planned reduction.

The final development which propelled Cromwell towards the appointment of the major-generals was the disastrous failure of the Western Design to the West Indies in the summer of 1655. When the news of the humiliating defeat suffered by Penn and Venables at Hispaniola reached London in late July 1655, it was interpreted by Cromwell as a clear sign of divine displeasure. Shortly after hearing of the reverse, he wrote to Vice Admiral William Goodson that 'it is not to be denied but the Lord hath greatly humbled us in that sad loss sustained at Hispaniola; no doubt we have provoked the Lord, and it is good for us to know and to be abased for the same.'[18] Over the next few weeks he seems to have spent a great deal of time deliberating about how his government had incurred God's displeasure, eventually arriving at the standard godly explanation that the cause was its failure to make real progress in the task of the moral reformation of the English people. His resultant conviction that this work needed to be undertaken as a matter of great urgency strengthened his resolve to push ahead with the plans for the appointment of the major-generals and to make the reformation of manners one of the chief priorities of their rule.[19]

Most of the detailed work on the construction of the major-generals' system took place during August and September 1655. At the beginning of August, John Lambert, John Desborough and Sir Gilbert Pickering were appointed to work with Cromwell on drawing up the detailed operational instructions for the officers of the new county militia troops.[20] Several days later, the officers of the new militia attended a banquet at Whitehall, at which Cromwell almost certainly outlined the reasons for their appointment and the government's expectations of the new force.[21] In order to ensure that they would cooperate closely with the leadership of the regular army, the council also now took the decision to group the county militias into ten regional associations, and to put each of them under the overall command of a prominent New Model Army officer. On 2 August, John Desborough, who already controlled all the regular forces in the west country, was given command of the twelve new militia troops which had been raised in Cornwall, Devon, Somerset, Dorset, Wiltshire and Gloucestershire.[22] A week later, the remaining militia troops were divided up between another nine high-ranking officers. Thomas Kelsey was given command in Kent and Surrey; William Goffe in Hampshire, Sussex and Berkshire; William Boteler in Northamptonshire, Rutland, Huntingdonshire and Bedfordshire; Edward Whalley in Lincolnshire, Nottinghamshire, Stafford-shire, Leicestershire and Warwickshire; James Berry in Herefordshire, Shropshire and Wales; John Lambert in Yorkshire, Lancashire, Durham, Northumberland, Westmorland and Cumberland; Charles Fleetwood in Norfolk, Suffolk, Essex, Hertfordshire, Cambridgeshire and the Isle of Ely, Oxfordshire and Buckinghamshire; Charles Worsley in Derbyshire, Cheshire and Worcestershire; and Philip Skippon in Middlesex and London.[23] While at this stage these men were meant to concern themselves only with the supervision of the new troops, the issuing of their commissions was clearly a major step in the construction of the rule of the major-generals.

On 22 August, Lambert presented the council with a set of seven draft instructions for these ten military governors. The text of the draft makes it very clear the subcommittee established three weeks earlier had decided to recommend the widening of their remit beyond the purely military and to give them responsibility for a wide range of other local governmental functions. The instructions required the regional commanders, whom it described as 'persons of knowne and approved integrity', to suppress all tumults, insur-rections and rebellions and to meet frequently with the captains of the county militias to discuss security matters. They were to disarm Roman Catholics and royalists, and to deposit all confiscated weapons in local garrisons. They were also required to keep all disaffected persons under close surveillance and to prevent any of them gathering together either in private houses or at horse race meetings, cock-fightings or bear-baitings, both because treason and rebellion was frequently hatched at such gatherings and also because 'much evell and wickednes' commonly occurred at them.

In addition to these security measures, however, the draft instructions proposed to make the new regional commanders responsible for apprehend-ing all idle and loose persons in their areas and for either putting them to work or organising their transportation out of the country. They were also to consider how the impotent poor of their regions could be better provided for, and were to be responsible for making the roads safer for travellers by seeking out thieves, robbers and highwaymen, offering rewards of up to £10 for information leading to their arrest. The final draft instruction directed them 'in their constant carriage and conversation to encourage and promote godli-ness and vertue and discourage and discountenance all prophaneness and ungodliness'. To this end, they were to be required to work closely with JPs, ministers and other local officials to ensure that the laws against 'drunken-ness, prophanenes, blaspheminge and takeing of the name of God in vaine by swearing and cursing and such like wickednes and abominations be put in more effectual execucon then they have been hitherto'. If they found any local officers 'remisse or careless therein and soe unfitt for their trust', they were to forward their names to the council so that action could be taken against them. Lambert and the other members of the subcommittee had thus drawn up a formidably wide brief for the new military governors and one which was clearly intended to involve them not only in the supervision of local security arrangements but also in the promoting of efforts to achieve the moral betterment of provincial society.[24]

The draft document presented to the council by Lambert on 22 August also declared that the government had decided to lay an 'extraordinary tax' on the estates of all those who had been sequestered for delinquency in the 1640s, and instructed the militia commanders to call before them the royalists of their associations and assess their liability for this new tax. Following discussions within the full council, however, this clause was for the time being discarded. Why it was decided to lay it aside at this point is not clear. It is possible that some members were still unconvinced of the wisdom of imposing a discriminatory tax of this kind and wanted more time to consider the proposal. Alternatively, they may have accepted that it should be levied but agreed to keep it secret until they had worked out more fully the details of how it would be administered. For whatever reason, two days later on 24 August the taxation clause was replaced by another instruction drafted by the subcommittee. This required the commanders to investigate what had been done within their areas to prosecute the 1654 ordinance for the ejection of scandalous and insufficient ministers and schoolmasters, and to take steps to ensure that the ejectors, who had not been very active in most counties during the previous year, performed their duties more conscientiously in the future.[25]

It was at this point, too, that the government began to select from amongst the ranks of its supporters in the localities the individuals who it would ask to assist the militia commanders. The first of these new county officials, who were to be known as 'commissioners for securing the peace of the commonwealth', were appointed on 24 August, when the council approved a number of names from lists of nominees which had almost certainly been put together by Lambert's subcommittee.[26] Subsequently, however, their selection was to prove a protracted and somewhat ad hoc process. Lambert's subcommittee seems to have remained the major source of the nominations, but following their arrival in their associations several of the major-generals took local soundings and either appointed individuals themselves or forwarded suggestions to Thurloe. Most of the Sussex commissioners, for example, appear to have been selected by William Goffe; following his arrival in the county at the beginning of November, Goffe sent Thurloe a paper containing 'the names of those I have resolved for commissioners, wherein I have used my utmost care and understanding upon the discourse I have hadd with the gentlemen I have spoken with'.[27] A few weeks later, he forwarded him a list of his Hampshire commissioners; sixteen of these had been 'put in by the council', another three had been named by him before he left London, and a further seven had been appointed after he had consulted the existing commissioners in the county.[28] In some areas the selection process had still not been completed by December. Writing to Thurloe in late November, Goffe assumed that it was the failure to complete the work which had prevented the government from publishing the major-generals' orders and instructions.[29] Goffe himself subsequently added several individuals to the Berkshire commission, and John Desborough appointed three additional commissioners for Wiltshire in December.[30]

During August 1655, then, Cromwell's government made considerable progress in constructing the rule of the major-generals, and by the final week of the month many of the most important elements of the system were already in place. At this point, however, Cromwell was taken seriously ill and was unable to take any further part in government business until the last week of September. Although the council frequently conducted important business when Cromwell was not in attendance, it was clearly reluctant to proceed with such a major initiative in his absence and, in a highly unusual move, decided to suspend any further consideration of it until he was well enough to return. The remaining decisions which needed to be taken before the major-generals could begin work were thus put off for nearly four weeks.[31]

The momentum was only resumed on 21 September, when the council considered drafts of two important documents which were again presented to it by Lambert's subcommittee: the commission for the militia commanders and a set of orders for the county commissioners for the securing of the peace of the commonwealth.[32] The draft commission to the commanders declared that the government had been forced to raise the new county militias because the royalist community remained 'restlesse and implacable in their malicious designes against the peace of this commonwealth', and that it had decided that they should be commanded by officers who had been chosen for their 'fidelitye, wisdome and circumspection'. The text was accepted by the full council, but only after it had made several very significant amendments. It discarded a clause which would have given the new militia commanders sweeping powers of martial law and authorised them to 'slay, destroy, and put in execution of death' as many 'enemyes and rebels' as they saw fit, without any recourse to the normal judicial process. It also rejected a proposal from the subcommittee which would have allowed them to appoint deputies to act on their behalf. Furthermore, it dismissed the suggestion that they should be referred to as 'lieutenants', a title which would have invited direct comparisons with the pre-civil-war lord lieutenants, and decided instead that they should be known as 'major-generals'.[33]

The second document which was adopted by the council on 21 September was the set of orders for the new county commissioners. These began by dividing the royalist community into three categories or 'heads'. In the first of these were grouped all those involved in the spring uprisings, who were to be imprisoned or banished and to have their estates sequestered. Encompassed in the second head were those royalists who, while they had not been conspicuously active in the spring, 'appear by their words or actions to adhere to the interest of the late king or of Charles Stuart his son and to be dangerous enemies to the peace of the commonwealth'; these, too, were to be imprisoned or banished, but would not lose their estates unless they returned from exile without permission. More controversially, within the third head were included all those who had fought against parliament or who had been sequestered for delinquency at any time since 1642. Although a great many of the individuals within this category had been politically quiescent for a considerable length of time, any of them who possessed land worth at least £100 per annum or personal property valued at £1,500 or more would now be required to pay an 'extraordinary tax' to the government to meet the costs of the new militia. The commissioners were instructed to impose what became known as the decimation tax at the rate of ten per cent of the rental value of land and £10 for every £1,500 worth of personal assets. They were to collect the money in two half-yearly instalments, at Christmas and midsummer, the first payment being due on 21 December 1655. Any royalist who refused to pay was to have his lands confiscated, the sequestration to continue until all the arrears had been satisfied and security given for future payment. As an alternative to paying the tax in regular instalments, royalists were given the option of making over to the state land of the equivalent value of their annual liability, on the understanding that it would be returned to them if the tax was at some point in the future discontinued.

The remaining orders imposed a range of further restrictions on the royalist community. No royalist was to be allowed to keep arms in his house, and any who were found to be 'persons of no estate' who 'live loosely and without labour' were to be apprehended and transported. The ejected royalist clergy were singled out for particularly severe treatment. From 1 November they were to be banned from preaching, administering the sacraments, celebrating marriages or acting as schoolmasters. Those caught performing such functions would suffer three months' imprisonment for a first offence, six months for a second, and banishment for a third. The only ejected clergy who would henceforth be permitted to earn a living as ministers were those who had been approved by the 'Commissioners for Approbation of Public Preachers', or 'Triers', after they had given 'signal and sufficient testimony' of their godliness and change of heart. Furthermore, from the same date all royalist householders were forbidden to employ any ejected clergymen as chaplains or tutors on pain of having their decimation tax doubled.

These orders authorised the commissioners for securing the peace of the commonwealth to undertake an unprecedented crackdown on those the state considered its enemies. They were at best of somewhat dubious legality; the Victorian historian, Samuel Gardiner, went so far as to claim that every one of them 'frankly relinquished the domain of law' and that 'political necessity alone could be pleaded in their favour.'[34] To assist them in these tasks, the new commissioners were given wide powers to administer oaths, summon individuals, requisition papers and imprison anyone who defied them. They were also promised an indemnity for all their actions.

Even after the council had accepted these two documents on 21 September, the launching of the major-generals' period of rule was further delayed by the need to finalise some remaining administrative details and by another bout of illness which kept Cromwell away from the council during the first few days of October. On 3 October, the council considered a draft of the bond which would be tendered to the royalist community, and on 5 October Lambert presented it with a further set of instructions for the commissioners.[35] Adopted with minor amendments on 9 October, these additional instructions further widened the scope of the major-generals' responsibilities. They were now required to assist in the apprehending of felons, to supervise the postal service within their areas, to suppress all isolated and disorderly alehouses, and to take security from and set to work all those with no trade or calling 'who harbour and lodge loose and dissolute persons'. They were also ordered to force all royalist householders to enter security bonds for the good behaviour of themselves and their male servants, and to send lists of those who had given security to a central register office which was to be established in London. As well as keeping a record of these names, this new register office would be responsible for recording the whereabouts of all royalists within the country, as well as the movements of all visitors arriving from abroad.[36] The major-generals for London and Middlesex were specifically instructed to improve the safety of the highways, to seek out and close down all brothels and gaming-houses in the capital, and to suppress all alehouses and taverns on the outskirts of London and Westminster which were not needed for travellers.[37]

During this first week of October 1655, some final adjustments were also made to the major-generals' districts. While the militia associations established in August were largely retained, several significant changes were approved: Whalley and Worsley exchanged Staffordshire and Derbyshire; Worsley gained Lancashire from Lambert and lost Worcestershire to Berry; and South Wales was taken away from Berry and not at this stage re-allocated.[38] One new name also now appeared, with John Barkstead being appointed major-general for Middlesex and Westminster. The areas of responsibility of the new major-generals were now as follows: John Barkstead, Middlesex and Westminster;

James Berry, Herefordshire, Shropshire, Worcestershire and North Wales; William Boteler, Bedfordshire, Huntingdonshire, Northamptonshire and Rutland; John Desborough, Cornwall, Devon, Dorset, Gloucestershire, Somerset and Wiltshire; Charles Fleetwood, Buckinghamshire, Cambridgeshire and the Isle of Ely, Essex, Hertfordshire, Norfolk, Oxfordshire and Suffolk; William Goffe, Berkshire, Hampshire and Sussex; Thomas Kelsey, Kent and Surrey; John Lambert, Cumberland, Durham, Northumberland, Westmorland and Yorkshire; Philip Skippon, London; Edward Whalley, Derbyshire, Leicestershire, Lincolnshire, Nottinghamshire and Warwickshire; Charles Worsley, Cheshire, Lancashire and Staffordshire.

The formal commissions to these men were issued on 11 October. Referring to the uprisings earlier in the year and the continuing conspiracies of the royalist community, they gave them full powers over the troops of the new militia and authorised them to raise extra forces if they deemed them necessary. They also ordered them to enforce the orders and instructions described above and informed them that the local officials within their counties would be commanded to assist them. Along with the commissions was sent the final form of the security bond which the generals were to tender to all those who had fought against parliament in the 1640s as well as all those who lived 'dissolutely or without calling or at a high rate'.[39] The details of the new system were finally made public several weeks later on 25 October, when Cromwell issued a proclamation requiring all royalists in and around London to return to their homes in the provinces and report to their local major-general.[40]

Almost as soon as it had constructed the new system, however, the council decided to introduce some fundamental amendments to it. Although in late September it had rejected the idea of allowing the major-generals to act through deputies, by mid October it had conceded that neither Lambert nor Fleetwood could be excused from attendance at the council and that both should be allowed to do so. On 19 October, therefore, Robert Lilburne and Charles Howard were appointed as Lambert's deputies, the former in Yorkshire and Durham, the latter in Cumberland, Northumberland and Westmorland. The same day Hezekiah Haynes was chosen as deputy for the whole of Fleetwood's association.[41] The arrangements for Lambert's association remained in place for the next year, but in Fleetwood's area further refinements were subsequently introduced. On 14 November, a second army officer, Tobias Bridge, was appointed to deputise for Fleetwood, possibly for the counties of Buckinghamshire, Hertfordshire and Oxfordshire. Bridge intervened in a quarrel over a disputed election at High Wycombe in Buckinghamshire later that month, but thereafter does not appear to have been active in this region. Haynes started work in East Anglia in early November and at the end of the month informed Thurloe that he did not feel he could cope with any of the three counties beyond this region. At the beginning of 1656, he was still officially acting as deputy for the whole of Fleetwood's association, but in February Buckinghamshire, Hertfordshire and Oxfordshire were formally taken from him and given to another deputy, William Packer. Appointed with Packer, as joint deputy major-general for Buckinghamshire, was George Fleetwood, a distant relative of Charles Fleetwood.[42]

While no official deputy was appointed for the city of London, the government seems never to have expected the elderly Skippon, who had been named primarily to reassure the capital's governors with whom he had some standing, to take any active part in the work. From the outset, therefore, John Barkstead acted as Skippon's deputy in the city of London, as well as major-general in his own right in Westminster and Middlesex. It is perhaps surprising that John Desborough, too, did not act through a deputy. The government may well have felt that the still volatile west country needed the presence of a soldier of his stature, but, like Lambert and Fleetwood, he was a very important member of the council and in the event his duties at London kept him away from his association for much of 1656. As another late amendment to the system, in January 1656 the council re-allocated Monmouthshire and South Wales to James Berry, appointing as his two deputies there John Nicholas and Rowland Dawkins.[43] When Charles Worsley died in June 1656, his north-western association was given to Tobias Bridge.[44] In all, a total of nineteen individuals received a commission as major-general or deputy major-general during 1655 and 1656, and no fewer than sixteen of these were active in the provinces in that capacity.[45]

In appointing this particular group of men to the position of major-general, Cromwell and his advisers had selected men who were competent and available, and whose loyalty to the new protectoral regime was beyond question. Several other potential appointees, such as George Monck, John Hewson, John Reynolds and Matthew Tomlinson, were probably ruled out on the grounds that they could not be spared from their strategically vital commands in Scotland and Ireland. Philip Jones and William Sydenham were likewise important and active members of the council who were needed at Whitehall, though it is possible that Cromwell did consider giving Jones responsibility for South Wales, an area where he possessed considerable influence, before deciding at the beginning of 1656 to return it to Berry.

A number of other possible candidates for the new post had disqualified themselves by expressing doubts about the new constitutional order ushered in by the Instrument of Government. No fewer than five colonels – Matthew Alured, Thomas Harrison, John Okey, Nathaniel Rich and Robert Saunders – had been deprived of their commissions during 1654 and 1655 for suspected disaffection. Robert Overton, meanwhile, was being held in the Tower of London, where he would remain until 1658. Thomas Pride may also have been overlooked because of his staunch republican views, though he did serve both as sheriff of Surrey and a commissioner for securing the peace in London during 1656. Once these men had been discounted, there remained a relatively small pool of reliable and available senior officers, out of which Cromwell selected those he considered most able and trustworthy and with whom he had had the longest personal association.

Another significant feature of the choice of these men was that it enabled the government to incorporate pre-existing local military jurisdictions into the new structure and thus disguise the novel nature of the experiment. No fewer than eight of the officers who were appointed as major-generals or deputies in the autumn of 1655 were already exercising important military authority within some part of the association they would now control in their new capacity. John Barkstead had been lieutenant of the Tower of London since 1652; Rowland Dawkins, governor of Camarthen since 1648; Charles Howard, governor of Carlisle since the early 1650s; Thomas Kelsey, governor of Dover since 1651; Robert Lilburne, governor of York since 1654; and John Nicholas, governor of Chepstow since the early 1650s. Hezekiah Haynes had been commanding Charles Fleetwood's regiment of horse stationed in East Anglia for several years before 1655, and John Desborough had been in overall command of the west country forces since the early 1650s and major-general of the west since the spring of 1655.

As a result of the convoluted administrative process outlined above, by early 1656 England and Wales had been divided up into twelve distinct associations, each of which was controlled by an active major-general or deputy major-general exercising full executive authority under the council.[46] The size of these associations varied greatly. After he had been reallocated South Wales at the beginning of 1656, James Berry controlled the largest, with an area of around 11,000 square miles. The next largest was Desborough's in the south-west, which covered an area of around 9,000 square miles. Haynes, Howard, Lilburne and Whalley were each responsible for middle-sized associations of between 5,000 and 6,000 square miles, and Goffe and Worsley controlled slightly smaller ones of around 3,000 square miles. Boteler, Kelsey and Packer each governed relatively small associations with areas of around 2,000 square miles. The smallest association of all in terms of geographical area was Barkstead's, which comprised London, Westminster and Middlesex, but this was, of course, by far the most densely populated of the twelve.

With all the key components of the new system now in place, on the last day of October 1655 the government published a declaration in which it presented to the nation the detailed rationale behind its decision to establish the major-generals. It began by outlining the events of the previous decade and showing how the royalist community had steadfastly refused to become reconciled to the fall of the Stuarts and the establishment of the commonwealth. Specific

Map 1 The major-generals' associations

Table 1 The major-generals' associations

Association	Major-general
Cumberland, Northumberland and Westmorland	Charles Howard (as John Lambert's deputy)
Durham and Yorkshire	Robert Lilburne (as John Lambert's deputy)
Cheshire, Lancashire and Staffordshire	Charles Worsley (and after his death Tobias Bridge)
Derbyshire, Leicestershire, Lincolnshire, Nottinghamshire and Warwickshire	Edward Whalley
Bedfordshire, Huntingdonshire, Northamptonshire and Rutland	William Boteler
Essex, Cambridgeshire, Isle of Ely, Norfolk and Suffolk	Hezekiah Haynes (as Charles Fleetwood's deputy)
Buckinghamshire, Hertfordshire and Oxfordshire	William Packer and, in Buckinghamshire, George Fleetwood (as Charles Fleetwood's deputies)
Middlesex, London and Westminster	Sir John Barkstead (as Philip Skippon's deputy in London)
Kent and Surrey	Thomas Kelsey
Berkshire, Hampshire and Sussex	William Goffe
Cornwall, Devon, Dorset, Gloucestershire, Somerset, Wiltshire	John Desborough
Herefordshire, Shropshire, Worcestershire and Wales	James Berry (with John Nicholas as his deputy in Monmouthshire and Rowland Dawkins as his deputy in Carmarthenshire, Cardiganshire, Glamorgan and Pembrokeshire

reference was made to the 1652 Act of Oblivion, which it claimed had been invalidated by the continued refusal of the royalists to become reconciled to the regime and by their decision to remain 'implaceable in their malice and revenge and never to be drawne from their adhering to that cursed interest'. It went on to argue that, as additional forces were necessary to defend the state, it was right that the charge 'be not put upon the good people who have borne the heat and burden of the day but upon those who have beene and are the occasion of all our danger'.

In a frank acknowledgement that the legality of the new system was at best doubtful, the declaration then argued that 'if the Supream Magistrate were in these cases tyed up to the ordinary rules and had not a liberty to proceed upon illustrations of reason against those who are continually suspected, there would be wanting in such a state the meanes of comon safety.' It added that the new measures were intended to be 'exemplarie for the terrifying men from such attempts for the future', and roundly denounced the supporters of the Stuarts who had kept themselves 'separate and distinguished from the well affected of this nation' and had 'bred and educated their children by the sequestered and ejected clergie and very much confined their marriages and alliances within their owne party as if they mean to entail their quarrel and prevent the meanes to reconcile posterity'. In the final section of the declaration, the government offered to exempt from the decimation tax and the other restrictions all those royalists who were prepared to give public testimony of their change of heart, and expressed the hope that the work of the major-generals would encourage the 'good and well affected people of the land' and help to achieve 'the settlement and reformation which every good man longs for'.[47]

Historians have disagreed about who actually wrote this declaration. Samuel Gardiner accepted the claim by the contemporary royalist, Edward Hyde, that the author was Nathaniel Fiennes.[48] How Hyde could have known that the declaration was Fiennes's work is by no means clear, however, and W. H. Dawson has argued instead that John Lambert was involved in drawing it up.[49] The passages which deal with the Act of Oblivion and the subsequent determination of the royalists to remain unreconciled to the government do closely resemble later remarks of Lambert on the same theme during the debates on the decimation bill at the end of 1656.[50] As head of the government's intelligence system, John Thurloe would have been best placed to draft the document's detailed analysis of recent royalist plotting, while some of the comments about the need for reconciliation and godly reform at the end of the document could well have been composed by Cromwell himself. While the identity of the declaration's author cannot be established with any certainty, it is likely that it was composed collectively by the council, before being amended and approved by Cromwell.

A few weeks later, the arguments outlined in the declaration of 31 October were rehearsed in a proclamation by Cromwell ordering the keeping of a national day of fasting and humiliation on 6 December 1655. While the dispatch of the major-generals to the provinces was not explicitly referred to as a reason for the holding of this traditional puritan means of seeking repentance and reconciliation with God, the proclamation did allude to both royalist conspiracy ('the secret and open practices of those that, bearing evil will unto Sion, have Balaam-like attempted') and the failure of the Western Design ('the late rebukes we have received'). It went on to declare that 'settlement and reformation' were 'the weight of the work of this generation', and in what was almost certainly a reference to the new major-generals, it concluded with the hope that God's presence would be with

> those that are more especially engaged in and entrusted with the great affairs of the nation ... that they may bear some proportion of serviceableness to the great works, designs and promises of God concerning the kingdom of his Son, our blessed Lord, in these later times, and may be used as instruments in his hand for the continuance and increase of reformation and the security and settlement of these nations.[51]

The construction of the major-generals' system was, then, a long and tortuous process and one which increasingly came to dominate council business during the summer and autumn of 1655. This was largely because the government was moving into uncharted waters and was operating from first principles with very few precedents to guide it. For the same reason, for all the council's care and attention to detail, the arrangements which emerged in late October were, in some important respects, imprecise and contradictory. As we shall see in later chapters, once the system was up and running a great deal of additional advice and clarification would need to be given to the major-generals and their commissioners.

A number of the historians who have studied the origins of the rule of the major-generals have argued that its original instigator and architect was John Lambert, who saw it primarily as a security measure, and that Cromwell intervened during the construction process to give the major-generals their additional responsibilities with regard to moral reformation. Samuel Gardiner, for example, suggested that their orders and instructions can be divided into two distinct categories: a practical and administrative set which were the work of the pragmatic Lambert, and a moral and religious group which originated from the more godly Cromwell. He further asserted that it was the disputes within the council over the scope of the major-generals' duties which caused the launching of the system to be delayed from August to October 1655.[52] Gardiner's line has been followed by several subsequent writers. Maurice Ashley, for example, has argued that Lambert was 'the inventor and perfector' of the system and was probably opposed to Cromwell's wish to add a moral dimension to their work, and Lambert's biographer, W. H. Dawson, has claimed that 'the idea of converting the major-generals into a corps of moral police was altogether in the Protector's spirit and not at all in that of his adjutant.'[53]

The claim that Lambert was the main driving force behind the creation of the major-generals' system is almost certainly correct. He was undoubtedly deeply frustrated by the royalist community's steadfast refusal to abandon its loyalty to the Stuarts and become reconciled to the protectorate. Moreover, as chair of the council subcommittee which carried out most of the detailed work of constructing the system during August and September 1655, he had both the opportunity and authority to shape government thinking. There is, furthermore, some evidence to suggest that the decimation tax may have been Lambert's brainchild. Dawson has shown that the idea of imposing a punitive tax upon royalists was one which had been discussed by some of Lambert's parliamentarian associates in Yorkshire as early as 1642, and in her contemporary memoir the Nottinghamshire gentlewoman, Lucy Hutchinson, claimed that Lambert was widely viewed as the instigator of the tax.[54]

The theory that Lambert and Cromwell harboured conflicting visions of the role of the major-generals is, however, less convincing. While little mention was made of the need for godly reform in the spring of 1655, this dimension was very much in evidence in the original set of instructions drawn up by Lambert's subcommittee in August, which, as has been seen, required the military governors to work closely with the justices of the peace and other local officials to 'promote godliness and vertue and discourage and discountenance all prophaneness and ungodliness'.[55] The subsequent orders, which were again drawn up by Lambert's subcommittee and considered by the full council in late September, continued to deal with both security issues and moral reform, and there is no compelling evidence to suggest that they proceeded from a different source than the earlier ones. The process of construction clearly did involve considerable debate and much amendment of draft documents, but these were normal features of conciliar administration, and the delays which occurred in September and October coincided precisely with Cromwell's bouts of ill-health and were the product of incapacity rather than disagreement.

Furthermore, while Lambert was a more pragmatic and hard-headed politician than Cromwell, both men fully endorsed a fundamental principle that underlay much of the policy-making of the protectorate period: that security and reformation were indivisible goals and that, just as godly reform would only be realised once the regime was fully secure, so real security would only be established once the godly reformation had taken firm root. Cromwell specifically acknowledged this point at the opening of the second protectorate parliament, when he argued that these two objectives were 'scarcely distinct' and declared: 'I think reformation, if it be honest and thorough and just, it will be your best security.'[56] It was the government's unanimous adherence to this fundamental principle which determined that the major-generals would be burdened with the twin responsibilities of security and moral reform.

By the time copies of Cromwell's declaration of 31 October had begun to be read and discussed in the English provinces, most of the major-generals had already arrived in their associations. Boteler, Goffe, Haynes, Whalley, and Worsley were all active by the end of the first week of November 1655, and Berry and Kelsey began work a few days later. In the other associations there were some delays. Lilburne only began to act in Yorkshire in early December, and Howard was not active in the far north of the country until the end of the year. Desborough, meanwhile, did not begin his tour of the west country until early December, and little appears to have been done in London, South Wales, Buckinghamshire, Hertfordshire or Oxfordshire until the spring of 1656. Nonetheless, by early 1656 most of the country was under the direct control of a major-general with instructions from Cromwell to implement a wide and ambitious programme of reform. What kind of men these new military governors were will be considered in the next chapter.

NOTES

1 Abbott, *Writings and Speeches of Cromwell*, vol. 3, pp. 511, 582, 588; see also Maurice Ashley, *Financial and Commercial Policy under the Cromwellian Protectorate* (London, 1962 edn), p. 43.

2 Gardiner, *Commonwealth and Protectorate*, vol. 3, pp. 282–91. For more details of the royalist plotting which preceded these events, see David Underdown, *Royalist Conspiracy in England 1649–1660* (New Haven, 1960).

3 Austin Woolrych, *Penruddock's Rising 1655* (London, 1955); Andrea E. Button, 'Penruddock's Rising, 1655', *Southern History*, 19 (1997), 99–111.

4 PRO, SP.25.76A, pp. 22–4.

5 PRO, SP.25.75, p. 754; BL, E. 481.28, *A Perfect Diurnall*, 19–26 Mar. 1655.

6 PRO, SP.25.75, pp. 696–7; BL, E.481.18, *A Perfect Diurnall*, 5–12 Mar. 1655.

7 PRO, SP.25.76A, pp. 26–33. An earlier reorganisation of the militia had occurred in the summer of 1650. As the New Model Army was preparing to march north to meet the threat posed by a Scottish army loyal to Charles Stuart, the Rump had passed an act which appointed new militia commissioners in every county to replace the old pre-war deputy-lieutenants and instructed them to recruit the regime's well affected supporters to a new military reserve. For more details see Gardiner, *Commonwealth and Protectorate*, vol. 1, p. 267, and Firth and Rait, *Acts and Ordinances*, vol. 2, pp. 397–402.

8 PRO, SP.25.76A, pp. 36–7.

9 PRO, SP.25.76A, pp. 34–6.

10 PRO, SP.25.76A, pp. 37–9.

11 BL, E.481.32, *Certain Passages of Everyday Intelligence*, 23–30 Mar. 1655.

12 BL, E.831.6, *Perfect Proceedings of State Affairs*, 29 Mar.–5 Apr. 1655.

13 Birch, *State Papers of John Thurloe*, vol. 5, p. 504.

14 Gardiner, *Commonwealth and Protectorate*, vol. 3, pp. 296–7, 316–18; BL, E.841.4, *Certain Passages of Everyday Intelligence*, 25 May–1 Jun. 1655; BL, E.842.1, *A Perfect Diurnall*, 28 May–4 Jun. 1655; PRO, SP.25.77, pp. 861–80; SP.46.97, fols 164–5. For more details of the structure of the militia, see chapter 7.

15 Bod. Lib., Rawlinson MSS, A 32, fols 171–4.

16 H. M. Reece, 'The Military Presence in England, 1649–60' (Unpub. D.Phil. thesis, University of Oxford, 1981), p. 287.

17 Birch, *State Papers of John Thurloe*, vol. 5, p. 504. The work of Richard Williams on local government in the west country in the 1650s has confirmed that no regular forces in that area were reduced during 1655 and 1656; see Richard Williams, 'County and Municipal Goverment in Cornwall, Devon, Dorset and Somerset, 1649–60' (Unpub. Ph.D. thesis, University of Bristol, 1981), p. 279.

18 Abbott, *Writings and Speeches of Cromwell*, vol. 3, p. 859.

19 Barry Coward, *Oliver Cromwell* (London, 1991), pp. 135–6.

20 PRO, SP.25.76, p. 218.

21 BL, E.850.24, *A Perfect Diurnall*, 30 Jul.–6 Aug. 1655; E.851.2 *The Weekly Post*, 31 Jul.–6 Aug. 1655; C. H. Firth (ed.), *The Clarke Papers*, vol. III, Camden Soc. Publs, new series, 60 (1899), 47. The captains were paid 6s 8d a day while in London; PRO, SP.25.76, p. 217.

22 PRO, SP.25.76, p. 217.

23 PRO, SP.25.76, pp. 226–7.

24 PRO, SP.18.100.42.

25 PRO, SP.18.100.42, 43; SP.25.76, p. 246.

26 PRO, SP.25.76, pp. 248, 341. Gardiner, *Commonwealth and Protectorate*, vol. 3, pp. 321–2; J. T. Cliffe's assertion that 'the selection of the commissioners was left to the major generals' is not entirely accurate; see J. T. Cliffe, 'The Cromwellian Decimation Tax of 1655: the Assessment Lists', *Camden Miscellany*, Camden Soc. Publs, 5th series, 7 (1996), 409. For more details on the commissioners, see chapter 4.

27 Bod. Lib., Rawlinson MSS, A 32, fols 171–4.

28 *Ibid.*, A 33, fols 738–9.

29 *Ibid.*, A 32, fols 809–12.

30 *Ibid.*, A 33, fols 105–8, 233–6.

31 Abbott, *Writings and Speeches of Cromwell*, vol. 3, pp. 817, 819, 825. Council business was further disrupted in September by the unexpected arrival of Penn and Venables from the West Indies; see Gardiner, *Commonwealth and Protectorate*, vol. 3, p. 369.

32 PRO, SP.25.76, p. 297.

33 PRO, SP.18.100.133.

34 PRO, SP.18.101.136; Gardiner, *Commonwealth and Protectorate*, vol. 3, p. 323.

35 PRO, SP.25.76, pp. 319–20, 324, 325, 327.

36 For more details of this register office, see chapter 7.

37 These orders were printed in full in several government newsbooks at the end of the year. See BL, E.491.9, *Mercurius Politicus* 20–27 Dec. 1655; E.491.10, *The Public Intelligencer*, 24–31 Dec. 1655; BL, E.491.11, *Mercurius Politicus*, 27 Dec. 1655–3 Jan. 1656. They are also given in full in Abbott, *Writings and Speeches of Cromwell*, vol. 3, pp. 844–8.

38 PRO, SP.25.76, p. 329.

39 Abbott, *Writings and Speeches of Cromwell*, vol. 3, pp. 349–51.

40 BL, E.489.9, *The Public Intelligencer*, 22–29 Oct. 1655.

41 PRO, SP.25.76, p. 338.

42 PRO, SP.25.76, pp. 338, 376, 378, 525; Bod. Lib., Rawlinson MSS, A 32, fols 931–4; BL, Additional MSS, 19516, fols 2r, 20r.

43 PRO, SP.25.76, p. 457.

44 PRO, SP.25.77, p. 262.

45 For more details on these men, see chapter 3.

46 Most previous accounts of the major-generals' system state that there were ten or eleven associations, but they seem to have overlooked the division of Lambert and Fleetwood's areas into four distinct associations under their own deputy major-generals.

47 PRO, SP.25.76A, pp. 169–81; *A Declaration of his Highness in Council, Showing the Reasons of their Proceedings for Securing the Peace of the Commonwealth, on Occasion of the Late Insurrection.*

48 Gardiner, *Commonwealth and Protectorate*, vol. 3, p. 327–8; BL, E.884.2, *A Letter from a True and Lawfull Member of Parliament* (London, 1656). Posing as an anonymous member of the 1654 parliament, Hyde declared that the arguments of the declaration were 'inconsistent with the elements of law, equity and religion' and 'destructive to the private interest of those for whose preservation it seems to be intended'.

49 W. H. Dawson, *Cromwell's Understudy: The Life and Times of Colonel John Lambert* (London, 1938), pp. 203–4.

50 Rutt, *Diary of Thomas Burton*, vol. 1, pp. 240–1.

51 BL, 669 f.20.19.

52 Gardiner, *Commonwealth and Protectorate*, vol. 3, pp. 324–7.

53 Maurice Ashley, *Cromwell's Generals* (London, 1954), pp. 151–3; Dawson, *Cromwell's Understudy*, p. 205.

54 Dawson, *Cromwell's Understudy*, pp. 203–4; Lucy Hutchinson, *Memoirs of the Life of Colonel Hutchinson*, ed. John Sutherland (Oxford 1973), p. 209.

55 PRO, SP.18.100.42.

56 Abbott, *Writings and Speeches of Cromwell*, vol. 4, p. 270.

Chapter 3

The men:

backgrounds, careers and beliefs

When Cromwell and his advisers dispatched the major-generals to the English provinces in the autumn of 1655 they did so in the belief that the very survival of their government rested upon their collective shoulders. For this reason they were careful to select as the new provincial governors individuals whose support for the regime was beyond question and whose competence and reliability had been proved on numerous occasions over the course of the previous decade. These criteria were emphasised in the wording of their commissions, which declared that they had been chosen because of their 'approved fidelitye, wisdom and circumspection'.[1] This chapter will investigate the backgrounds, careers and beliefs of the major-generals, and consider what other characteristics these soldiers may have shared beyond their loyalty to the protectorate.

Before this can be done, the more basic question of precisely how many major-generals there were needs to be clarified. In all, between October 1655 and June 1656 a total of nineteeen individuals received a commission as a major-general or deputy major-general. As was seen in chapter 2, three of these nineteen were never active in the provinces. Charles Fleetwood, major-general for East Anglia, Buckinghamshire, Hertfordshire and Oxfordshire, and John Lambert, major-general for Cumberland, Durham, Northumberland, Westmorland and Yorkshire, were both important members of Cromwell's council and remained in London throughout the period of the major-generals' experiment. The third inactive major-general was Philip Skippon, who was appointed to control London largely on the grounds that he was regarded favourably by the city's governors, but who left the day-to-day running of the capital entirely to his deputy, John Barkstead, who was lieutenant of the Tower of London and major-general for Westminster and Middlesex in his own right. These three have been excluded from the ensuing prosopographical analysis of the major-generals on the grounds of their inactivity.[2]

Of the sixteen remaining active individuals, nine – John Barkstead, James Berry, William Boteler, Tobias Bridge, John Desborough, William Goffe, Thomas Kelsey, Edward Whalley, and Charles Worsley – were full major-generals in their own right, although Bridge was only appointed as Worsley's replacement in the north-west after the latter's death in June 1656. Five of the remaining seven – George Fleetwood, Hezekiah Haynes, Charles Howard, Robert Lilburne and William Packer were deputy major-generals with no active superior who thus exercised full executive power within their regions. The remaining two – Rowland Dawkins and John Nicholas – were deputies in South Wales to the active major-general, James Berry, and reported directly to him. It is these sixteen men who will now be investigated in an attempt to achieve a group portrait of the active major-generals.[3]

While it is not possible to ascertain the precise dates of birth of all the major-generals, an approximate age can be calculated for all of the active sixteen, with the exception of John Nicholas. A comparison of these estimates reveals that, while the gap between the eldest and youngest of the major-generals was quite wide, the majority of them had been born within a few years of each other and were still relatively young in 1655. The four eldest generals were Berry, Desborough, Lilburne and Whalley, all of whom were over forty in 1655. Another ten generals – Barkstead, Boteler, Bridge, Dawkins, Fleetwood, Goffe, Haynes, Kelsey, Packer and Worsley – were aged between thirty and forty years old in 1655. The youngest was Charles Howard, who was still in his late twenties in 1655. At least eleven of the sixteen were entrusted with substantial political power before they had reached the age of forty. They were thus significantly younger than many of the prominent royalists against whom they proceeded, and their relative youth may well have been a contributing factor in the antagonism they aroused in their opponents. Furthermore, with the exceptions of Desborough, Whalley and Berry, they would have seen Oliver Cromwell, who was fifty-six in 1655, as belonging to an older generation. It is clear from their letters that some of them regarded the protector as a revered father-figure, and that they were anxious to gain his respect through the successful prosecution of their duties.

The identification of the geographic and social origins of the major-generals is a far from straightforward task, but enough information can be discovered to allow several important points to be made.[4] In the first place, it is clear that the central government was keen to ensure that individual major-generals were assigned to parts of the country with which they had some pre-existing connection. The families of nine of the sixteen major-generals – Barkstead, Boteler, Dawkins, George Fleetwood, Haynes, Howard, Lilburne, Whalley and

Worsley – had all been settled within their respective associations prior to the outbreak of the civil war, and all of these men had been born within the areas they would later rule. Most of the other seven possessed rather less clear-cut, but nonetheless significant connections to their areas. While James Berry's place of birth is unknown, he was certainly living in the west midlands in the 1630s and had probably been born in that area. William Goffe was brought up in London, but his father had been a minister in Sussex in the early seventeenth century. Thomas Kelsey was also a Londoner, but he had been living in Kent and acting as the governor of Dover Castle for four years before 1655. William Packer had acquired crown lands and a residence at Theobalds in Hertfordshire in the early 1650s, and John Desborough had been put in overall charge of the New Model Army regiments in the west country in 1650 and had been stationed at Plymouth during the early 1650s. The only active major-general with no meaningful connection with his association before 1655 was Tobias Bridge, who was only appointed after Worsley's death in the summer of 1656.

In setting up the system, therefore, the council clearly decided that it would be advantageous to send into the provinces men who possessed some knowledge of the areas for which they would be responsible. The counter-argument that they might, as a consequence, be more likely to succumb to local pressures was presumably either dismissed or simply not considered. Some of those who subsequently worked with the major-generals certainly valued the fact that they possessed local connections. Writing to Cromwell in late January 1656 to thank him for appointing Edward Whalley as their major-general, the Nottinghamshire commissioners described him as 'our native countryman, of an ancient and honourable family, and of singular justice, abilitie and piety'.[5]

But if Whalley's commissioners were impressed with his family background, many of their contemporaries were quick to denounce the other major-generals on account of their lowly social origins. According to the diarist, Thomas Burton, a number of the MPs in the second protectorate parliament were extremely dismissive of their social origins. Burton claimed he had been told that Barkstead had begun life as a thimble-maker, that Kelsey had sold 'leather-points', and that Bridge had been a common dragooner; he added that some of his fellow MPs had 'reckoned up the mean extraction of many more major-generals'.[6] The Nottinghamshire gentlewoman, Lucy Hutchinson, meanwhile, called the major-generals 'a companie of silly meane fellows'.[7] Even the protector's daughter, Elizabeth Claypole, was reported to have looked down her nose at them and their families. According to one of Edward Hyde's informants, shortly after the defeat of the militia bill in January 1657 the major-generals and their wives stayed away from the wedding of a kinswoman of the president of the council, Henry Lawrence. Asked where the major-generals' wives were, Elizabeth was said to have replied: 'I'le warrant you washing their dishes at home as they were use to doe', a comment which reportedly outraged not only the women in question but also their husbands.[8]

Investigation into the social origins of the major-generals reveals that, while such dismissive comments do somewhat overstate the humbleness of their origins, there was nonetheless more than a grain of truth in them. The families of only three of the sixteen – George Fleetwood, Howard and Lilburne – can be clearly identified as belonging to the pre-war magisterial elites of their respective counties. Another six – Boteler, Dawkins, Desborough, Goffe, Haynes and Whalley – were members of pre-war landed families of more minor status, but most of the other seven appear to have been of below gentry status before the civil war. James Berry was working as a clerk in an iron-works in Shropshire in the 1630s, Barkstead and Kelsey were active as tradesmen in London, and Worsley's father was a prosperous merchant in Manchester, who had only just begun to acquire significant landed property. In the early 1650s, John Lilburne claimed that William Packer's army career had raised him from 'a dung-hill'.[9] The fact that the family origins of the other two, Bridge and Nicholas, are obscure strongly suggests that they too were of below gentry status. With only just over half the major-generals able to boast a landed background and only one in five coming from the established provincial elites, as a group they were the clear social inferiors of both the pre-war magisterial elites of the areas they governed and of most of the royalists against whom they acted. Richard Baxter later remarked that his local major-general, James Berry, had been 'scorned by the gentry that had known his inferiority', and suggested that he might have been more respected if he had been given control of a different part of the country where his background would have been less well known.[10]

If the social origins of most of the major-generals were modest, as a direct result of their extended military service during the 1640s and early 1650s the majority of them were significantly wealthier in 1655 than they had been fifteen years earlier. As many as thirteen of the sixteen active major-generals – Barkstead, Berry, Boteler, Bridge, Dawkins, Desborough, Goffe, Haynes, Kelsey, Nicholas, Packer, Whalley and Worsley – are known to have purchased estates which had been confiscated from the crown, church or individual royalists. The most substantial buyers appear to have been Whalley, who acquired property worth over £9,000, and Kelsey, who bought an interest in property in six counties.[11] Only three of the active major-generals – George Fleetwood, Howard, and Lilburne – do not appear to have purchased confiscated lands. Charles Howard's family already possessed extensive land-holdings in the far north-west of the country. Robert Lilburne's decision not to become involved may well have stemmed from a principled objection to the exploitation of the land market by the army's leading figures, and in particular by his own superior, Lambert.[12]

The means by which men of such modest origins had risen to prominence by 1655 was, of course, their distinguished military service during the 1640s and early 1650s. Four of the major-generals – James Berry, John Desborough, William Packer and Edward Whalley – were counted among Oliver Cromwell's longest-standing military colleagues. All of them had enlisted in his famous 'Ironsides' regiment during the early stages of the first civil war and had fought alongside him throughout the 1640s and early 1650s. Whalley was made a colonel of horse in the New Model Army in 1646, Desborough in 1649, and Berry in 1651. Packer became a major in 1652. While the relationships of the other major-generals to Cromwell were of shorter duration, their military records were no less impressive. William Goffe was a captain in the New Model by 1645; he commanded Cromwell's regiment at Dunbar, and was made a colonel during the Worcester campaign in 1651. Thomas Kelsey had risen to the rank of lieutenant-colonel by the end of the first civil war; he subsequently served as deputy-governor of Oxford and from 1651 as governor of the strategically vital Dover Castle. William Boteler had been appointed a colonel of horse by 1646. Robert Lilburne became a colonel of foot in 1647; he subsequently served as governor of Newcastle and during the early 1650s commanded the New Model forces in Scotland, returning from there to take up the post of governor of York in 1654. Hezekiah Haynes was a captain of foot at the start of the civil war and a major of horse by 1645; he fought at Preston and in Scotland, and during the early 1650s commanded Charles Fleetwood's cavalry regiment stationed in East Anglia.

John Barkstead served as a colonel of foot in the New Model Army during the first civil war and as governor of Reading and Yarmouth, before taking up the post of lieutenant of the Tower of London in 1652. Charles Worsley was a captain of foot in Lancashire in 1644 and in 1650 was appointed lieutenant-colonel and given command of a new regiment of foot raised in Lancashire for Cromwell. Tobias Bridge served as a captain during the first civil war, was made a major of horse in 1649, and was active in Scotland in the early 1650s. George Fleetwood raised a troop of dragoons for parliament in Buckinghamshire in 1643. Rowland Dawkins served in South Wales throughout the 1640s and was appointed governor of Camarthen and Tenby in 1648. His fellow deputy in South Wales, John Nicholas, was governor of Chepstow Castle during the same period. Charles Howard was too young to serve during the 1640s, but he fought at the battle of Worcester in 1651, and was a member of Cromwell's lifeguard and governor of Carlisle during the early 1650s. Despite their relative youth, therefore, by 1655 the sixteen active major-generals had amassed a very substantial collective fund of military knowledge and experience.

They had not, however, acquired anything like the same amount of political experience. A small majority of them could claim some brief involvement in the political process. Barkstead, George Fleetwood, Goffe, Lilburne and Whalley had sat in judgement on Charles I in 1649 and had signed the king's death warrant. Desborough had been a member of the republican council of state in the early 1650s. Both George Fleetwood and Charles Howard had been members of Barebone's Parliament, and Barkstead, Dawkins, Desborough, Fleetwood, Goffe, Howard, Kelsey, Whalley and Worsley had all been elected to the 1654 parliament. But while these ten had had some limited involvement in civilian politics before 1655, the remaining six major-generals – Berry, Boteler, Bridge, Haynes, Nicholas and Packer – appear to have lacked any significant experience of the exercising of political power.

Investigation into the personalities and beliefs of the sixteen active major-generals reveals that they differed markedly in terms of character, outlook and approach to their duties. James Berry was an old friend of the presbyterian divine, Richard Baxter, and had shared with him in the 1630s both a house and a moderate puritan standpoint in religion. After Berry joined Cromwell's regiment in 1642, however, a rift had opened up between the two. According to Baxter, Berry became one of Cromwell's 'favourites' and under his influence adopted more radical separatist beliefs, and became filled with a 'spiritual pride' which caused him to look down on his old, more conservative friends. Following this defection to nonconformity, Baxter commented that Berry lived 'as honestly as could be expected in one that taketh error for truth and evil to be good'.[13]

Berry was certainly one of the more radical of the active major-generals with respect to his religious beliefs and was conspicuous for his lenient attitude towards the Fifth Monarchists and Quakers of Wales and the west midlands. Soon after his arrival in his association he invited the Welsh Fifth Monarchist, Vavasour Powell, to dinner.[14] He later released a number of Quakers from Evesham gaol and told the Worcestershire justices that they should be allowed to worship freely if they behaved peaceably.[15] It is possible that Berry may himself have been attracted to Quakerism. In 1657, George Monck complained to Cromwell that most of the men and many of the officers of Berry's regiment were Quakers, and two years later Berry appointed two Quakers as cornets in his regiment.[16] Berry was also deeply shocked by the absence of preachers in Wales, which he described as 'a great evill', and he warned the government that 'if some course be not taken, these people will some of them become heathens'.[17] For all his godly zeal, he was not lacking in a sense of humour. After he had been forbidden from returning home to Lincoln, where he had bought the old bishop's palace, for a few days' rest in January 1656, he told Thurloe: 'when I intend next to steale a little time, I will tell noe body'; and when South Wales was added to his district a few weeks later, he commented wryly: 'I … cannot but acknowledge my Lord's kindness in his endeavour to keepe me from idleness, though I am perswaded I could have made a shift to have found my selfe worke without any such enlargement of my limitts.'[18]

William Goffe was conspicuous both for his radical religious and political beliefs, and for his strong millenarian conviction that he was living through the last days of human history. During the late 1640s, he had played a significant role in the political developments within the army, attending both the famous army debates at Putney in late 1647 and the Windsor prayer meeting the following spring. On the first day of the discussions at Putney, he expressed his fears that the army might have wandered from the purpose God had entrusted to it, and he called for time to be put aside for a prayer meeting on the grounds that no project would prosper 'unless God be first sought'. The following day, he referred to his own researches into the Book of Revelation and intimated that the promised rule of Christ's saints was imminent.

Goffe also made clear at Putney that he believed the army leaders should end their attempts to reach a settlement with Charles I and instead bring him to justice. On the first day he declared: 'God does seem evidently to be throwing down the glory of all flesh', and he later added: 'it seems to me evident and clear that this hath been a voice from heaven to us, that we have sinned against the Lord in tampering with his enemies.'[19] Six months later at the start of the army prayer meeting at Windsor in April 1648, he referred his fellow officers to the first chapter of the Old Testament Book of Proverbs, in which God ordained that disaster would befall those who refused to follow His plans and purposes. Again, his intention was to suggest that the resurgence of the royalist cause was the direct consequence of the army's negotiations with Charles I and its failure to bring him to justice. According to a later eyewitness account of the meeting, Goffe's words engendered in those present a deep sense of 'shame and loathing' for their sins and led them to resolve to put the king on trial as soon as they had the opportunity.[20] Goffe retained his millenarian beliefs throughout the remainder of his life. The letters he wrote to his wife from America, where he took refuge after the Restoration, reveal that despite the failure of the puritan revolution he still confidently expected the imminent return of Jesus Christ. They also make clear that he was deeply troubled by the reports he received about developments in England. In 1672 he told his wife: 'I cannot but tremble to think what may become of poor England whose sins are grown to a great heigth', and two years later he declared:

> Oh that the inhabitants of poor England would learn righteousness … I am at a great distance yet methinks I see the Lord shaking both your earth and heaven. Oh that

He would give us the grace to seek a kingdom that cannot be shaken, and to serve Him acceptably with reverence and godly fear, for our God is a consuming fire.[21]

During the early 1650s, Goffe was a member of John Rowe's Independent congregation which met at Westminster. In 1652 he was one of the twenty-seven individuals who supported John Owen's proposal to the Rump for the establishment of a state church with a wide, but not unrestricted, degree of religious toleration, and two years later he was appointed one of the triers charged with vetting candidates for the parochial ministry.[22] Unlike Berry, he was extremely hostile to the Quakers. In January 1656, he told Thurloe that George Fox and several other itinerant Quaker preachers had been active in Sussex, 'doing much work for the devil and deluding many simple souls', adding: 'I have some thoughts to lay Foxe and his companions by the heels if I see good opportunity.'[23] His deep antipathy to Fox's movement was further revealed during the debates in parliament at the end of 1656 about how to punish James Nayler for his blasphemous entry into Bristol earlier that year. Goffe declared that the Quakers 'go about to revile the ordinances and ministers of Christ and would tear the flesh off the bones of all that profess Christ', and claimed that Nayler was a false Christ who was sent to deceive the godly and as such should be punished by death.[24]

Despite the strength of his convictions and his absolute commitment to the godly cause, Goffe's letters to Thurloe during 1655 and 1656 reveal him to be an anxious individual who lacked confidence in his own abilities and was easily discouraged when he encountered problems. Shortly after his appointment as major-general he expressed the hope that Cromwell would not regret putting his trust in 'so poore and inconsiderable a creature', and later admitted to Thurloe that he had on occasions become discouraged 'because things were soe exceeding long in settling'.[25] He was frequently preoccupied by domestic and family concerns, such as the reimbursement of his personal expenses and his wife's difficulties in settling at Winchester, where he had set up house in the early summer of 1656.[26] He also seems to have found his work as major-general taxing; in March 1656, for example, he told Thurloe that he had returned to Winchester from Sussex 'so much tyred' that he could hardly find the energy to write to him.[27]

William Boteler was another uncompromising puritan zealot. A long-time member of a congregationalist church which met at his home at Oundle in Northamptonshire, he declared in parliament in 1656 that 'we all sit here, I hope, for the glory of God' and 'the greatest care in the world we ought to have of God's glory'.[28] He was also an individual whose immoderate and tactless behaviour earned him an unenviable contemporary reputation as a bully and bigot. The aggression he displayed as major-general against both his religious and political enemies was frequently commented upon. A document drawn up by some Northamptonshire Quakers in the early 1650s denounced him as 'a man whom prid hath overcome'. It accused him of imprisoning Quakers without trial and of violently breaking up their meetings, and claimed that there might be 'a greate volume written of the wicked tyrannicall actions of this man'.[29] In 1656, the Quaker leader, George Fox, also denounced him to his face as a 'cruel persecutor in Northamptonshire' and 'a shame to Christianity and religion'.[30] In the course of the James Nayler debates in parliament, Boteler denounced the Quakers as 'despisers of your government [who] contemn your magistracy and ministry and trample it under their feet'. He advocated putting Nayler to death by stoning, on the grounds that the 'law made against blasphemy in Leviticus is as binding to us this day as surely as that against murder, which follows in the next verse'.[31]

Boteler was equally uncompromising in his approach to his royalist enemies. When James Compton, earl of Northampton, refused to sign a security bond with no time limit in November 1655, Boteler imprisoned him and only reluctantly set him free several months later after receiving direct orders from the council to do so.[32] It may have been this incident which prompted one of Sir Edward Nicholas's royalist informants to report in January 1656 that Boteler had 'carried himself insolently to a royalist of quality, calling him "Sirrah" and telling him he would make him proclayme Charles Steward … a traytor or eate his sworde'.[33] Three years later in 1659, Boteler was censured by some of the members of Richard Cromwell's parliament for his high-handed treatment of another Northamptonshire royalist. Several MPs argued that as major-general he had acted more arbitrarily than Charles I's hated councillor, the earl of Strafford, and one claimed that 'his crimes are generally all over Northamptonshire cried out against'.[34] In 1665, another contemporary reacted to the news of Boteler's imprisonment for alleged involvement in a conspiracy against Charles II by remarking that he had 'exercised all imaginable afflictions on the king's subjects in Northamptonshire'.[35] Such testimony was, of course, far from unbiased, but Boteler himself admitted to Thurloe in March 1656 that as major-general he exceeded his powers on an almost daily basis.[36]

Boteler has sometimes been identified as the 'Maj. Butler' who, in 1652, opposed the plans of John Owen to restrict the degree of religious toleration within the state church, and whose arguments were outlined by Roger Williams in *The Fourth Paper presented by Maj. Butler to the Honorable Committee of Parliament for the Propagation of the Gospel of Christ Jesus*. This is almost certainly, however, a mistake as the future major-general had been a colonel since the 1640s. The author of the paper was probably the Captain William Butler who had argued in favour of universal toleration at the Whitehall debates in 1649.[37]

John Desborough was Cromwell's brother-in-law and the major-general with the longest personal association with the protector, whom he had known since well before the outbreak of the civil war. Like Cromwell, he was a godly East Anglian and possessed a reputation as a blunt, straightforward and uncultivated countryman. Contemporaries commented on his 'rustic origins and manners' and described him as 'blunt and honest'. Desborough was a religious radical with strong Baptist associations. Before the civil war he had appointed the radical puritan and subsequent General Baptist, Henry Denne, to the living of his home parish of Eltisley in Cambridgeshire and Eltisley subsequently became notorious as a centre of radical, sectarian worship.[38] As major-general, he was uncompromising in his dealings with his opponents. He admitted to Thurloe in late December 1655 that he had dealt 'very plainly and indeed very roundly' with some royalists who had objected to giving security and paying the decimation tax, and the following month he used threats and intimidation to secure the resignation of several Bristol aldermen whose support for the regime he doubted.[39] George Fox, who was imprisoned by him at Launceston in Cornwall in early 1656, described him as 'a hard-hearted man'.[40] He was also quite untroubled by the reliance of Cromwell's government on military force. In December 1656, he introduced into parliament a bill to make the decimation tax permanent; in the course of the ensuing debate he declared: 'It was blows not fair words, that settled and must settle the peace of England', adding: 'It is our swords must indemnify us. It is that [which] must procure our safety.'[41]

Unlike Boteler, however, Desborough did have a milder, more conciliatory side to his character. In early 1656, he told Thurloe: 'it's unplesant for me to act without rule' and during the decimation debate he commented of the royalists: 'It is their reformation, not their ruin is desired. If they become our friends, let them benefit by their change.'[42] He was also one of the main advocates of mercy for James Nayler. He argued that he should be banished rather than executed and, after the rejection of the death penalty, he opposed a proposal to slit the Quaker's tongue on the grounds that this might kill him anyway.[43] Desborough's other commitments meant he was only able to be present in the west country from early December 1655 until mid February 1656, and again for a few weeks during the election campaign in August 1656. During the latter stages of the first tour, moreover, he was distracted by his wife's serious illness and was very anxious to complete his duties and return to London to see her.[44]

Edward Whalley, Oliver Cromwell's cousin and William Goffe's father-in-law, was arguably the most eirenic and moderate of the major-generals. While he himself was an Independent and a member of Thomas Goodwin's congregation during the 1650s, he was on good terms with some of those who favoured a national church structure. During the first civil war he invited the presbyterian, Richard Baxter, to act as chaplain to his New Model regiment, and in 1652 he supported John Owen's proposal to the Rump for the establishment of a comprehensive state church with a wide, but not unrestricted degree of religious toleration.[45] In 1649, during the discussions within the army at Whitehall about how to proceed with the re-conquest of Ireland, he adopted a more conciliatory stance than most of his colleagues, arguing that 'no ill terms be imposed on them as either to eradicate the natives or to divest them of their estates'.[46] In 1655, he expressed his support for the re-admission of the Jews into England, which he argued was justifiable for 'both politique and divine reasons', the principal of these being the economic benefits to the state and the increased opportunity it would allow to bring about their conversion.[47] During the Nayler debates in parliament in December 1656, he attempted to cool the passions of his fellow members and to reconcile the conflicting positions, declaring at one point: 'I would have this agreed upon in peace and charity; that those that are for a low punishment might not be censured for coldness, nor those for a higher punishment censured for preposterous zeal.' He himself favoured the death penalty for Naylor, but was prepared to offer him a reprieve if he recanted after sentence.[48]

Whalley also dealt with the royalist community with rather more moderation than some of his fellow major-generals. He had acted as Charles I's gaoler while he was held in army custody in 1647 and, when the king escaped from Hampton Court in November of that year, he left him a letter thanking him for his kindness. As major-general he allowed the annual horse race for Lady Grantham's Cup to be run at Lincoln in the spring of 1656, and he later told Cromwell that he had assured the earl of Exeter that 'it was not your highnes intention in the suppressing of horse races to abridge gentlemen of that sport'.[49] Whalley also showed more interest than most of his fellow major-generals in issues of social justice. In March 1656, he praised the assizes judge, Matthew Hale, for the great concern he had shown for poor litigants while on circuit in the east Midlands, and he subsequently wrote to Thurloe to urge the government to take action to prevent fraudulent practices in markets, depopulating enclosure, and profiteering by tradesmen and alehouse keepers. He also commissioned a survey of the effects of enclosure in Leicestershire, and in December 1656 tried unsuccessfully to introduce into parliament a bill to prevent further enclosures which might result in depopulation.[50] During July 1656, he was distracted from his work as major-general by his wife's serious illness following a miscarriage.[51]

During the 1640s Charles Worsley had antagonised his Lancashire gentry neighbours and made substantial financial gains by acting as an informer for the parliamentary sequestrators and revealing to them royalists who had concealed parts of their estates.[52] A religious Independent, his beliefs were markedly apocalyptic and millenarian in flavour. In 1653 in the preface to *Refreshing Drops and Scorching Vials*, a devotional work by the godly London minister, Christopher Goad, he declared: 'We are the children of the last times and upon us are the ends of the world come. Prophesies and promises which have been hid from ages and generations are now enriching us by their revealing and fulfilling in us.' He also predicted that:

> Whatever hath been captived into Babylon shall be brought back and set upon Mount Sion: the redeemed of the Lord shall return and, being filled with the spirit and restored to their first state, shall shine in the perfection of beauty and holiness and then shall all saints sing in the unity of the spirit the song of Moses, the servant of God, and the song of the Lamb, saying great and marvellous are thy works, Lord God Almighty, just and true are thy ways, O thou King of Saints.[53]

The strength of Worsley's commitment to the godly cause is demonstrated by the vigour with which he attempted to implement a godly moral reformation within his association in the north-west.[54] His strenuous efforts in pursuit of this end exhausted him and probably contributed to his premature death in June 1656. On his death-bed he directed that an estate formerly belonging to the royalist, Sir Cyril Trafford, which he had bought from the sequestrators, should be returned to the state as he 'would not for all the world wrong the commonwealth'.[55] At the time of his death his estate was worth £1,679, of which £489 was paid out to creditors; his widow was given his salary for a further year and also granted an allowance of £100 per annum.[56]

Hezekiah Haynes came from a strongly puritan East Anglian family, which had emigrated from Essex to New England in 1633 to escape from the Laudian harassment of the godly. Hezekiah's father, John, had subsequently served as governor of both Massachusetts and Connecticut.[57] Hezekiah himself returned to England in the late 1630s and served in the parliamentary armies throughout the 1640s and early 1650s. In the late 1640s, he was acting as elder for the parish of Birch within the Essex presbyterian association.[58] He was a close friend of the puritan minister of Earls Colne in Essex, Ralph Josselin, and is frequently mentioned in Josselin's diary.[59] His letters to Thurloe during his time as major-general reveal that he was deeply hostile to Fifth Monarchists and Quakers.[60] After the rejection of the death penalty for James Nayler in December 1656, he argued that the Quaker's tongue should be slit or bored through and that he should be branded with the letter 'B' for blasphemer.[61]

Little is known of Haynes's personality, although he was described by one of Sir Ralph Verney's friends in November 1655 as 'a civell gentleman'.[62] For much of the time he served as major-general he suffered from ill-health. He was unwell in November 1655 and again in March 1656.[63] In late August 1656, he was troubled with 'an auguish fever, the country illness', which left him 'so indisposed at tymes that I am fit for nothing'.[64] A year later, he had a relapse which once again incapacitated him for several months, and Josselin at this point thought he might not live.[65] It is possible that this 'country illness' was a strain of malaria, which may well have been endemic in the fenlands of East Anglia in the seventeenth century.

William Packer was one of the most radical of the major-generals in terms of both his political and religious beliefs. He had been accused of anabaptism as early as 1644, and shortly after serving as major-general he was cashiered from the New Model Army by Cromwell on the grounds of his disaffection to the government.[66] In 1658, George Monck described him as a 'discontented and dangerous person' and claimed that, as a result of his influence, Cromwell's regiment, which he commanded, had become 'the worst regiment in the army for disaffection to the present government'.[67] During the early 1650s, Packer attended some of John Simpson's Fifth Monarchist meetings in London, and on one occasion he defended Simpson's preaching against an attack by William Erbury.[68] He himself was a noted lay preacher and in 1653 he received a licence to preach from the council of state. In 1654, he was appointed one of the triers charged with vetting candidates for the parochial ministry.[69] He denounced the celebration of Christmas in 1656, and while acting as major-general he reportedly launched a violent attack on a royalist who he believed had appeared before him drunk.[70] During 1655, he participated in several heated public disputations with the Quaker leader, George Fox, in the course of which, according to Fox, 'he railed against Friends and truth' and declared he would rather see the restoration of Charles II than the granting of liberty to the sect.[71] After hearing Packer preach, Fox accused him of speaking 'with a light chaffy mind of God and Christ and the scriptures' and of being 'of one spirit' with a number of Ranters with whom he consorted.[72]

Despite his vehement opposition to the Quaker movement, in December 1656 Packer strongly opposed the proposal to execute James Nayler, arguing in parliament that 'a free exercise of their consciences' was 'the native liberty' of the English people.[73] He was also a firm advocate of religious freedom for other radical groups. In 1659, he delivered an extraordinary speech in parliament, in the course of which he expressed a profound sense of betrayal by Cromwell and regret for some of his own actions as major-general. Arguing against the confirmation of Richard Cromwell as protector, he stated that Oliver had dismissed him 'without trial or appeal, with the breath of his nostrils', adding: 'God hath left it upon record that he did not answer all the trust that was put in him.' He went on to express the hope that 'the two great interests of religious and civil liberty shall never be parted' and, in a probable reference to his work as a deputy major-general, declared: 'I say it to my shame ... I have been one of those that have opposed some of those liberties ... I am ashamed to tell you how far fear, respect and hope of preferment have made me swerve from what my conscience thought just.'[74]

While Robert Lilburne's beliefs were somewhat more moderate than those of his more famous younger brother, the Leveller leader John Lilburne, he nonetheless displayed a conspicuously radical approach to both politics and religion. During the late 1640s, he was prominent in the army's campaign to secure its political and religious rights, and he strongly opposed parliament's plan to re-conquer Ireland. His regiment gained a reputation as one of the most radical within the New Model Army and in November 1647 was heavily involved in the mutiny at Ware. Lilburne was a radical Baptist and displayed an extreme hostility to presbyterianism. In the late 1640s he appointed the Baptist preacher, Edward Hickhorngill (or Hickeringill), as his regimental chaplain and, while governor of Newcastle in the late 1640s, he was probably involved in the establishment of the early Tyneside Baptist congregations. There is some evidence to suggest that, during the 1650s, he may have been attracted to Quakerism. Following his appointment as governor of York in 1654, the Quaker Thomas Aldam reported that 'we have great friendshipe and love from the governor of the towne', and he seems to have been supported by some Yorkshire Quakers when he stood for parliament in 1656. Two officers of his regiment also subsequently defected to Quakerism. He did not, however, speak out in support of James Nayler in parliament in December 1656. It is possible that, like his brother John, he may have converted to Quakerism before his death in 1665.[75]

Sir John Barkstead was one of Cromwell's most reliable colleagues. He was knighted in January 1656 for his services to the state, and in his speech at the opening of the second protectorate parliament in 1656, the protector praised his efficiency as lieutenant of the Tower of London, commenting that 'there never was any design on foot but we could hear of it out of the Tower'. His enemies, however, were very critical of his behaviour in that capacity. In March 1656, a correspondent of the duke of Ormonde described him as 'a most severe man', and in the anonymous pamphlet, *Invisible John made Visible, or a Grand Pimp of Tyranny Portrayed*, published in 1659, he was denounced as 'the most indefatigable drudge in the nation to the late tyrant'. The author of the tract accused him of acting cruelly and insolently to prisoners and of amassing a large fortune by charging extortionate fees from them, a practice which 'stincks in the nostrils of both good and bad'. He was a congregationalist in his religious affiliation.[76]

Charles Howard was the most atypical of the group. The youngest of the major-generals, he had been brought up as a Roman Catholic and had only converted to Protestantism in 1645. Some earlier writers have claimed that he fought for Charles I in the 1640s and, as a result, was sequestered for delinquency. In fact he seems only to have been involved in a minor skirmish near Skipton Castle in 1646 when under the control of his uncle, and the subsequent short-lived sequestration of the family estates was not for delinquency but for non-payment of money arising out of his brother's wardship.[77] Howard's religious views following his conversion are far from clear. He was chosen to sit in Barebone's Parliament, and during the protectorate he was a member of the London congregation led by George Cokayne, which met at St Pancras, Soper Lane. Cokayne was a godly cleric with Fifth Monarchist connections but, if Howard shared his minister's religious views at this time, he rapidly jettisoned them after the Restoration, when according to Austin Woolrych his outlook was 'decidedly unpuritan'.[78] The strong suspicion must remain that, rather than holding deep convictions, as an adult Howard was a trimmer in religion. His decision to serve Cromwell and the Interregnum state may have stemmed primarily from a wish to advance his own career and protect the dominant position that his family enjoyed in the far north-west of England.

Information about the characters and personal beliefs of the remaining major-generals is rather more patchy. Thomas Kelsey was probably one of the more radical of the major-generals. During the early 1650s, he was a member of John Simpson's Fifth Monarchist congregation in London, but when the congregation split over the establishment of the protectorate he came out strongly in support of Cromwell.[79] In December 1656, he opposed the proposal to execute James Nayler, arguing that it was 'dark and difficult to know what the mind of God is in this thing', and that 'this court ... must mix mercy with judgement'.[80] While Rowland Dawkins was undoubtedly also godly in his religious outlook, historians have disagreed about his denominational affiliation in the 1650s. While Philip Jenkins has argued that he was a Baptist, Stephen Roberts has stated that he attended his parish church in the 1650s and was never a member of the Baptist congregation at Ilston in Gower, which was near his home. Dawkins served both as a commissioner for the Propagation of the Gospel in Wales and as an ejector and trier for South Wales. He was also very hostile to Quakers. After 1660 he refused to conform to the restored church and was summoned before the ecclesiastical authorities for refusing to have his children baptised.[81] Nothing of significance is known about the personalities or beliefs of Tobias Bridge, George Fleetwood or John Nicholas.

This attempt to draw up a collective biography of Cromwell's major-generals has shown that they were a very diverse group in terms of their ages, social and geographical origins, and personalities. It has also revealed, however, that they shared some important characteristics and beliefs. All of them had risen to prominence as a result of distinguished military careers during the 1640s and early 1650s, and all had consistently displayed a strong personal devotion to Oliver Cromwell. Their most important common denominator, however, was their radical puritanism. With the possible exception of Charles Howard, as a group they were both deeply committed to the task of religious and moral reform and utterly convinced they were being sent to the provinces to implement the express will of God.

Their strong collective belief that their work as major-generals was a divinely inspired mission and that they could thus rely on God's providence to bring them eventual success pervades the correspondence they sent back to London from their associations during 1655 and 1656. James Berry, for example, declared that he was confident that he 'came forth in this worke as sent of God', and Charles Worsley told Thurloe that: 'I cannot but observe a visible hand of God goeinge along with us in this work.'[82] Edward Whalley commented that 'God hath in a very great measure blest our endeavours', and Rowland Dawkins told Cromwell: 'wee are not onely satisfied in the mind of God as to these extraordinary proceedings ... but especially that the cause of God and his people is promoted.'[83] William Packer, meanwhile, commented of the election campaign of August 1656: 'The Lord, in whose hand alone is the greate worke, I hope will order and dispose thereof for the refreshment of the hearts of his owne deere children, for perfecting the worke of reformation and for exalting his owne great name on the earth.'[84]

Some passages in the major-generals' letters closely resemble the sermons and extempore prayer which were such prominent features of the puritan worship in which they were such eager participants. Hezekiah Haynes, for example, commented of the decimation tax that 'every tongue must confess it was of the Lord, who is a righteouse god in the execution of his judgements; and when his hand is lyfted up he shall not onely make them (though most unwilling) to see, but also make them ashamed for their envy to his people.'[85] William Goffe told Thurloe that he would 'be watchfull in the station God hath set me', adding: 'except the lord watch the citty, those that watch, watch in vain.'[86] Several months later, he declared: 'it is the lord himself that must be our support, on whome wee have greate reason to trust. He hath hetherto helped us in all the straights wee have beene in, and I am persuaded will yet bee our helper and, notwithstanding all our unworthynes, will save us and bless us for his owne name's sake.'[87] Reporting to Cromwell on the disastrous election results in Kent in August 1656, a mournful Thomas Kelsey wrote:

> If the Lord shall take pleasure in us, hee will cause his face to shine upon us and carry us well through the seas of blood that are threatened against us and the vast howling wilderness of our straits and difficultyes, and at length bring us to that blessed haven of reformation endeavoured by us, and cause all our troubles and

disquiett to end in a happy rest and peace, when all his people shall bee one and his name one in all your dominions.[88]

What such comments demonstrate very clearly is that, above all else, the major-generals were a set of godly governors who were convinced that they were doing God's vital work and that He would therefore not let them fail. This unshakeable godly conviction was to prove both their greatest asset and their greatest handicap. For, while it engendered in them great energy and enthusiasm for the work and gave them the strength to persevere when opposition must have appeared insurmountable, more than anything else it ensured that the local communities they were sent to govern viewed them as an alien and unwelcome intrusion – one that was to be resisted and, at the first opportunity, repelled.

NOTES

1 PRO, SP.18.100.133.

2 Charles Fleetwood, the younger son of a Northamptonshire gentleman, fought for parliament throughout the first civil war. He acted as lord-deputy for Ireland in the early 1650s and married Bridget Cromwell, the protector's daughter. John Lambert originated from Yorkshire and also fought for parliament throughout the 1640s. By the early 1650s he was one of Cromwell's closest advisers and, as was shown in chapter 2, he was the chief architect of the major-generals' experiment. Philip Skippon, who originated from Norfolk, fought as a mercenary soldier in Europe in the 1620s and 1630s and on the outbreak of the civil war was given command of the London trained bands. He later fought in the New Model Army and was badly wounded at Naseby.

3 Unless otherwise stated, the subsequent biographical material in this chapter is taken from references to the major-generals in the following sources: *Dictionary of National Biography*; C. H. Firth and G. Davies, *A Regimental History of Cromwell's Army* (2 vols, Oxford, 1940); R. L. Greaves and R. Zaller (eds), *A Biographical Dictionary of British Radicals in the Seventeenth Century* (3 vols, Brighton, 1982); Maurice Ashley, *Cromwell's Generals* (London, 1954); and Anthony Fletcher, 'The Religious Motivation of Cromwell's Major-Generals', in D. Baker (ed.), *Religious Motivation: Biographical and Social Problems for the Church Historian*, Studies in Church History, 15 (1978), 259–66. Also consulted were the following studies of individual major-generals. Paul H. Hardacre, 'William Boteler: A Cromwellian Oligarch', *Huntington Library Quarterly*, 11 (1947), 1–11; W. L. F. Nuttall, 'Hezekiah Haynes: Oliver Cromwell's Major-General for the Eastern Counties', *Transactions of the Essex Archaeological Society*, 3rd series, 1 (1964), 196–209; J. Berry and S. G. Lee, *A Cromwellian Major-General: The Career of Colonel James Berry* (Oxford, 1938); Roger Howell, 'The Army and the English Revolution: The Case of Robert Lilburne', *Archaeologia Aeliana*, fifth series, 9 (1981), 299–315; and A. R. Williams, 'John Desborough: Gloucestershire's Major-General', *Transactions of the Bristol and Gloucestershire Archaeological Society*, 89 (1970), 123–9.

4 Information on geographic origin has been ascertained for all sixteen, except John Nicholas.

5 Bod. Lib., Rawlinson MSS, A 34, fols 767–80.

6   Rutt, *Diary of Thomas Burton*, vol. 1, p. 331.

7   Lucy Hutchinson, *Memoirs of the Life of Colonel Hutchinson*, ed. John Sutherland (Oxford, 1973), p. 209.

8   Bod. Lib., Clarendon MSS, vol. 53, fols 262–3.

9   Lilburne made the comment in his tract *The Upright Mans Vindication* (London, 1653), p. 2. See also Murray Tolmie, *The Triumph of the Saints: The Separate Churches of London, 1616–1649* (Cambridge, 1977), p. 157.

10 Richard Baxter, *Reliquiae Baxterianae* (London, 1696), part 1, pp. 97–8.

11 For details of these land purchases see Ian Gentles, 'The Debentures Market and the Military Purchases of Crown Lands, 1649–1660', (Unpub. Ph.D. thesis, University of London, 1969), pp. 161, 171, 173, 249, 253, 259, 273, 274, 286, 294, 304, 315, 318, 351. None of the active sixteen could match two of the non-active major-generals, John Lambert and Charles Fleetwood, both of whom bought lands worth in excess of £20,000.

12 David Farr, 'The Military and Political Career of John Lambert, 1619–1657' (Unpub. Ph.D. thesis, University of Cambridge, 1996), pp. 143, 151.

13 Baxter, *Reliquiae Baxterianae*, pp. 53, 57.

14 Bod. Lib., Rawlinson MSS, A 32, fols 715–18.

15 N. Penney (ed.), *The First Publishers of Truth* (London, 1907), p. 283.

16 Firth and Davies, *Regimental History*, vol. 1, p. 247; Barry Reay, *The Quakers in the English Revolution* (London, 1985), p. 90.

17 Bod. Lib., Rawlinson MSS, A 35, fol. 277.

18 *Ibid.*, A 34, fols 217–20, 431–4. In May 1655, Berry had requested the council to arrange for the removal from the palace of the cathedral pulpit, which had been stored there; see, PRO, SP.25.76, p. 72.

19 A. S. P. Woodhouse, *Puritanism and Liberty* (London, 1951), pp. 20–1, 39–42, 100–1.

20 William Allen, *A Memorial of the Remarkable Meeting of Many Officers of the Army in England at Windsor Castle in the Year 1648* (London, 1659), *passim*.

21 The letters are printed in two volumes of the *Collections of the Massachusetts Historical Society*: 'Hutchinson Papers', 3rd series, 1 (1865), and 'Letters and Papers Relating to the Regicides', 4th series, 8 (1868). The quotations are from the latter volume, pp. 136–42, 155.

22 *Commons Journal*, vol. 7, pp. 258–9; Firth and Rait, *Acts and Ordinances*, vol. 2, p. 856.

23 Bod. Lib., Rawlinson MSS, A 34, fols 395–6.

24 Rutt, *Diary of Thomas Burton*, vol. 1, pp. 52, 80, 108–11, 155.

25 Bod. Lib., Rawlinson MSS, A 32, fols 381–4; A 39, fols 424–5.

26 *Ibid.*, A 32, fols 659–60; A 38, fols 125–8.

27 *Ibid.*, A 36, fols 630–2.

28 Rutt, *Diary of Thomas Burton*, vol. 1, pp. 25, 115.

29 PRO, SP.18.102.50.

30 John L. Nickalls (ed.), *The Journal of George Fox* (London, 1952), p. 275.

31 Rutt, *Diary of Thomas Burton*, vol. 1, pp. 25–6, 113–15.

32 Bod. Lib., Rawlinson MSS, A 32, fols 385–8; PRO, SP.25.76, p. 512.

33 George F. Warner (ed.), *The Nicholas Papers, vol. III: Correspondence of Sir Edward Nicholas, Secretary of State*, Camden Soc. Publs, new series, 57 (1897), 261–2.

34 Rutt, *Diary of Thomas Burton*, vol. 4, p. 403.

35 *Calendar of State Papers Domestic, 1664–65*, p. 538.

36 Bod. Lib., Rawlinson MSS, A 36, fols 590–1.

37 BL, E.658.9, *The Fourth Paper presented by Maj. Butler to the Honorable Committee of Parliament for the Propagation of the Gospel of Christ Jesus* (London, 1652); Richard L. Greaves, *Saints and Rebels: Seven Nonconformists in Stuart England* (Macon, Georgia, 1985), p. 170; and Woodhouse, *Puritanism and Liberty*, p. 170.

38 Margaret Spufford, *Contrasting Communities: English Villagers in the Sixteenth and Seventeenth Centuries* (Cambridge, 1974), pp. 227–8, 286.

39 Bod. Lib., Rawlinson MSS, A 33, fols 529–32; A 34, fols 305–8.

40 Nickalls, *Journal of George Fox*, p. 241.

41 Rutt, *Diary of Thomas Burton*, vol. 1, pp. 316–17.

42 Bod. Lib., Rawlinson MSS, A 34, fols 899–902; Rutt, *Diary of Thomas Burton*, vol. 1, p. 237.

43 Rutt, *Diary of Thomas Burton*, vol. 1, pp. 31, 39, 54–5, 71–2, 153.

44 Bod. Lib., Rawlinson MSS, A 34, fols 899–902.

45 *Commons Journal*, vol. 7, pp. 258–9; Firth and Davies, *Regimental History*, vol. 1, pp. 208–9, 212.

46 H. N. Brailsford, *The Levellers in the English Revolution* (London, 1961), p. 494.

47 Bod. Lib., Rawlinson MSS, A 33, fols 355–8.

48 Rutt, *Diary of Thomas Burton*, vol. 1, pp. 101–4, 154.

49 Bod. Lib., Rawlinson MSS, A 36, fol. 371.

50 *Ibid.*, A 36, fol. 709; A 37, fols 229–32; H. Stocks (ed.), *Records of the Borough of Leicester, 1603–1688* (Cambridge, 1923), pp. 428–9; Rutt, *Diary of Thomas Burton*, vol. 1, pp. 175–6. For more details, see chapter 8.

51 Bod. Lib., Rawlinson MSS, A 40, fols 499–502.

52 Morrill, *Cheshire*, pp. 276–87. For Worsley's family background, see John Booker, *A History of the Ancient Chapel of Birch in Manchester Parish*, Chetham Soc. Publs, 47 (1859), 23–70.

53 Christopher Goad, *Refreshing Drops and Scorching Vials* (London, 1653), second preface; for brief details on Goad see Keith Lindley, *Popular Politics in Civil War London* (Aldershot, 1997), p. 58, note 99; and Tai Liu, *Puritan London* (Newark NJ, 1986), p. 117.

54 For more details, see chapter 8.

55 PRO, SP.18.130.129.

56 PRO, SP.25.77, pp. 261–2, 362–3, 459, 576; Manchester Local Studies Archive Service, Carill Worsley Papers, M35/5/4/2.

57 For John Haynes, see Roger Thompson, *Mobility and Migration: East Anglian Founders of New England, 1629–40* (Amherst, 1994), pp. 14, 32, 40, 41, 42, 44, 187.

58 William A. Shaw, *A History of the English Church during the Civil Wars and under the Commonwealth 1640–1660* (2 vols, London, 1900), vol. 2 , p. 388.

59 Macfarlane, *Diary of Ralph Josselin*, pp. 30, 110–11, 196, 268, 302, 340–2, 348, 356–7, 362–3, 365, 374–8, 381, 388, 392, 394–5, 400–1, 406–8, 411, 419–20, 430, 445, 449, 451, 458, 484, 509, 553.

60 For examples see Bod. Lib., Rawlinson MSS, A 37, fols 233–6, 611–14; A 40, fols 121–4.

61 Rutt, *Diary of Thomas Burton*, vol. 1, p. 153.

62 Buckinghamshire Record Office, Claydon House Letters, M11/14. Sir William Waller to Sir Ralph Verney, 20 Nov. 1655.

63 Bod. Lib., Rawlinson MSS, A 32, fols 711–14; Macfarlane, *Diary of Ralph Josselin*, pp. 363, 365.

64 Bod. Lib., Rawlinson MSS, A 41, fols 858–9.

65 Macfarlane, *Diary of Ralph Josselin*, pp. 406–8.

66 Firth and Davies, *Regimental History*, vol. 1, pp. 35, 70, 71, 73.

67 *Ibid.*, p. 73.

68 Greaves, *Saints and Rebels*, pp. 107–9.

69 Firth and Rait, *Acts and Ordinances*, vol. 2, p. 856.

70 Rutt, *Diary of Thomas Burton*, vol 1, p. 229; Bod. Lib., Clarendon MSS, vol. 55, fols 12–13.

71 Nickalls, *Journal of George Fox*, pp. 195–6, 358.

72 *Ibid.*, p. 195.

73 Rutt, *Diary of Thomas Burton*, vol. 1, pp. 99–101.

74 *Ibid.*, vol. 3, pp. 159–69.

75 Frances Dow, *Cromwellian Scotland 1651–60* (Edinburgh, 1979), pp. 78–114; Reay, *Quakers*, pp. 19, 38.

76 Bod. Lib., Carte MSS, 131, fols 189–90; BL, E. 985.11; Abbott, *Writings and Speeches of Cromwell*, vol. 4, p. 266.

77 *DNB*, Charles Howard, first earl of Carlisle (1629–1685); *Lord's Journal*, vol. 8, pp. 296, 469, 477, 499. For more information on Howard's later career, see Stephen Saunders Webb, *The Governors-General: The English Army and the Definition of the Empire* (Chapel Hill, 1979), pp. 69–79.

78 Austin Woolrych, *Commonwealth to Protectorate* (Oxford, 1982), p. 201.

79 Bernard Capp, *The Fifth Monarchy Men* (London, 1972), pp. 276–8.

80 Rutt, *Diary of Thomas Burton*, vol. 1, pp. 122–3, 163–4.

81 Philip Jenkins, *The Making of a Ruling Class: The Glamorgan Gentry, 1640–1790* (Cambridge, 1983), pp. 110–13; Philip Jenkins, '"The Old Leaven": The Welsh Roundheads after 1660', *Historical Journal*, 24 (1981), 809; Stephen Roberts's view is taken from his entry in the *New DNB*, which he kindly allowed me to see prior to publication.

82 Bod. Lib., Rawlinson MSS, A 32, fols 715–18; A 33, fols 571–4.

83 *Ibid.*, A 35, fol. 4; PRO, SP.18.126.50.

84 Bod. Lib., Rawlinson MSS, A 40, fols 341–2.

85 *Ibid.*, A 32, fols 647–50.

86 *Ibid.*, A 36, fols 331–3.

87 *Ibid.*, A 39, fols 424–5.

88 PRO, SP.18.129.156.

Chapter 4

The helpers:
the commissioners for securing
the peace of the commonwealth

A t the same time as it appointed the major-generals in the autumn of 1655, Cromwell's government also selected groups of men to act as their helpers within England and Wales and appointed them to the new post of commissioner for the securing of the peace of the commonwealth. Virtually every county was allocated its own commission, although Cumberland and Westmorland shared a set of commissioners as did a number of Welsh shires. As was pointed out in chapter 2, the selection process for these new commissioners was lengthy and rather imprecise. While the great majority of them were chosen centrally by the council, others were added after the major-generals had arrived in their associations in the late autumn and taken local soundings.[1] Despite the delays, by the end of 1655 the government in London had issued commissions to around a thousand individuals whom it believed it could trust with the vitally important task of supporting the major-generals in the work of collecting the decimation tax, improving local security and promoting godly reform.

The names of several hundred of those appointed to the commissions for more than thirty English counties, and for London, Bristol, North Wales and Camarthenshire can be found amongst the state papers of John Thurloe and other extant records.[2] While the great majority of these men were named only to their local commission, a few individuals, such as Cornelius Holland, who served in Berkshire and Buckinghamshire, and James Chadwick, who served in Derbyshire and Nottinghamshire, were appointed in several counties. The major-generals themselves served as commissioners in each of the counties of their associations, and several of them were also named in other counties with which they had personal connections; John Barkstead, for example, was appointed in Berkshire and Hampshire, and James Berry in Lincolnshire, where his principal residence lay.

These new commissioners have been dismissed both by hostile contemporaries and later commentators as inept and unscrupulous non-entities.

According to the Suffolk royalist, Roger Coke, they were 'mean and profligate rascals', while for the eighteenth-century Tory historian, Laurence Echard, they were 'the dregs of the people, tho' others of better note were sometimes mingled with them'.[3] Such assertions can only properly be examined by undertaking a detailed prosopographical analysis of the commissioners, but any attempt to carry out such a study is hamstrung by two major problems: the apparent absence of any official list of the commissioners amongst the surviving records of the protectorate government, and the relative obscurity of many of those who can be identified as holders of the new office.

Exhaustive searches among the Interregnum state papers in the Public Record Office have failed to uncover a definitive national list of commissioners, and in the absence of such a document the names of a large number of the commisioners must remain unknown. Moreover, the relatively low social status of many of those who can be identifed often makes it difficult to uncover any meaningful evidence which throws light on their material situation or ideological outlook. For these reasons, most modern historians of the protectorate have generally avoided commenting in detail on the identity and character of the commissioners, who as a consequence have remained, in John Sutton's phrase, 'the invisible men of Interregnum politics'.[4] Although these problems will inevitably impose limitations upon it, the following investigation will attempt to go some way towards remedying this situation by outlining some of the most important characteristics shared by those who are known to have been named to the commissions in Cheshire, Kent, Sussex, Hampshire, Cornwall, Staffordshire, London and Bristol.[5]

The Cheshire commission contained a number of representatives from the highest ranks of county society, such as John Bradshaw, Jonathan Bruen, Edward Hyde, Sir Thomas Mainwaring, Thomas Marbury and Thomas Stanley, as well as a number of gentleman of substantial, if somewhat lesser status, such as Henry Birkenhead, Henry Brooke, William Compton, and Thomas Croxton. It also contained around ten serving soldiers, including Colonel Henry Brooke, Captain Thomas Malbon, Colonel Thomas Croxton, Colonel Thomas Howard and Captain John Griffiths. Croxton was governor of Chester and captain of the county militia troop; Howard was second-in-command of Charles Worsley's regular forces; and Griffiths was a close associate of John Thurloe and lieutenant of the county militia troop. The commission could boast a fair degree of administrative experience. Brooke and Stanley had served on the county bench of justices since the 1630s, and Birkenhead, Croxton, Hyde, Mainwaring and Marbury had served as committeemen or JPs in the 1640s. A number of the commissioners, including Birkenhead, Brooke, Bruen, Compton, Hyde and Mainwaring, were conspicuous for their godly religious outlook. While the Cheshire commission clearly, therefore, possessed a distinctly military and godly flavour, it also contained a reasonable representation of the traditional ruling families of the county.[6]

As a result of the strength of royalism in Kent, the commission for that county contained fewer county magnates than its Cheshire counterpart. While the leading county gentry families were represented on the Kentish commission by Thomas Monins and Henry Oxinden of Deane, the great majority of the commissioners, including Richard Beale, Charles Bowles, John Browne, Thomas Foach, Augustine Garland, Robert Gibbon, Lambarde Godfrey, Robert Hales, Sir Michael Livesey, John Parker, Alexander Roberts and Augustine Skynner, were gentlemen of lesser status. The commission also contained several prominent townsmen, such as Andrew Broughton of Maidstone and William Cullen of Dover, as well as a strong military representation. No fewer than half of the thirty-two commissioners were soldiers, including the New Model Army colonel, Robert Gibbon, and two of the three commanders of the county militia troops, John Browne and Thomas Monins. A number of the Kentish commissioners had significant experience of public adminstration, and Beale, Bowles, Broughton, Godfrey, Monins, Roberts and Ralph Weldon had all been active as members or officers of the local county committee in the 1640s or early 1650s. The commission also contained a number of conspicuous religious and political radicals; both Garland and Livesey were regicides, and Broughton had acted as clerk of the court which had tried Charles I. Livesey and Hales, meanwhile, were prominent within Kentish Independency.[7]

Among those nominated to the Sussex commision were several members of the powerful local magnate gentry, notably John Busbridge, Anthony Shirley and John Stapley. Again, however, these prominent county figures were far outnumbered by more minor landowners, such as Arthur Bettesworth, Walter Everenden, William Freeman, Nathaniel Studley and Richard Yates, and by influential townsmen, such as Thomas Ballard, mayor of Arundel, and Richard Maning, mayor of Chichester. This preponderance of the middle ranks of society within the commission was specifically acknowledged by the local major-general, William Goffe, who reported to Thurloe shortly after his arrival in the county that 'the stresse of this businesse must lie upon the middle sort of men.'[8] Once again, the military was well represented; all three captains of the county militia troops, Busbridge, Freeman and Thomas Jenner, were appointed to the commission, as were a number of other local officers, such as Colonel Richard Broughton, Captain Edward Madgwick and Captain Walter Everenden. Like their counterparts in Kent and Cheshire, the Sussex commissioners were not without administrative experience; Freeman and Yates had served as county committeemen in the 1640s, and Bettesworth, Busbridge, Everenden, Richard Knowles and Studley had all served on the local bench of justices before Goffe's arrival. According to

Anthony Fletcher, Goffe chose his commissioners for their godliness, and a number of them were certainly conspicuous for their radical religious beliefs. Maning was, in Fletcher's phrase, 'a fierce puritan' who had led a long battle against 'the corrupt party' in Chichester, and Goffe described Walter Everenden as one whom 'the honest party of the country were apt to follow'. Numbered amongst their godly allies on the commission were Freeman, Knowles and Studley.[9]

The Hampshire commission, too, contained several representatives from the leading county families, including Richard Norton and Richard Major, who as father-in-law of Richard Cromwell had a close family connection to the protector. Yet again, however, they were greatly outnumbered by men of lower social standing. Particularly active in Hampshire was a group of individuals who exercised considerable power within the principal towns of the county, including John Hildesley and Thomas Muspratt of Winchester, and Thomas Cole and Robert Wroth of Southampton. The two captains of the county militia troops, John Dunch and John Pitman, were both named to the commission as were a contingent of regular army officers, including Colonel Norton, the governor of Portsmouth, Colonel John Fiennes, Major Azariah Husbands, Major Richard Bull, Major Edward Hooker and Captain Thomas Chase. Many of the commissioners, including Thomas Bettesworth, Thomas Cole, William Jephson, John Hildesley, Edward Hooker, Richard Major, Richard Norton and Thomas Muspratt, were conspicuous for their support for the godly cause.[10]

The Cornish commission contained several leading county gentlemen, such as Anthony Nicoll and John St Aubyn, as well as a number of more minor gentlemen and individuals with a mercantile background, such as Edward Nosworthy and Peter Ceeley. The military was represented here by the local militia captains, William Braddon and Peter Ceeley, and by John Fox, the governor of Pendennis castle. Here too, there was a fair degree of administrative experience on the commission, as Nicoll, St Aubyn, Ceeley, Braddon and James Launce had all served on earlier parliamentary committees for the county. Most of the Cornish committeemen appear to have been presbyterian in religious outlook.[11] Elsewhere in the west country, the picture appears to have been very similar. Richard Williams, who investigated the social composition of the commissions in four of Desborough's western counties, concluded that in Devon, Dorset and Somerset as well as in Cornwall they were dominated by 'the lesser gentry and the professional soldiers under the tutelage of a handful of JPs'.[12]

By far the most detailed investigation into the backgrounds of the major-generals' helpers in the provinces has recently been undertaken by John Sutton for the commission in Staffordshire.[13] His findings confirm the above picture. The twenty-two men named in Staffordshire were drawn in roughly equal proportions from all parts of the county. While they ranged in age from late twenties to mid sixties, the majority were aged around forty-five. Most were eldest sons and just under a third had attended a university or inn of court. Seven of the twenty-two commissioners – George Bowes, John Chetwode, Thomas Crompton, Edward Mainwaring, Thomas Whitgreave, Sir John Wryley and John Young – belonged to the elite group of county gentry families. Another six – Thomas Adshead, Peter Backhouse, George Bellot, Edward Brett, Thomas Malkin and Thomas Pudsey – were gentlemen of more minor status, and a further five – William Gent, Thomas Minors, Robert Smith, Henry Stone and John Symcox – were townsmen, who were still active in commerce within the county's boroughs. Of the four remaining commissioners, Zakariah Babbington, Daniel Watson and Thomas Worswick were lawyers, whilst Matthew Worswick was an apothecary in Stafford.

Only around half of these Staffordshire commissioners were armigerous, and most of those who did possess a coat of arms had only acquired one relatively recently. While the richest commissioner, Edward Mainwaring, enjoyed an annual income of around £1,000, nearly half of his colleagues were worth no more than £200 per annum. Sutton's conclusion as to their social status is that most of them were clearly located within 'the lesser gentry or the more prosperous "middling sort of people"'. They nonetheless possessed what he has described as 'impressive records of both national and local expertise'. Fourteen had served as JPs before 1655, nine of them for more than five years, and five others had held important municipal office. Five had sat in parliament before 1655, and six had been active on parliamentary committees in the county during the 1640s. Nine of the twenty-two either possessed recent military experience or were serving as officers of the county miltia troop.

With regard to the religious complexion of the Staffordshire commission, Sutton has argued that at its godly nature was 'beyond doubt' and that six of its members – Backhouse, Bowes, Brett, Stone, Matthew Worswick and Young – were 'particularly pious'. On the other hand, he has also suggested that as a group the commissioners exhibited a 'basic religious conservatism' and that most of them 'seem to have been on the conservative ends of the Puritan spectrum'. Five of them – Babbington, Crompton, Minors, Smith and Stone – were in Sutton's view presbyterians, and two of them – Mainwaring and Wryley – Anglicans. These religious findings are not, however, entirely reliable. In the context of the fluid, ill-defined nature of the Interregnum religious settlement, precise attributions of religious affiliation during the 1650s are frequently problematic and misleading. Sutton's attempts to prove that neither John Chetwode nor Daniel Watson deserved their contemporary reputations as religious radicals are not convincing. More worryingly, his two 'Anglicans' are classified as such solely on the basis of their conformity to the restored church after 1660, a course of action which reveals little about their earlier views. Sutton is right to point out that the godly zeal of the commissioners should not be equated with religious fanaticism, but in his overeagerness to protect the commissioners from such a charge, he underplays the importance of their shared godly outlook and obscures the fact that even as 'conservative puritans' they were very clearly marked out from the great majority of their ungodly Staffordshire neighbours.

Unsurprisingly, the commissions for two of the country's largest urban communities, London and Bristol, contained a very large representation of prosperous merchants with strong godly credentials. The London commission, established in March 1656, was dominated by the capital's political Independents, many of whom had a long history of political and religious radicalism; among those who fell into this category were Thomas Atkins, Thomas Andrews, Charles Doyley, John Fowke, Mark Hildesley, John Ireton (Henry Ireton's brother), William Kiffin, Isaac Pennington, Owen Rowe, John Stone and Robert Tichborne. Most of these men were also new merchants, engaged in the colonial interloping trade. They shared a wealth of administrative and military experience. A number of them, in particular Atkins, Andrews, John Dethick, Pennington and Tichborne, had exercised high office in the city's government. Atkins, Pennington and Sir John Woolaston had served as colonels of the city militia, and Nathaniel Camfield, Thomas Juxon, Owen Rowe, Robert Tichborne, William Thomson and William Underwood had all served as more junior officers in that force. Some of them, including Tempest Milner, Thomas Stone and William Underwood, also enjoyed a contemporary reputation for what Keith Lindley has labelled 'parish zealotry', and William Kiffen was a prominent Baptist minister.[14] Like its counterpart in the capital, the Bristol commission was also dominated by the godly members of the city's merchant community, including important figures such as James Powell, and the leading Baptists, Thomas Ellis and Robert Purnell.[15] These two urban commissions appear to have been significantly more radical in composition than those in some of the rural counties such as Cheshire and Staffordshire.

The above investigation into the origins, status and attitudes of the commissioners in six rural counties and two cities clearly reveals that the majority of them were minor gentlemen or prosperous townsmen, and that many of them had served as members or officers of parliamentary county committees and as justices of the peace in the 1640s and 1650s. Significant numbers had also either been in arms for parliament during the civil war or were still serving as army officers and most were conspicuous supporters of the godly cause. The great majority had also been named to the commissions of local ejectors set up in each county in 1654, and charged with the task of purging 'scandalous and insufficient' clergy from the parochial ministry.[16]

Not all of those appointed by the government to serve on these new commissions, however, proved willing and eager to play an active role as assistants to their local major-general. In most counties a number of those originally nominated either sent their excuses or simply failed to turn up for the early meetings of the commission. In December 1655, James Berry informed Thurloe that several of the commissioners for North Wales were 'disatisfyed or rather not satisfyed to act' and that 'there is some little scruple in some, and they scarce know what it is.'[17] Shortly afterwards, John Desborough reported from Bristol that 'sundry' of the commissioners there had 'craved tyme to consider ... and at last made their excuses', with the result that he had been forced to replace them with others 'that will effectually carry it on'. He encountered similar problems in Gloucestershire, where two of the commissioners excused themselves for attendance, pleading toothache and gout respectively. Clearly not convinced of the genuineness of these ailments, Desborough commented wryly to Cromwell: 'but the best is they are diseases not catching, for the work goes pleasantly on.'[18] In Kent, three of the commissioners – Lambarde Godfrey, Henry Oxinden, and Colonel Ralph Weldon – failed to attend a single meeting.[19] Often it was the more socially elevated nominees who declined to serve. In Hampshire, Richard Norton sent his apologies to Goffe in late November; in Sussex the magnate gentlemen, John Busbridge and John Stapley, failed to appear; and in Derbyshire Colonel Thomas Sanders decided not to get involved.[20]

The best documented case of refusal to act concerned the Wiltshire presbyterian, Thomas Grove. In early December 1655, John Desborough wrote to Thurloe and Cromwell to inform them that all the Wiltshire commissioners were prepared to serve, with the one exception of Grove, whom he described as 'honest and able, though tender'. He enclosed a letter which Grove had sent him, in which he had explained that ill-health had prevented him from attending the commissioners' first meeting, but that even if he had been well he would have requested more time to consider whether or not to act, on the grounds that: 'I cannot undertake any business of consequence till I have had some serious thoughts about it and have debated it with mine own weak judgement, that so my conscience may be clearly satisfide in what I doe.' Grove went on to state that he had no objection to 'the grounds of the design' and was sure that 'the old enimies have their old hearts and old hatred still', but that he was concerned that 'there may be some scruple in the manner of doing this'. He assured Desborough that if he could convince himself that 'the way and manner be as righteous and warrantable as the thing is good and desirable', he would act 'as cordially as any man in England'.[21] Unsurprisingly, he failed to resolve his doubts and remained inactive.

A number of other commissioners who did put in an initial appearance seem also to have lacked any real enthusiasm for the work. William Boteler

encountered some initial hesitancy amongst the Northamptonshire commissioners. In early November 1655, he informed Thurloe that only a few of
them had turned up for their first meeting in Northampton, and that some of
those that had attended 'were not very harty in our worke' but rather 'a little
timorous and seeming averse'. Whether through threats or encouragement,
within a day or two he had persuaded them to act and could report back that
'they have all of them putt their hands to the plough; and shame will not let
them now looke back.' A week later he confirmed that 'they came on (some of
them especially) a little slowly at first, yet now go on without any rubb.'[22]

Some of the commissioners who decided they would serve seem to have
done so not because they sympathised with the aims of the major-generals but
rather because they wished to gain or retain local power, or to protect their
royalist friends and relations and minimise the damage inflicted upon their
local communities. Christopher Guise, one of the Gloucestershire commissioners, for example, was the son of a royalist and possessed a distinctly
ungodly reputation as a womaniser; his attempts to shield some of his friends
from the decimation tax enraged his fellow commissioners and prompted
Desborough to denounce him during the election campaign in the summer of
1656.[23]

Another individual who should perhaps be added to the list of commissioners with ulterior motives for acting is Colonel James Chadwick, the recorder
of Nottingham and Derby, who was a member of both the Nottinghamshire
and Derbyshire commissions. According to the godly Nottinghamshire
gentlewoman, Lucy Hutchinson, Chadwick was a time-serving opportunist
whose apparent godliness was a sham and who was addicted to 'a thousande
cheates and other base wayes'.[24] On the other hand, Edward Whalley, who
encountered Chadwick soon after his arrival in the east Midlands, was far
more positive about him, describing him as someone who was particularly
keen to help with the work and 'very able and well esteemed, even amongst
honest and godly men, as far as I can hitherto learne'. Whalley was clearly
aware that the government in London had earlier received unfavourable
comment about Chadwick, for he went on to claim that Cromwell had not
previously been given a true account of his character.[25] It is difficult to know
which of these assessments is the more accurate. Lucy Hutchinson had
probably known Chadwick for longer then Whalley and had observed at close
range his rapid rise to power in Nottingham. She was, however, clearly
prejudiced against him on account of his plebeian origins.

A few of the commissioners also went out of their way to remain on
amicable terms with their royalist friends and neighbours. In Cheshire, Henry
Birkenhead and Sir Thomas Mainwaring wrote to the council on behalf of a
royalist who was seeking an exemption from the decimation tax, and
Mainwaring continued to dine regularly with his royalist friends throughout

his time as a commissioner.[26] In early December 1655, one of the Staffordshire commissioners, Robert Smith, lent his support to his royalist neighbour,
Sir Hervey Bagot, who was attempting to escape the decimation, and wrote to
him to assure him that he would be 'ready to serve you in what lawfully I may,
and at all times remain your friend'.[27] A few days later, his fellow Staffordshire
commissioner, Thomas Crompton, wrote to his royalist friend, Sir Richard
Leveson, to apologise about the new requirement to give security to the
authorities. To avoid giving Leveson the trouble of travelling in 'difficult and
tedious' weather, he offered to come to his house, and he went on to assure
him: 'you may be confident I will use you with what civility my commission
and instructions give me leave.'[28]

In most counties, however, the reluctant commissioners and those less than
fully committed to the work of the major-generals played at best only a minor
role on the commissions, leaving the brunt of the work to be carried out by
their more enthusiastic colleagues. These more ardent commissioners were
in the main local military figures and zealous puritans; they were unswerv-
ingly committed to the work of the major-generals and utterly uncompromising in their approach to those of their neighbours whom they
considered their enemies. In Kent, in addition to the three commissioners
mentioned above who declined to serve at all, another thirteen attended fewer
than seven of the commission's twenty-three meetings. As a consequence,
most of the work in that county was left to a subgroup of thirteen active
commissioners, which included no fewer than nine soldiers as well as the
unpopular regicide, Sir Michael Livesey.[29] In Warwickshire, the equivalent
subgroup of active commissioners included the two godly merchants from
Coventry, Thomas Basnet and Robert Beake; the governor of Warwick Castle,
Colonel Joseph Hawkesworth; the former sequestration commissioner,
William Thornton; and the former county committeeman and major of foot,
Waldive Willington.[30] The active subgroup in Dorset, meanwhile, was similarly
dominated by godly soldiers, including the former governors of Bridport,
Poole and Portland, John Lea, John Bingham and John Arthur respectively,
and the captain of the county militia troop, James Dewey.[31]

The eagerness of these subgroups of active commissioners to assist the
major-generals was a central theme both of the reports the major-generals
sent back to London in the weeks following their arrival in their associations
and of the commissioners' own correspondence with the government over the
same period. Most of the major-generals reported to Thurloe in the autumn of
1655 that they had found them 'ready', 'cheerful' and 'very forward' to help
with the work.[32] James Berry, for example, wrote from Herefordshire that the
active commissioners there had set about the work 'with much readines and
(indeed I thinke) joy'. He added that 'some that have seemed disatisfyed and

have declined action formerly have now declared their hopes of good by this dispensation and are resolved to assist in this worke and are persuaded it will bring forth some desirable reformation.'[33] Thomas Kelsey similarly commented that the active commissioners in Kent were 'very hartie and cordiall to the work', and William Boteler remarked of those in Bedfordshire that 'God hath wrought a good promptitude in the harts of our honest friends in other places to this great worke; yet I am apt to thinke more than ordinary in these gentlemen.'[34] In January 1656, William Goffe reported to Thurloe that the godly Sussex gentleman, Walter Everenden, was so keen to assist in the decimation work that he regularly travelled more than sixty miles from his home near Rye to Chichester to attend meetings of the commissioners.[35] An account of Charles Worsley's first meeting with the Lancashire commissioners, meanwhile, which appeared in the government newspaper, *Mercurius Politicus*, suggested that: 'there appears daily more and more ground of encouragement for acting, for the good people doe not a little rejoyce and seem to be abundantly affected therewith and promise to set heart and hand to this good work.'[36]

Several of the major-generals, who had clearly not set out for their districts with very great expectations, were genuinely taken aback by the degree of enthusiasm shown by the active commissioners. Hezekiah Haynes wrote from Norwich in early November 1655 to inform Thurloe: 'I did not expect it would have had so good an acceptance with them; and I desire to bless the Lord for his goodness therein and to take encouragement from this good beginning to trust him in what remains.'[37] Several weeks later, he again commented: 'Truly I could not have expected that readyness to this worke as I find in the gentlemen now mett', and a few days afterwards he declared, this time from Cambridge: 'still it pleaseth the lord to unite the hearts of our friends beyond expectation in this worke.'[38] Thomas Kelsey was another who was surprised by the zeal displayed by some of his Kentish commissioners; in late November 1655 he informed Thurloe from Maidstone: 'I must confess the Lord hath given my unbelieving hart the ly, by vouchsafing unto mee more of his presence and comfort in thes uncouth imployment then I could expect.'[39]

Some of the active commissioners also sent their own letters to Cromwell and Thurloe in the weeks following their appointment. In this correspondence they thanked the government profusely for sending down the major-generals, expressed their great eagerness to assist with the work, and promised to carry it out as speedily and diligently as possible.[40] In a typical example, sent to Thurloe on 16 November, eleven of the commissioners for Bedfordshire declared themselves highly satisfied that the government had decided 'to purpose such a way for settling the hearts and quieting the minds of all good people by this course now proceeded in'.[41] A few days later, around twenty of the Suffolk commissioners declared to Cromwell: 'We are very clear in our opinions that this undertaking is not only honourable in itself but also the most probable and likely means to secure the peace and happiness of this commonwealth.'[42]

The commissioners' letters reveal that what particularly appealed to them about their new position was that it provided them with what seemed to be an excellent opportunity to punish and emasculate their royalist enemies. The active Suffolk commissioners thanked God for making Oliver Cromwell 'the instrument of our deliverance from that implacable generation of men', and expressed great satisfaction that the imposition of the decimation tax would reduce the financial burden on 'the good and peaceable people of this nation who have a long time born the heate of the day'.[43] In late November 1655, Thomas Kelsey informed Thurloe that the Kentish commissioners 'rejoyce to see such a checke and discourgement is put upon their old enemy', and a week later the Cheshire commissioners told Cromwell they had 'long been desirous that the first and continued causers of the disturbance of our peace might not equally have shared our so dearly purchased freedom'.[44] In mid December, the Essex commissioners argued that it was right that 'those who will not be convinced, reclaimed and won by lenity should have the straighter reins of government imposed for a curb and terror unto them', adding: 'it is also reasonable that they who by their restlesse designes endeavour continually to interrupt and undermine all those dearly bought liberties which the proud hand of God have wrought out for us should be made instrumentall (though against their wills) to conserve that which they soe labour to destroy.'[45]

In January 1656, the Nottinghamshire commissioners informed Cromwell that in their view their work was 'composed of great justice and mercie, wisdom and equitie of justice, in chargeinge the guiltie and easing the guiltlesse', and in March the Buckinghamshire commissioners claimed that the decimation tax should not be considered 'an extraction of vitals, but the correction of distempered humours, that the whole body may be brought into a right frame again'.[46] Such comments make very clear that, like the major-generals themselves, the great majority of the active commissioners saw their role as a God-given trust and believed it was their bounden religious duty to help in every way they could to secure the survival of Cromwell's regime and to further the work of religious and moral regeneration.

This investigation into the backgrounds of the commissioners for the securing of the peace of the commonwealth has shown that they were a mixture of old county gentlemen, minor landowners and prosperous townsmen, and that, while the respective weightings of these social groups within the individual commissions varied somewhat depending on the degree of support for the protectoral regime exhibited by local elites, in most counties minor gentlemen and prominent townsmen predominated. It has also shown that, as was the case with many other Interregnum commissions, significant numbers of those chosen to serve subsequently proved unwilling to do so. These reluctant commissioners, who were often the most socially elevated of those originally appointed, were not prepared to involve themselves in what they saw as the divisive and disagreeable work of assessing and collecting the decimation tax and disarming and taking security from their royalist neighbours. As a result of their non-appearance or withdrawal, in many counties this work was left to small cadres of godly zealots of generally lower social status. These newly empowered activists set about the tasks of levying the decimation tax, purging the ministry, and attempting to eradicate what they regarded as the endemic irreligion and ungodliness of their local communities with great commitment and enthusiasm. What impact they had upon the more traditional elements of local government will be considered in the following chapter.

NOTES

1 For more details, see chapter 2.

2 Most of the names can be found at the following references in the Rawlinson Manuscripts in the Bodleian Library: Bedfordshire, A 32, fols 529–32; Berkshire, A 33, fols 73–6; Bristol, A 34, fols 137–40; Buckinghamshire, A 36, fols 229–32; Cheshire, A 32, fols 887–90, A 35, fol. 106, A 39, fols 366–7; Cornwall, A 34, fols 699–702; Cumberland and Westmorland, A 34, fols 389–93, A 35, fol. 276; Derbyshire, A32, fols 609–12; Dorset, A 33, fols 359–62; Durham, A 35, fol. 165; Essex, A 33, fols 385–8, A 34, fols 569–74; Gloucestershire, A 33, fols 702–5, A 40, fols 301–4; Hampshire, A 32, fols 809–12, 817–20, A 33, fols 738–9; Hertfordshire, A 36, fols 117–20; Huntingdonshire, A 32, fols 719–22, A 33, fols 403–6; Lancashire, A 37, fols 669–72, A 40, fols 561–4; Leicestershire, A 33, fols 523–4; Lincolnshire, A 32, fols 335–8, 613–16, 801–4, A 33, fols 533–6; Middlesex and Westminster, A 38, fols 267–70; Norfolk, A 37, fols 183–90, 361–4, A 41, fols 324–5; Northamptonshire, A 32, fols 723–6; Northumberland, A 35, fol. 84; Nottinghamshire, A 34, fols 767–80; Oxfordshire, A 36, fols 340, 372; Shropshire, A 35, fol. 17; Staffordshire, A 34, fols 487–90, 511–12; Suffolk, A 32, fols 691–4, A 33, fols 23–6, A 34, fol. 518; Sussex, A 32, fols 171–4; Wiltshire, A 33, fols 157–60, A 36, fol. 427; Worcestershire, A 35, fols 174–5; Yorkshire, A 34, fols 315–18, A 40, fols 85–8, A 42, fols 339–40; North Wales, A 32, fols 617–20; Camarthenshire, A 36, fols 217–20. The commissioners for Kent can be identified from their minute book; see Peter Bloomfield, 'The Cromwellian Commission in Kent, 1655–57', in Alec Detsicas and Nigel Yates (eds), *Studies in Modern Kentish History* (Maidstone, 1983), p. 22. Bloomfield based this article on their minute book, then held at the Centre for Kentish Studies at Maidstone (reference U2341). Unfortunately, it could not be consulted for this study because it has subsequently been lost. The names of some of the active Warwickshire commissioners can be found at the Staffordshire Record Office, D793, 95. The names of the London commissioners are given at PRO, SP.25.77, p. 2.

3 Roger Coke, *A Detection of the Court and State of England during the Last Four Reigns and Interregnum* (2 vols, London, 1694), vol. 2 , p. 53; Laurence Echard, *The History of England from the Beginning of the Reign of Charles I to the Restoration of Charles II* (London, 1718), p. 777.

4 John Sutton, 'Cromwell's Commisioners for preserving the peace of the Commonwealth: A Staffordshire case study', in Ian Gentles, John Morrill and Blair Worden (eds), *Soldiers, Writers and Statesmen in the English Revolution* (Cambridge, 1998), p. 151.

5 These areas were chosen because the names of their commissioners are extant and their communities have been the subject of earlier detailed studies.

6 Information on the Cheshire commissioners is from Morrill, *Cheshire, passim*, but esp. p. 284; Paul J. Pinckney, 'The Cheshire Election of 1656', *Bulletin of John Rylands Library*, 49 (1967), 387–426; R. C. Richardson, *Puritanism in North West England* (Manchester, 1972), p. 96; Austin Woolrych, *Commonwealth to Protectorate* (Oxford, 1982), pp. 410–11 (for Birkenhead). For Bradshaw, see also *DNB*.

7 Information on the Kent commissioners is from Alan Everitt, *The Community of Kent and the Great Rebellion* (Leicester, 1966); Peter Clark, *English Provincial Society from Reformation to Revolution: Religion, Politics and Society in Kent 1500–1640* (Hassocks, 1977); and Woolrych, *Commonwealth to Protectorate*, pp. 414–5 (for Cullen). For Augustine Garland and Sir Michael Livesey, see also *DNB*.

8 Bod. Lib., Rawlinson MSS, A 32, fols 171–4.

9 Information on the Sussex commissioners is from Anthony Fletcher, *A County Community in Peace and War: Sussex 1600–1660* (London and New York, 1975), *passim* but esp. pp. 308–9; and Woolrych, *Commonwealth to Protectorate*, pp. 428–9 (for Studley). For the Everenden quote, see Bod. Lib., Rawlinson MSS, A 34, fols 225–8.

10 Information on the Hampshire commissioners is from Andrew Coleby, *Central Government and the Localities: Hampshire 1649–1689* (Cambridge, 1987) *passim*; W. H. Mildon, 'Puritanism in Hampshire and the Isle of Wight from the Reign of Elizabeth to the Restoration' (Unpub. Ph.D. thesis, University of London, 1934), pp. 201, 202, 276, 302–4, 318, 337, 362–4, 404, 435; Woolrych, *Commonwealth to Protectorate*, pp. 418–19, 422–5 (for Hildesley, Major and Norton).

11 Information on the Cornish commissioners is from Mary Coate, *Cornwall in the Great Civil War and Interregnum, 1642–1660* (Oxford, 1933), pp. 27, 103, 183, 194, 239, 242, 246, 262, 272, 289, 293–4, 308, 311, 313, 332.

12 Richard Williams, 'County and Municipal Government in Cornwall, Devon, Dorset and Somerset, 1649–60' (Unpub. Ph.D. thesis, University of Bristol, 1981), pp. 172–3.

13 John Sutton, 'Cromwell's Commissioners', pp. 151–182.

14 Information on the London commissioners is from Robert Brenner, *Merchants and Revolution: Commercial Change, Political Conflict and London's Overseas Traders, 1550–1653* (Cambridge, 1993), *passim*; Keith Lindley, *Popular Politics and Religion in Civil War London* (Aldershot, 1997), *passim* but esp. pp. 68–70, 208, 388; Woolrych, *Commonwealth to Protectorate*, pp. 420–1, 428–31 (for Ireton, Stone and Tichborne). For Thomas Juxon, see also Keith Lindley and David Scott (eds), *The Journal of Thomas Juxon, 1644–7*, Camden Soc. Publs, 5th series, 13 (1999).

15 Information on the Bristol commissioners is from David Harris Sacks, *The Widening Gate: Bristol and the Atlantic Economy, 1450–1700* (Berkeley, Los Angeles and London, 1991), pp. 270–1, 289, 308–10, 323–5.

16 Firth and Rait, *Acts and Ordinances*, vol. 2, pp. 968–90. For more details of the activities of the ejectors, see chapter 8.

17 Bod. Lib., Rawlinson MSS, A 33, fols 726–9.

18 *Ibid.*, A 34, fols 173–6.

19 Bloomfield, 'Cromwellian Commission in Kent', p. 22.

20 Bod. Lib., Rawlinson MSS, A 32, fols 769–72, 805–8, 809–12; Fletcher, *Sussex*, pp. 308–9.

21 Bod. Lib., Rawlinson MSS, A 33, fols 225–36.

22 *Ibid.*, A 32, fols 293–6, 385–8.

23 Godfrey Davies (ed.), *Memoirs of the Family of Guise*, Camden Soc. Publs, 3rd series, 28 (1917), 129–30.

24 Lucy Hutchinson, *Memoirs of the Life of Colonel Hutchinson*, ed. John Sutherland (Oxford, 1973), pp. 71–2.

25 Bod. Lib., Rawlinson MSS, A 32, fols 601–4.

26 Morrill, *Cheshire*, p. 279; Cheshire Record Office, DDX 384/1, Mainwaring's Diary, pp. 227–72.

27 Staffordshire Record Office, D/793, 96, 97.

28 Staffordshire RO, D 593 P/8/1, 46.

29 Bloomfield, 'Cromwellian Commission in Kent', p. 22.

30 Staffordshire RO, D793, 95; for more details on these men, see Ann Hughes, *Politics, Society and Civil War in Warwickshire, 1620–1660* (Cambridge, 1987).

31 Bod. Lib., Rawlinson MSS, A 33, 359–62. For more details on these men, see Tim Goodwin, *Dorset in the Civil War, 1625–1665* (Tiverton, 1996).

32 For examples, see Bod. Lib., Rawlinson MSS, A 32, fols 177–80, 381–4, 517–20, 621–4, 655–8, 683–6, 793–6, 809–12; A 33, fols 105–8, 225–8, 373–6; A 34, fols 755–8, 771–2; A 36, fols 217–20.

33 *Ibid.*, A 32, fols 793–6.

34 *Ibid.*, A 32, fols 517–20, 683–6.

35 *Ibid.*, A 34, fols 225–8.

36 BL, E.489.14, *Mercurius Politicus*, 8–15 Nov. 1655.

37 Bod. Lib., Rawlinson MSS, A 32, fols 215–8.

38 *Ibid.*, A 32, fols 711–14, 931–4.

39 *Ibid.*, A 32, fols 683–6.

40 For examples see *ibid.*, A 32, fols 529–32, 691–4, 719–22; A 33, fols 157–60, 355–8, 359–62, 702–5; A 34, fols 767–70; A 36, fols 117–20.

41 *Ibid.*, A 32, fols 529–32.

42 *Ibid.*, A 32, fols 691–4.

43 *Ibid.*, A 32, fols 691–4.

44 *Ibid.*, A 32, fols 683–6, 887–90.

45 *Ibid.*, A 33, fols 385–8.

46 *Ibid.*, A 34, fols 767–70; A 36, fols 229–32.

Chapter 5

New local government
and old local government

When Cromwell and his advisers sent the major-generals into the
provinces and appointed sets of county commissioners to assist them
in the autumn of 1655, they neither wished nor intended that these new local
officials should replace entirely the traditional structures and personnel of
English and Welsh local government. Rather it was their hope that they would
work alongside the magistrates, sheriffs, assize judges, constables, freeholder
juries and town corporations that had traditionally been responsible for the
regulation of the localities, and that they would re-invigorate these established
organs of local government, purge them of disaffected elements, and
cooperate with them to enhance the security of the protectorate and promote a
godly reformation of manners.

To a degree, both the new and the old local governors realised that they
were intended to be partners rather than rivals and thus made some effort to
treat each other with respect and consideration. William Goffe's first act in
arriving in Hampshire in November 1655, for example, was to pay his respects
to two prominent local justices, Richard Cromwell and Richard Major.[1]
Similarly, when James Berry heard a rumour at the end of 1655 that a new oath
was to be imposed upon justices of the peace, he wrote to John Thurloe to
suggest that the government 'be tender in this', on the grounds that few of
them would be 'better fixed by it'.[2] In some parts of the country, the traditional
elements in local government reciprocated by according the major-generals
honour and dignity. Edward Whalley, for example, was lavishly entertained by
the corporations of Coventry and Leicester, and James Berry by the mayor of
Shrewsbury.[3] John Desborough was on one occasion the guest of the mayor of
Devizes, and when he visited godly Dorchester with the western circuit assizes
judges in the summer of 1656, he was presented with gifts of a gallon of sack,
a sugar loaf and a fat sheep, and was lodged in the house of a prominent
member of the corporation.[4] A number of the major-generals were also

offered the freedom of the main boroughs within their associations.[5]

For all such displays of mutual respect and civility, however, relations between the old and the new local governors were also frequently marked by unease, suspicion and a good measure of mutual distrust. On one, not unimportant level, tensions were created by uncertainties over respective status and authority. Edward Whalley experienced difficulties of this nature within days of arriving in his association. In late November 1655, he reported to Thurloe that although he had been 'solemnly welcomed' in every town he had so far visited, at Leicester the mayor and his colleagues had met him without 'bearing up theyr mace before the mayor', as they would have done if had they been receiving an acknowledged superior authority. Asking for guidance as to 'where the precedency is', he explained that, while he did not consider himself a proud man, he did not want to collude in challenges to the government's authority.[6] A few days later, similar strains emerged at Coventry. To avoid the same problem with regard to the mace, the local mayor, Robert Beake, absented himself from the official delegation which welcomed Whalley to the town, and a few days later he protested when Whalley 'upon a mistake' occupied a more prominent position than him in church.[7] Significantly, Beake's concern over these issues of 'precedency' did not proceed from any lack of sympathy for the regime or its new local representative, for he possessed an impeccable godly pedigree, was engaged in his own vigorous campaign to combat immorality and ungodliness in Coventry, and over the course of the next few months was to be one of Whalley's most active commissioners in Warwickshire.

If such a strong supporter of the major-generals' experiment was concerned to prevent his traditional civic dignity and authority being undermined by the new structure of local government, the many other local officeholders who did not share Beake's enthusiasm for the major-generals resented their inter-ference a great deal more and reacted to their reform initiatives with at best indifference and at worst overt hostility. As a consequence, power struggles developed and the major-generals and their commissioners frequently found themselves at loggerheads with some of those who had wielded local power prior to their appointment. This chapter will consider the interaction between the major-generals and their commissioners and the various agencies of traditional local government. It will attempt to discover how the new local governors regarded those who operated the older system, what efforts they made to bring about its reform, and whether these efforts had any meaningful long-term impact upon local administration.

The linchpins of seventeenth-century local government were, of course, the county justices of the peace. These elite groups of local landowners had been responsible for a wide range of administrative and judicial functions for over three centuries and, since the Tudor period, they had conducted the bulk of their business at the regular quarter sessions meetings held four times a year in the major urban centres of their shires. During the 1640s and early 1650s, the county benches of justices had frequently been purged and many of the regime's most conspicuous opponents had been removed from office. These expulsions, however, had left many vacancies which had not always proved easy to fill. Moreover, throughout the early 1650s the government's most enthusiastic supporters persistently complained that many of the JPs who had either survived from the pre-war period or been appointed since 1646 were far from diligent in the exercise of their duties and often displayed only a lukewarm attachment to the regime they served.

In the weeks following their arrival in the localities, a number of the major-generals echoed such complaints, reporting to the central government that there were few justices they could rely upon for support and that some were actively hostile to them and working to frustrate their objectives. Edward Whalley told John Thurloe in November 1655 that 'what some justices in order to reformation doe, others undoe; and the spirits of the best are very low for want of such an officer to encourage them.'[8] Several weeks later, he added that in the boroughs of his association 'wicked magistrates by reason of their number over-power the godly magistrates. They no sooner suppress alehouses but they are set up agayne.'[9] Charles Worsley similarly reported from the north-west in early 1656 that there was 'a greate want of justices of the peace in these countys, both by reason of those that refuse to act, as alsoe of the smallnesse of the number'.[10] James Berry was also very disturbed by the calibre of the JPs he encountered in Wales. In December 1655, he told Thurloe that a number of them were former royalists who were liable to pay the decimation tax. The following month, he commented: 'I beseech you be carefull in disposeinge powers and places to put them in good hands, or you undoe us', and in February 1656 he reported from Monmouth: 'I am much troubled with these markett townes, every where vice abounding and magistrates fast asleep.'[11]

Some of the major-generals provided details of the kind of obstructive activities in which these 'wicked' justices had been engaging. Hezekiah Haynes informed Thurloe in June 1656 that he had been told that one of the Suffolk justices, Robert Lane, had issued warrants for the arrest of local sequestrators and encouraged some to take out lawsuits against the godly with the result that 'honest men stand in feare of him, that they dare hardly venture home to their own houses least he should imprison them'.[12] Edward Whalley reported that one of the Coventry JPs, Joseph Chambers, had similarly instigated lawsuits against godly constables and had helped to protect the town's many unlicensed alehouses from those who wished to close them.[13] Whalley and his Lincolnshire commissioners also investigated complaints against a local justice, John Hobson, who was accused of misappropriating money allocated to the poor, taking bribes to release prisoners, and overcharging couples to marry them.[14]

In an attempt to remedy these magisterial deficiencies, the major-generals added themselves and their allies to the local benches, while at the same time purging them of justices whom they believed were defaulting on their duties or were actively working to frustrate the government's aims. Within a few days of arriving in the localities several of the major-generals realised that their presence on the bench was of vital importance to their work. Edward Whalley wrote to Thurloe at the beginning of November 1655 to tell him it was 'very needful' that they be made JPs, and a few weeks later he reiterated the point, declaring that it was 'of absolute necessity you put us in commissions of the peace where we are major generalls'.[15] Some of them were already members of the bench in one or more of their counties at the time of their appointment as major-generals: John Barkstead, for example, was a JP in Middlesex; William Boteler in Northamptonshire; John Desborough in Devon; and Hezekiah Haynes in Essex.[16] Over the next few months this presence was considerably enhanced. By the end of 1655, William Goffe had been appointed in Berkshire, Hampshire and Sussex; William Boteler in Bedfordshire, Huntingdonshire and Rutland; Charles Worsley in Staffordshire and Cheshire; James Berry in Herefordshire, Shropshire, Worcestershire and most of the counties of North Wales; John Desborough in Gloucestershire, Wiltshire and Dorset; Robert Lilburne in the three ridings of Yorkshire; and Hezekiah Haynes in Suffolk, Cambridge and the Isle of Ely. The following spring, Berry and Rowland Dawkins were appointed to a number of benches in south and mid Wales.[17] By early 1656, a clear majority of English and Welsh county benches contained their local major-general.

Because of their many other commitments, not all of the major-generals were regular attenders at quarter sessions within their associations, but some did make a point of being present whenever they could and attempted to take an active part in the work of the local magistracy. Barkstead, for example, regularly attended the Middlesex sessions in London; Goffe was present at the 1656 Epiphany meetings in Hampshire and Berkshire, and again at the Easter and summer meetings in Hampshire; Desborough attended the 1656 Epiphany sessions for Somerset; Boteler was present at the 1656 Easter sessions for Northamptonshire; and Berry at the Epiphany and summer sessions for Shropshire.[18]

There is some evidence to suggest that, as well as taking part themselves in the work of the justices, the major-generals presided over an ambitious attempt to remodel the county magistracy. In their letters to John Thurloe, individual major-generals regularly put forward the names of 'well affected' individuals whom they wished to see added to their local benches. John

Desborough was one of the most active in this respect. In December 1655, he forwarded to Thurloe the names of two men he considered suitable to be added to the Dorset bench and another five he wished to see appointed for both Somerset and Gloucestershire, 'in respect there is not one justice in either of these counties near the city of Bristol and yet much vice raigneinge'.[19] During early 1656, he suggested a number of further additions for Devon, Gloucestershire and Cornwall.[20] On several occasions, William Goffe also sent Thurloe the names of men he wished to see added to the Sussex bench.[21] In November 1655, Edward Whalley suggested adding to the Lincolnshire bench Richard Brownlow, 'a gentleman of very good report, a hopefull young man', and promised to send more names for both that county and Nottinghamshire 'there being as yet scarce enowe to carry on the publique service'.[22] The following February, he duly nominated another seven men who he believed were suitable to serve in Lincolnshire.[23] The same month, Thomas Kelsey asked Thurloe to add Martin Pike of Penshurst in Kent to the commission of the peace for that county 'there being such want of acting men in that part of the county'.[24] In the summer of 1656, William Packer sent Thurloe the names of several 'persons fearing God and ... at least of sober and orderly conversation' whom he wished to see added to the Buckinghamshire and Hertfordshire benches, and in a subsequent letter he recommended the appointment in Hertfordshire of Richard Godfrey, 'a very godly and able man, living in a corner where there is great need'.[25] In July 1656, Hezekiah Haynes similarly asked that Francis Brewster, 'a right honest man', be inserted in Suffolk.[26] Altogether, around thirty individuals are mentioned by name in the major-generals' correspondence as suitable candidates for the bench, and the great majority of them were subsequently appointed JPs by the government.[27]

As well as requesting additions, the major-generals also on occasions asked the council to remove JPs whom they considered unsuitable. In December 1655, for example, Hezekiah Haynes penned a memorandum to Thurloe calling for the expulsion of several Suffolk magistrates, and the following summer he requested the removal from the same bench of the 'highly disaffected' Robert Lane.[28] In several cases, where the charges against the recalcitrant JP were considered particularly serious, the major-generals and their commissioners personally conducted an investigation. The Lincolnshire commissioners called John Hobson before them at Spalding and examined the witnessses against him; on receipt of their report the council in London directed that he should be punished at the next Lincolnshire assizes.[29] Joseph Chambers, the Coventry magistrate who was alleged to have protected the city's ungodly, was similarly examined by Whalley, Robert Beake and several other aldermen. After considering the testimony of 'diverse godly men that came in against him in writing', they forced him to resign his office.[30]

According to the government's official record of additions and omissions, the scale of the changes to the composition of county benches may have been much greater than is revealed by these cases which are specifically mentioned in the major-generals' correspondence. The Chancery crown office docquet book for the Interregnum reveals that in the twelve months from November 1653 to October 1654 forty-eight men were added to the county benches throughout the country and only seventeen removed. The following year, from November 1654 to October 1655, another 137 were added and thirteen removed. Over the period of the major-generals' presence in the localities from November 1655 to October 1656, however, no fewer than 276 men were added and 106 removed. The changes in the composition of the local benches reached a peak in March and July 1656; in both of these months new commissions of the peace were issued for more than twenty English and Welsh counties and nearly a hundred new JPs were appointed nationally. It may be significant that the extensive alterations of these months came shortly after visits by the major-generals to London in February and May 1656.

The scale of the changes to some individual benches was quite dramatic. In March, there were eleven additions and eight omissions in Surrey, and twelve additions and eight omissions in Kent. In July, there were seven additions and nine omissions in Norfolk, nine additions and nine omissions in Suffolk, fourteen additions and three omissions in Hertfordshire, and two additions and no fewer than twenty omissions in Buckinghamshire. This level of turnover was sustained during the year following the major-generals' departure from the provinces, with another 243 individuals added and 110 omitted between November 1656 and October 1657. The following year, however, the number of changes fell back to the level they were at before the major-generals had arrived, with 159 additions and only sixteen omissions.[31] This marked increase in both additions and removals during their period in power does seem to indicate that the major-generals launched a serious attempt to create a 'well affected' local magistracy with which they could work to realise their reform aspirations. Their efforts in this direction were scathingly acknowledged in the autumn of 1656 by one of their severest critics, William Prynne, who accused them of having appointed as JPs 'sectaries and illiterate swordmen and other persons of mean quality who understand neither law nor justice'.[32]

Partly as a result of these changes to the local commissions of the peace, and partly because a significant number of those appointed as commissioners for securing the peace of the commonwealth in the autumn of 1655 were already serving as justices, in many counties there was considerable overlap between the membership of the bench and the major-generals' commission for securing the peace of the commonwealth. In Essex, for example, no fewer than fourteen of the twenty active commissioners had served as justices prior to their appointment as assistants to Haynes, and ten of them – Gobert Barrington, Samuel Champneys, Christopher Earle, Sir Richard Everard,

William Harlakenden, Sir Thomas Honeywood, John Paschall, Dudley Templer, Dionysius Wakering and Peter Whetcombe – were active as both commissioners and JPs during late 1655 and 1656. Indeed, both Everard and Honeywood served as *custos rotolorum* for the county in 1656.[33] The picture was similar in Staffordshire, where fourteen of the twenty-two commissioners were also justices of the peace.[34] Those serving in both capacities must have been extremely busy men during the months which followed the major-generals' appointment, but provided they were able to cope with the heavy workload, they were in a good position to coordinate policy across the two commissions and to impress upon the bench the need to work closely with the major-generals.

Assessing the national impact of the major-generals upon the county magistracy is a far from straightforward task. There is evidence to suggest that in some parts of the country their presence did produce a temporary invigoration of the local bench, and increased the JPs' commitment to carrying out their duties, particularly in the fields of poor relief and alehouse regulation.[35] Jean Mather's study of the attempt to enforce puritan moral legislation at a county level has revealed that in Middlesex the number of moral transgressions brought before the justices was three times higher in 1656 than it had been in 1652, a rise she attributes directly to the diligence of the 'formidable figure' of Sir John Barkstead. Her work also makes clear, however, that such a re-invigoration did not occur everywhere and that, where it did, it proved short-lived. By 1661, the percentage of moral cases brought to the attention of the Middlesex JPs had fallen back to the level of 1652. Furthermore, in both William Goffe's Sussex and Charles Worsley's Staffordshire the proportion of quarter sessions' presentments with a moral dimension remained broadly the same in 1652, 1656 and 1661, a fact which led Mather to conclude that in these rural counties the arrival of the major-generals had had little impact upon the justices' commitment to the enforcement of moral legislation.[36]

That much still remained undone when the major-generals departed for London in the autumn of 1656 is suggested by the declaration of the grand jury for Flintshire at the Michelmas quarter sessions in October of that year. The Flintshire jurors complained that, as a result of the continued lack of good justices in their county,

> good men desirous of reformation become much discouraged and vice and prophaneness, through want of fit magistrates to resort unto, happen often to pass unpunished; and the good laws made against sabbath-breaking, whoredom, prophane swearing, drunkenness, and other enormous crimes, and for provision of the poor and punishment of rogues, vagabonds and sturdy beggars, remain in great part unexecuted.[37]

As far as these Welsh jurors were concerned, the local major-general, James Berry, had signally failed to create a godly magistracy in Flintshire. That his failure was replicated by his fellow generals in other parts of England and Wales is suggested by comments made by both Richard Baxter and Oliver Cromwell in the period following the end of the major-generals' period of rule. In late 1656, Baxter was still complaining that: 'it will never be well till we have either more zealous justices than most are, or else there be greater penalties on magistrates and constables for neglect of their duty', and a few months later Cromwell remarked to a parliamentary committee that 'a justice of the peace shall from most be wondered at as an owl, if he go but one step out of the ordinary course of his fellow justices in the reformation of these things'.[38] For all their good intentions, the major-generals' campaign to remodel the local magistracy seems to have been both incomplete and short-lived.

After the magistracy, the next most important office in local government was the shrievalty. The county high sheriffs, who were chosen annually by the government at the end of November, exercised a number of important local functions. They were responsible for protecting and entertaining the judges and justices during quarter sessions and assizes, and for empanelling the juries for these courts. They acted as the key local officials in the execution of writs issued by the Westminster law courts and dealt with a number of minor offences in their own court, the tourn. When a parliamentary election was called, they presided over the county poll for the knights of the shire and they sent out the warrants to the local towns to hold the borough elections. For these reasons the government was naturally anxious to appoint sheriffs they could rely on, but for many years the office had proved extremely unpopular, primarily because the holder was required to stay in his county throughout his year of office and to meet the considerable expenses involved in the post out of his own pocket. As a result, many of the sheriffs appointed in the late 1640s and early 1650s had been less than fully committed to the regime and some had had active royalist pasts.

The major-generals arrived in their associations at the ideal time in the year to influence the choice of sheriffs for 1656 and one of their first tasks was to forward the names of suitable local candidates to the government at London. They found this a far from easy matter, primarily because most of those they considered appointable were extremely reluctant to be nominated. A number of the major-generals specifically referred to this problem in their early reports back to Thurloe. James Berry commented in mid November 1655 of one of his friends whose name had been suggested by the council as a possible sheriff for Worcestershire that: 'I fear it would be much to his prejudice to have the place, he having noe house or conveniency in the country'.[39] Several days later, he reported that 'the saying is here that a man had as good be sequestered as made sheriffe'.[40] In early December, he wrote from Shrewsbury to suggest that Colonel Thomas Hunt was an 'honest man' and would make a good sheriff for Shropshire, but that he was 'loath to doe him the discourtesy to put him to the charge'; a few weeks later he again reported that Hunt had specifically asked him to write 'to keepe him from being high sheriff'.[41] In several of these letters to Thurloe, Berry neatly summed up the regime's dilemma with regard to the appointment of sheriffs. On 1 December 1655, he commented from Shrewsbury: 'to put it upon our friends is to doe them a great discourtesy and to put it into other men's hands is to doe ourselves a greater'; and six days later he wrote from Wrexham: 'if you put it on friends it is a burthen and they cannot long beare it; and knaves will not do your worke.'[42]

A number of Berry's fellow major-generals experienced similar problems. William Boteler informed Thurloe in November 1655 that none of the government's suggestions for sheriffs within his association would be likely to 'lead or follow the commissioners in their work'. He did send him two names for both Bedfordshire and Northamptonshire, but added that he had nominated one of these, John Maunsell, extremely reluctantly because he was burdened with an 'extraordinary charge of children and debts'.[43] The same month, Hezekiah Haynes similarly reported that, while the government's suggestions for his East Anglian counties were quite unsuitable, it was very difficult to find fit men; he too added: 'I should be most unwilling to putt our friends uppon it to contract expenses.'[44] Charles Worsley also rejected the government's nominations for his counties in the north-west but struggled to find suitable alternatives.[45]

In a number of counties, including Bedfordshire, Buckinghamshire, Cornwall, Devon, Essex, Gloucestershire, Herefordshire, Kent, Norfolk and Oxfordshire, the problem was subsequently resolved and the shrievalty harnessed to the new local government arrangements by appointing as sheriff for 1656 one of the major-generals' commissioners or militia captains.[46] Elsewhere, however, the widespread reluctance to serve meant that a number of the appointments which were made were considered highly unsatisfactory by the local major-general. Robert Lilburne informed Cromwell in January 1656 that the choice of Richard Robinson as the new sheriff of Yorkshire had given 'great distast to many conscientious people', as he was 'too much addicted to tipling and that which is called good fellowship'. He added that, although Robinson was reasonably able, he believed it was better for the government 'to call good men to places of magistracy', on the grounds that this would be 'more acceptable to godly men and more honourable to your Highnes and tending more to the quieting of the spirits of all good people and to the stopping the mouths of those that may lay this as a stumbling block'.[47] Charles Worsley similarly complained about the sheriff of Cheshire for 1656, Philip Egerton, on the grounds that his 'pleasure and delight is onely in those who I verilie believe are the most dangerous enemyes we have in these countyes'.[48] In Sussex, the 1656 sheriff, John Busbridge, was both a commissioner for securing the peace of the commonwealth and a captain of the new militia, but his evident lack of enthusiasm for the regime led William Goffe to disband his militia troop in the spring of 1656.[49]

In November 1655, William Boteler informed Thurloe that he could have found better candidates in his association if the post of sheriff were made of longer duration and relieved of the heavy charges it involved.[50] The government may well have taken heed of this, for in the new year the issue was referred by the council to a subcommittee and in February 1656 John Lambert brought back to the full council a plan for cutting down the costs of the shrievalty. It proposed that in future the local major-general should provide a troop of horse to 'to wayt upon the judges and performe such other services as have so usually been required of the sheriffes men', and that the sheriff should no longer be required to provide entertainment for the assizes judges and JPs, or to give gratuities to the judges' clerks. It further suggested that the council should investigate how the costs incurred by the sheriffs in presenting their annual accounts could be lessened.[51] The council accepted these recommendations, and a few days later Cromwell issued a proclamation publicising the changes.[52] How much this move increased the attraction of the office is not clear. It may, though, have done enough to persuade those sheriffs appointed during the major-generals' period of power to remain in office after their year had elapsed, for, as Stephen Roberts has pointed out, many of them did in fact continue in office until the Restoration and the period 1655 to 1660 saw fewer appointments as sheriff than any other time in the seventeenth century.[53]

In addition to the justice of the peace and the sheriff, the other important figures in local government, albeit ones who only visited each shire for a few weeks each year, were the assizes judges. As well as hearing serious criminal cases, the distinguished judges who performed this function were responsible for supervising the activities of the local justices, giving them advice on complicated legal issues, and relaying the concerns of central government to the assembled representatives of the local community. Aware of the importance of these functions, a number of the major-generals worked closely with the assizes judges and journeyed with them around the shires of their associations, in order both to offer them assistance and to monitor their proceedings. William Goffe attended the spring assizes in Sussex and Hampshire in 1656 and the summer assizes in Sussex and Berkshire.[54] Edward Whalley followed the assizes judge, Matthew Hale, around all the counties of his association in the spring of 1656 and he was again present in some counties in the summer.[55] John Desborough attended the Dorset assizes in the summer of 1656, and Hezekiah Haynes followed his assizes judge through all his East Anglian circuit.[56] Most of the major-generals appear to have been happy with the judges' conduct of the courts; Edward Whalley, in particular, was full of praise for the way Matthew Hale had handled the cases which he heard in both the spring and summer.[57] The only major-general to voice serious criticism of an assizes judge was Charles Worsley. Worsley was unable to attend the spring assizes in Chester, but he afterwards reported to Thurloe that he had heard that the prominent local republican, John Bradshaw, who presided over the assizes in the county palatine of Cheshire in his capacity as chief justice of Chester, had done the government 'many ill-offices' during the proceedings.[58]

While the offices of magistrate and sheriff were the preserve of the elite sections of local society, large numbers of men of more modest social standing were also involved in local government, serving either as jurymen at the regular assizes or quarter sessions courts or as the constables and bailiffs who represented the government at the parish and hundred level. Following the major-generals' appearance in the counties, attempts were made to bring about reforms in these areas, too.

The freeholders who served on the grand, trial and petty juries at the quarter sessions and assizes courts were potentially a very influential element of local government. Summoned by the sheriffs, they were responsible for a variety of functions, including bringing presentments against offenders and notifying the authorities about issues of particular concern to the local community. Jury service had, however, long been highly unpopular. Freeholders went to great lengths to avoid selection and those that were prevailed upon to serve commonly showed little enthusiasm for their tasks. Cromwell and his advisers were well aware that juries made up of 'well affected' freeholders might play a useful part in the grassroots implementation of their policies and that those peopled by their enemies might conversely do much to frustrate their aims. This fact had been brought home to them in the aftermath of Penruddock's rising in the west country, when they had found it difficult to find local jurymen prepared to proceed rigorously against the indicted royalist conspirators.

In early 1656, therefore, the government instructed the major-generals to involve themselves in efforts to remodel local juries. In January of that year, Cromwell wrote a long letter to John Desborough on the subject of jury reform. He informed him that in the past the selection of bad jurors had frequently led to miscarriages of justice and that he had been 'much pressed to endeavour' the reform of the system. He ordered him to carry out a review of the west country freeholder books and to remove from them the names of anyone he considered unsuitable to serve. This, he argued, would allow the local JPs to choose from the purged lists 'freeholders of clearest integrity and prudence, of honest and blameless conversation' and to recommend them to the sheriffs and their deputies as jurors. He added that he was aware that in the past, when the names of those empanelled to serve had been made public, attempts had often been made 'to pre-engage them on one side or the other', with the result that 'justice is often perverted, the innocent wronged and the wrong-doer prevails and escapes'. To remedy this, he told him to report to the judges the names of any jurymen who had been approached by those involved in an ongoing lawsuit. He added that he hoped Desborough would be able to carry out these reforms 'without either distasting the weaker or giving advantage to the wilful and froward by our appearing in it'.[59] A letter to the same effect was also sent to several of the Devon justices, and at the Epiphany quarter sessions the Devon bench ordered that henceforth all returns of jurors should be vetted by the nearest justice of the peace.[60]

Desborough was not optimistic about the prospects of achieving meaningful reform of the jury system in the west country. He wrote back to Cromwell on 4 February 1656 telling him that, while he would do his utmost to follow his instructions, 'when I have done all, I fear it will be to little purpose'.[61] He may, however, have been being unduly pessimistic, for the work of Stephen Roberts into the structure of local government in Interregnum Devon suggests that some significant changes did in fact take place. According to Roberts, the Devon trial jury for the summer quarter sessions of 1656 was highly atypical in that it contained twelve men who had never served before and who were drawn from a much wider geographical area than was customary. Around three-quarters of the members of the grand jury were also newcomers.[62] These marked changes in personnel may indicate that Desborough and the Devon justices had had some success in purging the local freeholder books and securing more acceptable juries. The Devon justices' concern to vet juries persisted after the major-general's departure and only finally petered out in the mid 1660s. According to Anthony Fletcher, it 'may well have been the most sustained bid to tackle the overall problem during the whole century'.[63]

Around the same time, the other major-generals were also instructed to implement similar jury reforms in their associations and a number of them subsequently took action to this end.[64] William Boteler told Thurloe in mid February 1656 that he had personally drawn up draft lists of jurors for the counties of his association and was confident that his sheriffs would accept them.[65] In early 1656, Charles Worsley supervised the drawing up of lists of 'honest juditious freeholders' to serve on juries in the north-west, and he subsequently told Thurloe that this much-needed reform was 'a matter of singular use to the countyes' and 'much rejoiceth the people'.[66] In April 1656, Robert Lilburne wrote to the Yorkshire justices asking them to investigate 'grievances with regard to jurors'.[67] The same month, a report in *The Public Intelligencer* claimed that in Herefordshire the sheriff had taken great care to retain as jurymen 'gentlemen and the ablest of yeomen' and to exclude 'all common tales-men', with the result that at the spring assizes the grand jury had been made up of 'esquires and gentlemen of worth who presented very many grievances of concernment for the reformation and public welfare of the county'.[68]

But, if some of the major-generals did bring about some significant changes to the way juries were selected within their associations, others appear to have had little or no impact. During the election campaign in the summer of 1656, William Goffe was concerned that the grand jury in Hampshire still contained a number of royalists, several of whom he had only a few months earlier decimated.[69] Hezekiah Haynes, meanwhile, faced similar problems in Suffolk, where the sheriff had picked 'soe malignant a grand jury, who will have a great advantage to possess the country'.[70] Furthermore, even in those areas where some improvement was achieved, in most cases it failed to outlast the period of the major-generals' rule in the provinces.

No attempt to reform the local government of seventeenth-century England and Wales could hope to enjoy much success if it ignored the crucial work carried out by the thousands of high and petty constables, bailiffs, excisemen and the other minor officials who operated at the grassroots parish level. While these men had only limited power and often even less prestige, they were the only officials who were close enough to the population to observe the myriad minor infringements of law and custom which were endemic within their local communities and to report them to the higher authorities for punishment. Both the central government and the major-generals were well aware that, as Andrew Coleby has put it, the enforcement of government policy 'depended upon an amorphous mass of minor officials recruited locally with no necessary commitment to the regime or its objectives', and that any reform initiatives which were not fully supported by these local Dogberrys were likely to founder on the rock of their apathy and hostility.[71]

The way that unsympathetic minor officials could obstruct the reform efforts of their superiors is nicely illustrated by the case of Richard Gill, constable of Thurcroft in Yorkshire. In October 1656, Gill was indicted before the justices of the west riding for refusing to execute warrants from them to levy fines of twenty shillings on two spinster sisters of his village, Frances and Anne Brotherton, who had been brewing beer without a licence in their house. According to the justices, the result of Gill's show of neighbourly solidarity was that 'publike justice was contemned and the said Frances and Anne Brotherton have escaped unpunished in contempt of the lawes of this nacon, to the evill example of others in the like case offendinge'.[72] But, as Derek Hirst has pointed out, in such cases 'community solidarity' frequently 'proved stronger than godly zeal'.[73] The English and Welsh parishes almost certainly contained hundreds of other constables who shared Gill's reservations about the government's aspirations, and who like him attempted to subvert its reform programme by turning a blind eye to their neighbours' moral transgressions.

A number of the major-generals clearly regarded their minor officials as far from satisfactory and several of them specifically complained to their masters in London about them. Charles Worsley reported to Thurloe in December 1655 that many of the constables in the north-west were 'swerers and drunken idle parsons themselves and of the meanest sort of men'. He added that the small minority of diligent, godly constables were unclear about the extent of their powers and 'how farr they may proceed of themselves in punishing sin etc.', as 'the law is very darke in that; so that divers have suffred upon that account; and they find it hard to find justices that will encourage them in that worke.'[74] James Berry similarly reported from Shrewsbury in early January 1656 that 'we have such a pittifull company of officers in state affairs that it is a shame to see it', adding: 'I am filled with complaints of them and, when I can have while to search them out, shall trouble you with an account of them.'[75] A few days later, the commissioners for securing the peace for Yorkshire wrote to Cromwell to point out that there were

> many stewards of courts, solicitors, attornies and other officers in these parts who have been very stirring for the late king's party and are and have been very active in such places against well affected persons and do thereby act the cavaliers' revenge against honest men who have been instruments to the commonwealth's service which we do find a great discouragement to and the oppression of honest people.[76]

Despite the acknowledged importance of this bottom tier of local government, Charles Worsley seems to have been the only major-general to make a concerted effort to improve the calibre of his parish officers. On several occasions in late January and early February 1656, he told Thurloe he was taking measures to remove 'bad' constables and replace them with 'honest, faithfull and juditious men', whose absence from office he described as a 'great evell to this nation'.[77] In Lancashire, he prompted the justices to take more care over the appointment of constables by examining them in person at the time of their appointment, and he also ordered all the county's constables to appear before the commissioners for securing the peace of the commonwealth and provide them with a detailed breakdown of the state of their parishes.[78] In Cheshire, he went further by advocating the appointment of a new parish official who would work alongside the constable but report directly to the major-general's commissioners.[79]

For all his dedication, however, it is unlikely that these initiatives had much lasting impact. The sustained monitoring of the attitudes and actions of the hundreds of constables within much of the north-west of England was a task beyond the capacities of even the hyperactive Worsley, and once again any temporary amelioration he achieved quickly evaporated after his death. Preoccupied with their other responsibilities, his fellow major-generals do not seem even to have begun to tackle the problem and, as a consequence, the rule of the major-generals had no real impact upon the quality of grassroots local administration. Their inability to achieve reform here contributed substantially to the difficulties the major-generals faced in the sphere of moral reform, for, as Derek Hirst has remarked, 'in the failure of constables to delate, of grand juries to present, and of trial juries to convict, we see the failure of the godly cause to put down adequate roots.'[80]

The final area of local administration in which the major-generals became involved was municipal government. The central government had long been aware of the importance of vetting those who exercised power within towns. In 1647, the Long Parliament had passed an act barring former royalists and other enemies of the state from taking part in elections or holding public office in boroughs, and in October 1652 the Rump Parliament had extended this act for a further three years. On 21 September 1655, the same day as the commissions for the major-generals and the instructions for their commissioners were finalised, Cromwell issued a proclamation extending indefinitely the 1647 act's provisions.[81] As well as ensuring that the provisions of this act were observed, the major-generals were keen to do all they could to increase the influence of the godly minorities within the towns of their areas and to promote the reformation of urban communities within which they believed immorality was endemic. Charles Worsley told Thurloe in November 1655 that he had struggled to find a 'coram [quorum] of honest men' in Lichfield, and a few days later Edward Whalley confirmed to him that 'where the work of reformation should be most eminent, as in cyties and corporations, it is very much wanting'.[82] At the beginning of 1656, John Desborough reported to Cromwell that 'discountenancinge the godly and upholding the loose and prophane' was 'a disease predominatinge in most corporations'.[83] Six months later, William Packer reinforced the point, declaring: 'there are some very bad men in corporations under my power, as such as have been decimated and under bond, and others that are drunkards and prophane swearers and are magistrates.'[84]

The two main tactics employed by the major-generals in an attempt to improve the administration of towns were to purge their opponents from corporations and to encourage the urban godly to petition the government for new municipal charters which would cement their power and influence for the future. Although it was far from clear that they possessed the authority to remove men from municipal office, a number of the major-generals ignored the legal niceties and secured the removal of those they considered their enemies through threats and intimidation. The second ploy – charter reform – had been tried before. As early as 1650, the Rump had set up a committee for corporations to consider the remodelling of urban constitutions and over the next few years a number of English boroughs had requested new charters from the central authorities. The months which followed the major-generals' arrival in their associations, saw a significant increase in such petitions. Typical of them was the one John Patshall, a bailiff from Leominster in Herefordshire, sent to Cromwell in 1656. Patshall argued that the size of the Leominster corporation should be reduced from twenty-four to thirteen or even seven, so that the 'very few' well affected inhabitants who shared his outlook could gain the power that would allow them to combat the widespread 'vice and wickednes' in the town.[85]

In the spring of 1656, the council responded to the growth in these petitions by appointing a special subcommittee for municipal charters. This group, which included both John Desborough and John Lambert, received the petitions and, if it approved of them, sent them on to a group of four legal advisers, who were instructed to draft new charters which would encourage 'religion and good government' and discourage vice. One of these advisers, William Sheppard, would argue the following year in his tract *England's Balme* that it was necessary to reduce the power of corporations and extend the jurisdiction of the county magistracy into towns to ensure that the law was enforced. Once a new charter had been drawn up, it was scrutinised by the attorney general before finally being approved by Cromwell.[86]

Most of the major-generals employed one or both of these tactics in their dealings with the elites which controlled the towns of their associations. John Desborough removed a number of suspected aldermen and justices in Bristol, Gloucester, Tiverton and Tewkesbury from office in early 1656 by privately telling the mayors of these towns that they should advise their colleagues to resign before he made public examples of them.[87] Desborough's *modus operandi* was subsequently recommended by Thurloe to William Boteler, who employed it in March 1656 to engineer the removal of the mayor and a number of aldermen of Bedford. After investigating their activities and satisfying himself as to their delinquency, Boteler called them before him and pressurised them to stand down. Admitting afterwards to Thurloe that he had exceeded the bounds of his power in so doing, he justifed his actions on the grounds that it had united the godly party in the town and prevented 'many evill con-sequences that were at the very doore'. Two months later, he persuaded the purged corporation to repeal a by-law of 1650 which had given the freemen of Bedford considerable latitude in their choice of MP. He also forced them to admit himself and four of his allies to the corporation.[88]

Edward Whalley was similarly active in several of his east midlands' boroughs. In late 1655, he intervened in a long-running dispute within the corporation of Lincoln. After dismissing a mayor with a royalist past and threatening the corporation by what it protested was 'an usurped, illegal, pretended power' with the loss of its charter, he forced it to accept his own nominee as town clerk and to make both himself and James Berry freemen of the town.[89] As was mentioned above, in Coventry Whalley responded to the appeal of several godly constables by launching an investigation into the actions of one of the aldermen, Joseph Chambers, whom they had accused of encouraging lawsuits against them and of turning a blind eye to the existence of large numbers of unlicensed alehouses in the town. After examining him in the presence of the mayor, Robert Beake, and several other godly aldermen, Whalley pressurised Chambers to resign his office, a move which he later told Thurloe 'hath strucke the worser sort with feare and amazement; but exceedingly rejoyces the hearts of the godly'.[90]

Hezekiah Haynes was equally determined to stamp his authority over the towns of his association. Several weeks after arriving in East Anglia he warned Thurloe that Norwich was under the control of 'persons notoriously disaffected upon the worst principles', and urged him to consider imposing a new charter on the city, which he argued was 'as badd as any other in England as to persons in authority'.[91] Over the next few months, however, it was to be Colchester rather than Norwich which would demand most of Haynes's attention. During the early 1650s, Colchester had witnessed a long and bitter power struggle between a moderate party led by Thomas Reynolds and a radical, godly faction, headed by Henry Barrington. A few weeks before Haynes received his commission, Reynolds and his supporters had made major gains in the municipal elections. Soon afterwards, however, Barrington had petitioned Cromwell, claiming irregularities in the conduct of the poll, and the protector had ordered seven of the new Essex commissioners for securing the peace of the commonwealth to investigate the matter.

By early December, the government had decided to order fresh elections. Haynes was instructed to supervise these and to ensure that nobody who was forbidden by the 21 September proclamation was able to register a vote. By operating a stringent vetting process, he managed to reduce the electorate to 140. The godly 'honest interest' mustered seventy-four votes, enough now to overturn the September result and restore Barrington to power. Haynes afterwards reported to Charles Fleetwood that he had advised Cromwell that

> unlesse some speedy change be made in such malignant corporations, it's not for such honest men that would serve you to abide in their present stations; for no longer then such a severe hand as there was in this election be held over them will any good magistracy be countenanced; which if I may by any meanes provoke to the doing somethinge effectual in the character of corporations, I have my end, and I am sure the hearts of most that feare God wil be rejoyced.[92]

A few months later, the small godly majority on the Colchester corporation petitioned the government for a new municipal charter. They argued that under the present constitution 'too great a power is given to the people to slight the magistracy of the said towne and render them uselesse in their places, whereby wickednesse and prophanenesse is much increased to the great discouragement of honest men', and they called for the granting of a charter 'which may (by the countenancing of religion and sobriety) preserve that interest which God hath been pleased soe ominously to owne in our dayes'. The council responded by drawing up a new charter which turned the corporation into a close body, selected in the first instance by the protector and thereafter through cooption by the existing members. This new body was also given the power to choose the future borough MPs. Fifteen aldermen were subsequently purged from office and the size of the corporation was reduced from forty-two to thirty-four. Haynes even delayed the Colchester borough poll for the 1656 parliament until 12 September so that it could be held under the provisions of the new charter. The godly corporation repaid his trust by electing as its MPs Henry Lawrence, the president of the council, and John Maidstone, a prominent member of Cromwell's household.[93]

While the involvement of the other major-generals in municipal affairs is less well documented, there is evidence that most of them were responsible for some initiatives in this area. Shortly after his arrival in his association, Charles Worsley visited the boroughs of the north-west to encourage the well affected within them to set about the work of reformation.[94] At the same time as he was doing this, his eventual successor, Tobias Bridge, who at that stage was acting as Charles Fleetwood's deputy, was sent to intervene in a long-running dispute within the corporation of High Wycombe in Buckinghamshire.[95] In early 1656, James Berry put pressure on the corporation of Monmouth to instruct their bailiffs to act more decisively against those who sold beer without a licence, and William Goffe did his best to bolster the authority of the godly mayor of Chichester in Sussex, Richard Maning.[96] In April 1656, Charles Howard was ordered to investigate complaints made by some of the inhabitants of Carlisle about the governing body of that town, and the same month Rowland Dawkins forced the corporation of Haverfordwest in Pembrokeshire to dismiss its mayor.[97] Thomas Kelsey and his Surrey commissioners intervened to prevent several men who had been excluded from the corporation at Kingston from regaining their places through writs of *mandamus*.[98] In the summer of 1656, Robert Lilburne was involved in several enquiries into the behaviour of aldermen in York and Hull, and in September William Packer asked the Oxford corporation for a copy of their charter, a request it clearly found very threatening and politely, but firmly refused.[99]

Finally, the government's decision in the spring of 1656 to activate the major-generals' system within London represented a major challenge to the authority of the most powerful urban oligarchy in the country. Aware of the particularly sensitive nature of the move, Cromwell met with the capital's governing body in early March to explain to them his reasons for wishing to extend the system to the city and to assure them that 'due regard should be taken for the preservation of the liberty and privileges as also the civil government of that metropolis'.[100] Whether they were convinced or not is unclear, but when a few weeks later Sir John Barkstead began assessing the capital's royalists for the decimation tax and rounding up prostitutes and those profaning the sabbath, it was clear that the traditional autonomy of the capital's governors was being seriously challenged.[101]

Several historians have argued that Cromwell's regime had little interest in the regulation and reform of municipal government. Samuel Gardiner believed that it merely responded to local initiatives without displaying any concern for regulating borough affairs, and more recently Paul Halliday has argued that it had no real interest in charter reform and that, when requests for new charters were received from local factions, 'little advantage was taken on such occasions to make sweeping changes in terms of corporate governance'.[102] While these authors are right to point out that initiatives for borough reform most commonly originated from within the towns themselves rather than from the centre, their assessment gives insufficient weight to the facts that it was frequently the regime's godly supporters within corporations who were the most prominent in agitating for change, and that both the central government and the major-generals were keen to lend their considerable support to these well affected minorities and to do all they could to help them secure power. Its also underplays the effects of charter reform, for, as William Schilling has pointed out, one of the 'undeniable features' of most changes to town charters during the Interregnum was that 'they did work to the central government's advantage'.[103] While Cromwell and his major-generals may not have had a masterplan for the remodelling of borough constitutions, they did fervently believe that the godly should control England's urban as well as rural communities, and in a number of towns, such as Bedford, Bristol and Colchester, they did their utmost to bring this reality about.

The period from November 1655 to September 1656 saw, therefore, an ambitious attempt by the major-generals to forge a close partnership between themselves and their newly empowered commissioners on the one hand and the more traditional elements of local government on the other. As we have seen, this project was not a complete failure. In a number of counties substantial changes to the composition of the local benches were effected and as a consequence close links were developed between the commissioners and the county magistracy. In some counties, more reliable sheriffs and jurymen were appointed, and in a few towns power was placed in the hands of local godly cliques. Limitations of time and resources meant, however, that such improvements were patchy and hard to sustain, and ensured that in many parts of the country the major-generals had no lasting impact of any significance on the magistracy, shrievalty and the other traditional organs of local government. As a direct result, they and their commissioners were obliged to shoulder the daunting tasks of collecting the decimation tax, neutralising the threat from the royalist community and eradicating popular immorality and irreligion largely on their own, with little help from the traditional rulers of provincial England. How they fared in the implementation of these tasks will be the subject of the next three chapters.

NOTES

1 Bod. Lib., Rawlinson MSS, A 32, fols 797–800.

2 *Ibid.*, A 33, fols 35–8.

3 *Ibid.*, A 33, fols 39–40; L. Fox (ed.), 'The Diary of Robert Beake, mayor of Coventry, 1655–6', *Dugdale Miscellany Volume I*, Dugdale Soc. Publs, 31 (1977), 117; H. Stocks (ed.), *Records of the Borough of Leicester 1603–1688* (Cambridge, 1923), p. 440; J. Berry and S. G. Lee, *A Cromwellian Major-General: The Career of James Berry* (Oxford, 1938), p. 134.

4 B. H. Cunnington, *Some Annals of the Borough of Devizes* (Devizes, 1925), pp. 124–5; Richard Williams, 'County and Municipal Government in Cornwall, Devon, Dorset, and Somerset, 1649–1660' (Unpub. Ph.D. thesis, University of Bristol, 1981), p. 78; David Underdown, *Fire from Heaven: Life in an English Town in the Seventeenth Century* (London, 1992), pp. 215–16.

5 Howard was offered the freedom of Newcastle-upon-Tyne; Whalley, Nottingham; Whalley and Berry, Lincoln; and Packer, Oxford. See M. H. Dodds (ed.), *Extracts from the Newcastle-upon-Tyne Council Minute Book, 1639–1656*, Newcastle-upon-Tyne Records Committee, 1 (1920), 217; *Records of the Borough of Nottingham*, 5 (1900), 288; HMC, *14th Report Appendix 8*, MSS of Corporation of Lincoln, p. 103; Oxfordshire Record Office, C/FC/1/A1/03, Council Act Book, 1629–63, fol. 233r, C/FC/1/A2/03, Council Minute Book, 1635–57, fol. 309r.

6 Bod. Lib., Rawlinson MSS, A 32, fols 805–8.

7 *Ibid.*, A 33, fols 39–40; 'Diary of Robert Beake', p. 117.

8 Bod. Lib., Rawlinson MSS, A 32, fols 805–8.

9 *Ibid.*, A 33, fols 39–40.

10 *Ibid.*, A 29, fol. 297.

11 *Ibid.*, A 33, fols 525–8; A 34, fols 217–20; A 35, fol. 172.

12 *Ibid.*, A 39, fol. 496.

13 *Ibid.*, A 33, fols 41–4.

14 PRO, SP.18.124.51; SP.25.76, pp. 348, 555–6.

15 Bod. Lib., Rawlinson MSS, A 32, fols 485–8, 805–8.

16 Anthony Fletcher, 'Oliver Cromwell and the Localities: The Problem of Consent', in Colin Jones, Malyn Newitt and Stephen Roberts (eds), *Politics and People in the English Revolution* (Oxford, 1986), pp. 189, 196–7; Paul H. Hardacre, 'William Boteler: a Cromwellian Oligarch', *Huntington Library Quarterly*, 11 (1947), 1–11; Stephen Roberts, *Recovery and Restoration in an English County: Devon Local Adminstration, 1646–1670* (Exeter, 1985), p. 199; D. H. Allen (ed.), *Essex Quarter Sessions Order Book 1652–1661* (Chelmsford, 1974), p. xxxvi.

17 PRO, C.231.6, pp. 319–30.

18 Bod. Lib., Rawlinson MSS, A 34, fols 395–6; A 37, fols 505–8; A 39, fols 424–5; Joan Wake (ed.), *Quarter Sessions Records of the County of Northants, 1630, 1657, 1657–8*, Northants Records Soc. Publs, 1 (1924), 138; E. H. Bates-Harbin (ed.) *Quarter Sessions Records for the County of Somerset*, Somerset Records Soc. Publs, vol. III, 28 (1912), 278; O. Wakeman and R. L. Kenyon, (eds), *Orders of the Shropshire Quarter Sesssions Volume 1, 1638–1708*, Shropshire County Records, 11–12 (1908), 23, 26 ; J. C. Jeaffreson (ed.), *Middlesex County Records*, old series, vol. 3 (London, 1974), pp. 247–8, 249; Hampshire Record Office, Quarter Sessions Order Book, Q1/3, pp. 273, 281, 289.

19 Bod. Lib., Rawlinson MSS, A 33, fols 529–32, 744–7.

20 *Ibid.*, A 34, fols 177–8, 435–8; A 35, fols 51, 101.

21 *Ibid.*, A 32, fols 381–4; A 34, fols 225–8.

22 *Ibid.*, A 32, fols 485–8.

23 *Ibid.*, A 35, fol. 4.

24 *Ibid.*, A 35, fol. 170.

25 *Ibid.*, A 39, fols 526–7; A 40, fols 109–12.

26 *Ibid.*, A 40, fols 463–6.

27 A record of their appointment can be found in PRO, C.231.6, pp. 319–51.

28 Bod. Lib., Rawlinson MSS , A 33, fol. 329; A 39, fol. 495.

29 PRO, SP.18.124.51; SP.25.76, pp. 348, 555–6.

30 Bod. Lib., Rawlinson MSS, A 33, fols 101–4.

31 PRO, C.231.6, pp. 273–412. The figures are my own calculations; they exclude the appointment of assize judges and the major-generals themselves.

32 BL, E.892.3, William Prynne, *A Summary Collection of the Principal Fundamental Rights, Liberties, Proprieties of all English Freemen* ... (London, 1656), p. 63.

33 Allen, *Essex Quarter Sessions Order Book*, pp. xxxiii–xli, 69–95; the names of the commissioners are from Bod. Lib., Rawlinson MSS , A 33, fols 385–8.

34 John Sutton, 'Cromwell's Commissioners for preserving the peace of the Commonwealth: a Staffordshire case study', in Ian Gentles, John Morrill and Blair Worden (eds), *Soldiers, Writers and Statesmen in the English Revolution* (Cambridge, 1998), p. 168.

35 For more details of the justices' cooperation with the generals in these areas, see chapter 8.

36 Jean Mather, 'The Moral Code of the English Civil War and Interregnum', *The Historian*, 44 (1982), 207–228.

37 Bod. Lib., Rawlinson MSS , A 43, fol. 122.

38 Quoted by Anthony Fletcher in 'Oliver Cromwell and the Localities', p. 200; Abbott, *Writings and Speeches of Cromwell*, vol. 4, pp. 493–4.

39 Bod. Lib., Rawlinson MSS , A 32, fols 569–72.

40 *Ibid.*, A 32, fols 621–4.

41 *Ibid.*, A 33, fols 35–8, 726–9.

42 *Ibid.*, A 33, fols 35–8, 127–30.

43 *Ibid.*, A 32, fols 517–20, 777–80.

44 *Ibid.*, A 32, fols 647–50.

45 *Ibid.*, A 32, fols 679–82, 957–60; A 33, fols 221–4.

46 For a list of the 1656 sheriffs, see BL, E.491.16, *The Public Intelligencer*, 14–21 Jan. 1656. The list includes some mistakes; the sheriff for Kent, for example, was Sir Michael Livesey, not John Dixwell, and that for Cheshire was Philip Egerton, not Robert Duckenfield. For the lists of commissioners, see chapter 4, note 2.

47 Bod. Lib., Rawlinson MSS, A 34, fols 309–12.

48 *Ibid.*, A 37, fols 219–22.

49 For more details on Busbridge, see chapter 7.

50 Bod. Lib., Rawlinson MSS , A 32, fols 777–80.

51 PRO, SP.25.76, p. 534.

52 Abbot, *Writings and Speeches of Cromwell*, vol. 4, p. 101.

53 Stephen Roberts, 'Local Government Reform in England and Wales during the Interregnum', in Ivan Roots (ed.), *Into Another Mould: Aspects of the Interregnum* (Exeter, 1981), p. 57.

54 Bod. Lib., Rawlinson MSS , A 36, fols 221–4; A 40, fols 305–8; A 41, fols 248–51.

55 *Ibid.*, A 36, fols, 374, 709; A 37, fols 229–32; A 40, fols 499–502; A 41, fols 300–3.

56 *Ibid.*, A 40, fols 121–4, 463–6; Williams, 'County and Municipal Government', p. 78.

57 Bod. Lib., Rawlinson MSS , A 36, fol. 709; A 41, fols 300–3.

58 *Ibid.*, A 37, fols 219–22.

59 Abbott, *Writings and Speeches of Cromwell*, vol. 4, pp. 87–8.

60 BL, Add MSS, 44058, fols 40–2; Anthony Fletcher, *Reform in the Provinces: The Government of Stuart England* (New Haven and London, 1986), p. 120.

61 Bod. Lib., Rawlinson MSS , A 35, fol. 51.

62 Stephen K. Roberts, 'Initiative and Control: the Devon Quarter Sessions Grand Jury, 1640–1670', *Bulletin of the Institute of Historical Research*, 57 (1984), 169–70.

63 Fletcher, *Reform in the Provinces*, p. 120.

64 While no other copies of Cromwell's letter have survived, it is clear from the subsequent correspondence of some of the other major-generals that they had received a similar letter.

65 Bod. Lib., Rawlinson MSS , A 35, fol. 164.

66 *Ibid.*, A 35, fols 104–5, 135; A 36, fol. 610.

67 West Yorkshire Archive Service, QS 10/3, p. 186.

68 BL, E.493.2, *The Public Intelligencer*, 31 Mar.–7 Apr. 1656.

69 Bod. Lib., Rawlinson MSS, A 40, fols 305–8.

70 *Ibid.*, A 40, fols 463–6.

71 Andrew Coleby, *Central Government and the Localities: Hampshire, 1649–1689* (Cambridge, 1987), p. 56.

72 West Yorkshire Archive Service, QS 4/4, fol. 247r.

73 Derek Hirst, 'The Failure of Godly Rule in the English Republic', *Past and Present*, 132 (1991), 60.

74 Bod. Lib., Rawlinson MSS, A 33, fols 61–4, 369–72.

75 *Ibid.*, A 34, fols 217–20.

76 *Ibid.*, A 34, fols 315–18.

77 *Ibid.*, A 34, fols 877–80; A 35, fols 104–5.

78 Lancashire Record Office, QDV/29; QSO/2/28, 29; for more details of these initiatives, see chapter 8.

79 Cheshire Record Office, Diary of Thomas Mainwaring, DDX 384/1, p. 242; see also Morrill, *Cheshire*, p. 285.

80 Hirst, 'Failure of Godly Rule', p. 61.

81 PRO, SP.25.76A, pp. 125–6; William A. H. Schilling, 'The Central Government and the Municipal Corporations in England, 1642–1663' (Unpub. Ph.D. thesis, University of Vanderbilt, 1970), pp. 92–3.

82 Bod. Lib., Rawlinson MSS , A 32, fols 679–82; A 33, fols 39–40.

83 *Ibid.*, A 34, fols 305–8.

84 *Ibid.*, A 40, fols 341–2.

85 PRO, SP.18.131.82.

86 Schilling, 'Central Government and Municipal Corporations', pp. 105–9; B. L. K. Henderson, 'The Commonwealth Charters', *Transactions of the Royal Historical Society*, 3rd series, 6 (1912), 129–62. For Sheppard and his involvement in municipal reform, see Nancy L. Matthews, *William Sheppard: Cromwell's Law Reformer* (Cambridge, 1984), *passim*, but esp. pp. 48–59.

87 Bod. Lib., Rawlinson MSS , A 34, fols 305–8, 393–4; Schilling, 'Central Government and Municipal Corporations', pp. 99–100.

88 Bod. Lib., Rawlinson MSS, A 35, fol. 164; A 36, fols 590–1; Schilling, 'Central Government and Municipal Corporations', pp. 101–2; C. G. Parsloe, 'The Corporation of Bedford, 1647–1664', *Transactions of the Royal Historical Society*, 4th series, 29 (1947), 151–65.

89 Bod. Lib., Rawlinson MSS, A 32, fols 485–8; Schilling, 'Central Government and Municipal Corporations', pp. 94–5; Clive Holmes, *Seventeenth Century Lincolnshire* (Lincoln, 1980), p. 214.

90 Bod. Lib., Rawlinson MSS, A 33, fols 41–4, 101–4.

91 *Ibid.*, A 32, fols 647–50.

92 Birch, *State Papers of John Thurloe*, vol. 4, p. 330.

93 J. H. Round, 'Colchester during the Commonwealth', *English Historical Review*, 15 (1900), 641–64; Schilling, 'Central Government and Municipal Corporations', pp. 97–9.

94 Bod. Lib., Rawlinson MSS, A 32, fols 373–6.

95 Schilling, 'Central Government and Municipal Corporations', pp. 95–7.

96 Bod. Lib., Rawlinson MSS, A 32, fols 525–8; A 35, fol. 172.

97 Schilling, 'Central Government and Municipal Corporations', p. 100; PRO, SP.18.123. 147; SP.25.76, p. 484; B. G. Charles (ed.), *Calendar of the Records of the Borough of Haverfordwest, 1539–1660* (Cardiff, 1967), p. 129.

98 *Scandal on the Corporation: Royalists and Puritans in Mid Seventeenth Century Kingston from the Kingston Borough Archives* (Kingston, 1982), pp. 26, 28, 30–1.

99 PRO, SP.25.77, pp. 194, 909; Oxfordshire Record Office, C/FC/1/A1/03, Council Act Book, 1629–63, fol. 233r; C/FC/1/A2/03, Council Minute Book, 1635–57, fol. 309r; Birch, *State Papers of John Thurloe*, vol. 4, pp. 587–8.

100 Abbott, *Writings and Speeches of Cromwell*, vol. 4, pp. 112–13; Birch, *State Papers of John Thurloe*, vol. 4, p. 587–8.

101 For more details of Barkstead's activities, see chapter 8.

102 Gardiner, *Commonwealth and Protectorate*, vol. 3, p. 291; Paul D. Halliday, *Dismembering the Body Politic: Partisan Politics in England's Towns* (Cambridge, 1998), pp. 65–7. As part of his evidence for the major-generals' lack of interest in renewing town charters, Halliday states that Haynes advised Thurloe that the matter should be 'timorously' taken up. He in fact wrote that it should be 'timously' – or quickly – taken up; see Bod. Lib., Rawlinson MSS, A 32, fols 647–50.

103 Schilling, 'Central Government and Municipal Corporations', p. 107.

Chapter 6

The decimation tax

When Oliver Cromwell and his advisers concluded in the summer of 1655 that the continuing intrigues of their enemies necessitated the establishment of a national security system headed by the major-generals, they decided that the cost of this new initiative should be borne not by the nation as a whole but by the royalist community which they believed had steadfastly refused to acknowledge the legitimacy of the Cromwellian regime and still looked for a restoration of the Stuart monarchy. They therefore resolved that both those royalists who had been involved in the various conspiracies of the early 1650s and many of the much greater number who had remained quiescent but who, in their view, had given tacit support to their more active friends should pay a new discriminatory tax which would finance the work of the major-generals and pay for the new county militia troops. While this levy was officially labelled 'the extraordinary tax', it soon became widely known as the decimation tax.[1] This chapter will consider some of the most important questions raised by the imposition of this short-lived tax, including how efficiently it was assessed and collected, how the royalist community reacted to it, and whether ultimately it was able to provide sufficient funds to sustain the rule of the major-generals.

The arrangements for the introduction of the decimation tax were first outlined on 21 September 1655 in the printed orders and instructions drawn up by the council for the major-generals and their commissioners. The 'third head' of this document stipulated that 'an extraordinary tax be assessed, taxed and levied upon the estates of all and every person and persons in England and Wales whose estates have been sequestered for delinquency, or who were in actual arms for the late king against Parliament, or for Charles Stuart his son, or have adhered to, assisted or abetted the forces raised against the said Parliament'. All those who fell into one or more of these categories and who possessed an estate 'of inheritance' or 'for term of life' worth at least £100 per annum were required to pay £10 for every £100 of annual income. Those royalists who did not possess a landed estate of this value but who owned personal property worth at least £1,500 were to pay £100 for every £1,500. Those who qualified under the headings of both the real and personal estate could pay either a lump sum of £100 or an annual levy of £10 per annum for every £1,500 of their personal estate. The tax was to be paid in two half-yearly instalments, on 24 June and 21 December, the first payment being due on 21 December 1655. Those who refused to pay would have their estates sequestered until they complied. As an alternative to paying biannually, qualifying royalists were given the chance to convey to the state land of an equivalent annual value to their liability under the tax and were assured that this would be returned to them if the tax were at any time in the future rescinded.[2]

Shortly after publishing these arrangements, however, the government offered royalists a possible means of avoiding the new tax. In his declaration of 31 October, in which he outlined the reasons for the establishment of the rule of the major-generals and for the imposition of the decimation tax on the entire 'royal party', Cromwell declared that if any royalists had already dissociated themselves from the 'confederacy' and shown evidence of a change of heart, or if any decided now to forsake their former principles, 'wee shall much more esteeme of their reformation then desire their harme or preiudice'.[3] While this was a far from precise statement, it did genuinely offer an exemption from the tax to those who could provide evidence of a sincere change of heart and their acceptance of the protectorate. As we shall see, a number of royalists subsequently attempted to take advantage of this escape clause, and some were successful in persuading the government that they had abandoned their former allegiance and should thus be excused payment.

The task of assessing and collecting the decimation tax in the English and Welsh counties fell to the local commissioners for the securing the peace of the commonwealth. In most counties the bulk of the assessment work took place during November and December 1655, though in some areas it was not finished until well into January.[4] The commissioners held a series of meetings and summoned before them all those in their counties who they believed might be liable to pay. Suspects were required to bring with them accurate particulars of their estates, which were used to decide whether they possessed the minimum property requirement for eligibility and, if so, to calculate the amount they were required to pay. Each of the county commissions was assisted in the work by a clerk, two messengers and a doorkeeper; until June 1656 these officials were paid standard national salaries of £80, £30 and £10 respectively, but thereafter their pay was reduced and local variations developed. The decimation money was to be paid to county receivers, who were allowed a commission of 3*d* (old pence) for every pound they collected; in many counties this new post was held by the existing receivers of the assessment tax. By the summer of 1656, the receivers in at least one county were issuing royalists with specially printed receipts for payment.[5]

In most counties, the more active commissioners set about the assessment work with real urgency and enthusiasm. Those in Northamptonshire, for example, interviewed thirty of their royalist neighbours within one week in November, while during the same period their counterparts in Norfolk sat for ten days without a break.[6] They soon discovered, however, that the task was fraught with a range of procedural difficulties and that the orders and instructions they had received from the government failed to provide them with the detailed and precise guidelines that were required if they were to complete their task successfully.

In the first place, the orders of 21 September instructed the commissioners to ascertain the value of the real and personal estates of royalists both at the time of their appearance and as of 1 November 1653.[7] This earlier date was included to prevent royalists who had sold lands over the previous two years from avoiding payment for them. But, as the orders did not actually specify which of the valuations was to be used to assess the tax liability, some of the commissioners were clearly left rather confused. The issue was raised by the Lincolnshire commissioners in late November 1655, and a few days later the council ruled that the assessment should be based on the November 1653 value but charged on, and paid out of the estate currently owned.[8]

Another issue which complicated the commissioners' work was the question of what to do when some or all of a royalist's estate had been conveyed either by themselves or by the state to trustees. During the early 1650s, many royalists had voluntarily set up trusts to administer their estates on their behalf, and during the same period the government had also sold large amounts of forfeited royalist land to trustees, some of whom were clearly acting as agents for the original owners. The orders of 21 September instructed the commissioners to find out if any royalists had set up trusts to administer their estates and to determine whether these had been established for the 'use and benefit' of the previous owners.[9] This was to prove a complicated and time-consuming task, and in a number of counties the commissioners became embroiled in lengthy battles with royalists over the precise nature of their trusts. The sort of problems this issue could cause were illustrated in a letter Robert Lilburne sent to John Thurloe from Durham in February 1656. He told him that the Durham commissioners were finding it extremely difficult to assess the decimation tax in their county because 'many men's estates here are so encumbered by reason they were forfeited to the commonwealth for treason and purchased by several persons, as we suppose, in trust for the delinquents.' According to Lilburne, when such royalists appeared before the commissioners they claimed to be exempt from the tax on the grounds that, although they still lived on the lands, the real owners were now the trustees. He commented that this stance 'makes the case so dubious that as yet we have not yet completed our work'.[10]

William Goffe also encountered this problem. When he met the Hampshire commissioners for the first time in November 1655, he was told by some of them that the very large forfeited estate of John Paulet, marquis of Winchester, had been bought by trustees who were administering it for his benefit and that they thus considered it 'taxable'.[11] Several months later, the commissioners interviewed the agent responsible for the estate, who told them that, while the trustees did pay out some money to the marquis' wife and children, Paulet himself was excluded from any benefit. Informing Thurloe about this situation, Goffe requested him to try to find out the truth of the matter adding 'otherwise we can do nothing, though he would pay £300 pa'.[12] Despite their evident eagerness to tax the royalist peer, Goffe and his commissioners seem to have failed to prove that he benefited from the trust on his estates, as his name is absent from the list of those decimated in Hampshire drawn up after the Restoration.[13]

Goffe and his Hampshire commissioners faced the same problem when they tried to charge a decimation of £50 per annum on Sir John Meux of Kingston on the Isle of Wight. In May 1656, Meux petitioned Cromwell for a considerable reduction in his decimation assessment, on the grounds that most of his £500 a year estate had been conveyed away to trustees in 1640, and that since then he had received only £100 a year for his maintenance. In August, Goffe and two of his commissioners certified that in their opinion the trust was for Meux's 'use and benefitt' and that the original assessment should therefore stand. Meux was still being decimated in November 1656 when he again petitioned the government for a reduction. Whether he was successful is not clear, but his name does not appear on the later Hampshire decimation list.[14]

Another question which caused some confusion at the outset was whether the commissioners should allow reductions for taxes, debts, mortgages and other 'defalcations' and 'incumbrances' when making their assessments. Both William Boteler and the Lincolnshire commissioners asked Thurloe for guidance on this matter, and on 20 November 1655 Henry Lawrence, the president of the council, wrote to all the major-generals to inform them that, after considering the matter, the council had decided that no allowances should be made.[15] Boteler and Whalley were both pleased with this decision which they believed would make the assessment process quicker and more straightforward. Whalley commented that, if debts had been allowed, 'the tax would come to little, not half enough I dare say to pay the militia'.[16] His commissioners in Lincolnshire, on the other hand, were less pleased, both because they now needed to re-assess their royalists and because 'they thought it hard not to allow of mortgages'.[17]

A range of other queries also surfaced in the early weeks of the assessment process. Some of the commissioners were unsure how to proceed against the large number of royalists who possessed property in more than one county, but who fell beneath the threshold in some or all of them. On 20 November 1655, the council ruled that property throughout the country should be taken into account when deciding whether the £100 threshold had been reached, and that those royalists who were found to be eligible should then pay proportionately in each county where they held land.[18] The commissioners' orders also failed to give clear guidance about whether they should attempt to decimate the sons of deceased royalists; while this issue was never fully resolved, in most counties heirs seem to have escaped the tax.[19] Among the other questions raised by the commissioners were whether Roman Catholic recusants should pay the decimation on top of their other fines and charges; what should be done when royalists had leased property at low rents but had benefited from large entry fines; and whether those who owned valuable woodlands which did not produce a substantial annual revenue could none-theless be taxed.[20]

Yet another problem with the government's rather inadequate orders of 21 September was that each county seems initially to have received only one or two copies of them. Once they had begun work the major-generals and their commissioners quickly discovered that they needed their own personal copies to refer to for guidance, and that additional copies were required to give to any royalists who questioned their authority. During November 1655, a number of them wrote to Thurloe asking him to send them more copies as a matter of urgency.[21] At the end of the month, William Goffe suggested that the orders and instructions should be published in the official government newsbooks and this was done a few weeks later.[22]

One final, crucially important area where the government's orders and instructions failed to provide the commissioners with sufficiently clear guid-ance was the question of who precisely was liable to pay the decimation tax. As we have seen, the orders of 21 September required the commissioners to charge the tax not only on all those who had borne arms for the Stuarts and had suffered a consequent sequestration of their estates, but also on those who had in any other way 'adhered to, assisted or abetted' them.[23] This was a broad, imprecise definition of royalism which allowed the local commissioners a considerable degree of latitude in deciding who was and was not eligible to pay the tax. This fact was attested to by several of Sir Ralph Verney's friends during the first weeks of the assessment process. William Denton informed him on 17 November 1655 that 'sequestration and delinquency shall not be the only standard, but disaffection shall in due time have its place.'[24] Several weeks later, Sir Roger Burgoyne reported from Warwickshire that Whalley and the commissioners there were calling before them 'the sequestered and sequestrable, though they escaped the hands of the [county] committee'. He added that when one of those summoned, Sir Francis Willoughby, had declared that he had never been sequestered, Whalley had responded that 'the more the committee was to blame', and had proceeded to decimate him for sending two horses to Charles I.[25]

Other contemporary commentators disagreed markedly about how widely the commissioners had in fact cast their nets. Perhaps, not surprisingly, those who supported the tax argued that it was very limited in scope, while those who were hostile to it claimed that many men were decimated on the flimsiest of grounds. Edward Whalley claimed in parliament in December 1656 that it had not been levied upon any royalists 'that have laid down their arms and lived peaceably, or have given signal testimony of their affection', and several weeks later John Desborough supported this view, declaring: 'I believe no man has come under a decimation, but such as have either acted or spoken bitterly against the government, and for their young king, and drank his health', adding that 'many have escaped that have done such things'.[26] According to the royalist, Edward Hyde, however, many of those who were decimated

> never did, nor ever would have given, the king the least assistance, and were only reputed to be of his party because they had not assisted the rebels with a visible cheerfulness, or in any considerable proportion, and had proposed to themselves to sit still as neuters and not to be at any charge with reference to either party; or such who sheltered themselves in some of the King's garrisons for their own conveniency.[27]

The reality lay somewhere in between these partisan positions. The great majority of those decimated were undoubtedly committed royalists who had given active support to the Stuarts during the 1640s and early 1650s and who had as a consequence suffered sequestration and been obliged to compound for their estates. A significant minority, however, were deemed eligible to pay on other rather less clear-cut grounds. Some of these were decimated because they had lived in royalist garrisons during the first civil war. A few others, such as Sir William Halton and Sir Cranmer Herris in Essex, and John Lewkenor, Thomas May and Sir William Morley in Sussex, were taxed even though they had no clear association with the royalist cause and could with some justice have claimed to have remained neutral during the 1640s.[28]

In Essex and Kent, the commissioners taxed a number of individuals who had supported parliament until 1646, but then defected to the king during the uprisings of 1647 and 1648. Amongst this group were several former parliamentarian committeemen, including Sir William Hicks, Sir William Martyn and Robert Roe in Essex, and Sir Thomas Godfrey and Sir Richard Hardres and George Newman in Kent.[29] Some of those called before the commissioners had even held public office during the early 1650s. Sir Owen Wynn, for example, of Gwydir in Denbighshire was summmoned to appear in North Wales even though he had never been sequestered, had served as sheriff of Denbighshire in 1653, and had recently again been nominated as sheriff for 1656.[30] Most of the commissioners were keen to tax as many men as they could and proved reasonably efficient at identifying those of their neighbours who might be eligible to pay. There were, though, local variations in interpretation and efficiency. J. T. Cliffe has pointed out, for example, that a number of prominent royalists, including Thomas Chicheley of Cambridgeshire, Nicholas Steward of Hampshire and Sir John Harrison of Hertfordshire, seem to have escaped payment after being inexplicably overlooked by their local commissioners.[31]

If the commissioners were reasonably successful in finding royalists to decimate, how well did they carry out the process of arriving at accurate assessments of the value of their estates? As has been seen, all those who were summoned to appear in late 1655 were required to bring with them a particular of their estates as of November 1653. The commissioners were well aware that there was a very strong incentive for royalists to underestimate the value of their lands and personal property, and in some counties they attempted from the outset to verify royalist estimates by comparing them with other independent valuations. In mid November 1655, Hezekiah Haynes claimed that the Norfolk commissioners had checked the 'greatest part' of the valuations brought to them by local royalists extremely carefully, and around the same time Charles Worsley informed Thurloe that the Cheshire commissioners were trying to confirm the accuracy of the valuations by comparing them with other existing estate surveys and that they intended to conduct new surveys where they considered these to be deficient.[32]

Another method by which some of the commissioners hoped to obtain independent corroboration of the royalists' own assessments was by comparing them with the particulars of delinquent estates contained within the voluminous records of the old committee for compounding. In early November 1655, Edward Whalley and the Nottinghamshire commissioners asked Thurloe to arrange for them to be sent a list of those in their county who had compounded at Goldsmiths Hall during the 1640s, and a few days later a similar request was made by Whalley's commissioners in Lincolnshire and Derbyshire.[33] On 12 November, Thurloe accordingly wrote to the sequestration commissioners at Haberdashers Hall, who had taken over a number of the responsibilities of the Goldsmiths Hall committee in 1649, and asked them to prepare lists of all those who had compounded in each of the English and Welsh counties and to forward them to him at Whitehall. He stressed that the task was of 'great consequence' and required 'all possible speed'.[34] On 20 November, his request was backed up by the full council, which ordered the committee to compile lists of compounders and to attach to them copies of the particulars of their estates which they had submitted at the time of their composition.[35]

While the sequestration commissioners set about this task straightaway, they seem to have had little enthusiasm for it, and on 30 November they sent Whalley a long letter in which they explained why they felt any lists they produced would be of only very limited use to him and his commissioners. They told him that abstracting the information he needed from the 4,000 sets of composition papers they held would be 'a worke of some time' and added that, as many of those who had compounded possessed estates in more than one county, they could not identify all the royalists who held land in any one shire until they had completed lists for the whole country. They also pointed out that they had only been given responsibility for sequestration work in 1649 and that their knowledge of the dealings of pre-existing committees was patchy and incomplete. They concluded by arguing that in their view 'the particulars upon which the delinquents compounded here cannot be a certaine guide to the value of their present estates, for that many compounded for small personall estates to whom considerable estates have since come by dissent [descent], or marriage or otherwise.'[36] Had it suited them, they might equally have argued that many royalists now possessed much less property than they had at the time of their composition. Around the same time as they sent this letter to Whalley, the sequestration commissioners made similar representations to Thurloe and persuaded him to abandon the initiative.[37]

Soon after they had set to work, therefore, it became apparent to the major-generals and their commissioners that any attempt to carry out a systematic verification of royalist self-assessments would prove both difficult and time-consuming and make it quite impossible to collect the first instalment of the tax, due in late December. As a consequence, most of them concluded that in the short term at least they had little option but to accept the royalists' self-assessments more or less at face value. This was certainly the approach adopted by William Goffe and the commissioners in Sussex. When in late November Goffe sent Thurloe his preliminary list of those charged with the tax in Sussex, he told him 'it will cost much tyme and charge to come to an exact knowledge of men's estates', and he made clear that the present assessments were based either upon 'own consent' or 'general information'.[38] When Goffe's Hampshire commissioners interviewed Sir William Kingsmill of Sydmonton in December 1655 they did at least hold a 'debate' with him about the accuracy of his valuation. Such enquiries were not, however, likely to achieve very much, for as Kingsmill's mother, Bridget, remarked to him several days later, the commissioners would find it 'hard to prove more then what you confesse'.[39] Several major-generals pointed out that it was particularly difficult to check out the accuracy of valuations of personal property. Edward Whalley told Thurloe on several occasions in late 1655 and early 1656 that it was 'so hard a thing to discover personal property', and Charles Worsley commented in December 1655 'wee shall (I doubt) not find much of a parsonall estate.'[40]

At the beginning of 1656, William Orum, a steward to the marquis of Hertford, claimed in a letter to a friend that the Somerset commissioners were keen to 'act mildly' towards their royalist neighbours and were accepting without question drastic underestimates of the value of their estates.[41] In the absence of corroborating evidence, it is impossible to know whether or not this was true; but if it was, it certainly did not reflect the situation in other parts of the country, where many of their counterparts were anxious to maximise the yield from the tax and, as one of Sir Edward Nicholas's informants put it, were 'very severe in exacting the tenths'.[42] In mid November 1655, William Boteler told Thurloe that his commissioners in Bedfordshire were keen to 'go to the utmost bounds of their power' against one local royalist who was attempting to avoid decimation on the grounds that his substantial woodlands in the county yielded little in the way of annual income.[43] In Essex, the commissioners even decimated their major-general's elder brother, Robert Haynes.[44]

Furthermore, once the initial asssessments had been completed and the amounts due to be paid on 21 December had been determined, the commissioners in a number of counties did then set in train procedures to check the veracity of the royalists' own valuations. When Goffe sent Thurloe his initial decimation list from Sussex in late November, he assured him that if they had underassessed anyone it was only through lack of information and added: 'wee may go higher when we have clear grounds so to doe.'[45] In January 1656, Edward Whalley told Thurloe that the Lincolnshire commissioners, who had initially taxed local royalists on their own valuations, were now sending out messengers 'to find out the truth'.[46] In early March 1656, the council instructed all the English and Welsh commissioners to summon the decimated royalists within their respective counties before them once again and to demand new particulars of their estates. In an attempt to uncover lands liable to taxation which had been concealed during the initial assessment process, it also now ordered that the estate particulars of those royalists who held land in more than one association should be copied and circulated to all the relevant major-generals.[47] Some of the commissioners, including those in Charles Worsley's association in the north-west, acted on this directive and undertook a wholesale reassessment of liability under the tax during the spring and summer of 1656.[48]

The incompleteness of the extant records makes it impossible to come to any firm conclusions about the degree of accuracy achieved by the commissioners in their assessment of the tax. There can, however, be little real doubt that, as a direct consequence of their enforced reliance on the royalists' own valuations of their wealth, some of those who should have paid the tax were able to avoid it by claiming that they fell below the thresholds for payment, and that others who were decimated ended up paying less than they should have. J. T. Cliffe has uncovered a number of examples of royalists who appear to have paid far less than a tenth of their true annual income or who were decimated only in the county where they normally resided and avoided paying for estates they possessed in other shires.[49] It is perhaps to be expected that the individual county commissions would achieve differing degrees of success in this area of their work, for the numbers of royalists requiring assessment varied greatly from county to county and those commissioners with the lighter workloads would inevitably have had more time to check valuations than their more burdened counterparts. Finally, it is important to stress that any underassessment that did occur was, in the main, the result not of any lack of commitment on the part of the commissioners or any reluctance by them to impose a heavy fiscal burden on their royalist neighbours, but rather of the absence of any viable alternative to accepting the royalists' own estimations of their liability.

Most of the royalists summoned to appear before the commissioners seem to have concluded that they had little choice but to cooperate with them and to submit to assessment and taxation. At the beginning of November 1655, the Nottinghamshire commissioners informed Thurloe that they had found 'a willingness in those we have yet treated withal to submit to the instructions', and a few days later those in Lincolnshire reported that they had found a similar compliance in most of the royalists they had summoned.[50] James Berry, meanwhile, told Thurloe in mid November that the royalists interviewed by his Worcestershire commissioners 'seem not at all to quarrell att itt', and a few weeks later he claimed he had only encountered one 'refractory' person in the whole of North Wales.[51] Hezekiah Haynes reported that the Norfolk royalists had 'not one word to say why ought should be remitted'.[52] At the end of the November, Charles Worsley told Thurloe that the Lancashire royalists 'seeme to conforme to the particulars with much readines', and a few days later he reiterated that 'the malignant party seeme to submit to what is imposed with much redinesse'.[53] According to Robert Lilburne, the Yorkshire royalists summoned before his commissioners in mid December were 'very ready to doe what was required of them'.[54] While these reports indicate that open resistance to the commissioners was comparatively rare, they almost certainly exaggerate the willingness of the royalist community to pay the tax. Many of those summoned acquiesced only very grudgingly and like the Sussex royalist, Sir William Morley, who agreed to pay £150 a year but told William Goffe that he took it 'very much to hart that he should bee still reckoned a malignant', they resented the new exaction deeply.[55]

Those few royalists who did openly resist the commissioners were dealt with quickly and firmly. When Thomas Wriothesley, earl of Southampton, met Thomas Kelsey and the Surrey commissioners at Kingston on 22 November, he initially refused to show them a particular of his estate and had to be held for some hours before he complied.[56] When Sir John Monson refused to cooperate with the Lincolnshire commissioners, he was placed under house arrest, had fifty troops quartered on him and suffered sequestration of his property.[57] At a meeting of the Dorset commissioners in late December attended by John Desborough, three local royalists, Sir John Strangeways, Sir Gerard Napper and Sir Hugh Wyndham, objected strongly to the proceedings, and Wyndham in particular displayed 'much frowardness and averseness'; but after Desborough had dealt with them, as he put it, 'very plainely and indeed very roundly', they all submitted.[58] When Robert Henley of the Middle Temple refused to produce a particular of some land he owned in Cambridgeshire, the commissioners there ordered that if he did not comply by 2 January 1656 they would impose a decimation of £300 per annum on him. This proved an effective tactic, for Henley soon submitted and was assessed to pay £90 for the estate.[59] A number of other royalists initially cooperated with the commissioners, only to subsequently default on their payments. Arnold King had to be threatened with sequestration on several occasions by the commissioners in Kent before he paid up, and when Richard Thornhill of the same county also neglected to pay, the commissioners ordered several of his tenants 'to keepe soe much rent in their handes as is due to the state for payment of his decimation'.[60] The commissioners in North Wales adopted the same approach when John Bodvile of Anglesey failed to pay, and later threatened to distrain his cattle.[61]

As the names of the royalists who were assessed for the decimation tax survive for fewer than half of the English counties and for none of those in Wales, it is only possible to give a very rough estimate of the total number who paid the tax during 1655 and 1656. J. T. Cliffe found lists for fourteen counties in the published version of John Thurloe's papers and the commonwealth state papers and exchequer papers in the Public Record Office, and the present author has uncovered a further two county lists amongst the Rawlinson manuscripts in the Bodleian Library.[62] In all, around 500 royalists were assessed to pay the tax in these sixteen counties. The numbers decimated in the other twenty or so English counties and in London and in Wales can only be guessed at. Clearly, however, the overall total must have been well in excess of 1,000 and may well have been in the region of 2,000. Some 4,000 royalists had been obliged to compound for their estates over the previous ten years, but a number of these had died before the end of 1655, and many others would have fallen below the £100 per annum minimum threshold for the decimation.

Around 140, or somewhat over a quarter, of the 500 royalists who are known to have been assessed to pay attempted to avoid the tax by petitioning the central government for an exemption. Their cases were normally referred to the council subcommittee for petitions. Initially, Philip Jones and Walter Strickland were responsible for considering them but, due to the rapidly increasing workload, at the beginning of 1656 a further six members of the council were drafted in to help them.[63] The members of this expanded sub-committee normally recommended one of three options to Cromwell and the full council: that the petition should be rejected out of hand; that an exemption should be granted; or most frequently that the petition should be referred back to the relevant local commissioners to proceed 'as they shall in equity think meet and reasonable'.[64] While the majority of the petitioners were disappointed, a significant minority did manage to persuade the council to let them off and some others may have secured a release from their local commissioners.[65]

Most of those who sought a release from the tax did so on the grounds that they had changed their political affiliation and therefore satisfied the criteria for exemption laid down in the government's declaration of 31 October 1655. Amongst them were the eight prominent Staffordshire royalists, who sent Cromwell a joint petition in which they expressed the view that the protector would not wish to molest anyone who had lived peaceably since the passing of the Act of Oblivion and argued they should thus be exempted as they had given 'noe new occation to be distinguisht from the most obedient people of the commonwealth'.[66] Their confidence proved misplaced, as none was let off. Thomas Offley of Sussex, on the other hand, was luckier and won a discharge even though his statement that he judged it 'his duty to acquiesce in the wise proceedings of the most high God who pulleth down one and setteth up another as it pleaseth him' was hardly a ringing endorsement of Cromwell's regime.[67]

Although the government's reaction to these petitions was not entirely consistent or predictable, the majority of those who secured an exemption were successful for one of three main reasons: because they had won the backing of their major-general and commissioners or some other prominent local supporters of the government; because they had accompanied their petition with the offer of a substantial sum of money; or because they could exploit their pre-eminent social position, patronage and kinship connections within the corridors of power at London.

The Hampshire royalist, Parkinson Odber, secured a release from the tax after John Warner, a godly minster from Christchurch, had testified that he was a regular attender at his church not only on Sundays but also at additional meetings 'in private when the members of our church congregate themselves for their mutuall edification', and that 'his conversation hath bene such as becometh the gospell.'[68] Writing to Thurloe to recommend his release in

February 1656, William Goffe commented: 'as the Christians among whom he lyveth doe receive him into their godly society, so the commissioners have hitherto forborne to tax his estate.'[69] Edmund Jones of Monmouthshire was released after his local commissioners reported in April 1656 that since the mid 1640s he had 'shown himself very affectionate to the good people and uppon severall occasions hath bin very serviceable to them and given good testimony of his deserting the late king's interest'.[70] Jones had in fact served as attorney general for South Wales in the early 1650s and as MP for Brecon in 1654. In March 1656, two Denbighshire royalists, Kenrick Eyton and Francis Manley, were exempted after James Berry and the commissioners for North Wales had written to the government on their behalf. Eyton, who had been a commissioner of array in 1642, was discharged on their report that he had 'changed his interest', married a godly gentlewoman and had for some time frequented 'the society of godly people'.[71] Manley, meanwhile, was let off on the grounds that he too had 'really changed his interest and wholly deserted the late king's party and that he hath some reall worke of grace in him'.[72] Berry also supported the successful petition of Sir Edward Lloyd of Montgomeryshire.[73] Among those who were released after they attached to their petitions offers to contribute a substantial sum of money to the government were Sir William Walter of Oxfordshire and Sir George Pratt of Berkshire, both of whom donated £500; William Constantine of Dorset, who gave £80; Lawrence Washington of Wiltshire who gave £50; and Edmund Hall of Dorset who gave £40.[74]

That Cromwell's government was also susceptible to the privileges of social rank is suggested by the fact that a disproportionately high number of the royalist peers who were assessed for the tax, including the earls of Cork and Clare; lords Paget and Paulet; the countess of Middlesex; the earl of Bedford; and his brother, Edward lord Russell, subsequently secured a release. Some peers, such as John Holles, second earl of Clare; William, lord Paget; William Russell, earl of Bedford; and Edward, lord Russell, appear to have been exempted on the grounds that they had deserted the royalist cause before 1646. A number of others, including Richard Boyle, second earl of Cork, the elder brother of the Cromwellian supporter Lord Broghill; and Robert, lord Rich of Essex, the son of the parliamentarian admiral, the earl of Warwick, seem to have won a discharge simply through their kinship and patronage connections.[75] The government's marked willingness to respond favourably to aristocratic petitions did not go unnoticed by contemporaries and was, for example, commented upon by one of Sir Edward Nicholas's royalist informants in January 1656.[76] Other prominent, non-aristocratic royalists who also appear to have won a discharge through family connections included Henry Widdrington of Northumberland, brother of the speaker of the 1656 parliament, Sir Thomas Widdrington; and Sir Edward Ford of Sussex, brother-in-law of Cromwell's deceased son-in-law, Henry Ireton.[77]

By no means all those who relied upon the help of powerful friends, however, were successful in avoiding payment. Sir Hervey Bagot, who was one of the eight Staffordshire royalists whose joint petition had been turned down by Cromwell, subsequently attempted to escape the tax by exploiting his connection with his neighbour, Sir Charles Wolseley, a member both of Cromwell's council and the subcommittee for considering petitions. After receiving a request from Bagot for help, Wolesley wrote back in January 1656 acknowledging that he owed him 'respect and service' and promising to do 'his best endeavours' for him.[78] Several months later, however, he wrote again to tell him that, although he had delivered his petition to the council with 'the best advantage I could', it had been turned down. He added – not entirely honestly – that 'the truth is, they haveinge not done any thinge in cases of licke nature, did not thinke fitt to afford any favour in yours.'[79]

A small number of those who were assessed to pay sought an exemption on the grounds that their sequestration in the 1640s had been a mistake and had subsequently been discharged. Thomas Smyth of Essex was released after he produced a copy of his discharge from sequestration, and Henry Harpur of Cheshire was probably also released on this basis.[80] Not all those whose sequestrations had been discharged were so fortunate. Thomas, lord Coventry, remained under decimation even though his sequestration for acting as a commissioner of array in Worcestershire had been taken off by parliament in 1645, and Sir Charles Egerton of Newborough in Staffordshire failed to secure a release even though his sequestration had also been discharged.[81]

Sir Ralph Verney of Claydon in Buckinghamshire, who had spent much of the 1640s on the continent and who had also been sequestered and then discharged, was another gentleman who failed to win a reprieve on these grounds. When he appeared before the Buckinghamshire commissioners in March 1656 and informed them that his original sequestration had been taken off by parliament, they told him they were not 'judges of the justice of sequestration' and that he would have to appeal directly to Cromwell and the council for a release. After persuading the commissioners to postpone his decimation for three weeks, he journeyed to London to present his case to the government. Shortly after his arrival he told his friend, Sir Justinian Isham, that he was finding the business of petitioning the council to be 'very ill sport', adding that it involved 'soe great charge, trouble and attendance that most resolve to pay quietly rather than use this tedious and uncertain way of getting off'. At the end of April, he informed another friend that after attending the council daily for some weeks he had received some encouragement but as yet no discharge. In late May, the council finally referred the case back to the Buckinghamshire commissioners. On the morning of the second hearing in the county at the beginning of July 1656, Verney was so sure that his plea for an exemption would be rejected that he wrote to a kinswoman that were not Alisbery [Aylesbury] very neare to Claydon, I should scarce goe thether about it, unlesse it were to give an opportunity to the Maj. Gen. and commissioners to make their injustice shine more clearly, which you may guesse to be a needlesse errand, being most men are already fully satisffied in that point.

As he had anticipated, the Buckinghamshire commissioners did indeed proceed to confirm his decimation.[82]

But if Cromwell and the council failed to respond positively to the petitions of most of those who approached them for an exemption, they nonetheless released sufficient numbers to cause widespread disquiet among the major-generals and their commissioners. At the end of December 1655, James Berry wrote to Thurloe to advise him to be wary about 'protecting any from our power' without first consulting them. He declared that he and his commissioners were 'resolved to be impartiall and where any deserves favour we will commend them to you', but he added that 'it would much distracte our affaires at present if any check should be put upon us from above.'[83] Six weeks later in mid February 1656, he again wrote to Thurloe to inform him that 'the extraordinary taxe here will not be extraordinary great; especially if my Lord should be too liberall in distributing his indulgencyes amongst those unconstant people who have played with both hands.' He asked him to advise Cromwell 'not to interpose too much, least he bring upon us an odium and upon himself too great a trouble'.[84]

When Edward Whalley heard that Robert Sutton, Lord Lexington, of Averham in Nottinghamshire was seeking an exemption, he told Thurloe that he was known locally as the 'devil of Newarke' because of his harsh treatment of the parliamentary prisoners in that garrison during the civil war, and declared: 'should he escape your law, it would be looked upon like the spider's web, onely to take the litle flyes and let the great ones goe.' He added that, if Sutton were exempted, 'it would exceedingly weaken the hearts of your commissioners now acting vigorously for you'. This would undoubtedly have been the case, as Sutton possessed a very large estate valued by the commissioners at nearly £5,000 per annum.[85] As a result of Whalley's intervention, however, he almost certainly failed to win a reprieve.

A couple of weeks later, Whalley responded angrily to a request to suspend proceedings against William Cavendish, earl of Devonshire, commenting 'it makes the countrey thinke that great men have most friends as formerly'.[86] In February 1656, he wrote again to Thurloe to oppose the efforts of the Derbyshire royalist, John Frescheville, to secure an exemption. He dismissed Frescheville's petition on the grounds that 'at this time of day you shall have halfe the cavaleeres in England professe as much as he', and declared: 'Sir, this tax hath exceedingly pleased our friends, it haveing put a difference between well and ill affected; and certaynely it will much dissatisfye them to see you about to put them into your bosomes, especially eminent ones, before the Lord hath wrought a reall change and worke of grace in their hearts.'[87]

John Desborough was also distressed about the numbers securing exemptions. In December 1655, he told Cromwell that he had looked at the petition of Francis, lord Seymour, of Wiltshire, but had found in it 'no more than any cavalier in the west of England shall pretend for himself'; he added that, if he were let off, 'it will but open a dore and give occasion to the enemy to cry out of our partiallyty, especially if ffavour and respect shall be shown to him and denied to others that will doe as much if not more than he hath done.'[88] The following month, he again commented of the petitions of several Gloucestershire royalists who were seeking exemptions that they only stated what 'hundreds of cavalleirs shall in these parts freely declare, provided they may be exempted from this additionall tax; and yet if opportunity were, should be as free to set up that corrupt interest as ever'. He told Thurloe that he believed it unwise to release royalists 'without demonstration of a real work of grace or some eminent manifestation of integrity'.[89]

Most of the other major-generals were similarly disturbed by what they saw as the government's over-willingness to respond positively to petitions for release. Thomas Kelsey told Cromwell in early December 1655 that his commissioners in Kent were 'much discouraged that [the] chiefest enemies of greatest estates are like to be freed'.[90] The same month, Hezekiah Haynes requested that 'there be none, or as few as may be, of the fines and taxes upon delinquents suspended', and a few weeks later Robert Lilburne warned Thurloe: 'you clip our stocke too much with your suspensions.'[91] In February 1656, William Boteler expressed his frustration that, as a result of the release of a number of prominent royalists in his association, the yield from the decimation would be insufficient to pay the costs of his militia troops.[92] Several weeks later, he wrote to Thurloe to ask that 'care may be had to supply what the council shall see cause to take away'.[93]

On a number of occasions, the local commissioners also strongly opposed the petitions of those seeking exemptions. In December 1655, the Leicestershire commissioners wrote to Cromwell to tell him that six of their royalists who had petitioned for a release 'may obtain your favour through misrepresenting their cases', but that in their view they should all be decimated.[94] In March 1656, two of the Wiltshire commissioners wrote to Cromwell asking him not to grant the petitions of several royalists they were attempting to decimate; arguing that their petitions for release 'hinder just proceedings against them', they declared: 'all we aime at is that the maskes of these men may be pulled off and the countrey have a right knowledge of them.'[95] Some of the commissioners went so far as to disobey direct orders from London to release individuals. Although Cromwell had discharged Thomas Knyvett of Ashwellthorpe in Norfolk from payment in January 1656, the Norfolk commissioners continued to proceed against him, and in April they wrote to the protector to explain why they felt he should be decimated.[96] The commissioners for Middlesex and Westminster similarly ignored instructions to suspend proceedings against William Russell, earl of Bedford, and continued to demand that he pay the tax.[97]

Although in the opinion of the major-generals and their commissioners far too many royalists were being released from decimation by Cromwell and his advisers in London, the great majority of those assessed were required to pay the three instalments of the tax which were levied in December 1655, and June and December 1656. The total amount of tax charged on the 500 or so royalists in the sixteen counties for which decimation lists survive was in the region of £18,000 per annum.[98] While it is impossible to extrapolate from this figure the total amount levied on the royalist community throughout England and Wales, it seems highly unlikely that the tax could ever have brought in the £80,000 needed to meet the salaries of the militia troops, the major-generals and their commissioners' civilian officers for the twelve-month period beginning in June 1655. Theoretically, its yield might have approached the £67,000 which was required after the reduction of the national militia force in the summer of 1656, but in practice it is doubtful whether anything like this figure was ever assessed, let alone collected.

As a direct result, from the outset the government faced a serious problem over the financing of its new militia force. Because, however, both the numbers of troops needing to be paid and the incidence of taxable royalists varied greatly from county to county, the resultant underfunding of the militia was not of equal seriousness across the various associations. Some of the major-generals, such as John Desborough, Robert Lilburne, Edward Whalley and Charles Worsley, were able to collect not only enough money for their own needs but also substantial surpluses. Worsley informed Thurloe in early December 1655 that in Staffordshire the tax would raise enough for the local militia and 'a considerable sum for other uses', and in February 1656 he told him there was likely to be a surplus in Cheshire, too.[99] A number of his colleagues, however, realised from a very early stage that they faced serious financial difficulties. William Goffe, for example, warned Thurloe in mid November 1655 that in Sussex 'there are so many of the delinquents dead and so much of their estates sould that I fear the revenue raysed by the taxe in this county will not bee very considerable.'[100] A few days later, Hezekiah Haynes reported that Norfolk contained relatively few royalists eligible for decimation and that, as a result, what would be raised there would not be enough 'by a greate deale' to pay the local militia troops.[101]

Both the scale of the underlying problem and the way it varied in seriousness from county to county quickly become clear when the decimation totals for the sixteen counties for which records survive are compared to the salary bills of their respective militia troops. In Nottinghamshire the commissioners were in the comfortable position of having assessed over £3,000 per annum and needing to pay out only £1,189 for the one county troop and the commissioners' officials. In Essex, where they needed £2,189 to pay two troops, they had assessed around £2,500. In all the other fourteen counties for which decimation lists survive, however, the commissioners' financial commitments out-stripped their incomes from the tax. In several of them, the shortfalls were relatively small and might have been remedied by a modest increase in the tax. In Cumberland and Westmorland, for example, which shared one militia troop at a cost of £1,189, the decimation was assessed at £955 annually, while in Berkshire, where £1,189 was also required, £970 was assessed. Elsewhere, however, the situation was far worse. In Bedford-shire, Cambridgeshire, Derbyshire, Hertfordshire, and Huntingdonshire, where the commissioners again needed to raise £1,189 to pay the one county troop, the decimation amounted to only £668, £347, £828, £728 and £279 respectively. The Rutland commissioners needed to find £689 for a smaller troop of sixty men, but only managed to assess £348. In Hampshire, Northamptonshire and Sussex, where £2,189 was needed for two county troops, only £1,038, £1,600 and £982 respectively was levied; and in Kent and Suffolk, where £3,188 was required for three troops, only £2,622 and £1,469 respectively was assessed. Altogether, the salary bill for the twenty-three militia troops stationed in these sixteen counties was around £25,000, whereas, as we have seen, the total amount of decimation charged was only about £18,000.[102] In the great majority of these counties, and almost certainly too in most of those for which no records have survived, there was never any realistic prospect that the decimation tax would produce enough money to finance the new militia forces.

Further details of how this underlying problem with the new tax hampered the work of individual commissions is revealed by some of their surviving decimation account books. In Essex, which possessed two militia troops, the commissioners collected £1,313 from nearly 100 royalists under the first moiety of the tax due at the end of 1655. In the six months to December 1655, however, their disbursements totalled £1,500 and they were thus left with a deficit of £187. By the summer of 1656, they had managed to make this up and balance their books, but they were only able to pay Hezekiah Haynes £31 towards his salary of £666. After collecting the third moiety in December 1656, they were left with a surplus of £120, but they had paid Haynes nothing at all towards his salary for the second half of 1656.[103]

Elsewhere, the problems were much more acute. In Kent the commissioners managed to collect £1,551 under the first moiety, but were obliged to disburse £2,180 on the pay of the three militia troops and their own civilian officials, and were thus left with a deficit of £629 for the first half-year. Under the second moiety, they received £1,277; out of this they paid their officials' salaries of £138 and made up the deficit from the previous six months. This left them with a notional surplus of £509, but only because they did not pay the troops the money they were owed for their service from December 1655 to June 1656. By adding the £1,106 raised as the third moiety in December 1656 to the surplus of £509 from the summer, by early 1657 they had assembled a total of £1,615, which they then used to provide the militia troops with their pay for the first half of 1656. Some payments for service during the second half of 1656 were made later, but only in part and seriously in arrears.[104]

In Derbyshire the commissioners collected a total of £1,244 for the three half years' payments and altogether disbursed £1,256, but again they only achieved this balancing of their books by paying their militia troop less than they were due. In February 1656, the Derbyshire troop received £433, roughly all it was owed for its service to the previous December; in December 1656, however, it was paid only £233 of the money owed for the half-year period to June 1656, and in April 1657 it received only £364 of the money due for its service in the second half of 1656.[105] It is clear that in these counties, and probably in many others too, the commissioners were forced to operate a system of deficit finance, and that if they did manage ostensibly to balance their books, they only did so by paying their county troops much less than they were owed and seriously in arrears.

This dire financial situation was only worsened by the slowness with which many royalists paid in their money. In Kent, only three royalists paid the first moiety, due on 21 December 1655, on time; another six paid by the end of December, a further forty-six during January 1656, nine during February, and the remaining twenty-nine between March and mid July. Three Kentish royalists paid their first moiety after the second had become due. The second moiety, due on 24 June 1656, was collected somewhat more quickly; six paid this instalment by the end of June, forty-seven in July, fourteen in August, and the remaining nine by the beginning of October. The third moiety was due on 21 December 1656. Five had paid this by the end of the year; a further thirty-seven paid up during January 1657 when a decimation bill was going through the second protectorate parliament, and another fifteen paid in the period following its voting down on 29 January 1657.[106] That royalists were still prepared to pay up after the levy had effectively been declared illegal may seem surprising, but the official position appears to have been that despite the vote in parliament they remained liable for any arrears outstanding from the December 1656 instalment.[107]

The government in London responded to these acute financial difficulties in several ways. In an attempt to raise money quickly, during the second half of

1656 it allowed a few particularly wealthy royalists to compound for their decimation by paying a substantial one-off sum. In late June 1656, Warwick, lord Mohun, who several months earlier had signed a declaration pledging his support to Cromwell's government, was permitted to pay a composition fine of £500 for his west country estates.[108] A week later, William Cavendish, earl of Devonshire, compounded for his large landholdings throughout the country with a fine of £4,000, and in December 1656 Montague Bertie, earl of Lindsey, similarly compounded by paying £1,200.[109] Why these men were prepared to part with such large sums of money is far from clear, and when the tax was abolished a few months later they must surely have cursed their decision to follow this course. The advantage for the government, however, was obvious. The £4,000 paid by Cavendish, for example, was quickly allocated to William Boteler and Hezekiah Haynes, each of whom received £2,000 to ease their financial problems.[110]

The government further responded to the situation by encouraging the major-generals and their commissioners to redouble their efforts to increase the yield from the tax in their areas. On 1 January 1656, Henry Lawrence, the president of the council, asked them to consider what else might be done in those areas where the decimation would prove insufficient to pay the militia.[111] As was seen above, the following March the council ordered the commissioners to interview all their royalists again and attempt to obtain more accurate valuations of estates and full details of any lands in other counties which they might have been concealing.[112] When these initiatives failed to remedy the shortfall, they proceeded with a twenty per cent reduction in the size of the national militia force, and in June they handed over responsibility for the collection of the decimation and the payment of the troops to the central army committee.[113] Once again, however, these changes accomplished little, as the decimation money was insufficient to support even the reduced militia force and the actual collection of the tax continued to be carried out locally by the commissioners.

Several other more fundamental changes to the system were also considered before being rejected. In the summer of 1656, it was rumoured in royalist circles that the government was about to double the decimation tax and impose it at a rate of twenty per cent of annual wealth.[114] In addition, from a much earlier stage most of the major-generals and their commissioners had been arguing that the payment thresholds of £100 and £1,500 should be lowered to allow a much greater number of royalists to be taxed. William Boteler wrote to Thurloe in mid November 1655 to express his frustration that there were very few royalists in Bedfordshire who would reach the thresholds, and a few days later Thomas Kelsey told him that if the real property level was lowered to £50 the decimation revenue in Kent would be almost doubled.[115] In mid December, James Berry reported from Wrexham that 'the gentlemen of

Wales have more honour than inheritance', and that it was easier to find 50 men with £50 estates than five with £100.[116] The same month, John Desborough commented from Wiltshire that 'there are more dangerous persons under £100 pa then above', and Robert Lilburne reported that the Yorkshire commissioners were 'very desirous the rule might have been £40 and £500, for most of your desperate people, which are a more considerable number than those that are taxt, escape'.[117]

In late December 1655, Charles Worsley reported to Thurloe from the north-west that 'many in these countreyes that have been very active against the parliament and were looked upon to be men of good estate will hardly be brought within the compasse; for one hundred pound per ann is a good estate in these parts.'[118] Several days later he reinforced the point in a letter to Cromwell; informing him that he had found 'as many dangerous persons in these countys whose estates fall short of £100 pa as any of what quality soever', he claimed that if the thresholds were lowered to £50 and £500, 'we shall raise much more than else we can.'[119] Around the same time, William Goffe told Thurloe that 'men do now begin to be very industrious to bring in their estates to be under £100 per annum which makes us more earnestly desire an additionall order that those that have £50 per annum may be taxed'.[120]

The one major-general who dissented from this call for a lowering of the thresholds was Edward Whalley. Whalley wrote to Thurloe in mid December 1655 to tell him that he had discussed the possibility of a lower limit with the Nottinghamshire commissioners, but that they had opposed the move on the grounds that it would 'discontent many and ruinate some' and bring very little additional money into the treasury, 'the middling sort of men being almost all for the parliament, or neuters'.[121] Their atypical lack of enthusiasm for a lowering of the thresholds is unsurprising, for as we have seen they had already collected considerably more money than they needed to pay for their one county troop and as a result were not experiencing the same acute difficulties faced by their counterparts in other parts of the country.

At the beginning of 1656, Cromwell and his advisers decided to reject these calls for a reduction in the original lower limits. Why they did so is not entirely clear. They may perhaps have concluded that any resultant increase in the yield would be too small to justify the increased adminstrative burden on the commissioners. They may also have feared that an extension of the tax might provoke a backlash from the royalist community. John Desborough was nonetheless very disappointed when he heard of the decision, and he told Thurloe that he felt it had been a mistake to dismiss the proposal, claiming 'you will not loose [lose] one of them by it that otherwise might be gained, and, without a change of their principles, are better lost than found'.[122]

Just how much additional income would in fact have been produced if the thresholds had been lowered is difficult to estimate. The size of any increase would certainly have varied greatly from county to county. In Kent, where the persistence of the practice of partible inheritance meant the county possessed a higher than usual number of small estates, the commissioners were able to decimate only a quarter of the nearly 400 local royalists they interviewed, and, as was seen above, Kelsey believed that a lowering of the limit would have nearly doubled his yield.[123] In Suffolk, however, nothing like this scale of increase would have been achieved. The commissioners there, who decimated thirty royalists achieving a total of £1,069, sent Thurloe a list of the county's remaining twenty-seven delinquents who fell below the threshold. Between them, this latter group possessed lands worth £539 per annum and personal property worth £1,160; even if all of them had been taxed, the increased revenue would only have been around £54.[124] The fact that in the poorer parts of northern England and much of Wales, where estates worth £100 per annum were few and far between, the great majority of the royalist party did not possess sufficient income to qualify was undoubtedly extremely galling for the major-generals and commissioners who operated in these areas. But, while a lowering of the thresholds might well have raised their morale and would clearly have brought in a little extra money, there is no reason to believe it would have produced a large enough increase in the overall national yield to remedy the underlying problem.

In the event, none of the initiatives aimed at remedying the shortfall from the decimation proved effective, and the serious financial problems experienced by the major-generals and their commissioners in many parts of the country persisted throughout 1656 and on into 1657. In an attempt to help the most underfunded major-generals, in the spring of 1656 the council began to shift money from one association to another. In March 1656, Edward Whalley was ordered to pay £1,240 to Hezekiah Haynes, and six months later he was told to pay more of his 'overplus moneys' to William Boteler.[125] In September 1656, a large surplus of £5,500 from Desborough's six western counties was divided up between Haynes and Goffe, the former receiving £4,000 and the latter £1,500.[126] In January 1657, Robert Lilburne was ordered to pay Charles Howard £500.[127] Not all the major-generals, however, were keen to part with the money they had raised; Whalley, for example, had still not handed over the £1,240 he had been told to give Haynes eight months after the order.[128]

Despite these transfers, in November 1656 four of the generals were still in deficit to the tune of £5,700; Kelsey was £1,772 in arrears; Berry £1,337; Boteler £1,322; and Goffe £1,268.[129] In early March 1657, after Sir John Barkstead had reported that the pay for his Middlesex troops was still in arrears to the tune of £730, the council instructed the treasury commissioners to pay this sum over to him.[130] Several days later, it ordered that any remaining decimation money should be distributed equally throughout the country.[131] Despite all the government's efforts to remedy the problem, in many parts of the country the militia troops and the commissioners' civilian officials were never fully paid and the major-generals themselves only ever received a small fraction of their own salaries.

At the end of January 1657, the MPs of the second protectorate parliament brought the short-lived decimation tax to an end by voting down John Desborough's militia bill which would have established it on a permanent basis. Despite its brief lifespan, however, the decimation tax had a major impact on the politics of Interregnum England and Wales, in that it further polarised an already divided political nation and brought into sharper relief the differences between the supporters and opponents of Cromwell's regime. The depth of passion it could arouse is illustrated by an incident which occurred in a Sussex alehouse in early 1657, during the period when parliament was considering whether or not to make it a permanent levy. On 10 January 1657, a violent brawl erupted at the Bull Inn in Lewes after one drinker had defended the decimation tax on the grounds that 'it was a mercy in the protector and council in regard the cavaliers had forfeited both life and goods', and a fellow drinker had denounced him with the words 'God take the decimators and all that devised decimation.'[132]

Equally significantly, the tax also divided the regime's supporters, exacerbating pre-existing tensions between the puritan hardliners of the army, who saw it as a welcome and justifiable punishment for sedition and irreligion, and the protectorate's more moderate and pragmatic adherents, who believed it to be an unfortunate development which had set back the important process of healing and settling the nation's divisions. These contrasting views were expressed very forcefully during the debates in the second protectorate parliament on Desborough's militia bill in December 1656 and January 1657. On Christmas Day 1656, the radical godly Yorkshireman, Luke Robinson, declared:

> If you bear witness to that distinction, it will encourage your friends, though it be but a small tax. They grow fat and live at home; – we decrease; they increase … Most certain if the power were in their hands, they would spare their friends, and lay it upon us … It is but just they should feel it.[133]

Two weeks later the contrary viewpoint was expressed by the more conservative member, John Trevor, who declared:

> I am not ashamed to plead for my enemies, where justice and the faith of the nation plead for them. What do we by this but incorporate them against us, and put such a character of distinction upon them, that they will never be reconciled … You provoke and unite your enemies [by this], and divide yourselves and necessitate new arms and charges, and raise new dangers … To forgive our enemies is God's rule, and the only way to make them our friends.[134]

Several weeks after these comments had been made the decimation tax was voted down and both Robinson's hopes and Trevor's fears remained unrealised. Whether, if this defeat had been avoided and some fundamental review of its operation had followed, the decimation tax could have provided the long-term financial underpinning for a secure, godly commonwealth; or whether conversely it would in time inevitably have provoked widespread royalist resistance and revolt can only be matters for speculation. What is clear, however, is that the thinking behind the original decision to impose the tax was fatally flawed. Strongly attracted to the prospect of punishing their enemies, reducing the overall burden of general taxation and enhancing the security of the regime, Cromwell and his advisers instituted the decimation tax in the autumn of 1655 in a hurry, without giving sufficient thought to how they would overcome the administrative complexities attendant on its assessment and collection, and – more seriously – without having any real evidence that it could produce the kind of sums needed to support the major-generals and their new national militia. Had they been able to carry out a comprehensive valuation of the collective wealth of the royalist party, they would surely have realised that, as originally conceived, the decimation tax was from the outset doomed to failure.

NOTES

1 The term decimation was derived from the Latin *decem*, meaning ten. The Romans decimated mutinous or cowardly regiments by killing every tenth soldier and the word was used in this sense during the early seventeenth century to describe the process of selecting one soldier in ten by lot for execution. In medieval Latin the verb *decimare* also meant to tithe or take tithes; see the *Oxford English Dictionary*. While there were no precedents in English history for such a tax, in 1614 Sir Robert Dudley, the illegitimate son of the earl of Leicester, had published a pamphlet entitled *A Proposition for His Majesty's Service to Bridle the Impertinence of Parliament*. In this he had argued that forts should be established in every substantial town in the country, manned by a national force of 3,000 men, and that the £40,000 cost of the system should be met by imposing a universal decimation tax, 'being so termed in Italy', which would bring in much greater sums of money than the subsidy tax which it would replace. The tract was republished in 1629 under the title *A Project how a Prince may make Himself an Absolute Tyrant*; see John Rushworth, *Historical Collections* (London, 1659), Appendix to vol. 1, pp. 12–17.

2 PRO, SP.18.101.136.

3 PRO, SP.25.76A, pp. 169–181.

4 In Rutland, for example, William Boteler and his commissioners only informed some local royalists about their liabilities under the tax in the second half of January 1656, nearly a month after the date when the first moiety was due to be paid. See, BL, Egerton MSS, 2986, fol. 279.

5 PRO, SP.25.77, pp. 861–80, 884–901. For examples of the printed receipts, see

Northamptonshire Record Office, Isham Correspondence, IC 3332B, IC 3333B.

6 Bod Lib., Rawlinson MSS, A 32, fols 385–8, 647–50.

7 PRO, SP.18.101.136.

8 Bod Lib., Rawlinson MSS, A 32, fols 801–4; PRO, SP.25.76, p. 392.

9 PRO, SP.18.101.136.

10 Bod Lib., Rawlinson MSS, A 35, fol. 165

11 *Ibid.*, A 32, fols 809–12.

12 *Ibid.*, A 34, fols 639–42.

13 For the Hampshire decimation list, see J. T. Cliffe (ed.), 'The Cromwellian Decimation Tax of 1655: The Assessment Lists', Camden Soc. Publs, 5th series, 7, 437–9. I should like to record my debt to Dr Cliffe for his painstaking and meticulous work to locate the extant decimation records in the Public Record Office.

14 PRO, SP.23.231, 70–6; Cliffe, 'Assessment Lists', pp. 437–9.

15 Bod Lib., Rawlinson MSS, A 32, fols 293–6, 613–16, 801–4; PRO, SP.18.101.144; SP.25.76, p. 387.

16 Bod Lib., Rawlinson MSS, A 32, fols 777–80, 805–8.

17 *Ibid.*, A 34, fols 427–30.

18 PRO, SP.18.101.142; SP.46.97.158. Occasional exceptions to this rule, however, were permitted. Henry Nevill of Cressing Temple in Essex, for example, was allowed to pay the decimation due for his Essex estate in Leicestershire, where he also had lands; see PRO, SP.23.228.49a-c; Cliffe, 'Assessment Lists', p. 463.

19 Cliffe, 'Assessment Lists', p. 416. In the autumn of 1656, however, William Prynne accused the major-generals of having decimated the sons of dead royalists; see BL, E.892.3, William Prynne, *A Summary Collection of the Principal Fundamental Rights, Liberties, Proprieties of all English Freemen* ... (London, 1656), p. 59.

20 Bod Lib., Rawlinson MSS, A 32, fols 293–6, 655–8; A 33, fols 61–4.

21 *Ibid.*, A 32, fols 335–8, 485–8, 569–72, 793–6; A 33, fols 225–8, 233–6.

22 *Ibid.*, A 32, fols 809–12; BL, E.491.9, *Mercurius Politicus* 20–27 Dec. 1655; E.491.10, *The Public Intelligencer*, 24–31 Dec. 1655; BL, E.491.11, *Mercurius Politicus*, 27 Dec. 1655–3 Jan. 1656.

23 PRO, SP.18.101.136.

24 Buckinghamshire Record Office, Claydon House Letters, M11/14, Denton to Verney, 17 Nov. 1655.

25 *Ibid.*, Burgoyne to Verney, 10 Dec. 1655.

26 Rutt, *Diary of Thomas Burton*, vol. 1, pp. 235, 316.

27 Quoted in Cliffe, 'Assessment Lists', p. 414.

28 PRO, SP.18.105.4; Cliffe, 'Assessment Lists', pp. 463–4; Anthony Fletcher, *A County Community in Peace and War: Sussex 1600–1660* (London, 1975), pp. 310–11.

29 Cliffe, 'Assessment Lists', pp. 461–6, 471–7; Peter Bloomfield 'The Cromwellian Commission in Kent, 1655–57', in Alec Detsicas and Nigel Yates (eds), *Studies in Modern Kentish History* (Maidstone, 1983), pp. 14–19. Bloomfield consulted for this article the

extant minute book of the Kentish commissioners, held at the Centre for Kentish Studies in Maidstone (reference U2341). Unfortunately, it could not be consulted for this study because it has subsequently been lost.

30 *Calendar of Wynn (of Gwydir) Papers, 1515–1690* (Aberystwyth, 1926), pp. 343–4.

31 Cliffe, 'Assessment Lists', p. 416.

32 Bod Lib., Rawlinson MSS, A 32, fols 647–50, 871–4.

33 *Ibid.*, A 32, fols 159–62, 335–8, 609–12.

34 PRO, SP.23.172.620–1.

35 PRO, SP.23,172.617–18; SP.23.195.417; SP.25.76, p. 387.

36 PRO, SP.23.172.619–20.

37 PRO, SP.23.172.617–18.

38 Bod Lib., Rawlinson MSS, A 32, fols 809–16.

39 Hampshire Record Office, Kingsmill Papers, 19M61, 1371, 1372.

40 Bod Lib., Rawlinson MSS, A 33, fols 61–4, 355–8; A 34, fols 561–4.

41 HMC, *Bath MSS*, vol. 4, pp. 281–2.

42 PRO, SP.18.102.60a.

43 Bod Lib., Rawlinson MSS, A 32, fols 655–8.

44 Cliffe 'Asessment Lists', pp. 434, 461.

45 Bod Lib., Rawlinson MSS, A 32, fols 809–12.

46 *Ibid.*, A 34, fols 561–4.

47 PRO, SP.25.76, pp. 579–80.

48 Staffordshire Record Office, Bower Papers, D.793.110, Staffordshire commissioners to Sir Hervey Bagot, 26 Mar. 1656; Bod Lib., Rawlinson MSS, A 39, fols 366–7.

49 Cliffe suggests that among those who appear to have been under-assessed were Sir Thomas Fanshawe of Hertfordshire, John Frescheville of Derbyshire, and Sir Henry Appleton, Sir Benjamin Ayloffe, Sir William Halton, Sir Cranmer Herris, Sir Denner Strutt and John Fanshawe, all of Essex. Amongst those who appear to have avoided payment for lands in counties at a distance from their main residence were John Keeling of Hertfordshire, who escaped in Bedfordshire; John Tufton, earl of Thanet, of Kent, who escaped in Sussex; John Neville, lord Bergavenny, of Kent, who escaped in Suffolk and Sussex; James Compton, earl of Northampton, of Northamptonshire who escaped in Bedfordshire and Cambridgeshire; George Blundell of Bedfordshire, who escaped in Cambridgeshire; Sir Lodowick Dyer of Bedfordshire who escaped in Huntingdonshire; and Richard Thornhill of Kent who escaped in Essex. For more details, see Cliffe, 'Assessment Lists', pp. 416, 453–92.

50 Bod Lib., Rawlinson MSS, A 32, fols 159–62, 335–8.

51 *Ibid.*, A 32, fols 621–4; A 33, 519–22.

52 *Ibid.*, A 32, fols 647–50.

53 *Ibid.*, A 32, fols 957–60; A 33, fols 61–4.

54 *Ibid.*, A 33, fols 417–20.

55 *Ibid.*, A 32, fols 529–32.

56 *Ibid.*, A 32, fols 765–8.

57 HMC, *Portland MSS*, vol. 2, p. 141; Buckinghamshire RO, M11/14 Denton to Verney, 17 Nov. 1655.

58 Bod Lib., Rawlinson MSS, A 33, fols 529–32.

59 *Ibid.*, A 33, fols 656–8; see also Cliffe, 'Assessment Lists', pp. 431, 456.

60 Bloomfield, 'The Cromwellian Commission in Kent', pp. 14–16.

61 B. E. Howells (ed.), *A Calendar of Letters Relating to North Wales 1533–circa 1700* (Cardiff, 1967), p. 105; *Calendar of Wynn (of Gwydir) Papers*, pp. 344–5.

62 Cliffe found lists for Bedfordshire, Cambridgeshire, Cumberland, Derbyshire, Essex, Hampshire, Hertfordshire, Huntingdonshire, Kent, Northamptonshire, Rutland, Suffolk, Sussex, and Westmorland. He also identifed another fifteen royalists from various other counties; see Cliffe, 'Assessment Lists', pp. 429–52. The additional lists in Thurloe's papers are for Berkshire and Nottinghamshire; see Bod Lib., Rawlinson MSS, A 33, fols 734–7, and A 34, fols 141–4. The Nottinghamshire list gives the estimates for the annual value of the royalists' estates.

63 PRO, SP.23.228.29; SP.25.76, p. 445. The six new members were Charles Fleetwood; John Lambert; Sir Gilbert Pickering; Edmund Sheffield, earl of Mulgrave; Philip Sidney, viscount Lisle; and Sir Charles Wolseley.

64 The council order books for 1655 and 1656 also contain a great deal of information regarding these petitioners' cases; see PRO, SP.25, 76 and 77, *passim*. Some of their original petitions survive among the records of the committee for compounding; for examples, see PRO, SP.23.228.26, 29, 49a, 156–8,167; SP.23.229.80–1, 91–2, 108; SP.23.230.40; SP.23.231.42, 70, 75, 196–7, 241; SP.23.232.148–9; SP.23.233.19, 20; SP.23.234.55–6, 123–4; SP.23.235.20, 195; SP.23.236.77; SP.23.237.157a; SP.23.240.17.

65 In Essex, of the ninety-seven individuals who were assessed to pay the first instalment of the tax in December 1655, only sixty-four paid the third instalment a year later; Kent, too, saw a similar decrease from ninety to sixty-two payers. See Cliffe, 'Assessment Lists', pp. 434–7, 441–4.

66 Staffordshire RO, Persehowse Papers, D260/M/F/1/6/36. The petitioners were Sir Richard Leveson, Thomas Leigh, Randle Egerton, George Digby, Thomas Lane, John Persehowse, Thomas Warde and Sir Hervey Bagot. The petition is undated.

67 PRO, SP.18.127.58; SP.25.77, pp. 146, 854.

68 PRO, SP.23.234.53; SP.25.76, pp. 581–2.

69 PRO, SP.23.234.55.

70 PRO, SP.23.233.19, 20; SP.25.77, pp. 84, 137.

71 PRO, SP.25.76, p. 579.

72 PRO, SP.25.76, pp. 578–9.

73 PRO, SP.25.76, p. 465.

74 Bod Lib., Rawlinson MSS, A 36, fol. 373; PRO, SP.25.77, pp. 45, 114, 194, 248, 401, 428–9, 492.

75 PRO, SP.23.228.29–33; 234.124; SP.25.76, pp. 446, 461–2, 466–7, 487, 511, 518, 530–1,

539, 546; SP.25.77, pp. 104, 155–6, 227, 432; Bod Lib., Rawlinson MSS, A 34, fols 643–6; see also *DNB*, John Holles (1595–1666), Sir William Paget (1609–78), and Richard Boyle (1612–97).

76 George F. Warner, *The Nicholas Papers*, vol. III, Camden Soc. Publs, new series 57 (1897), 254.

77 PRO, SP.23.229, pp. 91–2; SP.25.76, pp. 581–2; and Fletcher *Sussex*, pp. 305–6.

78 Staffordshire RO, D793.106.

79 Staffordshire RO, D793.108.

80 PRO, SP.18.125.7; SP.25.76, p. 575; SP.25.77, p. 207; Birch, *State Papers of John Thurloe*, vol. 5, p. 22.

81 For Coventry see PRO, SP.25.76, pp. 553–4; Bod Lib., Rawlinson MSS, A 35, fols 172, 174–5. For Egerton, see BL, Additional MSS, 6689, fol. 320; Bod Lib., Rawlinson MSS, A 38, fols 129–32; PRO, SP.25.77, p. 231.

82 Buckinghamshire RO, M11/14, Verney to Denton, 21 Mar. 1656; Verney to Rhodes, 3 Apr. 1656; Verney to Burgoyne, 24 Apr. 1656; Verney to Gaudy, 3 Jul. 1656; Gaudy to Verney, 30 Jul. 1656; Northamptonshire RO, Isham Correspondence, IC393, Verney to Isham, 7 Apr. 1656; PRO, SP.25.77, p. 136.

83 Bod Lib., Rawlinson MSS, A 33, fols 726–9.

84 *Ibid.*, A 35, fol. 172.

85 *Ibid.*, A 33, fols 734–7, 758–9.

86 *Ibid.*, A 34, fols 561–4.

87 *Ibid.*, A 35, fols 77–8.

88 *Ibid.*, A 33, fols 437–40.

89 *Ibid.*, A 34, fols 595–8.

90 *Ibid.*, 33, fols, 143–6.

91 *Ibid.*, A 33, fol. 329; A 34, fols 313–16.

92 *Ibid.*, A 35, fol. 80.

93 *Ibid.*, A 35, fol. 181.

94 *Ibid.*, A 33, fols 523–4.

95 *Ibid.*, A 36, fol. 427.

96 *Ibid.*, A 37, fols 361–4; PRO. SP.18.128.5, 6; SP.25.77, p. 201; Abbott, *Writings and Speeches of Cromwell*, vol. 4, p. 82.

97 Bod. Lib., Rawlinson MSS, A 34, fols 357–60.

98 Cliffe, 'Assessment Lists', pp. 429–52; Bod Lib., Rawlinson MSS, A 33, fols 734–7; A 34, fols 141–4.

99 Bod. Lib., Rawlinson MSS, A 33, fols 221–4; A 35, fol. 135.

100 *Ibid.*, A 32, fols 525–8.

101 *Ibid.*, A 32, fols 647–50.

102 The figures are taken from Cliffe, 'Assessment Lists', pp. 429–51, and the militia establishment for June 1655; see PRO, SP.25.77, pp. 861–80. The annual decimation

liabilities for the sixteen counties are my calculations from Cliffe's figures. The expenditure requirements would have lessened somewhat when the troops were reduced to 80 men in the summer of 1656. The financial picture was in fact even worse than these figures suggest because the expenditure totals do not include any element for the major-generals' own salaries, which should also have come out of the decimation money.

103 PRO, SP.28.153, unbound document; see also Cliffe, 'Assessment Lists', pp. 434–7.

104 PRO, SP.28.159, unbound document; see also Cliffe, 'Assessment Lists', p. 441–4.

105 PRO, SP.28.226, unbound document; see also Cliffe, 'Assessment Lists', p. 433–4.

106 PRO, SP.28.159, unbound document; see also Cliffe, 'Assessment Lists', p. 441–4.

107 For the comments of one of Sir Justinian Isham's royalist friends on this subject, see Northamptonshire RO, IC 391, Simon Horsepool to Isham, 22 Mar. 1657.

108 PRO, SP.25.77, p. 207; Bod. Lib., Rawlinson MSS, A 35, fols 1, 21.

109 PRO, SP.25.77, pp. 216, 217, 353–5; *Calendar of Committee for Compounding*, vol. 2, p. 1504. For details of Cavendish's estate see PRO, SP.18.123.32, 48, 481, 51; SP.18.124.17; SP.18.125.69; SP.18.126.2, 21

110 PRO, SP.25.77, pp. 292–3, 305.

111 PRO, SP.25.76, p. 445.

112 PRO, SP.25.76, pp. 579–80.

113 PRO, SP.25.77, pp. 902–4; Cliffe, 'Assessment Lists', p. 422. For more details of the reduction of the militia troops, see chapter 7.

114 PRO, SP.18.128.107, Ross to Nicholas, 29 Jun.–9 Jul. 1656.

115 Bod. Lib., Rawlinson MSS, A 32, fols 655–8, 683–6.

116 *Ibid.*, A 33, fols 373–6.

117 *Ibid.*, A 33, fols 413–16, 417–20.

118 *Ibid.*, A 33, fols 515–18.

119 *Ibid.*, A 33, fols 571–4.

120 *Ibid.*, A 33, fols 618–21.

121 *Ibid.*, A 33, fols 355–8.

122 *Ibid.*, A 34, fols 435–8.

123 *Ibid.*, A 32, fols 683–6; Bloomfield, 'Cromwellian Commission in Kent', pp. 14, 23–7.

124 Bod. Lib., Rawlinson MSS, A 34, fols 513–14.

125 PRO, SP.25.76, p. 613; SP.25.77, p. 357.

126 PRO, SP.25.77, p. 357.

127 *Ibid.*, p. 608.

128 *Ibid.*, p. 470.

129 *Ibid.*, pp. 524–5.

130 *Ibid.*, pp. 743–4.

131 *Ibid.*, p. 748.

132 Bod. Lib., Rawlinson MSS, A 46, fol. 131.

133 Rutt, *Diary of Thomas Burton*, vol. 1, p. 232.

134 *Ibid.*, vol. 1, p. 315.

Chapter 7

Securing the peace
of the commonwealth

Paramount amongst the tasks entrusted to the major-generals in the autumn of 1655 was the guaranteeing of the peace and security of the state. During the mid 1650s, the survival of the protectorate regime continued to be threatened both by the intrigues of the exiled Stuart court on the continent and its royalist allies within England, and by the activities of those religious and political radicals who felt deeply let down by what they regarded as Cromwell's betrayal of the 'good old cause' of republicanism. Aware of the precarious nature of its position, the government expected the major-generals to provide the leadership for a set of local security forces which would be well-informed of local conditions, able to provide it with regular and good quality intelligence information, and capable of responding quickly to any potential threats. Accordingly, the major-generals and their local allies devoted much of their time and energy to monitoring the activities of those known to be hostile to the government and attempting to thwart those who wished to undermine Cromwell's regime. This chapter will attempt to evaluate the effectiveness of this aspect of their work.

As was seen in chapter 2, one of the major catalysts for the launching of the major-generals' system was the royalist insurrection of March 1655. During the weeks which followed the rising, the government instituted a series of measures to punish those involved and to prevent any further trouble. John Penruddock and the other ringleaders of the western rising were tried and executed, and in the south-west and elsewhere large numbers of royalists who were suspected of being implicated in the plots or considered to represent a security risk were arrested and interned without trial. While it is difficult to estimate the precise number held throughout the country, it was probably in the region of several thousand; in late June 1655, Peter Coyet, a Swedish diplomat in London, estimated that 2,200 royalists were being held by the government, and several weeks later the Venetian ambassador claimed that the figure was as high as 3,000.[1] The government seems to have been undecided about what to do with these men and one army newsletter reported that 'the cavalleare partie now under restraint hath taken up much debate'.[2] In early June 1655, two newsbooks claimed that they were all to be transported. In the event, no such mass deportation took place, although around seventy royalists who had been arrested in the aftermath of Penruddock's rising and were being held at Exeter were shipped to Barbados in the summer after two of their number had requested that they be sent there rather than prosecuted at law.[3] Some of those being held were released in August and most of the remainder were set free in the autumn shortly before the major-generals were dispatched to their associations.[4] As a condition of their liberty, they were required to enter into substantial bonds, which would be forfeited if they were found to have conspired against the government in the future.[5]

Although the government had acted quickly and decisively to restore control and punish its enemies in the south-west, it had been rather slower to prosecute those involved in the spring risings in other parts of the country, and in the autumn of 1655 the responsibility for the punishment of these men was handed over to the major-generals and their commissioners. As was seen in chapter 2, the commissioners' orders authorised them to proceed against any royalists within their associations who were known to have been actively involved in the March risings, as well as all those who, while their involvement could not be proved, nonetheless appeared 'by their words and actions to adhere to the interest of the late king or of Charles Stuart his son and to be dangerous enemies to the peace of the commonwealth'. The former group, which fell within the first head of the orders, were to be imprisoned and have their estates sequestered; the latter group, which came within the second head, were also to be imprisoned but would be allowed to retain their property. An additional instruction sent to the major-generals in late February 1656 authorised them to allow any royalists who fell within either of these heads to leave the country if they wished, on condition that they entered into a bond not to return without permission.[6]

The major-generals who were most involved in pursuing those who fell under the first head were naturally those whose associations contained the locations of the March uprisings. In early 1656, Robert Lilburne, Lambert's deputy in Yorkshire and Durham, conducted examinations of those suspected of involvement in the royalist gatherings at Morpeth and Hessay Moor, and several months later he took charge of the proceedings against Sir Henry Slingsby and several of the other leading conspirators in Yorkshire.[7] Edward Whalley similarly examined and imprisoned several royalists whom he suspected of being implicated in the attempted rising at Rufford Abbey in Nottinghamshire. In July 1656, however, he admitted to Thurloe that he was not confident that any local jury would find them guilty if he put them on trial, and he suggested instead that he should take security from them and let them leave the country.[8] Charles Worsley, meanwhile, took action against those he believed had planned the abortive uprising in Cheshire.[9] A number of the major-generals also imprisoned royalists under the second head of their orders. Shortly after arriving in his association in early November 1655, Hezekiah Haynes gaoled several individuals who, in his view, fell into this category, including the royalist poet, John Cleveland, whom he secured at Yarmouth on the grounds that he was 'a most desperate enemy to God and good men'.[10] William Boteler likewise arrested a number of individuals, including an itinerant Catholic priest, and the commissioners in Shropshire imprisoned several local royalists whom they believed to be major security risks.[11]

It was not only, however, the relatively small numbers of royalists who fell within the first two heads of the orders who were affected by the crackdown which accompanied the major-generals' arrival in the provinces. Many hundreds of their fellow royalists, who had remained quiet during the spring but who were deemed to have supported Charles I or his son over the previous fourteen years, were also now subjected to a number of new security measures. The third head of the major-generals' orders stipulated that they were to be disarmed, forced to give security for their own and their male servants' future good behaviour, and obliged to submit to a number of irksome restrictions on their freedom of movement.[12]

The disarming process seems to have been both thorough and rapid. Worsley told Thurloe in early November 1655 that he was intending to disarm all the royalists in his association on the same day, 'that wee may not be in the least prevented'. The operation, which was carried out by his militia troops, had been accomplished in all three of his counties by early December.[13] At the end of 1655, Sir Roger Burgoyne wrote from Warwickshire to his friend Sir Ralph Verney to inform him that Edward Whalley and the commissioners for that county would not allow his royalist neighbours 'so much as a birding piece [a gun for shooting fowl], no not a sword'.[14] Several months later in February 1656, Verney himself warned his son who was returning from the continent not to bring any weapons with him. He told him that the soldiers had taken away his pistols and his own and his manservant's swords, that 'fusills [light muskets] are taken away as ordinarily as pistolls', and that the soldiers had even confiscated a birding piece belonging to the young son of one of his friends.[15]

In addition to this work of disarming, during November and December 1655 the major-generals and their commissioners devoted a great deal of time to the business of taking security from the royalist community. As the government had not made its intentions in this area entirely clear in its original orders, there seems to have been some initial confusion about whether all royalists were required to enter into bonds, or only those who fell under the first and second heads of the orders. Thomas Kelsey testified to this uncertainty when he told Thurloe in November that, while his instructions stated that he was to take security only from those who had been in arms or were 'dangerous', he now understood that all those of 'the partie' were to give it.[16] Most of his colleagues seem likewise to have concluded that they were expected to take security from the entire royalist community within their respective associations. Even those royalists who had been held during the summer and had entered into bonds prior to their release were now obliged to sign new ones with higher penalties for defaulting.[17]

Those required to sign the bonds were expected to attend their local major-general or his commissioners and to bring with them two individuals who would act as their sureties. The wording of the bond obliged them not to 'plot, contrive or act, or cause or consent unto, to be plotted, contrived or acted any thing against the person of his Highness the Lord Protector or the peace of the Commonwealth', and to reveal to the authorities any information they possessed about the subversive activities of others. It also required them to report to their local major-general whenever summoned and to inform him if they changed their main residence. Those royalists wishing to travel to London were expected both to inform their local major-general before they left and to report to a newly established central register office within twenty-four hours of their arrival in the capital. If either they themselves or any other male member of their households was subsequently found to have broken the terms of the bond, they would forfeit the specified sum and probably as a result lose their estates.[18] To ensure that they were not able to escape giving security by absenting themselves from their country estates, Cromwell issued a proclamation at the end of October 1655 ordering all royalists who were temporarily resident in London and Westminster to leave the capital within a fortnight and to return home and report to their local major-general.[19]

During late 1655 and early 1656, the major-generals and their local commissioners imposed bonds for good behaviour on more than 14,000 royalist suspects and their male servants, and subsequently forwarded lists of their names, addresses and social positions to the new national register office in London. Included in the lists were individuals from right across the social spectrum, from noblemen and greater gentry to tradesmen and servants. The numbers who were obliged to enter into the bonds varied greatly across the different associations. John Desborough's commissioners took security from nearly 5,000 individuals in the west country, Robert Lilburne's from around 4,500 in Yorkshire and Durham, and Charles Worsley's from over 2,000 in Cheshire, Lancashire and Staffordshire. In marked contrast, within each of the other nine associations the commissioners took security from only a couple of hundred individuals.[20] Such wide variations can partly be explained by the unequal size of the associations, the uneven distribution of royalists across the country, and the particularly acute concerns about the security situation in the west country and Yorkshire, where the troubles of the previous spring had been concentrated. The fact, however, that the disparities were so great, with Worsley and his commissioners enforcing several thousand bonds in the north-west and Edward Whalley and his only around 125 in the east Midlands, suggests that they were also a reflection of the differing priorities of individual major-generals and sets of commissioners, and perhaps also of some inconsistency in their interpretation of the government's wishes.

For the royalist community, the requirement to enter into security bonds proved at best a major irritation and at worst a cause for serious alarm. The sums liable to forfeiture were very high, ranging from £5,000 for those who had been in arms in the 1640s to £1,000 for other suspects and £100 for servants. Many royalists were naturally very concerned about jeopardising their own and their families' futures by entering into an obligation which appeared to them vague and open-ended, where a hostile government would be the sole arbiter of whether or not it had been breached, and where the repercussions of forfeiture would be extreme. William Dugdale reported to a friend in October 1655 that many royalists 'doe stagger at the latitude the words have' and that many of their potential sureties believed it was 'too dangerous to seal such bonds where the condition is subject to the inter-pretation of those that are not their friends; for what they say is prejudiciall must then expose them to the dangers of the forfeiture'.[21]

Some royalists, such as James Compton, earl of Northampton, took particular exception to the absence of any time limit in the bonds. While Compton was prepared to give security for one year, he baulked at signing an indefinite bond, on the grounds that it would seriously undermine his already precarious financial position. Petitioning Cromwell in December 1655 and again in February 1656 to be allowed to give security for one year only, he argued that an unlimited bond 'would lye as a perpetuall incumbrance uppon his estate and make him altogether uncapable to raise moneye for the satysfying of his great debts, annuities, porcons and mortgages charged upon his lands, so that his estate would inevitably be forfeited without any hope of redempcon and he and his family utterlly ruined'.[22] The requirement to enter into bonds for the good behaviour of male servants seems to have particularly annoyed many royalists and to have prompted a number of them to dismiss some or all of them. Writing to his friend Sir Justinian Isham about this requirement in November 1655, Sir Ralph Verney commented wryly: 'you and I are now soe chast that wee had better hazard ourselves amongst our young maydens then enter unto such engagements.'[23]

As well as seeing the requirement to give security as a serious threat to their financial positions, some royalists appear also to have regarded it as a slur upon their honour and reputation. Writing to Thurloe in December 1655, the Kentish royalist, Sir Edward Hales, who had recently given what he called his 'bail' to his local commissioners in Maidstone, declared that "tis not so much the charge which troubles mee as the reproche.'[24] Sir Ralph Verney, who was held in St James's Palace in London from mid June to early October, was only released after he had very reluctantly signed a bond which in his opinion was 'soe full of barbarous conditions' that he was ashamed to report them to his friends.[25]

Despite their misgivings, the vast majority of royalists decided they had no choice but to accede to the government's wishes and enter into a bond. The small number which initially refused to do so received short shrift from the major-generals and their commissioners and were soon forced into submission. Thomas Kelsey informed Thurloe in late November 1655 that, at a recent appearance of a number of local royalists before the Surrey commissioners in Kingston, the earl of Southampton and 'many others' had refused to give security. He had arrested them but did not know where to hold them as the town had no gaol.[26] As was noted above, James Compton, the earl of Northampton, was reluctant to sign a bond with no time limit. According to William Boteler, his 'publique and peremptory' refusal to do so at a meeting of the Northamptonshire commissioners in November 1655 might have proved 'an unhansome slurr to our proceedings' and encouraged others to resist had he not immediately secured him. Boteler commented to Thurloe that in his view 'if a man will not engage for his peaceable living under the government, he declares himself to be an enemy.'[27] He subsequently kept Compton in prison, only reluctantly releasing him in February 1656 after the council had finally agreed that he could sign a bond for one year only.[28]

One royalist who does appear to have avoided giving security without suffering such ill consequences was Henry Coke of Thorington in Suffolk, a younger son of the famous legal theorist, Sir Edward Coke. The lengthy account of his case, which was published some forty years later by his son, Roger, gives an interesting insight into one royalist family's reaction to the new security measures. When Roger Coke was informed by the governor of Yarmouth that his father, who was being held in the town on suspicion of involvement in gun-running, would be required to give security before being released, he replied that 'no man who is bound for his good behaviour is taken as a man of good behaviour.' Henry Coke was subsequently set free and told to appear before the Suffolk commissioners at Bury St Edmunds, but Roger went instead and argued that his father should be exempted from both the bond and the decimation tax on the grounds that his sequestration in the 1640s had subsequently been rescinded. When he could not prevail upon the commissioners with this argument, he travelled up to London where, probably because he was Sir Edward Coke's grand-son, he was granted an audience with Cromwell. He claimed that the protector had promised him that the family's case would be looked at sympathetically, and in the event, while Henry Coke failed to secure an exemption from the decimation tax, he was not pursued to give security. Roger Coke was unsure whether this was because he had challenged the government over the matter or because 'the humour of giving security abated'. He was nonetheless emphatic that his father's avoidance of the security bond 'was all I cared for', and he concluded his account by commenting: 'I believe my father was the only man who was sequestered in England who escaped it [giving security] without imprisonment.'[29]

As a result of the efforts of the major-generals and their commissioners, by the spring of 1656 the vast majority of royalists in England were bound to the government in very large sums for their good behaviour and were acutely aware that, if in the future they were discovered to be involved in, or aware of, any plots against the government, they faced the very real prospect of financial ruin. It was perhaps this realisation which prompted the royalist William Walsh to visit Sir John Barkstead in March 1656 to inform him about a design against the government currently being planned in London.[30] While the imposition of the bonds did not, of course, persuade every royalist to inform on his friends or to refrain from conspiring against Cromwell, there can be little doubt that it proved a major deterrent to a great many of them, and was thus responsible for a considerable reduction in the scale of the royalist threat. The fact that there is no evidence that any of the bonds were actually forfeited may also suggest that the government believed they had largely achieved their purpose.

A crucial element in the coordination of these new security measures was the establishment of a national register office in London, which was entrusted with the formidable task of monitoring the whereabouts and movements of the entire royalist community. While the government had made clear its intention to set up such an office in its original instructions for the major-generals drafted in the autumn of 1655, the registration system was not in fact fully operational until the beginning of 1656. In late October 1655, Thomas Dunn was appointed by the council to the new post of 'register in the city of London', and by the end of November he had appointed a clerk and begun to record the names of royalists who appeared before him.[31] It was not, however, until the end of December that he finally received from the council a formal order to establish a permanent office, along with detailed instructions about how it was to function.

The new London register office was to be open for personal appearances from Monday to Saturday, from nine to eleven in the morning and from two to four in the afternoon. The names of all royalists who visited it were to be entered into a ledger along with the date of their appearance and information about where they had come from in the country, where they intended to lodge in the capital, and how long they intended to stay. Within a few days of an appearance a letter was to be sent to the relevant major-general informing him of the royalist's temporary residence in London. The register and his clerks were also required to check that the names of individuals who reported to them were included in the ledgers containing the names of all those who had given security in the provinces, which they had compiled from the lists sent to them periodically by the major-generals and their commissioners. If anyone appeared at the office who was not recorded as having previously given security, the register was immediately to inform Thurloe.[32]

When setting up the new system in October 1655, the council had discussed the possibility of meeting the costs of the office by charging royalists for appearances, but this idea was shelved and in December Thomas Dunn was granted a salary of £300 to be paid out of the decimation money.[33] On 1 January 1656, he wrote to all the major-generals and their deputies informing them that he had now received the council's orders and that initially he would be operating from a room in the house of 'Mr John Tuttie, silk-stocking seller in the backside of the Old Exchange in London'.[34] The search for a more dignified location for the office did not prove straightforward, and it was only in mid April that Dunn eventually found suitable premises in Fleet Street at a rent of £60 per annum.[35] This house, near the Three Kings' Inn, became the permanent location of the office from the end of April 1656.[36]

During the period of the major-generals' rule in the provinces a total of around 750 royalists apppeared at Dunn's office, making between them in the region of 1,450 visits. Around 300 individuals appeared more than once, and a few whose trades necessitated regular visits to London made multiple appearances: John Monger of Godalming in Surrey, for example, appeared twenty times; William Glascock of Farnham in Essex nineteen times; and John Turner of Bletchingley in Surrey sixteen times. The attenders came from a wide range of social backgrounds and included some of the leading noblemen in the country as well as obscure tradesmen. While the vast majority were men, two women, Lady Anne Farmer and Lady Sarah Redmayne, were also recorded as having made visits. Initially, the number of appearances was very low. Dunn saw only eleven royalists in November 1655 and a further eighteen the following month. After the major-generals had been notified of the office's establishment in the new year, however, the numbers picked up steadily. There were ninety visits in January 1656, 280 in February, and over 600 in May. By the early summer, the office was very busy and three clerks were needed to cope with the average daily total of around thirty visits. The busiest day of all was 10 May 1656, when as many as forty-five royalists appeared.[37]

Dunn and his assistants were extremely conscientious about reporting back to the major-generals the names of those who had reported at the office. During 1656, they sent the major-generals and their commissioners more than 600 letters, containing detailed and up-to-date information about the movements of royalists from their associations who were absent from their homes.[38]

In addition to the surveillance of royalists living within England, Dunn's Fleet Street office was also responsible for monitoring the movements of all visitors to the country from abroad. By the spring of 1656, deputy-registers answerable to Dunn were at work in many of the country's most important ports, including Dover, Deal, Gravesend, Rye, Plymouth, and those on the Isle of Wight. All English and foreign travellers arriving in these ports from abroad were required to report to these deputy-registers and to supply them with their names, destinations and intended lodgings. Those travelling on to London were ordered to present themselves at Dunn's office within twenty-four hours of their arrival, and those going into the country were told to report to the local major-general. If any of those questioned on disembarkation could not provide an address where they could be found later, they were required to enter into an engagement to appear at Fleet Street. In October 1656, Christopher Tidey, the deputy-register at Rye, suggested that he should prevent those without addresses in London from continuing on with their journeys; even Dunn, however, baulked at this, pointing out that 'they must first be offenders before any course can be taken against them.'[39]

The deputy-registers sent regular express letters to Dunn, notifying him of the names of those who had landed at their ports. He then acknowledged receipt of their communications and directed his staff to enquire after anyone who failed to report to the register office. Altogether, nearly 1,000 new arrivals in the country reported to Dunn between February 1655 and August 1657, the great majority of them in the summer of 1656.[40] Dunn clearly considered this aspect of his work to be of great importance. When Thomas Reynolds, the deputy-register at Dover, wrote to him in November 1656 to query whether it was worth continuing to inform him of the very small numbers now arriving at that port, he told him that 'in regard the service concerns the state, I shall expect to hear from you when and as often passengers shall land at Dover.'[41]

In addition to his formal duties, Dunn also operated as an unofficial conduit for intelligence, passing information between London, the ports and the major-generals in the provinces. In January 1656, he assured James Berry that 'as any thing of publique concernment cometh to mee from the major-generalls for your notice, you shall not fail of an accompt thereof.'[42] In late July 1656, he wrote to the major-general for London and Middlesex, Sir John Barkstead, to inform him that several days before one William Stephens had appeared at the office after arriving from the Netherlands by way of King's Lynn and had told his staff that he was carrying letters from Utrecht for an unnamed English gentleman.[43] In mid September, he sent the Dover deputy-register, Thomas Reynolds, a copy of a current newsbook, presumably because he was interested in reading about the opening of the new parliament.[44]

The operation of the register office was not without its problems, but Dunn moved quickly to rectify anything he believed to be hampering the work. During the weeks which followed the establishment of the system, some royalists did not find it easy to find Dunn. Henry Hudson of Melton Mowbray in Leicestershire, for example, claimed that he had had to search for ten days in December 1655 and make enquiries both at the Tower and with the city marshal before he located him.[45] Occasionally, too, Dunn found his instructions defective; when Robert Lilburne informed him in July 1656 that the Yorkshire royalist, Jeremy Langdale, was moving permanently to Bedfordshire, he was forced to admit that he was unsure about what he was expected to do in such cases.[46] He also frequently received from local commissioners lists of those who had given security in the country which he considered to be unsatisfactory, either because they were illegible or because they had omitted the residences or social positions of those named. When this happened, he was quick to criticise the senders and occasionally even returned lists to them for redrafting.[47]

There were also a number of problems with the liaison between the London office and the deputy-registers in the ports. Dunn frequently complained to his deputies that their letters were not sufficiently legible or lacked important information, such as the intended lodgings of travellers. In August 1656, for example, he upbraided the Deal deputy-register, John Kingsland, for sending a list without lodgings, explaining to him that such lists were of little use, for 'if they appear not, wee have no way to make enquiry after them.'[48] The following October, he sent back a list of passengers from the Rye deputy-register, Christopher Tidey, on the grounds that 'it is very inconvenient for us to have proper names intermixt with other writings when we come to make a search in your list.'[49]

He was particularly critical of deputies whom he suspected of having given inadequate or misleading instructions to travellers. In May 1656, he sent an abrupt letter to Kingsland at Deal, complaining that he had apparently told some travellers to report not to Fleet Street but to the Golden Cock on Ludgate Hill, 'a place utterly unknown to me nor to be found by any person whome you give directions unto, some whereof complayning of such advice they had from you'.[50] Several weeks later, he sent an even more scathing letter to Reynolds at Dover in which he declared:

> To what purpose should I give you such particular notice of the street and signe from whence I send my letters, but for your informacon where your returns will finde mee out, and for your excuse implying you might notwithstanding suppose the office to be elswhere, it would have had some satisfaccon therein if, after you

had such a hint of the place whence I sent my letters, you had informed persons engaged to appear that, if they had beene disappointed in one place, they might have found mee in the other; but for the future there will, I hope, bee no occasion of such kind of writeing as this.[51]

In December 1656, he criticised Christopher Tidey after some travellers who had failed to report to Fleet Street and had subsequently been arrested by Barkstead had excused themselves on the grounds that they had never been told that they were required to appear there.[52]

One further problem that Dunn faced was the failure of the government to provide him with sufficient funds for the running costs of the office and for his own and his clerks' salaries. With the yield from the decimation tax proving insufficient even to meet the costs of the militia in the counties, Dunn's chances of receiving regular funds from that source were slight, and his pay and expenses were always greatly in arrears. In October 1656, he complained to the council that he was still owed £400 which the army committee had been ordered to pay him for his rent and salaries. The following January, he received £200 out of the surplus from the decimation tax collected in Tobias Bridge's association, but by May 1657 he had still not received the other £200.[53]

Despite such niggling problems, the London register office seems to have carried out its work with reasonable efficiency. As the linchpin of the new security system, much depended on it, and it did a great deal to satisfy the government's expectations both by providing it with comprehensive lists of those from whom the major-generals had taken security, and by furnishing it with an unprecented level of information about the movements of the royalist community. Undoubtedly, some of those who should have reported to the office must have simply ignored the regulations and continued to travel around the country and to and from the continent without registering their movements. The number of such defaulters is impossible to estimate with any accuracy, but the vigour with which Dunn acted to close loop-holes in the system and to pursue those whose non-compliance was brought to his attention would suggest they were never more than a small minority. Overall, there can be little question that the establishment of Dunn's office did severely restrict the ability of royalists to engage in conspiracy, and as a consequence did a great deal to enhance the safety of Cromwell's regime.

If the royalist community continued to present the most serious challenge to the protectorate during 1655 and 1656, Cromwell's government could not afford to ignore the potentially damaging activities of its enemies from the other end of the religious and political spectrum. A number of the major-generals were thus closely involved in measures to nullify the threats from republicans, Fifth Monarchists, Quakers and other radicals within their associations. Many of those who adhered to these groups had supported Cromwell until the establishment of the protectorate, and a number of them had fought alongside the major-generals in the New Model Army during the 1640s and early 1650s. For this reason, some of major-generals were rather more indulgent towards them than they were towards their royalist enemies. On the other hand, several of the major-generals displayed a deep hostility towards Quakers, and dealt with them every bit as harshly as they did with those who continued to support the Stuarts.

The major-general who seems to have taken the most relaxed attitude to the activities of the government's radical critics was James Berry. Soon after arriving in the Welsh borders in November 1655, he had a long interview at Worcester with the Fifth Monarchist leader, Vavasour Powell. Informing him that Cromwell believed he was 'about some designe that tended to put things into distraction', he told Powell he would not tolerate any subversive activity from him or his supporters and dismissed him 'upon a promise not to meddle with any thing of difference'. The following Sunday, however, he allowed him to preach four sermons in Worcester and even invited him to dinner.[54] When, several months later, Powell published the tract *A Word for God*, in which he was highly critical of the government, Berry expressed his disappointment but was still not unduly alarmed. He described his followers as 'affectionate, tender-spirited people that want judgement' and added that 'they live farre off and want information and, haveing got a little prejudice, stumble at every straw.'[55] Berry also released from gaol in Hereford the former New Model Army officer and staunch supporter of the rights of parliament, John Birch, after he had told him: 'he is for the same things that we are but could have been glad to have them annother way, but seeing the time is not yet for it, nor we fit for it, he thinks we had better have it as it is then make disturbance.'[56]

Most of Berry's fellow major-generals, however, were much more concerned about the activities of Fifth Monarchist and anabaptist groups within their associations. In January 1656, Edward Whalley intercepted a number of anabaptist tracts which had been sent to Boston in Lincolnshire and subsequently interrogated those to whom they were addressed.[57] In April 1656, Hezekiah Haynes warned the members of a Fifth Monarchist group at Eye in Suffolk, who had told him that the New Model Army no longer marched with God and his saints, that if they caused any form of disturbance he 'should as heartely engage against them as others who had bin of us and had espoused that interest'.[58] Several months later, he reported to Thurloe his concerns about some Fifth Monarchists from North Walsham in Norfolk, who he believed had access to arms and might resort to violence.[59] William Goffe, meanwhile, informed Thurloe at the beginning of May 1656 about the activities of the General Baptist, John Sturgeon, who had lost his position in

Cromwell's lifeguard and been imprisoned in London after criticising the protector in print. He told him that, following his release from confinement, Sturgeon had travelled to Reading where he held a public meeting every evening, and that when the captain of the Berkshire militia troop had questioned him, he had been 'very peremptory'.[60] Thomas Kelsey, meanwhile, arrested the prominent Ranter, Richard Coppin, on the grounds that he had been attempting to subvert the soldiers of the garrison in Rochester.[61]

Several of the major-generals were particularly keen to ensure that the Quakers of their districts did not cause unrest. At the beginning of 1656, William Goffe informed Thurloe that George Fox and several other leading Quakers were travelling around Sussex 'doing much work for the devil and deluding many simple souls', and that he intended to expel them from the county if he got a chance.[62] In March, he imprisoned at Horsham one Lacock, a Quaker preacher, and confiscated several hundred of his pamphlets which contained 'many desperate words'. He also ordered one of the county militia captains to prevent crowds of his supporters from flocking to the town to visit him.[63] Hezekiah Haynes was similarly alarmed by the threat from Quakers within East Anglia, who had held 'considerable meetings' and 'greatly molested' his counties. After arresting a large number of them and imprisoning them at Bury St Edmunds, he reported that some of the clergy of his association believed they were 'ripe to cutt throates', adding: 'I think their principles would let them if they dared.'[64]

The major-general, however, who seems to have been most severe in his dealings with the Quakers was William Boteler. A number of Northamptonshire Quakers claimed that Boteler had imprisoned them without trial and had ordered his militia troops to break up their meetings and physically assault them. They also declared that 'there might be a great volume written of the wicked, tyrannicall actions of this man ... a shame to this nation'.[65] Their partial testimony was corroborated by an account in one of the official government newsbooks at the end of May 1656, which reported how a meeting of 800 Quakers at Hardingstone near Northampton had been violently broken up by the Northamptonshire militia, acting on direct orders from Boteler.[66]

The threat posed to the government by such anabaptist, Fifth Monarchist and Quaker activists was probably never as serious as that posed by royalist conspirators. It was, nonetheless, real enough and the major-generals' constant surveillance of such religious and political radicals provided the government in London with valuable intelligence about the activities of these potentially dangerous groups and individuals.

Before the overall effectiveness of the major-generals' security work can be evaluated, it is important to consider two other vital components of the new arrangements over which they presided: the posts and the new militias.

Cromwell, Thurloe and their colleagues in the council were well aware that the success of the major-generals' government would to a large degree depend upon the speed and reliability of communications between London and the provinces. During the the summer of 1655, therefore, as the new security system was being devised, Thurloe issued new regulations for the delivery of official letters and assumed personal responsibility for the operation of the government posts. Letters signed by the major-generals were henceforth to travel by an express service which would be expected to cover seven miles an hour in the summer and five miles an hour in winter.[67]

Following their arrival in their associations, several of the major-generals dismissed the existing postmasters, either because they had been found to be unreliable or because their attitude to the regime was considered lukewarm. Charles Worsley examined the postmasters of his association in December 1655, and in July 1656 Thomas Kelsey and his commissioners in Kent advised Thurloe to replace the postmaster of Dartford.[68] William Sweetman, the former postmaster of Shaftesbury in Dorset, failed to recover his position after it was alleged that he had thrown some official communications away and passed on other letters to those disaffected to the government.[69] After examining a former postmaster of Durham, who had petitioned him to be reappointed following his earlier dismissal, Robert Lilburne advised Thurloe not to give him back the position on the grounds that, while he was reasonably diligent, 'he would doe his office rather upon grounds of prudence and policy rather than affection'; he added that it was important 'to have cordiall men in places of trust'.[70]

In some places, this latter aim was achieved by appointing one of the local militia captains as postmaster. During the election campaign of August 1656, William Goffe was kept informed about who was writing to whom in Hampshire by the postmaster of Southampton, who was an officer of the county militia.[71] While such measures did not entirely eradicate delays and non-delivery, by the summer of 1656 the official posts were operating reasonably efficiently. The London register, Thomas Dunn, expected to receive letters from his deputies in the Kentish ports in not much more than twenty-four hours, and dispatches from Thurloe to the major-generals in the far north of England and in Wales normally arrived within two to three days.

Far more important, however, to the new security system than the regulation of the posts was the new militia raised during June 1655. Technically this new force was a 'select militia', which complemented the 'general militia' which had last been reorganised in 1650. Both types of militia were reservist forces which maintained their own weapons and were called out only at times of particular tension or danger. As J. G. I. Ive has shown, the advantages of the new select militia were that it was an almost entirely mounted force, which could respond rapidly to threats over a wide geographical area, and that it was made up of volunteers who were generally firmly committed to the regime. Its drawback, on the other hand, was that it was less closely connected to the communities it was responsible for protecting, and might thus be viewed by them as an unwelcome intrusion.[72]

The new national select militia was divided into sixty-six county troops, all but two of which were cavalry.[73] Their distribution was determined by the relative size and strategic importance of individual counties. Thus, there were four troops for Yorkshire, three for Devon, Kent, Norfolk and Suffolk, and two for Cambridgeshire and the Isle of Ely, Cornwall, Essex, Gloucestershire, Hampshire, Lincolnshire, Northamptonshire, Somerset and Wiltshire. Sussex originally had three troops, but one was disbanded by William Goffe in March 1656. All the other English shires had one county troop, except for Cumberland and Westmorland which shared one. Another four troops were raised in Wales: one for the six northern counties; one for Glamorgan, Brecknock and Radnor; one for Camarthenshire, Pembrokeshire and Cardigan; and one for Monmouthshire. In addition to these cavalry units, there were two troops of foot for the city of Norwich. All the other English cities came under the jurisdiction of their local county force; London, for example, was controlled by Barkstead's Middlesex troop.

Until June 1656, all but two of the sixty-four cavalry troops consisted of 100 men, the exceptions being those in Rutland and the Isle of Ely, each of which had sixty men. The officer corps was made up of a captain, who was paid £100 per annum; a lieutenant, who received £50; a cornet, who was paid £25; a quartermaster and trumpeter who each received £13 6s 8d; and three corporals who were paid £10 each. With the exception of Yorkshire, where Lord George Eure was appointed as colonel of the county militia and given overall command over all four troops, the militia captains reported directly to their local major-general. In two cases, indeed, the major-general was himself an officer of the militia; Sir John Barkstead, major-general for Middlesex, London and Westminster, was captain of the Middlesex troop, and George Fleetwood, who was Charles Fleetwood's deputy in Buckinghamshire, was also the captain of that county's troop. To ensure that the soldiers liaised closely with the major-generals' civilian helpers, all the militia captains and many of the lieutenants were appointed as commissioners for securing the peace of the commonwealth within their respective counties

The ordinary troopers each received £8 a year as a retainer, which was augmented by the pay of a regular soldier for every day they were on active service. The total cost of a cavalry troop of 100 men was £999 13s 4d. The two foot companies in Norwich also comprised 100 men, each of whom received £3 a year. The total cost of each of these troops was £434 16s 8d. In all, the national force contained 6,250 men, and its total annual salary bill was in the region of £64,000. An additional £8,000 had to be found annually from the decimation money to pay the twelve major-generals' salaries of £666 13s 8d, and around another £8,000 to pay the salaries and expenses of the commissioners' civilian officials. The total annual cost of the new security system, therefore, was just over £80,000.

Both because some counties contained more troops than others and because the number of counties within the twelve associations differed, the number of militia troops commanded by individual major-generals and the amount of money required to pay them varied considerably. Desborough and Haynes were each responsible for twelve troops; Berry for seven; Goffe and Whalley for six each; Lilburne and Boteler for five each; Kelsey for four; Packer and Worsley for three each; Howard for two; and Barkstead for only one. Thus, while Desborough and his west country commissioners had to find in the region of £14,000 annually from local royalists to pay their militia troops, Sir John Barkstead was required to find only around £2,000 from Middlesex and London.[74]

The government was keen that the new force should be made up of experienced soldiers who were firmly committed to the regime. To this end, it ensured that a number of the captains and lieutenants of the county troops had previously served as officers in the New Model Army. Alban Cox of Hertfordshire, Brampton Gurden of Suffolk, and Thomas Honeywood of Essex had all been colonels in the regular army; Wroth Rogers of Herefordshire had been a lieutenant-colonel; John Browne of Kent had been a major; and William Goodrick of Yorkshire had commanded a troop of Lambert's horse. Other former New Model Army veterans in the militia officer corps included Lewis Audley of Surrey, Talbot Badger of Worcestershire, Francis Blethin of Monmouthshire, Thomas Croxton of Cheshire and Richard Wagstaffe of Bedfordshire.[75] While lists of the ordinary troopers have not survived, it is highly probable that a great many of them too had previously served in the New Model Army. A report from Yorkshire published in a newsbook of early 1656, stated that the four troops of that county consisted 'much of reduced officers in the parlement's service and old soldiers', and that 'those few that have not bin soldiers are such whose affections have been tried and having good estates are freely engaged in the work.' It added that if they were called into service they would uphold 'that honest interest of the nation so much owned by God in the hands of his Highness'.[76]

As the above report suggests, in addition to being militarily experienced, the great majority of the militia troops were also conspicuous supporters of Cromwell's regime. The instructions sent out by the council to the newly appointed militia captains at the beginning of June 1655 had required them to recruit men of good life and conversation who were prepared to promise to be 'true and faithfull' to the protector.[77] Most of them seemed to have taken these directions very seriously. After Charles Worsley had met with the officers of his militia troops on his arrival in the north-west, he told Thurloe: 'truly I find in them a spirret extraordinarily bent to the worke, and I plainly discerne the finger of God goeinge along with it.'[78] Hezekiah Haynes similarly commented in the spring of 1656 that his militia troops in East Anglia were 'persons we can mostly confide in', and during the debate on the militia bill in parliament in January 1657 John Desborough claimed that 'the honestest men in the country' had been recruited to the force.[79] Cromwell was sufficiently confident of the goodwill of the troopers to suggest that they should be used as a secret police force for the government. He told the corporation of London in March 1656 that, as they were all local men, they could act as 'watchmen' and 'spies' for the major-generals by informing on their idle and dissolute neighbours.[80] Some of the regime's opponents also acknowledged the commitment of the 1655 militia; speaking in a debate in parliament on the militia in 1661, Sir John Holland declared: 'I cannot forget that in the late usurping time the ancient militia raised out of the freeholders and persons of interest in this nation was laid by and a troop of eight pound men raised in every county, who were to be in readiness at all times and upon all occasions to be execcutors of that tyrant's will.'[81]

That many of those who volunteered for the Huntingdonshire force in the summer of 1655 were ideologically motivated is revealed by the letter Robert Baker, a cornet in that troop, sent to Edward Montague in late June 1655 to inform him of the progress in raising the new troops in that shire. The letter makes clear that, for the most part, it was the local godly who were joining up and that their presence in the troop was a source of irritation to their less zealous neighbours. Baker told Montague that he and his fellow officers had so far enlisted between sixty and eighty men all of whom possessed a horse, sword and a case of pistols and were ready to serve at an hour's notice. The success of the recruitment had, he claimed, made 'some of the envious partie to swell with spight to see men so willing to a business so contrary to their complection'. Some of the recruits had been 'tampered with' by their neighbours, who had asked them 'why they would be listed to march up and downe in England, have pay when they could get it, and at last be sent to the Barbadoes'. Baker commented of such statements that, while they were meant to 'discourage and weaken the hands of our men, yet God turned it to good, for thereby our friends were fastened to us, who resolve to march whithersoever we are commanded'.[82]

Both the government and the major-generals took great care to preserve the reliability and ideological purity of the new militia troops, moving quickly to purge them of any inadequate or suspect elements. William Boteler told Thurloe in November 1655 that he was reforming the Northamptonshire militia, 'putting out and putting in ... and must do more for that many men are unfitt and many had not horses of their own which was altogether insufferable, especially for that we may have enough that can provide theire owne horses'.[83] In November 1656, the council instructed George Fleetwood to remove the lieutenant of his Buckinghamshire troop after he was discovered to be an innkeeper, and in January 1657 it ordered the dismissal of a cornet in the Northamptonshire troop who had criticised Cromwell's son-in-law, John, lord Claypole.[84] In March 1656, William Goffe advised Thurloe to take away the commission of Stephen Adams, a lieutenant of one of the Sussex troops, on the grounds that he had allowed local Quakers to hold meetings in his house and was suspected of being a Quaker himself.[85]

Goffe was also responsible for disbanding one of the three Sussex troops after he developed serious doubts about the loyalty of its captain, John Busbridge. In early January 1656, he told Thurloe that Busbridge had not attended any of the commissioners' meetings and that he had a new wife with royalist sympathies who was discouraging him from acting for the government. He added: 'I could wish the man a greate deal better then he is, if all be true that I have heard reported of him.' Several days later he wrote again, this time in cipher, reporting that another Sussex commissioner had told him that Busbridge had spoken against the government, was a friend of disaffected persons, and had attended 'malignant meetings' at which gaming and drinking occurred. The government was sufficiently concerned to order Goffe to disband Busbridge's troop, which he did in mid March 1656. Busbridge and his men were far from pleased. The captain claimed he was the victim of 'some ill doing by his countrymen' and declared he would 'never appeare in publicke businesse more'; his troops, meanwhile, angrily demanded nine months' pay rather than the six months' Goffe had offered them.[86] It is likely that Busbridge's deficiencies had initially been brought to Goffe's attention by his fellow militia captain, William Freeman, who felt that he lacked godly zeal and was insufficiently committed to the government's reform programme.[87]

As a result of such efforts by the major-generals and their allies, the militia raised in 1655 was potentially a much more effective body than its predecessors and one which retained a firm commitment to the regime which had created it. Even an experienced soldier like John Desborough was impressed by it; writing to Cromwell in February 1656, Desborough told him that the 700 soldiers serving in the militia in Cornwall, Devon and Somerset were strong supporters of the government and were 'well armed, stout men in appearance and well horsed, except in Cornwall, where their horses are but small.'[88]

In practice, however, the effectiveness of the new militia as a security force was greatly reduced by the government's failure to find sufficient funds to provide it with regular pay. The costs of the county troops was supposed to be met out of the receipts from the decimation tax, but for several reasons this source of funding soon proved inadequate. In the first place, whereas the troops had begun to serve in the summer of 1655, the first instalment of the decimation was not due until the end of December and in many counties was only received by the local treasurers during the first few months of 1656. This in-built time-lag meant that the troops could only ever be paid in arrears, a situation which was far from acceptable to many of them. As early as the end of November 1655, William Goffe informed Thurloe that 'pay was earnestly expected' by his troops in Hampshire, and that as he had no money to provide this he was unable to muster them. He added that the officers had told him that 'the country beginns to jeare the soldiers, telling them they are but cheated and must never expect any pay'.[89]

Furthermore, as was shown in chapter 6, once the commissioners had begun the work of assessing their royalist neighbours for the decimation tax in the autumn of 1655, it soon became clear that in many areas the sums raised would be insufficient to cover the costs of the local troops. In those counties where there was either a substantial number of royalists or one or two with exceptionally large estates, the sums did add up and the money needed for the militia could be found from the decimation receipts. John Desborough and his commissioners, for example, managed to raise the £14,000 needed for their twelve west country militia troops, and Charles Worsley collected enough money in the north-west not only to pay his militias but also to provide 'a considerable sum for other uses'.[90] In other areas, however, even the most vigorous exaction of the decimation tax could not prevent major shortfalls, and a number of the other major-generals, in particular Berry, Boteler, Goffe, Haynes and Kelsey, were soon struggling to find ways to pay their troops.

At the end of January 1656, Cromwell instructed the major-generals to give their militia troops six months' pay out of the receipts of the first instalment of the decimation tax, or, if they had not yet received enough money to do this, to pay them what they could, making sure that each troop within their association received the same amount. Several days later, William Goffe wrote back to Thurloe to voice his misgivings about this method of proceeding. He explained that, although he had collected enough money to pay his troops in Berkshire, he had only received half of what he needed for those in Hampshire and Sussex. He argued that to pay some of the soldiers in full and their counterparts in neighbouring shires only in part would be likely to produce 'a very great dissatisfaction to the soldiers who are underpaid and great prejudice to their major-generals and captains'. He also pointed out, however, that if he diverted some of the decimation money collected in Berkshire to pay the other troops, he would incense the Berkshire soldiers. He was unhappy about the idea of troops in different associations receiving varying amounts of pay, and argued that it was important that 'the whole militia of the nation as well as of the severall associations be paide in an equality of proportion'. He concluded that the best way to resolve the problem was to pay all the decimation money into a central treasury and disburse it in equal amounts to the militia throughout the country. If this were not done, he argued: 'I feare those associations that rayse the least money will have such a pittyfull militia that the major-general will have little honour or comfort in commanding them and, which is worse, the publicke safety little advantaged by them.'[91]

In late February 1656, the council responded to the crisis by ordering the major-generals to chase up all those who had still not paid in their decimations, and by deciding to reduce the size of the militia troops in eleven named counties from a hundred to eighty men.[92] This move did little, however, to help and by the spring some of the major-generals were desperate for cash. In mid March, Goffe was reduced to borrowing £500 from one of the regular army officers stationed in Sussex; imploring Thurloe to send him the funds which would allow him to pay the man back, he exclaimed: 'I am sorry to be thus scrapping for money, knowing of your other necessityes, but your affaires cannot goe on without it.'[93] When several months later he had still received no money, he declared in exasperation: 'if the worke and ourselves perish for want of our wages, it will not, I hope, be laied to our charge ... I know money is your greate want; but, under favour, I humbly conceive you must keepe your army and militia force in hart by constant pay, unlesse you intend all shall come to ruin.'[94] In June 1656, Hezekiah Haynes reported to Thurloe that it was a matter of 'some disgust' to his militia troops in East Anglia that they had received no pay for nearly a year's service. He told him he had not been able to muster them for want of pay, and added: 'I hope all possible care wil be had in makeing the door streight enough, else will the hearts of those that have cleaved to you in your late streights be sadde and a complyanc to other persons wil be but as the daubing with untempered mortar.'[95]

In the spring and early summer of 1656, the government took two further steps in an attempt to deal with the shortage of cash. In April 1656, it decided to reduce the overall size of the national miltia force by cutting all those cavalry troops which still contained one hundred men down to eighty. This left them with a force of 5,200 men, whose total annual wage bill, including the salaries of the major-generals and the commissioners' civilian officials, was around £67,000.[96] Then, on 13 June 1656, it followed Goffe's earlier advice and formally handed over responsibility for the collection and distribution of the pay for the national militia to the central army committee.[97] Once again, however, neither of these moves appears to have done much to alleviate the chronic problem of underfunding. Goffe was contacted by the army committee in July, but in mid August he was still waiting for money and he complained bitterly to Thurloe: 'wee and our business are ready to starve for want of necessary supplyes of money, the committee of the army having as yett taken noe course at all for us.'[98] Lack of money prevented Haynes from mustering his East Anglian militia during the election campaign in August, and dissuaded Goffe from calling out the Hampshire troop the following month for 'a word of exortation' before he left to take up his seat at Westminster.[99] Some members of the central government were well aware that these financial problems had considerably reduced the effectiveness of the new militia; in a letter to Henry Cromwell, probably written during the autumn of 1656, John Thurloe remarked ruefully that 'our rule here is that noe militia is of any value, nay that it will be dangerous, if it have not pay.'[100]

The council continued to struggle with this problem well into 1657. On several occasions in late 1656 and early 1657, it ordered those major-generals with spare money to send it to their impoverished colleagues.[101] It also gave Haynes and Boteler £2,000 each of the £4,000 which had been received from William Cavendish, earl of Devonshire, in exchange for his release from the decimation, and in November 1656, after being informed that nearly £6,000 was still owed to the militia troops serving under Berry, Boteler, Goffe and Kelsey for their pay to the previous June, it in desperation allocated them the contents of a recently captured Spanish prize.[102] Nonetheless, despite all these expedients, the pay of a number of troops was still badly in arrears long after the major-generals had withdrawn from their associations, and the major-generals themselves only ever received a fraction of their own salaries.[103]

The new security system established by the government in 1655 and presided over by the major-generals was extremely ambitious in scope. It attempted to regulate the movements and activities of a substantial section of the English population to an extent that had never been seen before in England and indeed would not be seen again until the industrial era. It was also without parallel elsewhere in seventeenth-century Europe. Given the scope of the experiment, it inevitably fell short of its aims, but there is both contemporary evidence and later scholarly analysis which suggests that it nonetheless achieved a considerable degree of success. In mid November 1655, William Sancroft wrote to a relative that it was 'the opinion of all knowing men I meet with that there is the greatest and sharpest persecution now falling upon the whole royall party that ever they yet felt', and shortly afterwards Thomas Watson declared to a friend that as a result of the new security arrangements the royalists had become 'the most excellent slaves in the world'.[104] In December 1655, the Venetian envoy informed his master that, although the English royalists remained embittered towards their government, they were

> so heavily burdened and their fortunes so delapidated that, without money, leaders or support, they are better able to grumble than to vindicate themselves. The government adopts such strict precautions that they have not only forbidden meetings and conventicles aimed against the present rule, but they will not permit a

gathering of 12 or 14 persons, even in the streets, for any sort of business, not excepting trade or conversation.[105]

The same month Henry Oxinden of Barham in Kent testified to the pervading sense of fear and suspicion that prevailed in the country at the time when, in a letter to his wife from London, he wrote:

> Thy advice concerning not trusting any with secrets I like well and thank thee for it; There can be nothing sayd more true then what thou hast sayd ... pray seal your letters well and write nothing but what if they broake open may bee seene ... as for public newes, men are afrayd to speke one to another, though friends ... let none of my letters bee seene, nor report any newes against the present proceedings, times are now so as a man can hardly walke securely.[106]

This contemporary testimony to the effectiveness of the major-generals' attempts to make Cromwell's regime safer has been confirmed by the work of David Underdown, who has carried out a detailed investigation of royalist conspiracy during the 1650s. Underdown has argued that 'in the second half of 1655 and the early months of 1656 Royalist activity was confined to the discussion of futile assassination projects and more constructively to the old preoccupations of intelligence and financial supplies.' In his view, the security measures enacted by the major-generals and their supporters were 'completely successful in eliminating whatever danger remained of a repetition of the March rising'. Once the major-generals had withdrawn from their associations in the autumn of 1656, the royalist underground was able to begin the process of reconstructing itself, but it was only in the spring of 1658 that it regained anything like the level of organisation it had enjoyed at the beginning of 1655, and not until 1659 that it was once again able to launch an armed insurrection against the Interregnum state.[107]

From late 1655 to the early months of 1657, the members of the English royalist community found themselves living in a police state, within which the major-generals, their commissioners, their militia troops, and the staff of the central register office in London worked together to circumscribe their freedom to a degree which would have been inconceivable in pre civil-war England. At the start of the second protectorate parliament in September 1656, Cromwell told the new MPs that the major-generals had proved 'effectual for the preservation of your peace' and that without them 'you had not had peace two months together'.[108] While the latter claim was rhetorical hyperbole, the former was broadly accurate, for whatever their record in the other aspects of their work, the major-generals had undoubtedly succeeded in making it far more difficult and dangerous to engage in conspiracy against Cromwell's regime, and had thus done a great deal to ensure that, while they continued to exercise their jurisdiction in the provinces, the protectorate would be likely to survive.

NOTES

1 Michael Roberts (ed.), *Swedish Diplomats at Cromwell's Court, 1655–1656*, Camden Soc. Publs, 4th series, 36 (1988), 89; *Calendar State Papers Venetian, 1655–1656*, p. 79.

2 C. H. Firth (ed.), *The Clarke Papers*, vol. III, Camden Soc. Publs, new series, 60 (1899), 47.

3 BL, E.841.4, *Certain Passages of Everyday Intelligence*, 25 May–1 Jun. 1655; BL, E.842.1, *A Perfect Diurnall*, 28 May–4 Jun. 1655; Gardiner, *Commonwealth and Protectorate*, vol. 3, pp. 338–9; Rutt, *Diary of Thomas Burton*, vol. 4, pp. 256–9.

4 BL, E.852.22, *Certain Passages of Everyday Intelligence*, 24–31 Aug. 1655; PRO, SP.25.76, pp. 319–20.

5 PRO, SP.25.76, pp. 319–20.

6 PRO, SP.18.101.136; SP.46.97, fols 162–3.

7 Bod. Lib., Rawlinson MSS, A 34, fols 771–2; A 35, fol. 103; A 48, fol. 167.

8 *Ibid.*, A 34, fols 975–6; A 35, fol. 4; A 40, fols 117–20.

9 *Ibid.*, A 34, fols 693–4; A 35, fol. 2.

10 *Ibid.*, A 32, fols 331–4, 647–50.

11 *Ibid.*, A 32, fols 655–8; A 35, fols 17–20, 49–52; A 36, fol. 705.

12 PRO, SP.18.101.136.

13 Bod. Lib., Rawlinson MSS, A 32, fols 373–6, 377–80, 871–4; A 33, fols 221–4.

14 Buckinghamshire Record Office, Claydon House Letters, M11/14, Burgoyne to Verney, 10 Dec. 1655.

15 Buckinghamshire RO, M11/14, Sir Ralph Verney to Edmund Verney, 15 Feb. 1656.

16 Bod. Lib., Rawlinson MSS, A 32, fols 765–8.

17 Buckinghamshire RO, M11/14, Isham to Verney, 10 Nov. 1655; Verney, to Sir William Waller, 19 Nov. 1655.

18 The text of the bond was published in the official newsbooks in December; see BL, E.491.7, *Mercurius Politicus*, 13–20 Dec. 1655.

19 PRO, SP.25.76A, pp. 137–8. This proclamation extended a ban originally imposed in July; see PRO, SP.25.76A, pp. 73–5. The Venetian ambassador stated that searches were carried out for any who might have disobeyed the proclamation and stayed in London but that the vast majority had complied, *Calendar of State Papers Venetian, 1655–1656*, p. 88. The royalist historian, James Heath, later claimed that three individuals, who were arrested and held at St James's Palace for breaching the proclamation, killed a soldier while attempting to escape and were subsequently convicted of manslaughter; see James Heath, *A Brief Chronicle of the Late Intestine Wars in the Three Kingdoms of England Scotland and Ireland* (London, 1663), p. 700.

20 BL, Additional MSS, 34011–3, 34016. The individual major-generals' approximate totals are as follows: Desborough, 4,932; Lilburne, 4,653; Worsley, 2,181; Barkstead, 564; Goffe, 505; Howard, 347; Kelsey, 239; Packer, 212; Haynes, 188; Berry, 163; Whalley, 125; and Boteler, 98. The ledger which contains returns from Desborough's association (Additional MSS, 34012), and which is labelled on the cover as containing the names of

those who gave security in all six of his counties, does not in fact record any names for Cornwall. The number of actual bonds tendered would have been considerably fewer than 14,000, as many of those named in the lists were servants, who were subsumed within those signed by their royalist masters.

21 Staffordshire Record Office, Leveson Correspondence, D868/5/8; for comments on the size of the bonds see J. W. Willis Bund (ed.), *The Diary of Henry Townshend of Elmley Lovett 1640–1663*, Worcestershire Historical Soc. Publs, 31 part 1 (1920), 30–1.

22 PRO, SP.18.102. 64; SP.18.124.1.

23 Buckinghamshire RO, M11/14 Verney to Isham, 19 Nov. 1655. See also Bod. Lib., Rawlinson MSS, A 33, fols 770–3; and George F. Warner (ed.), *The Nicholas Papers*, vol. III, Camden Soc. Publs, new series, 57 (1897), 254.

24 Bod. Lib., Rawlinson MSS, A 33, 770–3.

25 Buckinghamshire RO, Claydon Letters, M11/14, letter of Sir Ralph Verney, 8 Oct. 1655.

26 Bod. Lib., Rawlinson MSS, A 32, fols 765–8. The main seat of Thomas Wriothesley, the fourth earl of Southampton, was at Titchfield in Hampshire, but he also had a residence within a few miles of Kingston and he seems to have been staying there with his mother at that point.

27 *Ibid.*, A 32, fols 385–8.

28 PRO, SP.25.76, p. 512.

29 Roger Coke, *A Detection of the Court and State of England during the Last Four Reigns and Interregnum* (2 vols, London, 1694), vol. 2, pp. 55–62.

30 Bod. Lib., Rawlinson MSS, A 36, fol. 179.

31 BL, E.491.9, *Mercurius Politicus*, 20–27 Dec. 1655; E.491.10, *The Public Intelligencer*, 24–31 Dec. 1655; E.491.11, *Mercurius Politicus*, 27 Dec. 1655–3 Jan. 1656; BL, Add. MSS 19516, fol. 2r, 5r; PRO, SP.18.126.71. In November several of the major-generals asked Thurloe for information about the office; see Bod. Lib, Rawlinson MSS, A 32, fols 381–4, 647–50.

32 PRO, SP.25.76A, pp. 181–2.

33 PRO, SP.25.76, pp. 324, 327, 440.

34 BL, Add. MSS 19516, fol. 2r.

35 PRO, SP.18.126.71.

36 BL, Add. MSS 19516, fol. 36r.

37 These approximate figures were compiled using the information in BL, Additional MSS, 34014, the register office's book of appearances between 17 Nov. 1655 and 11 Jun. 1656; and BL, Additional MSS, 19516, its letter book of correspondence with the major-generals and their commissioners from 1 Jan. 1656 to 29 Jan. 1657.

38 BL, Add. MSS, 19516.

39 BL, Add. MSS 19516, fol. 108v.

40 The names of foreign travellers who reported to Fleet Street are given in BL, Additional MSS, 34015; copies of Dunn's letters to the deputy-registers in the ports can be found throughout BL, Additional MSS, 19516.

41 BL, Additional MSS, 19516, fol. 116v.

42 *Ibid.*, fol. 3r.

43 *Ibid.*, fol. 92r.

44 *Ibid.*, fol. 106r.

45 *Ibid.*, fol. 24v.

46 *Ibid.*, fol. 94r.

47 *Ibid.*, fols 21r, 24r, 64r.

48 *Ibid.*, fol. 97r.

49 *Ibid.*, fol. 108v.

50 *Ibid.*, fol. 36r.

51 *Ibid.*, fol. 44r.

52 *Ibid.*, fol. 126v.

53 PRO, SP.18.130.61; SP.25. 77, pp. 441–2, 459, 813.

54 Bod. Lib., Rawlinson MSS, A 32, fols 715–18.

55 *Ibid.*, A 34, fols 217–20.

56 *Ibid.*, A 32, fols 793–6.

57 *Ibid.*, A 34, fols 427–30.

58 *Ibid.*, A 37, fols 233–6.

59 *Ibid.*, A 40, fols 333–4.

60 *Ibid.*, A 38, fols 22–3.

61 *Ibid.*, A 34, fols 649–52.

62 *Ibid.*, A 34, fols 395–6.

63 *Ibid.*, A 36, fols 630–2.

64 *Ibid.*, A 40, fols 121–4.

65 PRO, SP.18.102.50.

66 BL, E.493.21, *Mercurius Politicus*, 22 May–5 Jun. 1656.

67 *Calendar State Papers Domestic, 1655*, p. 285–6.

68 Bod. Lib., Rawlinson MSS, A 33, fols 369–72; A 34, fols 487–90; A 40, fols 665–8.

69 *Ibid.*, A 33, fols 377–8, 379–84.

70 *Ibid.*, A 33, fols 93–6.

71 *Ibid.*, A 41, fols 248–51; A 42, fols 337–8.

72 For more details, see the chapters on the select militia in J. G. I. Ive, 'The Local Dimension of Defence: The Standing Army and Militia in Norfolk, Suffolk and Essex, 1649–1660' (Unpub. Ph.D. thesis, University of Cambridge, 1986).

73 The following information on the structure of the militia comes from the two militia establishments in the Interregnum State Papers; see PRO, SP.25.77, pp. 861–80, 884–901.

74 The detailed figures for the individual generals are as follows; Desborough, £13,802; Haynes, £12,162; Berry, £8,994; Whalley, £7,614; Goffe, £6,234; Lilburne, £6,145;

Boteler, £6,104; Kelsey, £5,045; Packer and Worsley, £4,235; Howard, £3,045; and Barkstead, £2,046. These include their own salaries and those of the commissioners' civil officers.

75 The names of the militia officers are given at PRO, SP.25.77, pp. 861–80; for their earlier military careers, see C. H. Firth and G. Davies, *A Regimental History of Cromwell's Army* (2 vols, Oxford, 1940), and R. L. Greaves and R Zaller (eds) *A Biographical Dictionary of British Radicals in the Seventeenth Century* (Brighton, 1982).

76 BL, E.492.3, *Mercurius Politicus*, 31 Jan.–7 Feb. 1656.

77 PRO, SP.46.97, fols 164–5.

78 Bod. Lib., Rawlinson MSS, A 32, fols 113–16.

79 *Ibid.*, A 39, fol. 495; Rutt, *Diary of Thomas Burton*, vol. 1, p. 316.

80 Abbott, *Writings and Speeches of Cromwell*, vol. 4, pp. 112–13.

81 C. Robbins, 'Five Speeches 1661–3 by Sir John Holland', *Bulletin of the Institute of Historical Research*, 28 (1955), 199–200; quoted in Anthony Fletcher, *Reform in the Provinces* (New Haven and London, 1986), p. 322.

82 Bod. Lib., Carte MSS, vol. 74, fol. 35.

83 Bod. Lib., Rawlinson MSS, A 32, fols 155–8.

84 PRO, SP.25.77, pp. 479, 637.

85 Bod. Lib., Rawlinson MSS, A 36, fols 630–2.

86 *Ibid.*, A 34, fols 225–8, 395–6; A 36, fols 630–2.

87 Anthony Fletcher *A County Community in Peace and War: Sussex 1600–1660* (London, 1975), p. 309.

88 Bod. Lib., Rawlinson MSS, A 35, fol. 102.

89 *Ibid.*, A 32, fols 809–12.

90 *Ibid.*, A 33, fols 221–4; A 35, fols 102, 135.

91 *Ibid.*, A 35, fol. 15.

92 PRO, SP.25.76, p. 565. The eleven counties were Berkshire, Buckinghamshire, Cambridgeshire, Hampshire, Hertfordshire, Huntingdonshire, Norfolk, Oxfordshire, Rutland, Suffolk and Sussex.

93 Bod. Lib., Rawlinson MSS, A 36, fols 630–2.

94 *Ibid.*, A 39, fols 424–5.

95 *Ibid.*, A 39, fol. 495.

96 PRO, SP.25.77, pp. 41, 49, 50, 841, 884–901.

97 *Ibid.*, pp. 902–4.

98 Bod. Lib., Rawlinson MSS, A 40, fols 315–18; A 41, fols 698–9.

99 *Ibid.*, A 41, 488–91, 572–5, 860–1.

100 Birch, *State Papers of John Thurloe*, vol. 5, p. 504.

101 PRO, SP.25.77, pp. 357, 470, 608.

102 *Ibid.*, pp. 215, 292–3, 305, 524–5. In January 1657 Kelsey was reimbursed his £230

expenses for 'coach hyre and travelling charges' for bringing the Spanish plate up to London from Portsmouth. See BL, Additional MSS, 4196, fol. 24.

103 PRO, SP.25.77, p. 512.

104 Bod. Lib., Tanner MSS, vol. 52, fol. 97; *Calendar of State Papers Domestic, 1655–1656*, pp. 79–80.

105 *Calendar of State Papers Venetian, 1655–1656*, pp. 147–8.

106 BL, Additional MSS, 28003, fols 326–7.

107 David Underdown, *Royalist Conspiracy in England 1649–1660* (New Haven, 1960), pp. 169–70, 178.

108 Abbott, *Writings and Speeches of Cromwell*, vol. 4, p. 274.

Chapter 8

The struggle
for the godly nation

The major-generals were sent into the provinces in the autumn of 1655 with the aim not only of improving the security of Cromwell's protectoral regime but also of reforming the nation's morality and reducing what the government saw as the endemic irreligion and ungodliness of the English and Welsh people. As was seen in chapter 2, their instructions of 22 August 1655 required them to 'encourage and promote godliness and discourage and discountenance all prophaneness and ungodliness'. More specifically, they were ordered to work closely with the local magistrates to enforce strictly the laws against drunkenness, profanity and swearing; to outlaw horse-racing, cock-fighting and bear-baiting; to put to work or imprison the idle and dissolute; and to take measures for the better relief of the deserving, impotent poor.[1] Several days later, an additional instruction ordered them to review what progress had been made within their areas towards the implementation of the 1654 ordinance for the ejection of scandalous and insufficient ministers and schoolmasters, and to oversee the removal of any such individuals who still remained in post.[2] In late September, further orders widened the scope of the moral reform brief. They were now instructed to ensure that from 1 November 1655 no ejected cleric preached in public, kept a school or administered the sacraments according to the Book of Common Prayer on pain of imprisonment or banishment, and that no royalist employed any ejected clergyman as a private chaplain or tutor.[3]

While the attempt to implement such an ambitious programme of godly reform represented a formidable task, it was nonetheless one which all of the major-generals, with the possible exception of Charles Howard, regarded as absolutely central to their mission and embraced with great enthusiasm. As staunch puritans, a strong commitment to the concept of the godly society was at the very core of their collective religious vision, and they saw their appointments as a (literally) heaven-sent opportunity to suppress wickedness and to create, in Anthony Fletcher's words, 'an ordered and godly common-wealth, a nation in which men worked hard and read the bible, heard the word of God, lived honestly, and gave obedience where it was due'.[4] Several of them made explicit their relish for the work of moral reform in their early letters back from their associations. In mid November 1655, Charles Worsley reported to Thurloe that he had already toured the major towns of the north-west, encouraging the 'best people' within them to punish drunkards, swearers and those who profaned the sabbath, and had found that 'God hath alredy put into his people a prayinge sperit for this great and good worke.'[5] Several days later, William Boteler remarked that, once he and his commis-sioners had completed the work of assessing the royalists of their association for the decimation tax, 'I cannot but please myselfe to thinke how greedily we shall put down prophaneness.'[6] At the end of the same month, Edward Whalley commented: 'I hope a very good outward reformation, the Lord assisting us, will be caryed on', and about the same time James Berry told the Welsh Fifth Monarchist, Vavasour Powell, 'with what confidence I came forth in this worke, as sent of God'.[7]

The major-generals' deep commitment to the cause of moral reform and regeneration was shared by the great majority of their active commissioners, some of whom were quick to express their eagerness to undertake this aspect of their work. The Bedfordshire commissioners, for example, told William Boteler that they would 'make it their business to finde out and give me notice of all their prophane and idle gentry and others whose lives are a shame to a Xn [Christian] commonwealth'.[8] In Huntingdonshire, meanwhile, they expressed their thanks that 'God hath alsoe put it into his Highnesses heart soe well to provide for the glory of God in the suppression of prophaneness and extirpation of scandalous and malignant ministers and schoolmasters'.[9] Shortly after they had begun work in March 1656, the Buckinghamshire commissioners assured Cromwell:

> The whole tenour of the work speakes good, the uniting of the fellow sharers in the grace of Christ, the exciting of magistrates and ministers to the faithful discharge of their dutyes, the bridleing of idle and licentious persons, who threaten an innundacon of sinn and consequently of wrath and ruine.[10]

The puritan minorities in the provinces also fully shared these aspirations. When Charles Worsley consulted some of the Independent congregations of his association about their reform priorities, the gathered church at Altham in Lancashire responded that they wanted him to create a magistracy of 'just men fearing God and hating covetousness'; to purge from the ministry the 'profane and heretical ministers who fill most pulpits in the country'; to punish drunkards, swearers and sabbath breakers; to close down unnecessary ale-houses; to set the idle to work; and to restrict the number of markets and fairs.[11]

The godly moral reform agenda was, then, clear and unambiguous and the commitment of all the main protagonists to it unquestioned. It was, however, an agenda which groups of puritans all over the country had been pursuing without conspicuous success for nearly a decade before 1655. The major-generals had been given command over very large associations and charged with other onerous tasks in the areas of taxation and security which would inevitably distract them from the work of moral reform. Moreover, the time available to them from their first arrival in the provinces in November 1655 to their recall to Westminster in September 1656 was severely limited. Given these circumstances, what, if any, progress did they make in pushing forward the godly reforms which were so close to their hearts?

With regard to a number of the moral reform responsibilities highlighted in their original instructions, the major-generals' impact appears to have been very slight. One such area was swearing; while individuals had been indicted for this offence throughout the early 1650s, the arrival of the major-generals saw no significant increase in prosecutions. Another was sexual crime. Quarter sessions records from all parts of the country reveal that during late 1655 and 1656 regular prosecutions were brought against both men and women for the sexual crimes of fornication and adultery. Again, however, the period since the passing of the 1650 Adultery Act had seen a steady stream of such indictments, and in the great majority of counties the arrival of the major-generals does not seem to have led to any noticeable increase in such cases.[12] One possible exception might be the west riding of Yorkshire, where the incidence of indictments for sexual offences does appear to have been significantly higher in 1656 than in previous years.[13] At first sight, another might appear to be Devon, where the period from 1655 to 1660 witnessed a rigorous campaign by the county magistracy to reduce fornication. In this latter case, however, the drive against sexual crime had begun before Desborough was appointed major-general, and was sustained by local figures like Henry Hatsell both when he was absent in London during 1656 and after his final withdrawal at the end of that year.[14] The only major-general who is known to have conspicuously involved himself in attempts to reduce illicit sexuality was Sir John Barkstead. At the beginning of 1656, he ordered the arrest of several hundred 'loose wenches' and prostitutes in the capital, with the apparent intention of transporting them to Jamaica.[15] A few months later in June 1656, he personally examined three men from Stepney and Ratcliffe Highway, who had been accused of running a brothel.[16]

The level of involvement by the major-generals and their commissioners in efforts to restrict popular sports and pastimes and to ensure a better observance of the sabbath was only a little higher, and, as with sexual crime, it was London which appears to have been most affected. Both the relatively small size of the capital and the presence of large numbers of soldiers made a campaign to outlaw unruly gatherings feasible here, and during 1656 Barkstead was involved in a number of initiatives towards that end. In February, with the help of the sheriff of Middlesex, Thomas Pride, he closed down the popular Beargarden in Bankside, killing all the bears, dogs and the cocks which had performed there for the London crowds.[17] In March, he bound over to appear at the next Middlesex sessions several individuals who had been arrested at what was probably a Shrove Tuesday cockfight in Stepney, and the same month his soldiers seized a large number of horses which had been exercised on the sabbath, forcing their owners to pay a large ten shilling fine in order to recover them.[18] In June, he joined with his fellow Middlesex JPs in issuing warrants to the county high constables to prevent any re-occurrence of the recent midsummer gatherings at Moorfields for 'wrestling, casting the stone, pitching the bar and the like'.[19] The following month, his soldiers broke up a horse race meeting on Hackney Marsh at which around 150 individuals were present.[20] Jean Mather's finding that around three times as many moral trangressions were brought before the Middlesex justices in 1656 than in 1652 strongly suggests that Barkstead's determined attempt to improve the moral behaviour of those who lived in and around the capital was having some real impact.[21]

Beyond London, there are only a few isolated examples of similar action being taken by Barkstead's fellow major-generals. Charles Worsley arrested a number of people who attended a horse race meeting in Lancashire in early December 1655 and kept them in custody for some days.[22] Thomas Kelsey's commissioners in Kent ordered the parish officials of their county to ban the traditional Whitsun celebrations which they asserted 'produced no other fruits but drunkenes, swering and all other kindes of lowness and debauchery'.[23] In May 1656, perhaps with the encouragement of Robert Lilburne or his commissioners, some of the godly inhabitants of Woodkirk in the west riding of Yorkshire petitioned the council to suppress their annual harvest fair, claiming that since the opening of a new cloth market at nearby Wakefield 'noe other use is made thereof now but for tumultuous meetings of idle and loose persons in the country to the occasioning of drunkenness, bloodshed and disorders.' The council immediately wrote to the fair's patron requesting him to bring it to an end.[24] Several months later in July 1656, it ordered Rowland Dawkins to take action against those who had attended unauthorised fairs at Caerphilly at which 'many disorders' were committed.[25] Both Charles Worsley and Robert Lilburne also wrote to the government to request that regular weekly markets held on Saturdays and Mondays in their associations be moved to another day, on the grounds that they caused the sabbath 'to be much violated' by those travelling to and from them.[26]

Such action by the major-generals to suppress or control the populace's traditional leisure pursuits was, however, at best sporadic and uncoordinated. While something approaching a sustained campaign may have been mounted by Barkstead in London, elsewhere in the country the impact of their administration on this aspect of the godly reform programme appears to have been muted. Nor was the hard line against traditional festivities supported consistently by all the major-generals. In March 1656, Edward Whalley disregarded his instructions and allowed the annual running of the horse race at Stamford in Lincolnshire for Lady Grantham's Cup. In doing so he was probably influenced by the fact that his permission had been sought for the event and by his belief that Cromwell did not wish to 'abridge gentlemen of that sport' unless security was seriously threatened by it.[27]

With regard to the attempt to reform the parochial ministry, some of the major-generals put a great deal of effort into this area of their work, but once again without achieving any very significant results. In August 1654, Cromwell and his council had passed an ordinance for the ejection of scandalous and insufficient ministers and schoolmasters. This legislation had authorised county commissions of lay ejectors and clerical advisers to receive information against any local clergyman or schoolmaster who was suspected of having committed one or more of a long list of offences, including adultery, fornication, swearing, drunkenness, brawling, card-playing, profaning the sabbath, using the Book of Common Prayer, encouraging traditional festivities and dancing, harbouring Ranter or popish opinions, neglecting his liturgical or teaching duties, or publicly scoffing at or reviling 'the strict professors of religion or godliness'.

The new ejectors were empowered to summon before them all those accused of such offences by their parishioners or others and, after examining them and any witnesses, to remove from their parishes all those who they were satisfied had transgressed in one or more of them. Any clerics who were ejected would forfeit stipend, property and tithes associated with their livings, although those with young families who had no other means of subsistence might be granted a fifth of the profits towards their maintenance. The patrons of livings made vacant by an ejection could nominate a successor to a central body of Triers which had been given the responsibility of approving all new appointments to the ministry. All of the future major-generals, except Tobias Bridge and Robert Lilburne, as well as the great majority of those who would later be named as commissioners for securing the peace of the commonwealth, were named as ejectors in 1654, and William Goffe and William Packer were also appointed as Triers.[28]

Over the course of the following year, the ejectors appear to have been active in only a small number of counties. Those in Berkshire removed around eight of their local ministers from their livings in late 1654 and early 1655, and their counterparts in the west riding of Yorkshire dismissed around twenty.[29] Smaller numbers were also ejected in Devon, Durham and Wiltshire, and in the country as a whole around fifty ministers appear to have lost their livings during the period between the passing of the ordinance and the arrival of the major-generals in their associations.[30] As far as the government and its godly allies were concerned, this was an entirely inadequate response to the legislation. In April 1655, the council drew up a letter to be sent to the ejectors in ten counties and the cities of London and Bristol, complaining about their failure to take more action under the ordinance.[31] The following month, a deputation of the godly inhabitants of Gloucestershire presented Cromwell with a remonstrance, which blamed the lack of progress under the ordinance on 'the paucity of persons impowred and the neglecting or refusing of so many of them to act, both in our county and in most others'.[32] The ensuing summer months saw several initiatives aimed at speeding up the work. In May 1655, the London ejectors began to hold weekly meetings; in August the Lincolnshire ejectors were given authority to act in the city of Lincoln; and in September the council made some minor amendments to the membership of the ejection commissions in Leicestershire and Oxfordshire.[33] Nonethelesss, when the major-generals were dispatched to their associations in the late autumn, the government clearly believed that much remained to be done and were hopeful that their new agents would now galvanise the ejectors into adopting a more rigorous and systematic approach to their work.

Most of the major-generals considered the reform of the ministry to be of the utmost importance. Addressing them and some of their fellow officers in March 1657, Cromwell claimed that he had been 'pressed' by them 'for the rooting out of the ministry'.[34] James Berry was certainly deeply shocked at the situation he found on his arrival in Wales. He reported to Thurloe from Wrexham in December 1655 that 'reformation hath many enemies and indeed here wants matter'. He went on to explain that many of the parishes in Anglesey were without a minister, and that in North Wales as a whole there were few good ministers to be found and 'the sequestered ministry and schoolmaisters are become like the branch of an unfruitful vine; a man cannot make a pin of it to hange a garment on and they are in a sad condition.'[35] Several months later, he wrote from Brecon in mid Wales that the want of preachers in that area was 'a great evell' and that unless the government took some action to remedy the problem, 'these people will some of them become heathens.'[36]

The two major-generals who were quickest to take up the challenge of reforming the ministries of their areas were Edward Whalley and Charles Worsley, both of whom took action within a few days of their arrival in their associations. Whalley began by prompting the Lincolnshire ejectors to begin work in November 1655. The following month he met with those in

Leicestershire and Nottinghamshire, and by that stage the Warwickshire commissioners were also active.[37] Worsley, meanwhile, spoke with both the Cheshire and Lancashire ejectors in November, and in early December he sat with those in Staffordshire. In all three counties, he prevailed upon the ejectors to send out notices inviting individuals to submit their complaints about the clergy. At the end of December, he reported to Thurloe that a great many articles had been received by the Lancashire ejectors and that summonses had been sent to those named in them requesting their personal appearance before the committee.[38]

This burst of activity against the clergy was substantial enough to come to the attention of two of the foreign diplomats resident in London. During December 1655, both the Venetian and Swedish envoys reported it in their dispatches to their masters, the latter claiming that suspect clergy were being 'pursued vigorously'.[39] In some other parts of the country, the major-generals' many commitments meant that action against the clergy was delayed. By the spring of 1656, however, at least partly as a result of encouragement they had received from the presence of the major-generals, local ejectors seem to have been active in the great majority of the English shires, and during the period of the major-generals' rule ministers were ejected from livings in more than thirty English counties.

According to the testimony of several of those forced to appear before them, some of the ejectors were particularly vindictive in their dealings with suspected clergy. Thomas Holbech, the rector of Chastleton in Oxfordshire, was ejected in early 1656 on the grounds that he had been sequestered from the living of Epping in Essex at the beginning of the civil war. Writing to his friend, William Sancroft, in March 1656, Holbech commented that he had hoped to keep his royalist past a secret but that 'the malice of some made that knowne soon enough to cut the throate of any such purpose.' He added that the local major-general, Charles Fleetwood, might perhaps have shown him some favour, 'but he acts not at all in person and his commissioners I have noe great fancy unto'.[40] Thomas Grantham, who was ejected from the living of Waddington in Lincolnshire, subsequently protested in print, denouncing the Lincolnshire ejectors as 'oppressing, hungry, barking, sharking, hollow bellyed committeemen' who 'do tyrannize under him [Cromwell] and do scratch and bite and test and worry the lives and estates of the peaceable subjects of God and man'.[41] Three of the five ejectors who proceeded against Grantham were also active in Lincolnshire as commissioners for securing the peace of the commonwealth. In many other counties, too, the same small groups of godly zealots served as both ejectors and commissioners.

Walter Bushnell, who was ejected from the living of Box in Wiltshire in 1656, subsequently accused some of the Wiltshire ejectors of maliciously hounding him out of his cure. His detailed – though not necessarily entirely objective – account of the way he was proceeded against during the first half of 1656 was published in 1660, probably as part of his successful attempt to regain the living from his successor. In January 1656, Bushnell received a warrant from the ejectors summoning him to appear before them to answer charges of profaning the sabbath, frequenting inns, gambling with his parishioners, using the Book of Common Prayer and the sign of the cross in baptism, attempting 'uncleanness' with several women, and associating with some of those involved in the uprising in the west country in the spring of 1655. In his account of the subsequent proceedings, he claimed that the small group of ejectors who were most active in pursuing the case against him suppressed evidence in his favour, interfered with witnesses and relied on the testimony of professional informers.[42]

But, although ejectors were active in many parts of the country during late 1655 and 1656, their initiatives did not bring about the wholesale purge of the parochial ministry they had been hoping to achieve. In most counties, fewer than five ministers were forced out and across the entire country only around 130 ministers seem to have been deprived during the time the major-generals were active in the provinces. This figure represents less than two per cent of livings in the country and only about six per cent of the total of somewhat over 2,000 clergy who suffered ejection at some point between 1640 and 1660. Nor was there any direct correlation between the level of involvement of individual major-generals and the number of ministers deprived within their associations. In Cheshire, Lancashire and Staffordshire, where Charles Worsley had pursued the matter with great urgency for more than six months, only around seven ministers can be positively identified as having been ejected during this period. By contrast, in the six western counties which John Desborough controlled and around which he made only two relatively short tours in 1655 and 1656, around forty ministers – or nearly a third of the national total – lost their livings at the hands of the local ejectors during 1656.[43]

This failure of the major-generals and their allies to carry out the more substantial purge that both their masters in London and their godly allies in the provinces had been calling for is attributable to a number of factors. In the first place, given that large numbers of those clergymen most opposed to the ideals of the godly English commonwealth had been removed from office during the previous decade, it is likely that the persistent godly jeremiads about the wide prevalence of ignorance and scandal within the ministry of the mid 1650s seriously overstated the need for further reform. While a few disaffected ministers remained in post and continued to behave in a manner which was wholly unacceptable to the Interregnum authorities, the great majority of their clerical colleagues had, by the mid 1650s, accommodated themselves to the new order and were, outwardly at least, conforming to the liturgical and moral precepts laid down by Cromwell's government.

Secondly, although the ejection process as outlined in the 1654 ordinance appeared straightforward enough, the reality on the ground proved rather different and the ejectors frequently found themselves embroiled in complicated and time-consuming procedures. Accused clerics could delay the proceedings by claiming they needed more time to prepare their defences; Worsley, for example, reported to Thurloe in March 1656 that, although the Lancashire ejectors had removed a few ministers, they had been unable to proceed against 'diverse others' who had argued they were 'not redy at that time'.[44] In addition, the ejectors' witnesses could not always be relied upon to appear at the appointed time and place, and on occasions inconveniently changed their testimony at the last moment. At least one such witness, Christopher Mead of Lastingham in Yorkshire, got into serious trouble for doing this. At the Easter quarter sessions for the north riding of Yorkshire held at Thirsk in April 1656, Mead was brought before the justices accused of 'deluding the commissioners for ejecting scandalous and ignorant ministers and schoolmasters and refusing to prove what formerly he offered to prove'.[45] Furthermore, examining the often conflicting evidence of those witnesses who did testify for or against an accused cleric could take the ejectors many hours and still fail to provide any conclusive proof of guilt. Robert Beake, the mayor of Coventry, sat with his fellow Warwickshire ejectors on at least five separate occasions in December 1655 and January 1656, but during these two months only one minister appears to have been removed from his living as a result of their investigations.[46]

The lengthy and complicated nature of the proceedings is illustrated by Walter Bushnell's acount of his ejection from the parish of Box. Following his summons in January 1656, he appeared before the Wiltshire ejectors on no fewer than seven separate occasions. The hearings were held in inns in Marlborough, Lavington, Calne and Salisbury and often lasted all day. Bushnell remarked of the sixth meeting at Lavington that a 'very long debate' occurred and that the ejectors 'met with more obstruction in the business then they dream't of'. As a result of such 'obstruction', it was a full six months before the protracted hearings had run their course and Bushnell was eventually removed from office along with a number of his fellow Wiltshire ministers in July 1656.[47]

Another important reason why no more ministers were deprived was that, beyond the confines of the small godly caucuses surrounding the major-generals, there appears to have been little appetite in the population for extensive ejections. Even some of those named to the ejection commissions appear to have been less than totally enthusiastic. The Gloucestershire remonstrance to Cromwell in the summer of 1655 had blamed the lack of progress on the refusal of many of those appointed the previous year to become involved in the work, and following their arrival in their associations a number of the major-generals came to the same conclusion. At the start of 1656, John Desborough told Cromwell that little progress had been made in Bristol and Gloucestershire 'and the reason is for want of active commissioners'.[48] Charles Worsley reported from Lancashire in mid January 1656 that 'in these countyes wee can hardly get a coram, there being so few named in it, and some that are dead, and some that will not act'; two weeks later, he added that fewer than five ejectors were active in Lancashire and that several meetings had consequently been abandoned as inquorate.[49] Robert Lilburne faced a similar struggle to meet the quorums for the ejection commissions in Yorkshire and Durham during the early months of 1656.[50]

The most obvious way to remedy this problem of a shortage of active ejectors was to appoint new men to the commissions. Desborough, Lilburne, and Worsley certainly sent Thurloe lists of names of those they believed would be willing to act, and some of their fellow major-generals may also have done so.[51] By December 1655, the council had set up a subcommittee headed by John Lambert to consider these nominations but this body was to prove very slow in its response to the problem.[52] Several of the major-generals were clearly frustrated by the delays. In March 1656, Worsley asked Thurloe to take action to appoint the men he had suggested some weeks before, adding in a somewhat aggrieved tone that he had gone to some trouble over them.[53] The same month, Lilburne requested Cromwell to send him an order for the appointment of new ejectors 'that the work of purging corrupt ministers may not sticke for the want of commissioners for the more effectuall carrying on that affaire'.[54] In early April, the council referred a list of suggested additions to Lambert's group, but it was not until four months later that it received its recommendations and finally took some decisive steps to remedy the problem by appointing well over a hundred new ejectors to commissions in fourteen counties. Thirty-eight of these, or around a third of the total, were appointed to serve in the north-western association which Tobias Bridge had inherited from Worsley following the latter's death in June.[55] This move, however, came far too late for the major-generals, for a few weeks later they were recalled to Westminster and as a consequence were unable to coordinate the work of these new expanded ejection commissions.

If some of those named in the 1654 ordinance were generally unwilling to take part in the work of ejection, the population as a whole was even less inclined to become involved in the harrying of their local ministers. One major-general who seems to have appreciated this was John Desborough. In the summer of 1656, he drew up an order which was to be read aloud in every parish in Bristol and afterwards nailed to the doors of the city's churches, in which he stated that some of the 'disaffected' parishioners and church-wardens of the city had encouraged 'malignant and scandalous' ministers to officiate at public services 'to the confirminge of the common people in their way of disaffection and to the discouragement of godly and faithful ministers'. He instructed the churchwardens to ensure that in future only those ministers approved of by the government be allowed to preach or administer the sacraments, and stipulated that if any of them disobeyed the order and continued to allow ejected ministers to officiate in their parishes, they should be reported to him so that he could refer them to the council 'to answer their contempt'.[56] The impression given by this order that many of Bristol's inhabitants were turning a blind eye to the continued involvement of 'malignant' clergy in public worship was probably an accurate one, and it almost certainly obtained in many other parts of the country too. Given this climate, it is no surprise that, for all the efforts of the major-generals and their allies, only a very small minority of the clergymen in the country were presented to the ejectors by their parishioners.

Those who were forced to appear before them had frequently been accused by small unrepresentative groups of hardline local puritans, sometimes with the support of those with a personal grudge against the minister or those who hoped to profit from his removal. Walter Bushnell's case again conforms to this pattern. One of the moving spirits behind his prosecution appears to have been the prominent local puritan from Bath, George Long, who had denounced him to the Wiltshire ejectors as one 'not well reported by the godly'. For his part, Bushnell likened Long, who had also given testimony against a number of other accused clerics in the west country, to the biblical Ishmael whose 'hand is against every man' and described Long's godliness as akin to that of 'the Chief Priest and elders, scribes and Pharisees'. The active Wiltshire ejectors and their allies such as Long were only able to persuade around seventeen men and women from the Box area to testify against Bushnell and, according to the accused cleric, even this small group was unrepresentative of the generality of his parishioners in that it included a number of Baptists and Quakers as well as a group of individuals who were notorious as sabbath breakers. Bushnell also claimed that one of the witnesses against him was a former innkeeper who had lost his licence after he had accused him of keeping a disorderly house and who had been promised he would get his licence back if he testifed against him, and that another was bribed into giving evidence with the promise of the post of parish register of Box.[57]

Bushnell, of course, was a far from unbiased commentator, but his distaste for the ejectors' proceedings was shared by a clergyman of a very different religious persuasion: Ralph Josselin, the godly minister of Earls Colne in Essex. Josselin, who had been a strong supporter of parliament since the early 1640s, was generally well disposed towards Cromwell's government and a close personal friend of his local major-general, Hezekiah Haynes. At the end of February 1656, he was summoned along with all the other clergy and schoolmasters in his county to a meeting of the Essex ejectors at Chelmsford. Although he himself was in little personal danger from the ejectors, he was deeply troubled by what he saw as the 'rigour' of their proceedings and the extreme anti-clericalism displayed by some of them, and he afterwards commented in his diary:

> for my part I saw no beauty in the day, neither doe I joy to see ministers put under the lay power, and thus on their head. Such is the affection of some that would be counted the first friends of god and religion, [that they] hoped wee should have been sent from thence to the Barbados, lord remember us for we are become a reproach.[58]

Such comments by one of the regime's supporters, would appear to confirm the impression that the population as a whole had little stomach for ejections and those that did take place were the result of agitation by unrepresentative minorities rather than any groundswell of popular opinion.

A final reason for the major-generals' failure to achieve a more substantial purge was the lack of support they received from the central government. As has already been seen, the council was very slow to react to the major-generals' requests for more ejectors. Moreover, as with the decimation tax, a number of the ministers who were proceeded against by local ejectors were subsequently allowed to retain their livings after they had petitioned Cromwell and his advisers in London, claiming that they had amended their ways and adopted a godly lifestyle.[59] The government's biggest climbdown with regard to the 'malignant' clergy, however, came over the order preventing ejected ministers from preaching or conducting public services using the Book of Common Prayer, or from acting as chaplains or tutors in private households. Originally due to come into force in on 1 November 1655, it was delayed first until the beginning of December and then again until the new year. On 30 November 1655, the diarist John Evelyn attended a Book of Common Prayer communion service at St Gregory's in London at which, as he put it, the minister, George Wild, preached 'the funeral sermon of preaching', taking as his text St Paul's farewell remarks to the Corinthians at the end of his second letter. Evelyn, who was clearly very distressed by the imminent ban, likened Cromwell to Julian the Apostate, who had tried to reintroduce paganism to the Roman Empire, and commented in his diary that 'this was the mournfullest day that in my life I had seene, or the church of England herselfe since the Reformation.'[60]

As it turned out, Evelyn need not have been so despondent. Although the ban did eventually come into force on 1 January, over the next few weeks a number of prominent conservative clergymen, in particular John Gauden and the archbishop of Armagh, James Ussher, made representations to Cromwell both in person and in print on behalf of their fellow conservative ministers.

Ussher, who was a cleric for whom Cromwell seems to have had real respect, was seriously ill at the start of 1656 and would die soon afterwards. He spent his last weeks organising a petition against the ban which he presented to the protector in February. It was probably his intervention which did most to persuade Cromwell that it would be unwise to enforce the order strictly, on the grounds that it would leave large numbers of clerics and their families utterly destitute and thus stiffen them in their animosity towards his regime. That Cromwell may as a result have become genuinely concerned about the social impact of a strict enforcement of the ban is suggested by comments he made to a group of army officers in March 1657, when he accused them of having urged him to purge the ministry and 'rather than fail, to starve them out'.[61] While the order was not officially withdrawn, it appears never to have been properly implemented. Ejected ministers like Wild continued to preach in public even in the capital and many others retained their posts as chaplains and tutors.[62] Numbers of them also continued to defy the 1653 civil marriage act and marry couples in private religious ceremonies and, while Charles Worsley arrested a number of ministers for officiating at these clandestine weddings, beyond the confines of his north-western association they seem to have done so with relative impunity.[63]

Overall, then, the effect of the major-generals' attempt to purge the parochial ministry was negligible. Despite their undoubted keenness to remove from it those elements hostile or lukewarm towards the godly reformation they were seeking, a combination of the shortage of time available to them, their many other commitments and the procedural issues outlined above ensured that only around two in every hundred ministers were removed from office while they were in power in the localities, and that another important element of the campaign to create the godly society would remain unrealised.

Another area where some of the major-generals made a real effort to achieve reform but were once again ultimately unsuccessful was the problem of how to deal with the poor. The standard early-modern approach to poverty emphasised the sharp divide between the deserving or 'impotent' poor, whose inability to fend for themselves was in no way their own fault, and the large numbers of itinerant 'sturdy beggars', whose straitened circumstances were believed to stem from their own idleness and immorality. While the former were considered to be deserving of various forms of practical help from their more fortunate neighbours, the latter were regarded as dangerous nuisances who defiled the well-ordered Christian state. As such, they were to be severely punished before being either returned to their parish of birth or set to work in houses of correction.

The attitude of the major-generals to the poor of their associations was clearly marked by this distinction between the deserving and undeserving poor, and most of their energies were directed towards the attempt to eradicate vagrancy by rounding up the idle and dissolute and holding them in local gaols while the government in London finalised the details for their transportation out of the country. James Berry, for example, reported from Shrewsbury in January 1656 that he had imprisoned in that town 'divers lewde fellowes', who he believed were 'fitt to grind sugar cane or plant tobacco', and in April Rowland Dawkins and the commissioners for Glamorgan sent the council a list of those in their county they wished to see transported.[64] Charles Worsley, meanwhile, supervised the arrest of a considerable number of 'wandring idle persons' in his three northern counties during December 1655 and January 1656, and contemplated tackling the problem by making the towns and villages on the borders of his association responsible for preventing wandering vagrants from entering his area.[65]

William Boteler began rounding up individuals in his district within a few weeks of his appointment as major-general, and in late March 1656 he sent Thurloe a list of those he had arrested in the four counties of his association. In Huntingdonshire he had secured a suspected highwayman who abused his wife 'by words and blows', and in Rutland a 'pitiful drunken wretch … every way as prophane as the devil can make him'. Several others had been held in Bedfordshire, and around a dozen in his native Northamptonshire. This last group included a Londoner who had been wandering around the county for a year and had persuaded two women to give him £10 after promising to marry them; two suspected highwaymen; a man who had brewed beer for many years without a licence and was suspected to run a brothel; a 'mad ranting blade' who had killed several men in a brawl at Wellingborough; and seven unemployed single men who were drunk and quarrelsome and 'fit for overseas service'.[66] Several weeks later in mid April, he wrote again to Thurloe to request that some action be taken to send these men out of the country, adding that he could round up several hundred more with only twenty-four hours notice 'and the countreys would thinke themselves well ridd of them'.[67]

It was, however, Edward Whalley who seems to have been most active in the attempt to eradicate vagrancy. On several occasions in January 1656 he informed Thurloe that he had been suppressing beggars and imprisoning idle and dangerous persons ready for deportation, and in February he requested Thurloe to 'cleere our prysons' as they were filling up with those he had arrested.[68] The same month, he ordered the mayor of Coventry, Robert Beake, to supervise the repair of his city's house of correction.[69] In April 1656, he went so far as to declare to Thurloe that 'you may ride all over Nottingham-shire and not see a beggar or wandering rogue', adding that he hoped soon to have cleared all his other counties of vagrants.[70] By the summer of 1656, he had filled most of the gaols of his associations with such vagrants and was becoming increasingly anxious that the government should relieve the burden this placed on the surrounding communities by moving quickly to deport them.[71]

In addition to taking such direct action themselves, in some parts of the country the major-generals stimulated other local officials into implementing more fully the laws against vagrancy. In March 1656, the London and Westminster justices of the peace issued a set of orders calling for a stricter enforcement of the laws concerning jugglers, tinkers, peddlars, petty chapmen, 'Eygptians and counterfeit Egyptians', and 'all idle persons going about in any countrey, either begging or using any subtile craft or unlawfull games and plaies or faining themselves to have knowledge of physiogomy, palmistrey or other like crafty science or pretending they can tell destinies, fortunes or such other like fantasticall imaginations.'[72] Similar orders were subsequently issued by a number of other county benches, including those in Hertfordshire, Nottinghamshire, Somerset, Warwickshire and Wiltshire.[73] In Nottinghamshire, the JPs also appointed two new marshals to apprehend rogues and vagabonds.[74]

The early months of 1656 saw a concerted effort by the governors of London to reduce the scale of the vagrancy problem in the capital. In February, the mayor and corporation ordered the constables of the city to enforce more vigorously the laws against beggars, 'the vermin of the commonwealth [who] doth now swarm in or about this city'. They instructed them to arrest anyone found begging and to dispatch those born in London to the capital's house of correction. Those from other parts of the country were to be whipped and then sent away to their places of birth. They also stipulated that all constables should display their staves of office outside their homes so they could be quickly found by anyone who wished to report a beggar, and that they should deliver lists of the vagrants they had dealt with to the city authorities at Weavers Hall on the first Wednesday of every month. The London corporation further emphasised its determination to tackle the problem by joining the Nottinghamshire JPs in appointing what the *Public Intelligencer* described as 'a competent number of able men under a sallary' to assist the unpaid force of city constables in the work of apprehending beggars.[75]

In some parts of the country, therefore, during the spring and summer of 1656 itinerant rogues and vagabonds experienced even more hostility and harassment from the settled communities through which they passed than they were normally accustomed to. Despite this, there is no real evidence that these initiatives by the major-generals and their allies resulted in any overall reduction in their numbers. To rid one area of its beggars was often merely to increase their prevalence elsewhere, a fact which was acknowledged by the grand jury at the Epiphany quarter sessions in Worcestershire in January 1657, which attributed the increase in the numbers of vagrants within their county to the 'activenesse of other counties in taking care and course to free themselves of such burthensome company'.[76]

The only way that the campaign against the idle poor might perhaps have met with some lasting success was if central government had acted decisively to ensure that those secured by the major-generals and their allies were quickly conveyed to convenient ports and then transported abroad. Here again, however, Cromwell and his advisers badly let down the major-generals. The council had established a subcommittee to consider the question of transportation by the beginning of March 1656, but the following months saw no significant moves to bring this about.[77] In April, Whalley complained to Thurloe that the government's inertia was discouraging his commissioners from securing more beggars and he implored him take some rapid action, commenting: 'a better worke for the safety and satisffying the country cannot bee; I wonder it should be so much neglected.'[78] The next few months, however, saw no response from the council and by midsummer the prisons of Whalley's east midlands' association were full of 'horse stealers, robbers and other condemned rogues'. In July and again in August, Whalley wrote to Thurloe to complain bitterly about the government's failure to organise the transportation of these prisoners.[79]

Perhaps as a result of Whalley's badgering, in mid August the council did finally stir itself into action and handed over direct responsibility for the proposed deportations to the new Jamaica committee. The major-generals were ordered to send lists of all those being held in custody in their associations to this committee, which was to select from them a thousand men for military service in Sweden and to negotiate with the merchant community about the provision of ships to transport the remainder to North America or the Carribean. Writing to all the major-generals on the 16 August to inform them of the council's decision, Henry Lawrence assured them that the removal of those in their gaols would now 'very easyly and speedily be effected'.[80] This proved, however, to be a wildly over-optimistic promise. Preoccupied by the imminent election, the major-generals had little time to organise the conveyance of their prisoners to the coast. Nor is there any direct evidence that the Jamaica committee ever produced any ships or that anyone was actually deported. After the major-generals had been recalled from their associations in mid September, many of the vagrants they had gaoled must subsequently have been released by local communities which could no longer bear the costs of keeping them incarcerated.

The only major-general who appears to have devoted a significant amount of time and energy to an attempt to improve the lot of the deserving poor of his association was Edward Whalley. In January 1656, Whalley reported to Thurloe that he had taken steps to provide for the poor of his association, and the following spring he heaped praise on Matthew Hale, who had presided over the assizes courts in the east midlands, for 'in speciall manner takeinge care of poore men in their causes without which some had suffered'.[81] Furthermore, in a letter to Thurloe at the end of March 1656, Whalley urged the government to find remedies for what he portrayed as the very serious problems of inadequate regulation of markets and false weights and measures. With regard to the first of these, he argued that, because markets did not generally begin until one o'clock in the afternoon, many small farmers who had to travel some distance to them were given only a relatively short time to sell their produce and were often forced to dispose of what they had left in the late afternoon to maltsters at reduced rates so that they could begin their homeward journeys. He suggested that the government should stipulate that markets should start at ten or eleven in the morning and that the major-generals should be required to enforce this regulation, which, he claimed, would give 'great satisfaction to the poore husbandmen who deserve what helpe you can affoard them'.[82]

Whalley also urged the government to take action against the many traders and innkeepers who he claimed either dispensed short measures or over-charged the public for their produce and services. When nothing had been done by midsummer, he raised the issue again with Thurloe. Pointing out that it had been identified as a grievance by the grand juries of all his counties, he commented that 'in vayne it is for either the countrey or us to propose good thinges if, after they come to you, they shal be buryed.' He urged the government to issue a proclamation establishing a standard system of weights and measures for the whole country, and to give the major-generals direct responsibility for its enforcement. He added that, if no remedy was forthcoming before the next assizes, he would be 'ashamed to appear before the face of the country'.[83] Once again, there is no record of any positive central government response to these suggestions.

Another important social problem which occupied Whalley's attention was enclosure. Over the course of the sixteenth and early seventeenth centuries, the counties of his east midlands association had seen a considerable amount of enclosure of common lands and conversion from arable to pastoral cultivation, and throughout the same period the social consequences of these agrarian changes had been hotly disputed. During the early 1650s, a deter-mined local campaign against enclosure had been led by the Leicestershire minister, John Moore, who was the author of several treatises critical of the practice and who, in 1653, had persuaded the corporation of Leicester to petition Barebone's Parliament for action to prevent depopulation.[84] When Whalley arrived in the east midlands in the autumn of 1655, Moore and the Leicester authorities attempted to enlist his help and soon found him sympathetic to their cause. In the spring of 1656, Whalley asked the Leicester corporation to draw up a detailed survey of the scale of depopulation resulting from local enclosure. On receipt of it, he called all the interested parties before him in early April and ordered that henceforth two-thirds of the county should be kept 'in tillage' and that 'for the performance of this, they were to enter large bonds to the protector and his successors'. Reporting his decision to Thurloe, he remarked: 'upon these terms I hope God will not be provoaked, the poor not wronged, depopulation prevented, and the state not dampnified.'[85]

Six months later at the end of 1656, Whalley attempted to take the issue further by introducing into the second protectorate parliament a bill 'for improvement of waste-grounds, and regulating of commons and common-able lands, and preventing depopulations'. Speaking in favour of the bill, which would have referred questions of the division of common land to three commissioners sitting with local juries, he stated that he himself would lose out if it became law as all his common lands were enclosed, but that it was nonetheless 'for the general good to prevent depopulation and discourage[ment] to the plough, which is the very support of the commonwealth'. His bill was, however, defeated on its first reading after coming under fierce attack from several MPs who clearly saw it as a serious threat to their property rights.[86]

While Whalley's attempts to introduce economic and social reforms favourable to the lower orders of his association were largely thwarted by the lethargy or hostility they encountered at Whitehall and Westminster, there is some evidence to suggest that his concern to ameliorate the lot of the impotent poor may have produced some positive, albeit temporary results in at least one of his counties. A. L. Beier's study of the operation of the poor relief system in Warwickshire has revealed that the county justices there dealt with a higher number of poor relief cases during 1656 than at any other time during either the 1630s or the Interregnum. While the average number of cases for the 1650s was fifty-four per annum, the figure for 1656 was sixty-nine. The only other year when more than sixty cases were recorded was 1650, when the plight of the poor had been worsened by several bad harvests. Beier's conclusion was that Whalley had 'clearly caused the volume of cases to swell by his militant activism' and that the marked rise in the total was the product of the 'injection of religious zeal into the civic arena'.[87]

The one aspect of the moral reform agenda where some of the major-generals may have had a rather more significant, albeit once again short-lived impact was the attempt to regulate alehouses and reduce drunkenness. All early-modern governments were well aware of the potentially harmful economic and social consequences of excessive drinking, and the supervision of the numbers and condition of the thousands of English and Welsh inns, taverns and alehouses had thus been an important part of the work of the local magistracy for many years. The godly were, of course, especially hostile to these establishments, which they regarded as 'dens of satan', and throughout the late 1640s and early 1650s puritan magistrates from all parts of the country had made strenuous efforts to regulate them and reduce their numbers. Even they, however, did not wish to eradicate all inns and taverns, for it was generally accepted that some such establishments were needed to provide board and lodging for travellers. Following their arrival in their associations, the major-generals' efforts in this context were focused on the attempt to reduce the overall number of alehouses by suppressing those where disorder was known to occur and which were sited away from main thoroughfares or had no overnight accommodation, and also to ensure that the licensees who ran the remaining establishments were respected members of their local comunities, who were well disposed towards the protectoral regime and would not tolerate drunkenness, gaming or sexual indiscretion on their premises.

Their impact in his area can be observed both in their own actions and in the initiatives taken by a number of county benches during their period of rule in the provinces. In December 1655, Edward Whalley told Thurloe that he intended to instruct the JPs of his counties to suppress all alehouses 'judged unnecessary' and to send him lists of those they had closed and those they had allowed to remain. A few weeks later he confirmed to him they were now 'depressing alehouses, which were growne to incredible numbers'.[88] As a result of his prompting, the justices who attended the Epiphany quarter sessions for Nottinghamshire in January 1656 complained about the excessive numbers of alehouses and tippling houses in their county and denounced

> the great disorder therein committed by harbouring of thieves and robbers and suspitious persons, as alsoe for suffering persons to continue and drink in their houses contrary to severall lawes and statutes in that behalf through the neglect of constables, jurors and other officers in not presenting the said offences to the end the same may be reformed.

To remedy these abuses, they instructed the high constables and grand jurymen of the county to compile a list of those alehouses suitable to be retained and to suppress all the rest.[89] The same month, their counterparts in Warwickshire decided that one third of the county's alehouses should be suppressed and again ordered their high constables to bring in lists of all those within their divisions, marking out those they believed should close.[90] In February 1656, Whalley wrote to the mayor of Coventry, Robert Beake, asking him to reduce the number of alehouses in his city, and the corporation responded by ordering that twenty-seven should be suppressed at the next licensing session for the city.[91]

Hezekiah Haynes similarly galvanised the justices of East Anglia into action. At their respective quarter sessions meetings at Easter 1656, the Essex and Norfolk JPs passed an identical set of orders for the suppression of local alehouses. These stipulated that henceforth all licences were to be issued at public meetings of the justices and signed by at least two magistrates; that they were to be granted only to men 'of honest life and conversacon' who had obtained a certificate of suitability signed by their local minister and three other well affected neighbours; that all licensees were to enter into recognizances for their good behaviour and provide two sureties who would do the same; and that licences should in future only be granted for alehouses which were on main highways and could accommodate strangers. In order that the total number of alehouses could be reduced to 'as few as may bee', both sets of JPs also committed themselves to 'use all possible diligence and care in the vigorous execucon of the lawes for the suppressing of unlicenced alehouses, and in causeing constables and other officers to bee dexterous in discharge of their dutyes for the discovering, presenteing, conviccon and punishment of all such offenders.'[92] All the Norfolk alehousekeepers were required to attend licensing meetings during Whit week. One of those who appeared at the King's Lynn meeting and, according to his local constables, falsely claimed to be able to provide accommodation and stabling, was later presented before the justices who ordered that his premises be inspected.[93] At the town sessions held at Yarmouth in September 1656, meanwhile, the exceptionally high number of ninety-six individuals were indicted for transgressing the new alehouse orders.[94] A similar set of orders to those issued in Essex and Norfolk was passed by the Hertfordshire bench in July 1656.[95]

In December 1655, the Caernarvonshire justices received a letter from James Berry in which he described alehouses as a 'spreading gangrene' and asked them to take action to reduce their number, 'like men that will be found faythfull to your trust'.[96] It is likely that Berry sent similar letters to the justices in his other counties, for the following month the Shropshire JPs issued an order calling on their constables to suppress superfluous alehouses which they described as 'the great nurseries of mischief and impiety in this commonwealth', and instructing them to bring a list of all their licensed alehouses to succeeding quarter sessions.[97] In February 1656, Berry informed Thurloe that he had prevailed upon the corporation of Monmouth to close down a number of the town's more disorderly alehouses and to impose heavy fines upon and imprison some of the municipal bailiffs who had run them. He added that the move had caused a considerable stir amongst the local godly 'who are in this place a pittiful people'.[98] At the Worcestershire quarter sessions at Easter 1656, the grand jury requested that for the 'suppressing of inordinate drinking (a vice now comon and very offensive to God and prejudiciall to the comon wealth)', no alehouse keepers should be 'permitted to suffer men to stay in their houses att unseasonable tymes or any longer than the statute allowes'. The following summer and autumn, they presented a larger than normal number of individuals for selling ale without a licence.[99]

At the beginning of 1656, the justices of the west riding of Yorkshire ordered their chief and petty constables to set about closing down all unlicensed alehouses situated outside towns and to report their progress to the next assizes. Several months later, Robert Lilburne sent the Yorkshire justices an order 'for the reformacion of several abuses', and at the Easter 1656 sessions held at Pontefract the west riding JPs responded by drawing up a detailed set of orders for the regulation of alehouses. These stipulated that no unincorporated town was to possess more than two alehouses, that those who 'clubbed for ales' in private houses were to be prosecuted, and that all 'hogg feasts, goose feasts, and revellings at country weddings' were to be prohibited. Local clergymen were enjoined to inform on any parish constables who neglected to enforce these new rules. The justices also wrote back to Lilburne, thanking him for putting them in mind of 'so necessary and needful a worke', and promising that they would publicise the new orders widely and enforce them vigorously. Over the following months, a number of individuals were indicted in the west riding for offences involving drinking, gaming and sabbath violation.[100] In Somerset, the grand jury for the 1656 summer assizes presented as one of their grievances 'the unnecessary number of alehouses' in their county and 'the common profanacion of the Lord's Day by the frequent resort of ill disposed persons to innes and alehouses on that day', and the Somerset justices subsequently mounted a campaign to close down such unlicensed alehouses.[101] Orders for the suppression of unnecessary alehouses and the regulation of licensees were issued in Kent in early 1656, and both before and after their publication the Kentish justices dealt with a number of petitions from alehousekeepers for the continuation of their licences.[102] August 1656 also saw a flurry of prosecutions for tippling at Salisbury in Wiltshire.[103]

Andrew Coleby's study of local government in seventeenth-century Hampshire has shown that the justices there had been working hard to control alehouses for some time before William Goffe's arrival.[104] One of the unintended effects of their activity, however, had been to prompt some of the county's inhabitants to organise private drinking parties, known as 'help-ales' or 'merry-meetings', in their own homes. As in the west riding, these involved groups of neighbours clubbing together to buy a barrel of beer and then gathering on a Saturday evening in the house of one of their number to drink through the night. In the summer of 1656, the Hampshire JPs decided to take action to outlaw these parties. They instructed their constables to search diligently for such help-ales and to publicise the fact that all those caught either attending them or supplying beer for them would be bound over to appear before the county bench.[105] At the following quarter sessions at Michaelmas 1656, several individuals were duly presented for allowing such disorderly events to occur in their houses.[106] Preoccupied by the collection of the decimation tax and his problems over the payment of his militia troops, Goffe left much of the work of alehouse suppression to the local justices. On at least one occasion, however, he did intervene personally, by persuading one William Boes of Winchester to bring an indictment against William Homard for keeping an unlicensed and disorderly alehouse in the city.[107]

The capital and its surrounding area also witnessed efforts to suppress disorderly alehouses. In December 1655, the Middlesex JPs banned constables from holding licences on the grounds that they sometimes kept those they had arrested in their own alehouses and charged them excessive amounts for their board and lodging.[108] The following March, a meeting of the London and Westminster justices attended by Sir John Barkstead issued a public warning to all those who kept inns and alehouses in the vicinity of the capital that they would lose their licences if they profaned the sabbath by receiving any travellers after midnight on Saturday or allowing any guests to depart before one o'clock on Monday morning, or if they were convicted of swearing or drunkenness or of allowing 'billiard tables, shovelboard tables, dice, cards, tables, nine pins, pigeonholes. bowling alley or bowling green or any other unlawful game' to be played on their premises.[109]

Undoubtedly, however, the part of the country which witnessed the most concerted effort to suppress alehouses was Charles Worsley's association in the north-west. Worsley's determination to reduce the numbers of what he described as 'the very wombe that brings forth all manner of wickednesse' verged on the obsessional.[110] Within a few days of arriving in his association, he had put pressure on the towns of his area to issue proclamations against drunkenness and to organise nightly searches for drunkards, and in mid November 1655 he reported to Thurloe that some of them, like Nantwich, had been quick to respond positively.[111] In mid January 1656, he attended the Epiphany quarter sessions meeting in Staffordshire at which the JPs passed an order calling for the suppression of unnecessary alehouses.[112] In his native Lancashire, meanwhile, he and his commissioners issued orders at the start of 1656 requiring all the petty constables, ministers and 'moste honeste and religious men' of the county to meet with them at Whalley on 22 January and bring with them a list of all the alehouses within their parishes along with the names of those that kept them.[113] Two days later, he wrote to Thurloe to inform him that the meeting had agreed to suppress around two hundred alehouses in the Blackburn area.[114] Shortly afterwards, several hundred others in the Salford area were also earmarked for closure.[115] Some of the Lancashire justices were particularly committed to Worsley's campaign and pursued alehouse offenders not only at formal quarter sessions' meetings but also at their own petty session hearings. As Derek Hirst has pointed out, during 1656 Edmund Hopwood, a justice from the south-east of the county, dealt in this way with more than seventy individuals accused of alehouse offences.[116]

A similar campaign was conducted in Cheshire. In January 1656, Worsley prevailed upon the Chester authorities to appoint five individuals to conduct nightly house-to-house searches for drunkards within their city.[117] The following month, he reported to Thurloe that he was supervising the suppression of considerable numbers of alehouses in the county, closing down a number of local breweries, and forcing those who were allowed to retain their licences or to continue brewing to give bonds for their 'good order and discipline'.[118] His Cheshire commissioners wrote the same day to confirm that the work was indeed proceeding with speed and to claim that around two hundred alehouses had already been closed in and around Chester.[119] That these initiatives had some real impact on the ground is revealed by the fact that more than twenty individuals petitioned the Cheshire justices in the summer of 1656 to protest about the suppression of their alehouses and to ask for their reinstatement as licensees.[120]

Assessing the national impact of these initiatives is a far from straightforward task. The patchiness of surviving quarter sessions records makes it impossible to give precise figures for the number of alehouses suppressed during 1656, but the total must clearly have run into hundreds. A large proportion of these was situated in Worsley's three counties, where for a short time at least it must have become quite difficult to conceal a disorderly house from the authorities. On the other hand, the total number of alehouses closed during the major-generals' period of power would still have represented only a small fraction of the tens of thousands of drinking establishments which existed throughout England and Wales. The great majority of these survived the major-generals' attentions and continued to offer their clients the same opportunities for refreshment, conviviality and – in the eyes of the godly – sin as they had for centuries.

Even in Worsley's native county of Lancashire, where reform had had the most impact, the results appear to have been less dramatic than some local puritans had hoped. In late 1656 or early 1657, twenty-five godly constables from the Salford area wrote to their local JPs to complain about the abortive nature of the moral reform initiatives in their locality. They began by stating that some months before they 'did not a little rejoice' that the justices had set about reforming 'severall things amisse amongst us, as the multitude of unnecessarie alehouses, bastardy, swearing and profanation of the Lord's day'. They pointed out that they had played a full part in the prosecution of this work and that the ungodly of their communities had begun to express genuine fears that they might suffer severe punishment for these offences. They then, however, went on to declare:

> And yet we see litle or no reformation therof, but (farre contrary to our expectation)

many alehouse keepers by us presented to bee unfit and unnecessary (and thereupon suppressed) have since from some of you procured licenses; soe that offenders are rather hardened in their bad practices, which is no small discouragement to us hereafter to be employed in a worke of that nature (as of late wee or some of us by your worships are again called unto).[121]

Endemic dissatisfaction with the progress of moral reform was a defining trait of the godly psyche, but this petition would nevertheless seem to indicate that even within Worsley's association many of the targets of the major-general's reform initiatives had found ways of shielding themselves from the onslaught.

In those few places where local campaigns to close down alehouses had achieved some success prior to 1655, moreover, the arrival of the major-generals seems to have had little real impact on the continuing work of reform. Andrew Coleby has shown that in Hampshire, where the justices had been making serious attempts to control alehouses throughout the early 1650s, local regulation was largely unaffected by the presence of William Goffe in 1656.[122] C. D Gilbert's study of King's Norton in Worcestershire has similarly revealed that, as a result of the combined efforts of the local minister and JP, Thomas Hall and Richard Grevis, half of the parish's alehouses had been closed down in the two years before James Berry assumed responsibility for the county and that the major-general's subsequent arrival had no real impact upon their efforts.[123] Such small-scale local campaigns were not always this successful, but when pursued with vigour by magistrates and ministers residing in or very near the parochial communities at which they were directed, they had a greater chance of achieving their objectives than the more ambitious reform initiatives of the major-generals, which were necessarily coordinated at the remoter, regional level.

That the major-generals' campaign to regulate alehouses and drinking had proved a failure was freely acknowledged by one of those who had supported it most vociferously, the prominent presbyterian divine, Richard Baxter. In an assizes sermon preached before the Shropshire justices at Shrewsbury in the late summer of 1656, Baxter was forced to admit that 'though there hath lately bin a sharper attempt against them [alehouses] than ordinary, yet do they stand up as it were in defiance of all your endeavours'. He went on to complain that even his own parish of Kidderminster, which he described as 'as honest a town as any I know in England', was plagued by large numbers of drunkards who posed a serious threat to public order. He further commented that both there and elsewhere in the country 'still iniquity aboundeth, still drunkards are raging openly in the streetes and still the alesellers keep open shop for them', adding that some justices protected unlicensed alesellers and denounced those who tried to prosecute them as 'bussy fellows'.[124] A year later, in a set of directions for godly magistrates, he again complained:

> Never were there stricter laws and endeavours, and yet drunkenness and wickedness rageth in our streets, as if it were to scorn or dare the magistrate; and many honest people are so tired in the costly and fruitless prosecution that they are tempted to sit down and meddle no more and to entertain unworthy thoughts of magistracy.

Here, too, he expressed his intense frustration with this situation, declaring: 'Oh how much is God abused in alehouses in one day. And hitherto they have stood as in despight of all we can do.'[125]

What overall degree of success, then, should the major-generals be credited with in pursuing their cherished aim of creating the godly society? The verdict of the major-generals themselves and their master in London was very positive. As early as January 1656, Edward Whalley had reported to Thurloe that he believed real progress was being made, commenting:

> our presence I fynde is desired in all places and gives lyfe to all proceedings; besides they look upon it as a favour to them to have us in theyre county ... You cannot imagine what an awe it hath strucke into the spirits of wicked men, what incouragement it is to the godly, yea and I may say through God's mercy how it reconciles them amongst themselves through our weake endeavours.[126]

Charles Worsley was another who believed his tireless efforts were bringing desirable results. He wrote to Thurloe from Cheshire in March 1656 to assure him: 'wee are in a very good condition in this county ... this worke stirs up the good people to informe us of the conversation of all men, their carridge and behaviour, so that, truly, I thinke the good sober people never were in better hart than now, and so much owned.'[127] The following month, Rowland Dawkins wrote to Cromwell to give him a similarly upbeat assessment of his progress in Glamorgan, declaring: 'the effects of our work are very observeable; our enemies being much terrifyed, our freinds encouraged, our peace as much as may be by ev'ry humane ordinance and more (for wee hope this is of God) secured, and sin and wickednesse suppressed.'[128]

Cromwell also declared himself very satisfied with the major-generals' record in the area of moral reform. In March 1656, he suggested to the corporation of London that as a result of their first few months' work the whole country had grown 'stronger in virtue'.[129] Six months later, he told the newly assembled MPs of the second protectorate parliament that the major-generals had been 'more effectual towards the discountenancing of vice and settling of religion than anything done these fifty years', adding that they had successfully put down 'horse races, cockfightings and the like' and that 'if God give you a spirit of reformation you will preserve the nation from turning again to these fooleries.'[130]

The findings of this chapter suggest, however, that these positive contemporary assessments greatly exaggerated the success of the major-generals' campaign to bring about moral reform. Throughout the whole of England and Wales, a few hundred alehouses were closed, a few hundred wandering beggars were held for a while in prison, and rather more than a hundred 'malignant' ministers were expelled from their livings. In some parts of the country, too, it became more difficult for a while to organise or participate in popular sports and pastimes. This, however, represented only a very modest achievement and one which fell far short of the religious and cultural transformation for which the major-generals had been aiming. Their campaign for moral reform must thus be regarded as a clear failure.

It was a failure which in the first instance is attributable to the excessive workloads that the major-generals were forced to shoulder. The onerous demands of their other duties, in particular the decimation and security work, meant that some of them were never able to get to grips with the task of moral reform and that those who did, like Whalley and Worsley, could never fully concentrate upon it. In January 1656, Whalley explicitly told Thurloe that, although he was busy ejecting ministers, closing down alehouses and tackling social problems, he could 'not thoroughly end all' because of the need to supervise the collection of the decimation tax.[131] Nor was the ten-months' period during which they were active in the provinces anything like long enough to give them a realistic chance of achieving lasting change.

Another equally significant reason for their failure was the extreme difficulty of the task they had set themselves. Attempts by national governments to bring about radical changes in popular attitudes and behaviour are immensely challenging undertakings, and are always more likely to end in failure than success. Throughout the 1650s, the English and Welsh peoples showed themselves to be both strongly attached to their traditional festive culture and deeply antagonistic to the new godly one that Cromwell's government was attempting to impose upon them.[132] Despite their undoubted commitment to the campaign, in the face of widespread popular hostility and resentment Cromwell's major-generals simply did not possess the means to force people to behave in the manner they believed they should. But, if their attempt to build the godly nation remained unrealised, the major-generals' failure in this area was not without serious repercussions for the government. For enough of them had devoted sufficient time and energy to the project to make it abundantly clear to the English and Welsh people what life would be like were they ever to succeed. The election campaign of August 1656 would reveal just how unappealing a prospect this was for the great majority of the population.

NOTES

1 PRO, SP.18.100.42.

2 PRO, SP.18.100.43.

3 PRO, SP.18.101.136.

4 Anthony Fletcher, 'The Religious Motivation of Cromwell's Major-Generals', in D. Baker (ed.), *Religious Motivation: Biographical and Social Problems for the Church Historian*, Studies in Church History, 15 (1978), 263–4.

5 Bod. Lib., Rawlinson MSS, A 32, fols 373–6.

6 *Ibid.*, A 32, fols 517–20.

7 *Ibid.*, A 32, fols 715–18, 805–8.

8 *Ibid.*, A 32, fols 655–8.

9 *Ibid.*, A 32, fols 719–22.

10 *Ibid.*, A 36, fols 229–32.

11 Henry Fishwick (ed.), *The Notebook of the Reverend Thomas Jolley*, Chetham Soc. Publs, new series, 33 (1895), 127–8.

12 Quarter sessions material from 19 counties was consulted for this chapter. The references are as follows. Bedfordshire Record Office, QSM/1; Cheshire Record Office, QJB 2/7, extracts published as J. H. E. Bennett and J. C. Dewhurst (eds), *Quarter Sessions Records ... For the County Palatine of Chester, 1559–1760*, Records Society of Lancashire and Cheshire Publs, 94 (1940); Essex Record Office, Q/SO1, published as D. H. Allen (ed.), *Essex Quarter Sessions Order Book 1652–1661* (Chelmsford, 1974); Hampshire Record Office, Q1/3, Q4/1; W. Le Hardy (ed.), *Calendar to Sessions Books and Session Minute Books, 1619–1657*, Hertfordshire County Records, 5 (1928); Centre for Kentish Studies, Q/SB 6–7, Q/SO, E1, W2; Lancashire Record Office, Q/SO/2, 28, 29; J. C. Jeaffreson (ed.), *Middlesex County Records*, old series, 3 (London, 1974); D. E. Howell James (ed.), *Norfolk Quarter Sessions Order Book*, Norfolk Records Society, 26 (1955); Joan Wake (ed.), *Quarter Sessions Records of the County of Northants, 1630, 1657, 1657–8*, Northants Records Soc. Publs, 1 (1924); H. H. Copnall (ed.) *Nottingham County Records* (Nottingham, 1915); O. Wakeman and R. L. Kenyon (eds), *Orders of the Shropshire Quarter Sessions: Volume 1, 1638–1708*, Shropshire County Records, 11–12 (1908); E. H. Bates-Harbin (ed.), *Quarter Sessions Records for the County of Somerset*, vol. III, Somerset Records Society, 28 (1912); Staffordshire Record Office, Q/SO/6; S. C. Ratcliff and H. C. Johnson (eds), *Warwick County Records III* (Warwick, 1937); West Yorkshire Archive Service, QS 10/3, QS 4/4; Wiltshire Record Office, A1/150/11; Worcestershire Record Office, 110/BA/ 90–93; and J. C. Atkinson (ed.) *North Riding Quarter Sessions Records*, North Riding Records Society, 5 (1887).

13 During 1656 there were 12 indictments for fornication, 3 for adultery and 1 for rape. Most of these were concentrated at the Easter sessions at Pontefract; see West Yorkshire Archive Service, QS 4/4, fols, 181–250. Ronan Bennett's researches into the enforcement of justice in Interregnum Yorkshire have revealed that not only were sexual prosecutions in the west riding significantly higher in 1656 than in previous years, but that 1656 saw the highest overall number of indictments in that county of any year between 1638 and 1665. See Ronan A. H. Bennett, 'Enforcing the Law in Revolutionary England: Yorkshire *c.* 1640–*c.* 1660' (Unpub. Ph.D. thesis, University of London, 1988), p. 47.

14 Stephen K. Roberts, *Recovery and Restoration in an English County: Devon Local Administration, 1646–70* (Exeter, 1985), pp. 199–204.

15 Bod. Lib., Carte MSS, 131, fols 183–5.

16 Jeaffreson, *Middlesex County Records*, p. 252. Macfarlane, *Diary of Ralph Josselin*, p. 363; J. W. Willis Bund (ed.), *The Diary of Henry Townshend of Elmley Lovett 1640–1663*, Worcestershire Historical Soc. Publs, 31 part 1 (1920), 30–1.

17 Willis Bund, *Diary of Henry Townshend*, pp. 31–2; Bod. Lib., Carte MSS, 131, fols 183–5.

18 Bod. Lib., Carte MSS, 131, fols 179–80.

19 BL, E.494.2, *Mercurius Politicus*, 12–19 Jun. 1656.

20 Bod. Lib., Rawlinson MSS, A 40, fols 171–2.

21 Jean Mather, The Moral Code of the English Civil War and Interregnum', *The Historian*, 44 (1982), 207–28.

22 Bod. Lib., Rawlinson MSS, A33, fols 369–72, 515–18.

23 Peter Bloomfield 'The Cromwellian Commission in Kent, 1655–57', in Alec Detsicas and Nigel Yates (eds), *Studies in Modern Kentish History* (Maidstone, 1983), p. 20.

24 PRO, SP.25.77, pp. 110–11, 846–7.

25 PRO, SP.25.77, pp. 230, 920.

26 Bod. Lib., Rawlinson MSS, A 33, fols 61–4; A 41, fols 304–6.

27 *Ibid.*, A 36, fol. 371.

28 Firth and Rait, *Acts and Ordinances*, vol 2, pp. 856, 968–990. The major-generals were named as ejectors in the following areas: Barkstead, Middlesex; Berry, Lincolnshire; Boteler, Northamptonshire; Dawkins, South Wales; Desborough, Devon and Somerset; George Fleetwood, Buckinghamshire; Goffe, Middlesex; Haynes, Essex and Norfolk; Howard, Cumberland, Durham, Northumberland and Westmorland; Kelsey, Kent; Nicholas, Monmouthshire; Packer, Hertfordshire; Whalley, Derbyshire and Nottinghamshire; and Worsley, Lancashire.

29 The totals given here for the ejections in the mid 1650s were derived from a study of all the clergy listed in A. G. Matthews, *Walker Revised* (Oxford, 1948). As neither Walker nor Matthews were able to be precise in every case about the exact date of ejection, they are necessarily approximate figures. For Berkshire see Matthews, *Walker Revised*, pp. 67–72. Among those ejected here was John Pordage, the Ranter influenced minister of Bradfield; for an account of his ejection see BL, E.840.1, *Daemonium Meridianum* (London, 1655). For the west riding see Matthews, *Walker Revised*, pp. 388–99, and Bod. Lib., Rawlinson MSS, A 31, fol. 376.

30 Matthews, *Walker Revised*, pp. 109–27, 140–2, 370–82.

31 PRO, SP.25.76, pp. 46–7. The areas named were Bristol, Derbyshire, Dorset, Leicestershire, Lincolnshire, London, Nottinghamshire, Rutland, Somerset, Staffordshire, Surrey and Wiltshire.

32 Bod. Lib., Rawlinson MSS, A 39, fol. 528; BL, E.841.1, *Perfect Passages of State Affairs*, 24–31 May 1655.

33 BL, E.840.5, *Perfect Passages of State Affairs*, 17–24 May 1655; PRO, SP.25.76, pp. 248, 274–6.

34 Rutt, *Diary of Thomas Burton*, vol. 1, pp. 383–4.

35 Bod. Lib., Rawlinson MSS, A 33, fol. 519–22.

36 *Ibid.*, A 35, fol. 277.

37 *Ibid.*, A 32, fols 601–4; A 33, fols 39–40, 101–4; A 34, fols 427–30, 561–4; L. Fox (ed.), 'The Diary of Robert Beake, mayor of Coventry, 1655–6', *Dugdale Miscellany Volume I*, Dugdale Soc. Publs, 31 (1977), 118–125.

38 Bod. Lib., Rawlinson MSS, A 29, fol. 297; A 32, fols 289–92, 373–80, 957–60; A 33, fols 321–4, 369–72, 515–18, 571–4.

39 *Calendar of State Papers Venetian, 1655*, pp. 137–8; Michael Roberts (ed.), *Swedish Diplomats at Cromwell's Court 1655–1656*, Camden Soc. Publs, 4th series, 36 (1988), 224.

40 Bod. Lib., Tanner MSS, vol. 52, fol. 113; see also fols 100, 104, 109, and 141.

41 BL, E.1710.2, Thomas Grantham, *A Complaint to the Lord Protector* (London, 1656), p. 15.

42 BL, E.1837.1, Walter Bushnell, *A Narrative of the Proceedings of the Commissioners appointed by Oliver Cromwell for the Ejecting of Scandalous and Ignorant Ministers in the Case of Walter Bushnell, Clerk* (London, 1660), *passim*.

43 The figures are my calculations from a study of *Walker Revised*. The approximate county figures are as follows: Bedfordshire, 3; Berkshire, 1; Buckinghamshire, 1; Cambridgeshire, 1; Cumberland, 3; Cornwall, 1; Devon, 12; Dorset, 4; Essex, 1; Gloucestershire, 1; Hampshire, 7; Herefordshire, 3; Hertfordshire, 3; Huntingdonshire, 2; Kent, 4; Lancashire, 4; Leicestershire, 4; Lincolnshire, 4; Middlesex, 1; Norfolk, 5; Northamptonshire; 8; Northumberland, 1; Nottinghamshire, 3; Oxfordshire, 5; Rutland, 1; Shropshire, 1; Somerset, 4; Staffordshire, 3; Suffolk 3; Sussex 8; Warwickshire, 6; Westmorland, 2; Wiltshire, 17; Worcestershire, 2; Yorkshire, 7. No ejections appear to have occurred in Cheshire, Derbyshire, Durham, Monmouthshire or Surrey during the major-generals' period of office.

44 Bod. Lib., Rawlinson MSS, A 36, fol. 341.

45 Atkinson, *North Riding Quarter Sessions Records*, p. 212.

46 Fox, 'Diary of Robert Beake', pp. 118–25. The minister was John Gilbert of Bourton-on-Dunsmore.

47 Bushnell, *A Narrative ...*, *passim*. The quote is from p. 209. A few weeks later, one of the ejectors who had removed Bushnell, Humphrey Chambers, denied his charges in print and claimed that 'hee preached in such a scholar-like way that his parishioners were little profited by him and that the scandalous miscarriages in the articles would be fully proved against him'; see BL, E.187.5, Humphrey Chambers, *An Answer of Humphrey Chambers, Rector of Pewsey ... to the Charges of Walter Bushnal* (London, 1660), p. 2.

48 Bod. Lib., Rawlinson MSS, A 34, fols 173–6.

49 *Ibid.*, A 34, fols 591–4; A 35, fol. 2.

50 *Ibid.*, A 36, fol. 633.

51 *Ibid.*, A 29, fol. 297; A 32, fols 31–2; A 34, fols 173–80, 435–8, 877–80.

52 PRO, SP.25.76, p. 437.

53 Bod. Lib., Rawlinson MSS, A 36, fol. 610.

54 *Ibid.*, A 36, fol. 633.

55 PRO, SP.25.77, p. 22, 320–4, 333. The number of the additional lay ejectors and clerical advisers appointed in each county was as follows: Cheshire, 13; Cornwall, 10; Cumberland, 4; Durham, 1; Gloucestershire, 10; Herefordshire, 8; Kent, 9; Lancashire, 18; Northumberland, 13; Staffordshire, 7; Surrey, 9; Westmorland, 1; Wiltshire, 13; the east riding of Yorkshire and Hull, 4.

56 Bod. Lib., Rawlinson MSS, A 39, fol. 529. The order is undated, but filed in Thurloe's papers as of late June 1656.

57 Bushnell, *A Narrative ..., passim.* Ishmael was the son of Abraham and Hagar. The reference is to Genesis: 16:12.

58 Macfarlane, *Diary of Ralph Josselin,* p. 362.

59 Examples include William Belke, Stephen Bound, Henry Chamberlain, Christopher Newstead, Robert Remington, Thomas Reynolds, Hugh Roberts, Nehemiah Rogers and Edward Woolley; see PRO, SP.18.102.68; SP.18.130.50–2; SP.25.76, pp. 440, 547, 578, 595, 613–14; SP.25.77, pp. 245, 427, 489–90, 618.

60 E. S. de Beer (ed.), *The Diary of John Evelyn* (6 vols, Oxford, 1950), vol. 3. p. 164.

61 Gardiner, *Commonwealth and Protectorate,* vol. 3 , pp. 334–6; BL, E.765.7, John Gauden, *A Petitionary Remonstrance Presented to Oliver Cromwell, 4th February 1656* (London, 1659); Rutt, *Diary of Thomas Burton,* vol. 1, pp. 383–4.

62 For Wild's continued preaching, see de Beer, *Diary of John Evelyn,* vol. 3, pp. 165–70. Examples of ejected clerics who were permitted to continue as chaplains and tutors include Richard Allestree, William Barker, Arthur Leonard, Jasper Mayne and Mirth Waferer; see PRO, SP.18.102.68–9; SP.18.129.19; SP.25.76, p. 592; SP.25.77, pp. 70, 215, 227, 386–7.

63 Bod. Lib., Rawlinson MSS, A 35, fols 104–6. One minister from the west riding of Yorkshire was indicted at the July 1656 sessions at Skipton for marrying a couple and subsequently refusing to enter into a bond for his future good behaviour; West Yorkshire Archive Service, QS 10/3, p. 192. For reactions to the civil marriage act, see Christopher Durston, *The Family in the English Revolution* (Oxford, 1989), pp. 69–86.

64 Bod. Lib., Rawlinson MSS, A 34, fols 217–20; PRO, SP.18.126.50.

65 Bod. Lib., Rawlinson MSS, A 33, fols 515–18, 571–4; A 34, fols 591–4, 693–4; A 35, fols 104–5; Morrill, *Cheshire,* p. 283.

66 Bod. Lib., Rawlinson MSS, A 33, fols 49–52; A 36, fol. 593.

67 *Ibid.,* A 37, fols 333–6.

68 *Ibid.,* A34, fols 427–30, 561–4; A 35, fol. 4.

69 L. Fox (ed.), 'The Diary of Robert Beake, mayor of Coventry, 1655–6', *Dugdale Miscellany Volume I,* Dugdale Soc. Publs, 31 (1977), 129–30.

70 Bod. Lib., Rawlinson MSS, A 37, fols 570–3.

71 *Ibid.,* A 40, fols 297–300; A 41, fols 538–9.

72 BL, E.1065.6, *Order by the Justices of the Peace of London and Westminster* (London, 1656).

73 Le Hardy, *Calendar to Sessions Books,* pp. 480–1; Copnall, *Nottingham County Records,* p. 20; David Underdown, *Somerset in the Civil War and Interregnum* (Newton Abbot, 1973), pp. 180–2; Ratcliff and Johnson, *Warwick County Records,* pp. 311–13; Wilts R.O, A1/160/2, p. 55.

74 Copnall, *Nottingham County Records*, p. 20.

75 BL, E492.6, *The Public Intelligencer*, 11–18 Feb. 1656.

76 Worcestershire RO, 110/BA/93/52.

77 PRO, SP.25.76, pp. 574–5.

78 Bod. Lib., Rawlinson MSS, A 37, fols 229–32.

79 *Ibid.*, A 40, 297 300; A 41, fols 538–9

80 PRO, SP.25.77, pp. 329–31.

81 Bod. Lib., Rawlinson MSS, A 34, fols 427–30; A 36, fol. 709.

82 *Ibid.*, A 37, fols 229–32.

83 *Ibid.*, A 37, fols 229–32; A 40, fols 297–300.

84 This discussion of midlands' enclosure is based on G. Jaggar, 'The Fortunes of the Whalley Family of Screveton, Notts: a study of some of its members *c.* 1540–1690, with special reference to Major-General Edward Whalley' (Unpub. M.Phil. thesis, University of Southampton, 1973), pp. 181–93. I am grateful to Geoff Jaggar both for lending me a copy of his thesis and for discussing Edward Whalley with me on several occasions.

85 Bod. Lib., Rawlinson MSS, A 37, fols 229–32.

86 Rutt, *Diary of Thomas Burton*, vol. 1, pp. 175–6.

87 A. L. Beier, 'Poor Relief in Warwickshire, 1630–1660', *Past and Present*, 35 (1966), 77–100.

88 Bod. Lib., Rawlinson MSS, A 33, fols 39–40; A 34, fols 427–30, 561–4.

89 Copnall, *Nottingham County Records*, p. 20.

90 PRO, E.492.3, *Mercurius Politicus*, 31 Jan.–7 Feb. 1656.

91 Fox, 'Diary of Robert Beake', pp. 129–30.

92 Allen, *Essex Quarter Sessions Order Book*, pp. 81–2; *Norfolk Quarter Sessions Order Book*, pp. 86–8.

93 *Norfolk Quarter Sessions Order Book*, p. 96.

94 Derek Hirst, 'The Failure of Godly Rule in the English Republic', *Past and Present*, 132 (1991), 55.

95 Le Hardy, *Calendar to Sessions Books*, pp. 480–1.

96 Caernarvonshire Quarter Sessions Records, 1655; quoted in J. Gwynfor Jones, 'Caernarvonshire Administration: Activities of the Justices of the Peace, 1603–1660', *Welsh History Review*, 5 (1970–1), 149.

97 BL, E.491.16, *The Public Intelligencer*, 14–21 Jan. 1656.

98 Bod. Lib., Rawlinson MSS, A 35, fol. 172.

99 Worcestershire RO, 110/BA/93/4, 10, 13, 29.

100 West Yorkshire Archive Service, QS 10/3, pp. 181, 185–6; QS 4/4. See also G. C. F. Forster, 'County Government in Yorkshire during the Interregnum', *Northern History*, 12 (1976), 99, and S. H Waters, *Wakefield in the Seventeenth Century from 1550–1710* (Wakefield, 1933), pp. 146–7.

101 J. S. Cockburn (ed.), *Somerset Assizes Orders, 1640–59*, Somerset Records Soc. Publs, 71 (1971), 46–7, Underdown, *Somerset*, pp. 180–2.

102 Centre for Kentish Studies, Q/SB 6; Q/SO E1, fols 7–18.

103 Hirst, 'Failure of Godly Rule', p. 63.

104 Andrew Coleby, *Central Government and the Localities: Hampshire 1649–1689* (Cambridge, 1987), pp. 54–5.

105 Hampshire Record Office, Q1/3, p. 292.

106 Hampshire RO, Q4/1, fols 110–11.

107 Hampshire RO, Q3/1, p. 301.

108 BL, E.492.3, *Mercurius Politicus*, 31 Jan.–7 Feb. 1656.

109 BL, E.1065.6, *Order by the Justices of the Peace of London and Westminster* (London, 1656).

110 Bod. Lib., Rawlinson MSS, A 34, fols 693–4.

111 *Ibid.*, A 32, fols 871–4.

112 Staffordshire Record Office, QSO6.

113 Lancashire Record Office, QDV/29.

114 Bod. Lib., Rawlinson MSS, A 34, fols 693–4.

115 Lancashire RO, QSP 140/7.

116 Hirst, 'Failure of Godly Rule', p. 56.

117 BL, E.491.19, *Mercurius Politicus*, 24–31 Jan. 1656.

118 Bod. Lib., Rawlinson MSS, A 35, fols 104–5.

119 *Ibid.*, A 35, fol. 106.

120 Cheshire Record Office, QJF 84, 1–4 (microfilm, 212/113–14), quarter sessions files 1656; See also Morrill *Cheshire*, p. 283.

121 Lancashire RO, QSP/140/28.

122 Coleby, *Central Government and the Localities*, pp. 54–5.

123 C. D. Gilbert, 'Magistracy and Ministry in Cromwellian England: The Case of King's Norton, Worcestershire', *Midland History*, 23 (1998), 71–83.

124 Dr Williams's Library, Baxter Treatises, vol. 20, no. 352; manuscript text of 'The Power of Magistrates in Religion', unpaginated.

125 Richard Baxter, 'Directions to Justices of the Peace especially in Corporations for the discharge of their Duties to God', in Richard Baxter, *The Practical Works of the Late Reverend and Pious Mr Richard Baxter* (4 vols, London, 1707), vol. 4, pp. 945–6.

126 Bod. Lib., Rawlinson MSS, A 34, fols 561–4.

127 *Ibid.*, A 36, fol. 341.

128 PRO, SP.18.126.50.

129 Birch, *State Papers of John Thurloe*, vol.4, pp. 587–8.

130 Abbott, *Writings and Speeches of Cromwell*, vol. 4., pp. 274, 278.

131 Bod. Lib., Rawlinson MSS, A 34, fols 427–30.

132 For a fuller discussion of this point, see Christopher Durston, 'Puritan Rule and the Failure of Cultural Revolution, 1645–1660', in Christopher Durston and Jacqueline Eales (eds), *The Culture of English Puritanism, 1560–1700* (Basingstoke, 1996), pp. 210–33.

Chapter 9

The major-generals and the 1656 election

By the summer of 1656, the growing financial problems of Cromwell's government had reached crisis point and, as the country was now effectively at war with Spain, it was imperative that some action be taken quickly to remedy the situation. After considering a number of possible courses of action, the government decided to call a parliament, in the hope that the political nation would be more willing to provide it with funds which had been sanctioned by its representatives at Westminster. Under the terms of the Instrument of Government, Cromwell was not obliged to call another parliament until 1657, and the second protectorate parliament which met in September 1656 was thus an additional assembly which the Instrument had stipulated could be summoned at times of national emergency.

The major-generals were fully involved in the discussions which culminated in the decision to call a parliament. Indeed, it was their collective enthusiasm for the idea and their belief that they could effectively manage the elections to produce a result which would be acceptable to the government that did much to persuade a sceptical and hesitant Cromwell to agree to the move. In the event, however, their confidence proved misplaced. The election campaign provided their opponents with an ideal opportunity to express their discontent with their rule, and the body of MPs which was eventually returned contained around a hundred individuals whom the government considered too hostile to the regime even to be allowed to take their seats. Many of those who were permitted to sit at Westminster were also highly critical of recent political developments and a few months later they would vote to bring the rule of the major-generals to a close. This chapter will consider the major-generals' involvement in the decision to call the second protectorate parliament, their attempts to influence the elections in the localities, and their reactions to what was for them a disappointing outcome.

While the government only began seriously to consider calling a parliament in the early summer of 1656, the idea may have been circulating amongst some of its supporters for some months before this. In early February 1656, John Desborough had written to Cromwell from Chard in Somerset to suggest that, if he called all the major-generals back to London, 'there might be somewhat propounded to your highnes which might be of great use and advantage to this poore nation; especially if they find the temper of the gentlemen where they come as I do generally in these parts'.[1] If this statement meant that Desborough had come to believe that a parliament should be called, he would almost certainly have discussed the matter with Cromwell, and perhaps also with several of the other major-generals who visited the capital in February, on his return from the west country several weeks later. It may well have been his influence that led the protector to summon all the major-generals to London in May 1656 to report on their progress and advise the government how best to tackle its financial difficulties.

These extensive discussions between Cromwell, the council and the major-generals began in the middle of May and lasted for almost a month. The major-generals' attendance was considered so important that William Goffe was refused permission to delay his arrival by several days to deal with what he argued were pressing domestic matters.[2] The first day was given over to fasting and prayer and subsequent meetings took up most of the protector's time for the next fortnight. The Venetian ambassador reported that the consultation process was so intense and protracted that those involved scarcely took breaks for food and that the discussions were marked by 'no little ruffling of tempers owing to sharp words passed between them upon points that they have never been able to agree about'.[3] Among the strategies reportedly under consideration were the doubling of the assessment tax, the collection of privy seal loans and the extension of the decimation tax. All these alternatives were eventually rejected, however, in favour of the major-generals' preferred option of the calling of a parliament. On 10 June 1656, Thurloe informed Henry Cromwell that this course of action had been unanimously agreed by Cromwell's advisers and that 'the major-generals are here and have fully consented to it'.[4] The following year, Cromwell claimed that he had been against the proposal, and he accused the major-generals to their faces of having been 'impatient' to hold a parliament, and of winning over the council through their confidence that by their 'strength and interest' they could obtain the election of 'men chosen to your hearts desire'.[5] After attending Charles Worsley's funeral in Westminster Abbey on 13 June, the other major-generals returned to their districts to prepare for the coming campaign. The writs for the elections, which were to be held in late August, were issued a couple of weeks later.

Campaiging began in earnest at the beginning of August, and on the 8th of that month Cromwell wrote to each of the major-generals to express his deep misgivings about the current political climate. He informed them that he believed there was a real danger of imminent invasion and asked them to be vigilant over the coming weeks to prevent hostile groups from taking advantage of the election to destabilise the regime.[6] While royalists were prevented by the Instrument of Government from either standing for the parliament or voting, no such disqualification applied to the government's republican opponents and Cromwell was clearly afraid that these 'dissatisfied spirits' might cause considerable trouble during the campaign. One of their number, Edmund Ludlow, later claimed that the letter had been specifically sent out to make it clear that the government would be unhappy if any 'who had continued faithful to the commonwealth' were returned to the parliament.[7]

A number of the major-generals replied to Cromwell's letter within a few days of receiving it. Berry, Bridge, Desborough, Goffe and Haynes all reported that they had shown it to their commissioners who had promised to be vigilant to prevent any disruption of the elections by the republicans and their allies.[8] Their replies reveal that, in line with their support for the calling of a parliament in May, they still believed that the elections would pass off peacefully and that the results would prove favourable to the regime. In his reply on 16 August, Robert Lilburne admitted to Cromwell that 'many at home are fraught with perverse spirits and labour to sett up some new interest, wherein they might be sharers', but he added that he was sure 'there will be sober men enough to ballance such.'[9] Writing a few days earlier on 11 August, Edward Whalley had been similarly upbeat. He had told Cromwell that 'so long as Charles Stewart or any of that line are alive, upon the approaching of every parliament we must expect the appearance of a black cloud', but had then gone on to declare that:

> after much labouring in the duty of my place, occasioning my converse with all sortes of people, I can with some assurance affirme that the heart is sounde ... the people generally knowe there is a present necessity for moneye; the partinge with it upon a settlement will not trouble them ... and I am very confident that not a man from hence would be chosen to sit in this parliament in whom they conceaved a spirit of opposition to the present govenment'.[10]

The election campaigning proved especially heated and hard-fought. John Desborough wrote to Thurloe from Cornwall on 12 August to inform him that 'there are great contendings and strugglings in all parts. I cannot say we are free here.'[11] The same day, Thurloe passed this message on to Henry Cromwell in Ireland, informing him that 'here is the greatest striveinge to get into the parliament that ever was knowne. All sorts of discontented people are incessant in their endeavours.'[12] Several weeks later, he again wrote to him to repeat that 'much adoe there hath beene about the elections here; every faction hath bestirred themselves with all their might.'[13] Hezekiah Haynes confirmed this picture, writing to Thurloe on election day that 'everie man layd about him as if his all was at stake.'[14] The main reason for this intense activity was that the election quickly came to be seen as a referendum on the rule of the major-generals. While those who opposed them saw it as an opportunity to strike a decisive blow against them, the puritan minorities who had supported them in their work over the previous few months concluded that what was at stake was nothing less than the future of the godly reformation for which they had been striving for so long. As a letter intercepted by John Thurloe in mid August put it: 'the country stande against the choosing of swordmen and the major-generalls would have them chosen.'[15]

Eloquent testimony to the seriousness with which the godly viewed the elections can be found in the comments made by the puritan minster of Lavenham in Suffolk, William Gurnall, in a sermon he preached at Stow-market on the morning of the Suffolk county poll on 20 August. Gurnall told his listeners that it was their bounden duty to elect to the coming parliament godly MPs who would carry on the work of reforming the nation. Likening a vote for an ungodly candidate to Cain's murder of Abel, he declared: 'O, it will pierce thy heart like a dagger when God shall ask another day What hath thou done in giving thy voice for such as will help to ruine, not to heal the land?' Warming to his theme, he then declared that:

> This day the temper of this nation will be discovered; [there is] no way that I know like this to feel how its pulse beats; and for my own part ... I cannot look upon it otherwise then as our owning or disowning God to be our God to rule over us; and if the nation do but vouch God to be their God, by a godly choice, I shall not bury my hopes for their future happiness ... drive him away and Oh how unhappy are thou O England, if thou mayst still have thy God and will not.

He went on to argue that any elector who voted for an unworthy candidate was 'a forsworne wretch' and that 'if thou gettest this brand upon thy forehead once, go where thou wilt, thou dragest a chaine after thee that will bind thee over to the fearful expectation of God's wrath.' This last comment was probably an implicit reference to the biblical Book of Revelation, where a brand on the forehead was identified as one of the defining marks of the Beast, condemning those who carried it to be 'tormented with fire and brimstone'. After once more exhorting his audience to elect men who feared God, were sound in faith and faithful to the ministry, Gurnall concluded by urging them to return home after the poll and pray for those chosen to sit at Westminster, and by assuring them: 'if you leave the curing of the nation's wounds to God, a happy people you will be.'[16] Such godly sentiments would, of course, have been fully endorsed by the great majority of the major-generals.

Their shared expectations of the elections had been summed up a few weeks earlier by William Packer, who had declared to Thurloe:

> The Lord, in whose hand alone is the greate worke, I hope will order and dispose thereof for the refreshment of the hearts of his owne deere children, for perfecting the worke of reformation and for the exaltinge of his owne great name on the earth.[17]

The 400 English and Welsh constituencies of the protectorate parliaments were distributed very unevenly across the major-generals' associations, but most of them were responsible for at least twenty different seats and several of them for considerably more. The area with by far the highest number was Desborough's with eighty-three seats. The next highest were Haynes's with fifty-six seats and Berry's with forty-seven. Whalley's contained forty seats; Goffe's, thirty-five; Kelsey's, twenty-eight; Lilburne's twenty-seven; Packer's and George Fleetwood's, twenty-three; Boteler's, twenty; and Bridge's, nineteen. The associations with the smallest number of seats were Barkstead's, with twelve, and Howard's, with only ten.[18] Given such large numbers, it was clearly logistically impossible for the major-generals to exert a decisive influence upon every contest which was fought within their areas. Most of them did, nonetheless, make a determined effort to secure the return of some godly candidates.

Details of the electioneering activities of the major-generals are contained in the letters they sent Thurloe during July and August 1656. While this correspondence gives only a patchy impression of their campaigning, it does seem to confirm Mark Kishlansky's contention that Cromwell and his councillors in London failed to provide them with a coordinated strategy for the elections, and left them instead to act on their own initiative to monitor the situation within their associations, support their preferred candidates, and keep the government informed about the activities of its opponents.[19] It also confirms that not even the most active of them could hope to have a decisive influence throughout their associations, and that most of them were forced to concentrate their efforts within one or two counties only.

Thurloe's papers contain meaningful evidence about interventions in the campaign by William Goffe, John Desborough, Edward Whalley, Robert Lilburne, Tobias Bridge and Hezekiah Haynes. William Goffe began to turn his attention to the forthcoming election as early as mid July, when he wrote to Thurloe in an attempt to enlist his support for his preferred candidate for the Berkshire county seat. In the same letter, he informed him that the grand jury for the Hampshire summer assizes had drawn up what in his view was a highly unsuitable slate of candidates, which included a number of decimated royalists, and he suggested that Cromwell's son, Richard, and another prominent local landowner, Colonel Richard Norton, should be prevailed upon to draw up an agreed slate for Hampshire, which he believed would then carry the election 'without dispute'. He assured Thurloe that his main priority would be 'to keepe out the badd man', and added: 'If in this or anything else I may serve his highnes in helping on a good choyse, I shall be gladd and doe hope I shall have your advice.'[20]

In another letter to Thurloe written three weeks later on 8 August, Goffe reported that he was closely monitoring the activities of a republican faction in Southampton, which was hoping to secure the election there of a radical candidate with Quaker sympathies. He also asked whether there would be grounds for taking into custody the Sussex royalist, Henry Bishop, who had begun to campaign against the government and who, he claimed, 'hath great influence upon some gentlemen'.[21] In the days immediately before the election, Goffe concentrated his efforts in Hampshire, where he met with some success, securing not only his own return but also that of one of the captains of the county militia and several county commissioners.[22]

John Desborough, meanwhile, who had travelled down to his west country association to oversee the elections there, reported to Cromwell in mid August that he had discussed the conduct of campaign with the 'honest people' of each of his counties and that they had resolved 'in divine strength to be unanimously active in electing such as are of known integrity to the present government'.[23] In another letter sent to Thurloe the same day, he confirmed that he had agreed with these honest people a godly slate of candidates for each shire and 'set them to work to elect sober and honest men'. He added that he had heard reports of individuals coming together into 'parties' in every county, and he assured Thurloe that 'my business is as much as in me lyes to prevent and break up all such contrivances.'[24] On the eve of the poll, he intervened personally to oppose the election in Gloucestershire of Christopher Guise, who had served as a commissioner for that county but who had angered his fellow commissioners by attempting to secure exemptions from the decimation tax for his royalist friends. According to Guise's memoirs, just before the election Desborough travelled from Salisbury to Gloucester to prevent his election, 'which by very foule means he did, expressing ... much hate against mee'.[25]

In early August, Edward Whalley was busy canvassing opinion in Lincoln-shire. On the 9th he told Thurloe he was confident that the electors there would only vote for those candidates who declared their support for the government. He added, however, that some might make such expressions of loyalty in order to deceive the voters, and suggested that John, lord Claypole, be prevailed upon to stand for the borough of Stamford against a local republican, John Weaver, who had caused trouble in the previous parliament. He also reported that, although Sir Henry Vane's republican friends were active on his behalf in Lincolnshire, he believed he had 'no great interest' in the county.[26] Two days later he wrote to Cromwell from Nottingham to inform him that 'the honest part of that county' had nominated Colonel John Hutchinson as one of their candidates, but that he had advised against this on the grounds that his loyalty to the regime was questionable. He added that he himself had 'a great influence' within the town of Nottingham and that the electors there 'will not chuse any without my advise'.[27]

During early August, Robert Lilburne was keeping a close eye on the activities of a number of Yorkshire republicans, including Richard Darley and Lionel Copley. He reported to Thurloe on the 9th that these two and several other local men had recently journeyed to London to discuss the election with a 'gang' of fellow republicans, including Sir Henry Vane and Henry Neville, and had then returned to the county to organise 'meetings and councils to keep the friends of the government out of parliament'. He added that he believed similar campaigns had been put into effect in Durham and Northumberland, though he was unsure whether the leading republican, Sir Arthur Haselrig, was involved. According to Lilburne, the result of all this covert activity was that 'the people ... are perfect in their lesson, saying they will have noe swordmen, noe decimator, or any that receives sallary from the state to serve in parliament.' Despite his apparent acknowledgement of the success of the regime's opponents, he nonetheless believed that they would 'miss of their ayme'.[28] As was seen above, a week later he re-affirmed his confidence about the outcome of the election in his reply to Cromwell's letter of 8 August.[29]

As a result of the sudden death of Charles Worsley, there was no direct intervention by a major-general in the election campaigns in Cheshire, Lancashire or Staffordshire until the final few days before the poll. Worsley's successor, Tobias Bridge, only received his commission as major-general for these counties in mid July and did not reach Cheshire until 13 August, by which time the local campaign had already been fully underway for several weeks. On his arrival, he discovered that a group of influential local gentlemen, including the high sheriff of the county, Philip Egerton, and two of the county commissioners, Jonathan Bruen and Thomas Stanley, had held several meetings and drawn up a slate of candidates which included the republican, John Bradshaw. Bridge's primary concern was to prevent Bradshaw's election, and he quickly called together the Cheshire commissioners and proposed to them his own alternative slate. After some discussion, he agreed to accept the original slate with the omission of Bradshaw, who was subsequently replaced by Sir George Booth. He also gave orders that the county militia troop and some of the regular soldiers who were stationed at Nantwich should march to Chester, where the county poll was to be held on the 20th. Having spent only two days in Cheshire, he then left for Lancashire on 15 August. Writing to Thurloe just before he set out, he told him he expected 'much thwarting there through the peevishness of some and disaffection of others'. He subsequently delayed the Lancashire county poll by several weeks in order to give himself more time to influence its outcome.[30] He appears to have had no involvement at all in the elections in his other county of Staffordshire.

In East Anglia, Hezekiah Haynes focused much of his effort on the attempt to prevent the election in Norfolk of the local gentleman and crypto-royalist, John Hobart, whom he described to Thurloe as 'a person as closely malinginge the government and good men as any other in Norfolk'. He was particularly alarmed by the return to Norwich from London of the ejected clergyman, John Boatman, who began preaching in the city in support of Hobart and whom he regarded as 'the captaine of all the more ordinary sort of people who have votes in the election'. He wrote to Boatman informing him that there was a government order preventing him from returning to Norfolk and ordering him to return immediately to London, but the cleric refused to leave. When he subsequently banned him from preaching within Norwich, he simply moved to a church a few miles outside the city and addressed 'multitudes' there instead. Haynes was clearly reluctant to intervene personally to break up these gatherings, perhaps fearing that Boatman's arrest might lead to civil unrest in the Norwich area.

As well as continuing to monitor events in Norwich, in the final days before the poll Haynes attempted to suppress a number of unlicensed tracts critical of the government which were being distributed by several East Anglian Fifth Monarchist groups. He also consulted the government's supporters in Suffolk about the progress of the campaign there, and wrote to Thurloe to advise him about his chances of securing election for the Isle of Ely. By mid August, however, he was clearly despondent about the situation in his association and on the 15th he expressed his concerns in letters to both Thurloe and Cromwell. He told the former that the government's supporters in East Anglia were now 'much discouraged by the potencie of the adverse party', and he informed the latter: 'such is the prevalency of that spirit which opposeth itself to the worke of God upon the wheele, that the spirits of those that are otherwise minded have been much perplexed and discouraged from almost appearing at the eleccon, seeing no visible way of ballancing that interest.' In an attempt to rescue the situation, he urged that money be found to pay the militia troops so he could deploy them in 'sufficient strength to secure the interest of these countyes'.[31] As was seen in chapter 7, however, the lack of adequate funds to pay the troops meant this was not a viable course of action.

In addition to his involvement in the shire elections, Haynes also intervened at Colchester, where he delayed the poll until mid September so that it could be held according to the provisions laid down in the town's new charter which had just been granted by the government. As a result, the new Colchester corporation, which had been personally approved by Cromwell and was dominated by the town's godly Barrington faction, ignored the townspeople's call for the election of two local figures and instead chose as its MPs the president of the council, Henry Lawrence, and a member of the protector's household, John Maidstone.[32]

While there is, then, clear evidence that the six major-generals mentioned above were deeply involved in the campaign, any electioneering activities undertaken by the remaining nine major-generals have gone largely unrecorded. This does not necessarily mean, however, that they had refrained from intervening in the contest. Six of them – Barkstead, Dawkins, Fleetwood, Howard, Nicholas and Packer – were never regular correspondents of Thurloe. The failure of the other three – Berry, Boteler and Kelsey – to comment in detail on the campaigns in their areas may perhaps be more significant, but does not on its own provide conclusive evidence that they were less involved.

While most of the major-generals attended one of the county polls in their associations on 20 August, only one of them is recorded as having intervened personally in an attempt to influence the outcome. William Boteler, who attended the county poll at Northampton, was reported to have ridden around the election site crying 'A Pickering!, A Pickering!', before peremptorily ordering the high sheriff to declare that he and Sir Gilbert Pickering, a local landowner and member of Cromwell's council, had been elected.[33] If the rest of the major-generals kept a lower profile on election day, a number of the other polls were nonetheless marked by dispute, acrimony and violence. According to the presbyterian, Edward Harley, at the Herefordshire county poll the sheriff secured the election of James Berry's favoured candidate, the local militia lieutenant, Benjamin Mason, by sending away all those who opposed him to an adjoining field.[34] At the Berkshire poll held at Reading, the government's preferred candidate was the local landowner, William Trumbull, who was supported by the high sheriff and local militia captain, William Thornhill. He was opposed by the prominent republican, Henry Neville, who also hailed from the county. According to a pro-republican pamphlet which appeared some weeks after the poll, Thornhill threatened and insulted Neville's supporters and, in league with the sheriff and the soldiers of the county militia, employed a number of other dubious tactics to prevent his election.[35] According to John Bradshaw's brother, Henry, the Cheshire sheriff similarly prevented the election of Bradshaw and Sir William Brereton by refusing to hold a proper poll.[36] At the Westminster poll, a number of soldiers clashed violently with a group of civilians who had declared their opposition to 'sword men' and 'marsonary men', and in the ensuing brawl several men were killed and a number of others wounded.[37] At the Middlesex poll at Brentford, meanwhile, a group of religious radicals clashed with the local justices, and a regiment of horse had to be called in to restore order.[38] Similar disputes arose at some of the borough polls.[39]

For all the efforts of the major-generals and their allies, the results of the 1656 elections proved a disappointing mixed bag for the government. Initially they seemed quite pleased with the results. John Desborough reported to Cromwell on 12 August that he saw no 'great danger' in the results from those west country boroughs which had so far selected their members.[40] Similarly, when several days after the county polls William Goffe received from Thurloe a preliminary list of those returned throughout the country, he responded that, in his view, 'though they be not so good as wee could have wished them, yet they be not soe badd as our enemies would have had them.'[41] On hearing of the results in Essex, the godly clergyman, Ralph Josselin, commented in his diary: 'the choice to view is not very good, nor very bad, [but] a strange mixture of spirits.' Significantly, however, he went on to add: 'Lord, I cannot trust them with our gospel concernments, but I will thee, and trust thou wilt looke after them, and not suffer the nacon to bee wrapt up by these men into any evill whatsoever.'[42]

All the major-generals, with the sole exception of George Fleetwood, were returned to Westminster.[43] A few of the officers of the county militia troops also secured election, as did some other conspicuous supporters of the regime, including a number of regular army officers and most of the members of Cromwell's council. Some of the results in those boroughs where the corporation had been purged by the major-generals or where a new charter had been sought from the government were also encouraging, and a number of conspicuous republicans, including Sir Henry Vane, failed to secure election.[44]

There was, on the other hand, little evidence of popular enthusiasm for the election of the major-generals or those closely associated with them. William Packer, for example, was defeated in the Oxford city poll in early August by a local dignatory, Richard Crooke, before being subsequently returned for the borough of Woodstock.[45] Sir John Barkstead's election for Reading further divided an already faction-ridden corporation and three years later led to the removal from office of all those involved in what were described in the borough's records as the 'great, insolent and notorious misdemeanours and offences' which occurred during his election.[46] In East Anglia, meanwhile, the fears expressed by Hezekiah Haynes on the eve of the county poll proved well founded, for his association witnessed several particularly embarrassing electoral reverses for the government. In Norfolk, John Hobart, whom he had worked so hard to oppose, amassed around 1,000 votes more than Haynes's superior, Charles Fleetwood.[47] In Suffolk meanwhile, Haynes's close ally, the godly gentleman, Sir Thomas Barnardiston, who had topped the county poll in 1654 and had subsequently been active as one of the major-general's commissioners for the county, was beaten into a humiliating tenth place and only just secured election.[48]

While many of those who had actively supported the major-generals struggled to secure election, large numbers of individuals who had been conspicuously critical of Cromwell's government or at best only lukewarm in their support were returned to Westminster. The ranks of the openly hostile MPs included the staunch republicans, Sir Arthur Haselrig, Thomas Saunders, Thomas Scot and John Weaver; the crypto-royalists, Thomas Adams, James Clavering, Sir John Gore, John Hobart, John Stanhope, Sir Horatio Townshend and Peniston Whalley (the nephew of Edward Whalley); and several notorious anti-puritans, notably John Buxton and Sir William Doyley. The still larger group of the uncommitted included John Bowyer, Richard Browne, Bernard Church, George Courtopp, John Fagge, Samuel Gott, Sir Ralph Hare, Herbert Morley, Sir Thomas Rivers, Thomas Southerton and Philip Woodhouse.[49]

Three of the major-generals, William Goffe, Hezekiah Haynes and Thomas Kelsey, recorded their reactions to these election results in some detail. Writing to Thurloe from Winchester on the day after the Hampshire county poll, Goffe expressed some satisfaction at the result there. He told him that 'considering the great efforts made to stop me being elected and the unkindness of some I had expected better from', he looked upon his election for the county 'as a speciall providence of God'. He added that the local militia captain and commissioner, John Pitman, had also been returned thanks to the support of a 'greate number of honest and resolute men that did cleave to him', and he declared: 'lett us, I beseech you, give ourselves to prayer and expect a blessed issue from the Lord to all the present greate affaires.'[50] Two days later, however, he wrote again to report that things had gone far less well in Sussex. There, the supporters of Herbert Morley, who had campaigned under the slogan 'noe soldier, decemator or any man that hath sallary', had 'ruled the rost by the help of a disaffected party, much to the griefe of the honest party'.[51] The outcome of the polls in these two southern counties would seem to confirm the impression that, while the major-generals were able to exert real influence over the campaign in those areas where they were present and upon which they concentrated their attentions, in the many other constituencies they were necessarily forced to neglect, their opponents could take advantage of their absence to promote their cause.

In his letter of 23 August, Goffe further informed Thurloe that a number of 'honest men' in Sussex were preparing a paper against one of those elected, George Courtopp, in the hope that he might be excluded from sitting.[52] A week later, he sent this paper to Thurloe and specifically asked him to consider whether the information contained in it, that Courtopp had been the 'principal promoter' of a Sussex petition calling for a treaty with Charles I, was sufficient grounds to bar him from parliament. He added that many 'honest people' in Sussex were very disturbed by Courtopp's election and were prepared to travel to London to petition against him taking up his seat.[53] The council seems to have taken notice of Goffe's information, for Courtopp was one of those subsequently excluded.

Hezekiah Haynes, whose results as we have seen were particularly depressing, was more despondent than Goffe. Late in the evening of the election day, he wrote to Thurloe from Norwich to tell him that the result of the Norfolk poll was 'as bad as it could well have bin made', and that there had been 'a clear combination' to return opponents of the government, 'by which choyce the prophaine, malignant and disaffected party and scandelous ministry are only gratified'. His immediate reaction was, like Goffe, to call for the exclusion of all those suspected of being disaffected, on the grounds that otherwise 'no good' could be expected of the parliament. He warned, however, that getting evidence against them would not be easy. Invoking a seafaring analogy which perhaps related to his personal experiences of crossing the Atlantic to New England and back in his youth, he concluded the letter with the comment: 'It is a difficult tyme: the allwyse God direct you and those at the sterne safely and resolutely to steere the shipp of this commonwealth in this troublesome and stormie season.'[54]

Over the course of the next few weeks, Haynes and his allies in East Anglia attempted to salvage something from the situation by dissuading some of those who had been elected from taking their seats and gathering together the evidence that might be used by the council to justify exclusions. John Balleston, one of the Norfolk commissioners, wrote to Haynes on 1 September to inform him that, when he had spoken to John Hobart, he had become 'extreame heightened' and declared that 'we were ruled by an arbitrary power, and not by any known law; and that he had suffered himself to be distrayned for taxes; and that major-generalls and such new raised forces were needless people, the army being to[o] great before.' Balleston had retorted that, if these were his principles, he should not sit at Westminster.[55] On the same day, another Norfolk commissioner, Ralph Woolmer, wrote to Haynes to tell him that he had been trying to gather together information against those elected in the county but that he had found 'noe man willinge to [give] it. When I aske them thereof, they saye it was to soe little purpose the last parliament that they resolve not to meddle any more therein; sayeinge alsoe it may prove theire utter undoeing if they should.' As a result of this lack of cooperation, Woolmer was reduced to sending Haynes an old paper which had been compiled at the time of the 1654 parliament, containing incriminating information against some of those who had been returned again for Norfolk in 1656.[56]

Thomas Kelsey's assessment of the results in Kent was even more gloomy than those of Goffe and Haynes, and he was particularly insistent that the government should move swiftly to exclude its opponents from Westminster. In a long letter to Cromwell written on 26 August, he informed him that in

Kent the royalists and presbyterians had joined forces against the government's supporters and that the 'generallity' of the county had displayed a 'bitter spirit against swordmen, decimators, courtiers etc.' He added that some of those elected in that county had declared that they 'would downe with the maior generalls and decimators and the new militia'. He also reported that his commissioners, who had met at Maidstone following the election, were 'full of feares' about those who had been elected and believed that 'if there were not a restraynt putt upon them ... they would putt all into blood and confusion.' They had told him that they had found 'such a perversenesse in the spirits of those that are chosen that, without resolution of spirit in Your Hignes and councell to maintayne the interests of God's people (which is to be preserved before a thousand Parliaments) against all opposition whatsoever, wee shall returne againe to our Egiptian taskmasters'.[57]

The Kentish commissioners had clearly discussed in some detail the possible mechanisms by which any exclusions might be carried out. In order that 'the honest party may know to whom to repaire', they had proposed to Kelsey that named individuals should be appointed to collect information against those returned. They had further suggested that if those elected were required to sign a 'recognition' of their support for the Instrument of Government this might 'keepe some that are most dangerous out', and had argued that it would be 'better that they bee kept out at first then afterwards Your Highnes bee forced to turne them out'. In a highly emotional conclusion to the letter, Kelsey expressed his own deep conviction that, despite the serious setback to the godly cause caused by the election results,

> if the lord shall take pleasure in us, hee will cause his face to shine upon us and carry us well through the seas of blood that are threatening against us and the vast howling wilderness of our straites and difficultyes and at lenth bring us to the blessed haven of reformacon endeavoured by us, and cause all our troubles and disquiett to end in a happy rest and peece, when all his people shall bee one and his name one in all your dominions.[58]

A week later Kelsey wrote again to Thurloe in a similar vein, to inform him that the 'honest people' of Kent were very anxious about the coming parliament and to call again for the drawing up of a 'recognition to own the government', which he believed might keep out the most dangerous individuals.[59]

After receiving this advice from the major-generals in the days following the polls, Cromwell's council carefully vetted the returns during the first half of September and decided to exclude from the parliament just over 100 of the 400 men who had been returned. As the extant lists of the debarred members do not correspond exactly, it is not possible to give precise figures for the numbers excluded in each of the major-generals' associations, but the approximate totals, compiled from a comparison of five of the lists, are as follows: Haynes, twenty-one; Desborough, eighteen; Whalley, seventeen; Goffe, twelve; Kelsey and Lilburne, nine; Packer and George Fleetwood, eight; Berry, seven; Barkstead and Bridge, five; Boteler, one; and Howard, none.[60]

By relating these figures to the totals of constituencies within each of the twelve major-generals' associations, it is possible to arrive at some approximate figures for the comparative incidence of exclusion across them. The exclusion rate for the whole parliament was roughly twenty-six per cent. The major-generals with a significantly higher rate than this included Whalley, with forty-two per cent of those elected in his association excluded; Barkstead, with forty-one per cent; Haynes with thirty-seven per cent; and Goffe, Kelsey, Lilburne, and Packer and Fleetwood with around thirty-three per cent. Those with especially low exclusion rates were Berry at fourteen per cent; Boteler at five per cent; and Howard, whose association saw no exclusions. In both Desborough's and Bridge's associations, meanwhile, the national average of around a quarter of those returned was excluded.

These figures reveal that the level of exclusion varied markedly from association to association. At first glance, they also appear to provide a basis for comparing the performance of the individual major-generals as electoral managers and for arguing that Berry, Boteler and Howard were much more successful in this role than Barkstead, Haynes and Whalley. The serious

Table 2 Numbers of parliamentary seats and exclusions in the major-generals' associations

Major-general	Number of seats	Number of exclusions	Percentage of exclusions
Barkstead	12	5	41
Berry	47	7	14
Boteler	20	1	5
Bridge	19	5	25
Desborough	83	18	22
Goffe	35	12	33
Haynes	56	21	37
Howard	10	0	0
Kelsey	28	9	33
Lilburne	27	9	33
Packer/Fleetwood	23	8	33
Whalley	40	17	42

administrative problems which bedevilled the exclusion process, however, would render any such conclusion highly suspect. The council's decisions about whether to exclude or admit those elected were taken quickly, often on the basis of insufficient or misleading information, and as a result a number of mistakes were clearly made. Furthermore, the varying levels of exclusion in the twelve associations were a reflection not only of the major-generals' impact upon the election campaigns, but also of the degree to which they liaised with the council in the period between polling day and the start of the parliament. It is far from clear, for example, whether Charles Howard's apparent success in the far north-west was due more to his competent electoral management or to his subsequent disinclination to send damning reports on those returned to the council in London. For these reasons, the temptation to place the major-generals in a league table of electoral managers on the basis of the number of exclusions within their associations should probably be resisted.[61] But, whatever the reasons for the varying exclusion rates within individual associations, the fact that the government felt compelled to exclude more than one in four of those returned to parliament in August 1656 clearly indicates that as a group the major-generals had signally failed to manage the elections and had roundly defaulted on the promise they had made to Cromwell in the spring to deliver him a godly parliament.

The 1656 election was, then, a major disappointment for the major-generals and their godly allies in central and local government. They had hoped to secure the election of a body of men which would give strong, unqualified support to Cromwell's regime and energetically drive forward the campaign for a godly reformation. In the event, however, as Ralph Josselin had put it, those chosen by the electorate could not be trusted with the 'gospel concernments' of the godly and, even after the substantial purge of early September, many of those who took up their seats displayed little enthusiasm for the government and its objectives.

While this failure to deliver a godly parliament may to some degree be attributable to the major-generals' shortcomings as electoral managers, it surely had more to do with three other factors: the failure of central government to coordinate the campaign and provide them with sufficient backing and resources; the extreme difficulty of controlling and managing the very large numbers of near simultaneous contests taking place within each of the twelve associations; and, above all, the fact that the activities of the major-generals and their commissioners in the provinces during the first half of 1656 had by August of that year rendered both themselves and the regime they represented odious to large sections of the English and Welsh political nations.

Apart from sending out Cromwell's letter of the 8 August, the government left the major-generals alone to devise their own election strategies. It did not take decisive action to back them when they requested advice and assistance, and it failed to provide enough of them with the money which would have allowed them to muster the county militias and thus provide an intimidating military presence both during the campaigns and on polling day. The second fundamental problem that the major-generals faced was that their associations, each of which contained an average of more than thirty constituencies, were simply too big to allow for effective electoral management. Although their county commissioners could exert some influence in their absence, the most important initiatives still demanded the personal presence of the major-generals, and as they could not be in two places at once, they were forced to concentrate their efforts within a small number of their constituencies and to leave the rest relatively free of outside interference. The result was that, while they secured their desired outcome in a small number of constituencies, their efforts were too limited and localised to have a substantial impact on the overall character of the parliament.

Finally, and probably most crucially, the major-generals had from the outset been wildly over-optimistic about the prospects of securing the return of a large body of godly MPs. Blinded by their own rhetoric and their inability to contemplate the possibility that the Lord's will might not prevail, they were unable to see that a large majority of English and Welsh people, who since the early 1650s had been far from enamoured with Cromwell's high-taxing military regime, were by the late summer of 1656 deeply resentful of the major-generals' presence within their local communities and determined to grab what seemed a golden opportunity to make their feelings known. Given this hostile climate of public opinion, as Cromwell had always suspected, the major-generals' original call for a parliament had been a serious mistake and their subsequent attempts to manage the elections had never had any realistic prospect of success. In this respect, the responsibility for the failure of the 1656 election campaign does lie squarely with the major-generals. As will be seen in the next chapter, they were subsequently to pay a heavy price for their serious misreading of the political mood, for six months later the parliament they had so eagerly called for would vote to bring the rule of the 'swordmen and decimators' to an abrupt end.

NOTES

1 Bod. Lib., Rawlinson MSS, A 35, fol. 102.

2 *Ibid.*, A 38 fols 125–8, 255–6.

3 *Calendar of State Papers Venetian, 1656–7*, pp. 240–1.

4 Thomas Carte (ed.), *A Collection of Original Letters and Papers Concerning the Affairs of England from the year 1641 to 1660* (2 vols, London, 1739), vol. 2, p. 110.

5 Rutt, *Diary of Thomas Burton*, vol. 1, pp. 383–4.

6 Abbott, *Writings and Speeches of Cromwell*, vol. 4, p. 226; Bod. Lib., Rawlinson MSS, A 41, fols 406–9. No copy of the letter appears to have survived, but its main thrust can be worked out from the major-generals' replies.

7 C. H. Firth (ed.), *The Memoirs of Edmund Ludlow* (2 vols, Oxford, 1894), vol. 2, pp. 16–17.

8 Bod. Lib., Rawlinson MSS, A 41, fols 436–9, 440–1, 488–91, 492–4, 495–7; A 42, fols 337–8.

9 *Ibid.*, A 41, fols 531–2.

10 *Ibid.*, A 41, fols 406–9.

11 *Ibid.*, A 41, fols 436–9.

12 Birch, *State Papers of John Thurloe*, vol. 5, p. 303.

13 *Ibid.*, vol. 5, pp. 349–50.

14 Bod. Lib., Rawlinson MSS, A 41, fols 572–5.

15 Birch, *State Papers of John Thurloe*, vol. 5, p. 310.

16 BL, E.889.6, William Gurnall, *The Magistrate's Pourtraiture* (London, 1656), *passim*. The relevant passage in Revelation is chapter 14, verse 9.

17 Bod. Lib., Rawlinson MSS, A 40, fols 341–2.

18 Vernon F. Snow, 'Parliamentary Reapportionment Proposals in the Puritan Revolution', *English Historical Review*, 74 (1959), 409–42, esp. pp. 426, 436–42; see also, Paul Pinckney, 'A Cromwellian Parliament: The Elections and Personnel of 1656' (Unpub. Ph.D. thesis, Vanderbilt University, 1962), p. 76.

19 Mark Kishlansky, *Parliamentary Selection: Social and Political Choice in Early Modern England* (Cambridge, 1986), p. 125.

20 Bod. Lib., Rawlinson MSS, A 40, fols 305–8.

21 *Ibid.*, A 41, fols 248–51.

22 *Ibid.*, A 41, fols 610–11.

23 *Ibid.*, A 41, fols 440–1.

24 *Ibid.*, A 41, fols 436–9.

25 Godfrey Davies (ed.), *Memoirs of the Family of Guise*, Camden Soc. Publs, 3rd series, 28 (1917), 129–30.

26 Bod. Lib., Rawlinson MSS, A 41, fols 300–3.

27 *Ibid.*, A 41, fols 406–9. See also, P. R. Seddon, 'The Nottinghamshire Elections to the Protectorate Parliaments in 1654 and 1656', *Transactions of the Thoroton Society of Nottinghamshire*, 102 (1998), 93–8.

28 *Ibid.*, A 41, fols 304–6.

29 *Ibid.*, A 41, fols 532–3.

30 *Ibid.*, A 41, fols 495–7; see also Paul J. Pinckney, 'The Cheshire Election of 1656', *Bulletin of John Rylands Library*, 49 (1967), 387–426; Morrill, *Cheshire*, pp. 287–91; and Pinckney, 'A Cromwellian Parliament', pp. 123–4.

31 Bod. Lib., Rawlinson MSS, A 40, fols 463–6; A 41, fols 306–15, 324–7, 488–94; John T.

Evans, *Seventeenth Century Norwich: Politics, Religion and Government, 1620–1690* (Oxford, 1979), pp. 217–19; for Hobart, see Carol S. Egloff, 'Settlement and Kingship: the Army, the Gentry and the offer of the Crown to Oliver Cromwell' (Unpub. Ph.D. thesis, Yale University, 1990), pp. 110–24.

32 J. H. Round, 'Colchester during the Commonwealth', *English Historical Review*, 15 (1900), 641–64. For more details, see chapter 5.

33 Peter Whalley, *The History and Antiquities of Northamptonshire Compiled from the Manuscript Collection of the Late Learned Antiquary, John Bridges Esq.* (2 vols, Oxford, 1791), vol. 2, p. 383.

34 HMC, *Portland MSS*, vol. 3, p. 208.

35 BL, E.891.8, *A True and Perfect Relation of the Manner and Proceeding held by the Sheriff of the County of Berks* ... (London 1656), *passim*.

36 Bod Lib., Top Cheshire MSS, e3, fols 20–1; Morrill, *Cheshire*, pp. 291–3.

37 Bod. Lib., Rawlinson MSS, A 41, fols 642–3.

38 *Ibid.*

39 Pinckney, 'A Cromwellian Parliament', p. 182.

40 Bod. Lib., Rawlinson MSS, A 41, fols 432–5.

41 *Ibid.*, A 41, fols 860–1.

42 Macfarlane, *Diary of Ralph Josselin*, pp. 377–8.

43 Their seats were as follows: Barkstead, Middlesex; Berry, Worcestershire; Boteler, Northamptonshire; Bridge, Chipping [High] Wycombe; Dawkins, Camarthenshire; Desborough, Somerset; Goffe, Hampshire; Haynes, Essex; Howard, Cumberland; Kelsey, Dover; Lilburne, the west riding of Yorkshire; Nicholas, Monmouthshire; Packer, Woodstock; and Whalley, Nottinghamshire.

44 For details of the borough elections, see Pinckney, 'A Cromwellian Parliament', pp. 179–200; for Vane's failure to secure election in Lincolnshire, see Clive Holmes, *Seventeenth Century Lincolnshire* (Lincoln, 1980), pp. 214–15.

45 Oxfordshire Archives, C/FC/1/A1/03, Council Act Book 1629–1663, fol. 232r.

46 HMC, *11th Report, Appendix 7*, Reading Corporation MSS, p. 193.

47 'MSS List of the Norfolk Poll, 1656', *Norfolk Archaeology*, 1 (1847), 67. See also, Carol S. Egloff, 'John Hobart of Norwich and the Politics of the Cromwellian Protectorate', *Norfolk Archaeology*, 42 (1994), 38–56.

48 Paul Pinckney, 'The Suffolk Elections to the Protectorate Parliaments', in Colin Jones, Malyn Newitt and Stephen Roberts (eds), *Politics and People in Revolutionary England* (Oxford, 1986), pp. 203–24.

49 For more details on the career and beliefs of these men see Egloff, 'Settlement and Kingship', pp. 90–171; and Carol S. Egloff, 'The Search for a Cromwellian Settlement: Exclusions from the Second Protectorate Parliament. Part 2. The Excluded Members and the Reaction to their Exclusion', *Parliamentary History*, 17 (1998), 301–23.

50 Bod. Lib., Rawlinson MSS, A 41, fols 610–11.

51 *Ibid.*, A 41, fols 698–9.

52 *Ibid.*, A 41, fols 698–9.

53 *Ibid.*, A 42, fols 59–62.

54 *Ibid.*, A 41, fols 572–5.

55 *Ibid.*, A 42, fols 7–10.

56 *Ibid.*, A 42, fols 11–14, 17–18.

57 PRO, SP.18.129.156.

58 *Ibid.*

59 Bod. Lib., Rawlinson MSS, A 42, fols 109–10.

60 The extant lists consulted can be found at Bod. Lib., Rawlinson MSS, A 37, fol. 317; Bod. Lib., Tanner MSS, 52, fol. 156; BL, E.889.8; BL, Harleian MSS, 1929, fol. 19; and *Commons Journal*, vol. 7, p. 425. For more details on the exclusions see Egloff, 'Settlement and Kingship', pp. 90–171; and Egloff, 'The Search for a Cromwellian Settlement', pp. 301–23.

61 I am grateful to Peter Gaunt for his advice on the interpretation of these exclusion totals.

Chapter 10

Defeat at Westminster
and fall from power

On 17 September 1656, Oliver Cromwell opened the second protectorate parliament with an address to the three hundred or so MPs whom the government had allowed to take up their seats at Westminster. During the course of his long speech he referred several times to the major-generals, whom he described as men 'of known integrity and fidelity', who had 'adventured their blood and lives for that good cause'. After attempting to play down the constitutional significance of their establishment by referring to their rule as 'a poor little invention' and 'a little thing invented', he expressed his strong personal commitment to their work, stating: 'if ever I think anything were honest, this was as anything I knew; and I would venture my life with it as anything I ever undertook.' He went on to declare: 'I will abide it notwithstanding the envy and slander of foolish men', and to add: 'if there be any man that hath a face averse to this, I dare pronounce him to be a man against the interest of England.' Conceding that there had been doubts in some quarters about the legality of the decimation tax which underpinned their rule, he argued defiantly that 'if nothing should be done but what is according to law, the throat of the nation may be cut till we send for some to make a law.' The major-generals, most of whom were among his audience that day, must surely have interpreted these words as a ringing endorsement of their work. There was certainly no suggestion in the speech that Cromwell's enthusiasm for their reform efforts had in any way diminished; indeed he specifically stated at one point: 'If this were to be done again, I would do it.'[1]

Both those who heard this speech and those who subsequently read reports of it could have been forgiven for concluding that the rule of the major-generals, which had taken so much time and effort to introduce and was apparently still so highly regarded by the protector, was set to become a permanent feature of local government. Few of them would have forecast that within five months the whole elaborate experiment would to all intents and purposes have been abandoned, following the voting down by parliament of a bill which would have established the decimation tax as a permanent levy. This chapter will attempt to explain this unexpected turn of events, and will suggest that the fall of the major-generals should be attributed to a number of factors, including their unpopularity in the country, their own mistakes and miscalculations, the hesitancy and indecision of Cromwell himself, and the activities of a well organised clique in the 1656 parliament who wanted the protector to break with the army and assume the crown.

The first issue to be considered, however, is whether it was sensible for the major-generals to remain at Westminster throughout the autumn of 1656. When the government received the election results in late August and discovered that all the major-generals, with the exception of George Fleetwood, had been returned to parliament, it decided that they should be temporarily withdrawn from their associations to attend not only the opening of the parliament but also the subsequent debates in the House over the next few months. This decision seems to have been relayed to the major-generals during the week following the county poll on 20 August. When William Goffe wrote to John Thurloe on 23 August to inform him that he had been returned for Hampshire, he was still not sure whether he would be required to leave Winchester for London; he told him he would delay making any arrangements to travel up to the capital until he had received further instructions, and added that he would continue to act where Cromwell 'thinks me most serviceable'. A week later, however, he had clearly been informed that his presence would be required at Westminister, for in his next letter to Thurloe on 29 August he talked of the need to find lodgings and reported that he had considered calling out the county militia so that he could 'leave them with a word of exortation' before his departure.[2]

Whether this decision was made by Cromwell alone or was arrived at collectively in the council chamber is unclear but, whoever was responsible for it, it appears to have been a tactical error. There is no doubt that the presence in parliament of these dependable supporters of the regime who were closely in touch with the situation in the counties was helpful to the government, but the major-generals' absence from their associations was bound to lead to a corresponding dilution of their work and to present those hostile to them with greater opportunity to coordinate their opposition. The government had been made aware of the potential disadvantages of withdrawing the major-generals from the provinces as early as February 1656, when Edward Whalley had warned Thurloe that their work required their 'constant attendance' if it was to be carried on 'effectually'.[3]

Nor is there much evidence to suggest that the major-generals performed any vital function for the government at Westminster. While they were well represented on the more important committees of the House, they do not appear to have worked closely together as a group. Indeed, during the long and heated debates in December 1656 about how to proceed against the Quaker, James Nayler, they were deeply divided. While William Boteler, William Goffe, Hezekiah Haynes and Edward Whalley argued that Nayler should receive the death penalty for his blasphemy in recreating Christ's entry into Jerusalem at Bristol the previous summer, their fellow major-generals, Tobias Bridge, John Desborough, Charles Howard, Thomas Kelsey and William Packer supported a lesser punishment.[4]

Given the widespread hostility which had been displayed towards the major-generals during the election campaign, the government may have feared that they would come under sustained attack in the House during the early weeks of the session and face a concerted call for their removal, and that they would thus need to be present to defend themselves in person. But, probably because the council's purge had removed their most outspoken opponents and those that remained were preoccupied by the need to find a way to finance the war against Spain, no such assault materialised during the early weeks of the session. As it became clear that they were not to face an early challenge to their authority from the new parliament, Cromwell and the council should surely have concluded that they would be of more use back in their associations and have ordered them to return to them. Their failure to do so contributed significantly to the loosening of the major-generals' hold on the provinces. In most counties the commissioners for securing the peace of the commonwealth remained active, but in time the prolonged absences of their masters inevitably blunted the edge of their operations.

When the parliamentary attack on the major-generals did eventually come, it did so only as a result of an initiative taken by one of their own number, John Desborough. On 25 December 1656, Desborough sought the leave of the House to introduce a militia bill which would have established the decimation tax as a permanent source of funding for the militia. It was almost certainly not a coincidence that he chose to make this move on Christmas Day. For some days prior to this, the House had been unusually thin, chiefly because around a hundred MPs had ignored the official suppression of the Christmas holiday and returned home to observe the traditional festivities in the country. On 20 December the remaining MPs had angrily ordered that all absent members should return by the end of the month, but when a roll-call was taken on the 31st nearly ninety were still not present. One MP who was in attendance, the diarist, Thomas Burton, was of the opinion that many of the absentees had no intention of returning during the current session.[5]

Desborough had probably calculated that the more hardline MPs who had stayed at Westminster would be well disposed towards providing the permanent financial underpinning which would allow him and his colleagues to continue indefinitely with their work. He was probably hoping that, if the House proceeded quickly, his 'short bill' might become law before those more moderate MPs who were planning to return began to drift back in January. This interpretation of the timing of the move was certainly the one favoured by Sir Ralph Verney's friend, William Denton, who in a letter to Verney on 29 December remarked: 'Decimacion had but a poore Xtmas dinner, no sweet plum broath nor plum pye, for they chose that day to bring it in when *armiger* was *in patinis.*'[6]

The presentation to the House several days earlier of a petition from Yorkshire in favour of the decimation tax was probably not purely coincidental and may well have been seen as a way of testing the likely reaction to Desborough's bill. On 23 December, Lord George Eure, who was a commissioner for Yorkshire and in overall command of that county's four militia troops, brought before the House a petition from some of the godly inhabitants of the north riding calling upon the MPs to reduce the burden of the excise and assessment taxes by laying the costs of the state's defence squarely upon the shoulders of the royalist community. The fact that the House reacted sympathetically and told Eure to inform the petitioners that their proposal had been well received may have helped to persuade Desborough that the MPs would look favourably upon a move to establish the tax permanently.[7]

Several other possible influences behind Desborough's action can be also be suggested. One may have been a desire to adjust the level of the tax upon royalists. The bill Desborough presented to the House in January 1657 conspicuously avoided using the word 'decimation', and during the subsequent debates both he and one of his supporters, the Yorkshire MP and commissioner in that county, Luke Robinson, argued that there might be grounds for both raising and lowering the incidence of the tax around the mean of one tenth. On 7 January, Desborough stated explicitly; 'I think it is too light a tax ... I would have it higher.'[8]

It is also possible that either Desborough or some of his fellow councillors felt that under the terms of the Instrument of Government they had no option but to seek parliamentary approval for the decimation tax. Article 4 of the Instrument stipulated that when parliament was sitting its consent was needed for the disposal of the country's military forces. This was a requirement which some of the regime's opponents had clearly not forgotten; when the excluded member, John Hobart, had set down his 'grounds for dissatisfaction with the Protector's proceedings' in September 1656, the first of his complaints against Cromwell was that he had violated article 4 of the Instrument.[9] Any suggestion, however, that this technical requirement for ratification of the new tax and militia left Desborough with no option but to introduce his bill is very much open to question. As has been mentioned above, during the entire three-month period from the meeting of the parliament in mid September 1656 to the introduction of Desborough's bill at Christmas, no MP appears to have raised the question of the need for parliamentary sanction of the new militia, or to have attempted to force a debate on the issue. Given this apparent absence of parliamentary pressure, there was no compelling reason why the financial underpinning for the rule of the major-generals could not, for the foreseeable future at least, have rested on the same executive directives which had established it the previous year. It is quite possible that, if Desborough had not introduced his bill, the decimation tax might never have come under attack in the parliament and might have continued to be collected after its dissolution.

The council was almost certainly aware of Desborough's intentions, for on 17 December it resolved to consider the question of the decimation tax the following week on the 23rd. The minutes of its meetings on the 23rd, 24th and 25th make no mention, however, of any discussion of the topic and whether it was ever debated is unclear. Nor is there any firm evidence about the precise degree of conciliar support Desborough enjoyed, though several councillors did speak in favour of his bill on 25 December. If the council did discuss the plan, it is unlikely that Cromwell, who was present both on the 23rd and 24th, gave his brother-in-law much encouragement. Speaking to a group of army officers at the end of February 1657 after the defeat of the militia bill, he gave the strong impression that he had been puzzled by the decision to introduce the bill and still failed to understand the reasoning behind it. After praising the major-generals, some of whom were amongst his audience, for performing their duties conscientiously, he added pointedly: 'You might have gone on. Who bid you go to the House with a bill, and there receive a foil?'[10] Whatever the thinking behind Desborough's decision to seek parliamentary approval for the militia and the tax which sustained it, in the light of subsequent events it is hard not to regard it as another serious and avoidable tactical miscalculation, and one which did much to seal the fate of the major-generals.

Even in the thin House of 25 December 1656 Desborough's proposal did not have an easy ride.[11] The major-general argued that a bill was necessary because the royalist community had refused to become reconciled to the protectorate and should thus be expected to bear the financial burden of the new militia which had been raised to protect the regime. He argued that, rather than expecting everyone to bear an equal share in the costs of defence, they should maintain a 'discrimination' and 'lay the saddle upon the right horse'. At the same time, he made clear he was prepared to exempt from the tax any royalist who 'shall come in to a cheerful compliance with us', and he declared: 'It is their reformation, not their ruin [that] is desired.'

He was opposed by a number of MPs, including the speaker, Sir Thomas

Widdrington, Bulstrode Whitelocke and Sir John Glynne. The principal argument of these and others was that parliamentary confirmation of the decimation tax would constitute a serious violation of the Act Of Oblivion passed by the Rump of the Long Parliament in February 1652, which had offered to all royalists who agreed to live peaceably under the commonwealth a pardon for their actions prior to the battle of Worcester in September 1651. Some of the MPs with a legal background were particularly worried about the implications of contravening this earlier act. The Master of the Rolls, William Lenthall, asserted that 'it is not for the honour of a parliament to break the faith of parliaments. Never was an Act of Oblivion violated by a parliament in any age of the world.' Another objector, Thomas Bampfield, MP for Exeter, argued that no matter how dishonourably some of the cavaliers had behaved, parliament 'ought to be honest with them'. He could not accept that it was right to punish all royalists for the offences of a few and believed that, if they now perpetuated an unjust exaction, God might come to 'plead' for their enemies. He was clearly acquainted with Machiavelli's *The Prince*, which had recently been published in English, and he intimated that Desborough and his supporters appeared to share the Italian writer's view that it was justifiable 'to place honesty only in safety'. He added, however, that in his view, 'God's rules are otherwise.'

It was Bampfield who drew the House's attention to the biblical precedent of the relations between the Israelites and their neighbours, the idolatrous Gibeonites. As the majority of his listeners would have been aware, the Old Testament books of Joshua and Samuel told the story of how the Israelite warlord, Joshua, had been tricked into making a treaty with the Gibeonites and how, after the deception had been discovered, he and his advisers had been roundly criticised by their own people. They had nonetheless refused to renege on the treaty, declaring: 'We have sworn unto them by the Lord God of Israel: now therefore we may not touch them.' Some years later, Joshua's successor, King Saul, had ignored the agreement and attacked the town of Gibeon, slaughtering a number of its inhabitants. As a result of this breach of faith, the Israelites had suffered three years of famine, and the blood guilt had only been removed when, at the wishes of the Gibeonites, King David had executed seven of Saul's sons.[12]

Bampfield warned his fellow MPs that the incident might 'run parallel with the case of the cavaliers'. Although Joshua had been cozened into making the original treaty and Saul had subsequently acted 'out of zeal to the House of Israel', the Israelites had still been severely punished for not keeping faith. By the same token, Bampfield argued, even though Desborough and his allies believed the royalists had tricked the Rump into granting an Act of Oblivion, they would still incur God's wrath if their zeal for the godly cause led them to violate its terms. This same biblical precedent was again referred to several weeks later by Roger Boyle, Lord Broghill, in a speech against the bill during the debate on its first reading on 7 January.[13] It had also been invoked several months earlier by the prominent exiled royalist, Edward Hyde, who, posing as an anonymous member of the 1654 Parliament, had published in July 1656 an answer to Cromwell's declaration of the previous October, which had outlined the government's reasons for establishing the major-generals in power.[14]

Desborough found support on the 25th from a number of other MPs, including several members of the council and some of his fellow army officers. The main argument presented on this side of the House was that the Act of Oblivion had been a contentious measure which had only offered pardons to the royalists on the implicit condition that they abandon their opposition to the new republic, and that this they had subsequently refused to do. Sir Gilbert Pickering declared that they remained 'implacable and irreconcilable to our interest', and John Lambert complained that 'they are as careful to breed up their children in the memory of the quarrel as can be' and would not be reconciled to the protectorate 'till time wear out memory'. According to these supporters of a bill, by remaining obdurate the royalists had forfeited all right to receive pardons, and the constant threat they posed to state security had forced the government to adopt as its maxim, *salus populi suprema lex.*

Another theme emphasised by those MPs who favoured Desborough's proposal was that the charging of the decimation tax upon their enemies had been a source of comfort to the 'well affected' godly minorities in the counties. Luke Robinson stated that 'the honest party look upon it as a great favour that there is a distinction made, a character set upon him, that you may know a Cavalier from a Roundhead', adding that 'if you will bear witness to that distinction it will encourage your friends.' Samuel Bedford, who claimed to have been involved in the assessment of the decimation tax in Bedfordshire, also reported: 'I know your friends were much satisfied that you put that distinction.' After declaring that he would only support the bill if he were convinced it was *bonum* as well as *utile,* John Lambert warned the House that the dangers from the royalists remained acute. He attempted to discredit Bampfield's biblical analogy by arguing that unlike the royalists the Gibeonites had never disturbed the peace nor 'made any insurrection against Israel'. Thomas Kelsey also spoke up strongly on Desborough's behalf and accused his fellow MPs of showing more consideration to their enemies than to the soldiers who had fought on their behalf. When the House divided at the end of the debate, Desborough was granted permission to introduce a bill by eighty-eight votes to sixty-three. This unexpectedly narrow result prompted William Denton to comment several days later: 'if the house fill, much good may be hoped for; if not, *actum est.*'[15]

The MPs had planned to debate Desborough's bill the following day, but other business intervened and it was not brought back until 7 January 1657. At the beginning of the discussion on that day, one member immediately stood up to complain that the bill which was now before the House was significantly different in content from the one discussed a fortnight earlier.[16] As well as seeking to perpetuate the punitive tax on royalists, it now also included an indemnity for the major-generals and their commissioners for all their activities over the previous eighteen months. It is unclear on whose initiative this indemnity clause had been inserted into the bill, but it is unlikely that it was Desborough's own idea. During the ensuing debate, he expressed his gratitude for the suggestion, but went on to declare: 'it is our swords must indemnify us.' Thomas Burton, meanwhile, overheard Robert Lilburne muttering to his neighbour during a speech in support of the clause that he 'scorned' to accept it.

The subsequent discussions on 7 January rehearsed many of the arguments of two weeks before. The opponents of the bill once again stressed the importance of upholding the Act of Oblivion and argued that parliament was obliged to deal justly and honourably with its enemies. Lord Broghill expressed his disquiet at the absence of any formal right of appeal against the decimation tax, and Bulstrode Whitelocke subjected the House to a lengthy historical survey of previous Acts of Oblivion before concluding: 'If you shake that act, you shake all foundations.' John Trevor gave voice to a more general objection to the rule of the major-generals, arguing that the bill would 'divide this commonwealth into provinces' and 'cantonize the nation' by sanctioning 'a power that was never set up in any nation without dangerous consequences'. In reply, Desborough once more claimed that the royalists had contravened the spirit of the Act of Oblivion and declared: 'it was blows not fair words that settled and must settle the peace of England.' He attempted to counter Trevor's argument by claiming that the power exercised by the major-generals was little different to that enjoyed by the pre-war lord lieutenants who had controlled the county trained bands.

One early intervention in the debate on 7 January, which was seen as highly significant by some observers, was the speech made by Cromwell's son-in-law and master of horse, Lord John Claypole. Claypole, who rarely spoke in the House, was one of the first to rise to his feet that day to express his opposition to the continuation of the decimation tax and his support for a separate indemnity bill. According to Edmund Ludlow, many of his fellow MPs interpreted his comments as a clear indication that Cromwell did not wish to see the bill passed and opposition to the measure consequently increased.[17] Claypole was a close associate of Cromwell, but there is no direct evidence that in making this speech he was acting on orders from the protector.

The MPs once again concluded their discussions with the intention of continuing with them the following day, but from 8 to 19 January parliamentary business was disrupted by the indisposition of the speaker. The debate on the militia bill was only resumed on 20 January and it then took up much of the House's attention for the next ten days. Regrettably, Thomas Burton's diary gives very few details of these debates, but other sources reveal that the MPs remained deeply divided and that a number of intemperate remarks were flung around. Contemporaries remarked that the House engaged in 'a serious debate and not without sharpness and reflexions', and that the outcome remained 'at soe even a cast that as yet it cannot be discerned'.[18] According to one report, when Sir George Booth commented that 'the maior generals were Cromwell's hangmen', Charles Howard gave him 'a sharpe reply' and the altercation nearly resulted in a swordfight.[19]

Two other members – James Ashe, and the protector's second cousin, Henry Cromwell – were later censured by the House for having made derogatory comments about the major-generals. According to the MP, Vincent Gookin, Henry Cromwell was so angered by a 'little too hot' speech made by William Boteler on 21 January, in the course of which the major-general argued that it was acceptable for all royalists to be held responsible for the actions of a few, that he sprang to his feet to point out that 'by the same argument ... because some of the major-generals have done amisse, which I offer to prove, therefore all of them deserved to be punished.' An outraged Thomas Kelsey immediately demanded that he should name whom he meant and Cromwell, who was almost certainly referring to Boteler, responded that he was prepared to do so. At that point, however, according to Gookin, 'this fire was putt out by the grave water-carriers in the house.'[20]

John Thurloe, who had made a short speech in support of Desborough's proposal on 25 December, may also have intervened again in the debates on one of these days. Amongst his papers is a document containing a draft in his own hand of a speech in favour of the militia bill; the notes outlined the crimes of the royalists in great detail and argued trenchantly that it was vital for state security that the militia and the tax which supported it should be continued.[21] Nonetheless, when the House finally took its decision on 29 January, it decisively rejected the bill by 124 votes to 88. Desborough's supporters had mustered exactly the same strength as they had a month before on 25 December but, as William Denton had predicted, they had been overwhelmed by the opposition of the more moderate members who had returned after the Christmas holiday. Significantly, nearly a hundred members had failed to vote at all.

Not surprisingly, the major-generals were bitterly disappointed by the result. On the day of the vote, William Denton reported to Ralph Verney that 'they do not a little storme' at the result, and another newsletter commented that they were 'very loath to surrender'.[22] John Thurloe was almost certainly referring to them when he told Henry Cromwell on 3 February that 'some gentlemen doe thinke themselves much trampled upon by this voet and are extreamely sensible thereof', adding that the debates on the bill had 'wrought such a heate in the house that I feare little will be done for the future'.[23] Vincent Gookin, meanwhile, reported that a few hours after the vote some of the major-generals had confronted Cromwell directly; complaining bitterly that their defeat had 'discouraged the godly', they told him that 'their ayme was to pass noething that might tend to his accomodation and that they would rayse no money, etc.'[24] If this was indeed their intention, the following day's proceedings revealed just how little influence they exercised over the House, for on 30 January the same MPs who had rejected the militia bill quickly pushed through a vote to supply the government with £400,000 in general taxation. Gookin again commented that 'those that were for the decimation-bill, it was plainely perceived, were exceeding cold in the debate for raysing money and seemed to repine that the parliament did soe well.'[25]

By depriving it of its financial underpinning, the vote of 29 January 1657 holed the major-generals' experiment below the water-line and did much to persuade Cromwell to abandon it. To explain how such a powerful and influential group of army officers could have suffered so humiliating a defeat it is necessary to consider the hostility their activities had aroused within the political nation, the reaction of Oliver Cromwell to the opposition they faced in parliament in January 1657, and the way their future became inextricably entangled with moves in the House to refound the government on a hereditary, or even monarchical basis.

As was seen in chapter 9, the August election campaign had made very clear the depth of the country's hostility towards the major-generals. While none of the elected members had gone so far as to launch an assault on them prior to the introduction of the militia bill, once Desborough had provided them with an opportunity to express their misgivings about their rule, many of them were prepared to lend their support to those leading the opposition to the bill. But, while the major-generals' unpopularity was undoubtedly a major factor contributing to the defeat of the militia bill, it by no means made it inevitable. For if the executive had remained steadfast in its support for them, the attack upon them need not necessarily have proved fatal to their rule. It is important, therefore, to consider whether a more fundamental reason for the fall of the major-generals was that their master decided to sacrifice them for his own political ends.

Any investigation of Oliver Cromwell's attitude to the problems faced by the major-generals during December 1656 and January 1657 can only arrive at tentative conclusions. Several contemporary observers were convinced that well before the House finally voted down the militia bill on 29 January the protector had decided that they should be put aside. Edmund Ludlow claimed in his memoirs that 'ambition corrupted his [Cromwell's] understanding to that degree that he made no scruple to sacrifice these men who, to say no worse, had enlarged their consciences to an extraordinary size in the execution of his orders, to those who in requital of the favour had promised to make him king.'[26] The Venetian envoy, Giavarina, also believed that by mid January Cromwell wished to see the militia bill defeated, having come to the conclusion that, if the major-generals were established permanently, the more ambitious of them like Lambert might gain a sufficiently strong power base from which to challenge him for his own position.[27] Vincent Gookin was also in no doubt that Lambert was behind the moves to establish the major-generals on a permanent basis as a way of increasing his own political influence. In a coded letter, dated 27 January, he informed the protector's son, Henry Cromwell, that 'Lambert is much for decimations ... I dare write no more of it, but if I could, I should convince you that my jealousy is not groundless.'[28] The following week, he reported to him that the protector had held a series of meetings throughout January with Oliver St John and William Pierrepont, in the course of which the possibility of adjusting the constitution to make Cromwell king had been discussed.[29]

As further confirmation that Cromwell had turned against the major-generals by mid January, Gookin also reported to Henry the sequel to the dispute in the House between his namesake and William Boteler. He related how soon after the incident Henry Cromwell had been accosted by several of the major-generals, who had told him that the protector would 'take it ill' that he had publicly criticised them. Henry thereupon went straight to see Oliver and told him that 'he had his blacke booke and papers ready to make good what he [had] said.' Oliver had 'answered him in rallary' and given him a cloak and some gloves, which Henry had worn in the House for the next few days 'to the great satisfaction and delight of some and trouble of others'. Gookin commented of the story: 'It was a pretty passage of his highness; pray consider it.' He clearly believed that this apparently trivial incident was highly significant, and that Oliver's relaxed attitude to his cousin's criticisms of one of the major-generals was evidence that he no longer supported the army colleagues about whom he had spoken so warmly just four months before.[30]

The testimony of these men cannot, however, be entirely relied upon. By the mid 1650s, Ludlow had developed a passionate hatred for Cromwell, whom he viewed as the cynical betrayer of the 'good old cause' of republicanism. Giavarina was heavily reliant on second-hand information and did not fully understand Cromwell's character, and in particular the strength of the ties of loyalty and comradeship that bound him to his fellow army officers. Gookin was a strong supporter of a return to monarchy and obviously realised that the recipient of his letters might look favourably upon the client who had reported to him the good news that he might soon be a royal prince and second in line to the throne.

There is, furthermore, other evidence which appears to argue against this reading of events and to suggest instead that, rather than being the orchestrator of the events of January 1657, Cromwell remained, as he had on a number of similar occasions in the past, an indecisive bystander torn between two opposing factions and uncertain about which to back. In a letter to Edward Montague written on 9 January, William Boteler revealed that he and a number of his fellow officers had met with Cromwell the previous evening and had come away much reassured, believing that the protector still shared their concern about the fiercely anti-army sentiments which had been expressed in parliament over the preceding days.[31] Several weeks later on 29 January, just a few hours after the defeat of the bill, Cromwell approached Lord Broghill and asked him why he had voted against the measure. The Irish peer had replied that he had done him a great service, 'by hindering your government from becoming disgustful', adding that if the bill had become law 'it would have made three kingdoms rise up against you; and they were your enemies not your friends who brought it in.' In Broghill's account of the encounter, Cromwell is portrayed as genuinely puzzled by the outcome of the vote, and the peer's comment that, as a result of the conversation, Cromwell '*began* to distrust those who had advised him' to support the bill would seem to argue against the theory that there had been a breach between protector and major-generals prior to the vote on the 29th.[32]

A month later, Sir Christopher Packe presented to the House a remonstrance, possibly drawn up by Broghill and his associates, calling upon Cromwell to take upon himself the title of king. Most of the major-generals and their fellow army officers objected vehemently to this proposal, and over the next few weeks they held a number of meetings with the protector to express their opposition. On several occasions during these audiences, Cromwell went out of his way to deny any personal involvement in either the defeat of the militia bill or the movement to make him king. According to one army officer, on the evening of the first debate in parliament on Packe's remonstrance

> some of the major-generalls were with his Highness, [and] tarried a quarter of an hower in the roome before one word passed from either. At length they began and complained of the parliament. His Highness answered hastily: 'What would you have me doe? Are they not of your own garbling? [choosing] Did not you admit whom you pleased and keep out whom you pleased? And now doe you complain to me. Did I meddle with it?' And so withdrew.[33]

On another occasion a few days later, Cromwell reportedly told a larger group of officers that he had first heard of the moves to make him king from one of those present, Colonel Mills, and declared that 'he had never been at any cabal about the same'. He also asserted:

> I have no design upon them or you. I never courted you, nor never will. I have a sure refuge; if they doe good things, I must and will stand by them. They are honest men and have done good things; I know not what you can blame them for unless because they love me too well.[34]

These protestations could, of course, have been little more than the disingenuous special pleading of a crafty politician. They are much more likely, however, to have been the honest testimony of a confused individual who had for some weeks been reacting to rather than dictating events. Indeed, probably the most telling comment about Oliver Cromwell's personal involvement in the process which led to the downfall of the major-generals was that made by his old friend, Sir Francis Russell, who in a letter to his son-in-law, Henry Cromwell, written after the 29 January, remarked:

> Suppose I should tell you he often knows not his owne mind ... the truth is your father hath of late made more wise men fooles than ever; he laughs and is merry, but they hange down theyr heads and are pittyfully out of countenance.[35]

This assessment of the events of January 1657 has been disputed by Carol Egloff who has argued that as early as the beginning of the month Cromwell had decided that the major-generals should be removed. In support of this theory, she has pointed to the fact that several members of the council who had spoken in favour of Desborough's bill on 25 December declined to do so again on 7 January. She has also claimed that, as a result of Cromwell's decision to dispense with the major-generals, Thurloe failed to deliver the second speech in their defence, the notes for which exist among his papers.[36] Her argument is, however, rather speculative and too dependent on negative evidence. According to Burton's diary, no fewer than eleven members who had supported Desborough on 25 December did not make a second speech on his behalf on 7 January; among them were three of the major-generals, who had certainly not changed their minds about the desirability of the bill. Furthermore, the thinness of the record of the parliamentary debates in late January make it impossible to state with any degree of certainty whether or not Thurloe and some of these others did in fact speak again in favour of the bill in the week preceding its rejection.

On balance, the evidence seems to suggest that, rather than positively seeking the defeat of the major-generals, Cromwell had stood hesitantly by in the wings while others engineered their fall. Within a few months he was expressing regret at their passing and the resultant loss of their work for moral reform, and in April 1657 he told the emissaries of parliament with whom he was negotiating the details of their proposed monarchical constitution that they had done 'excellent good service' and acted 'honourably and honestly and profitably.'[37] But, while he had almost certainly not actively sought the removal of the major-generals, he had singularly failed to offer them the clear and unequivocal support that might have ensured their survival. As a result most of them felt badly let down by him, and the belated endorsements referred to above did little to soothe their wounded feelings.

While Cromwell remained trapped in indecision, a small group of influential politicians was working steadily behind the scene in an attempt to remove the major-generals and bring about a return to the traditional monarchical constitution, a move they believed offered the best prospect of reconciling the nation to Cromwell's rule. At the core of this group was a small and highly organised nucleus of MPs with Irish seats, including John Bridges, Lord Broghill, William Jephson and Vincent Gookin. Around them clustered prominent lawyers like Oliver St John and Sir John Glynne; members of the council, such as Sir Charles Wolseley and Philip Jones; and several long-term associates of Cromwell, including William Pierrepont and Edward Montague.[38] Undoubtedly, the dislike these men felt towards the major-generals and their subordinates was a very important motivation behind their attempt to bring about a return to monarchy. When in late February 1657 Packe introduced to the House the remonstrance which offered Cromwell the crown, he launched a bitter attack on the soldiers, 'highly exclaiming against the major-generals and the decimations brought in by them'.[39] According to one contemporary commentator, those who supported him were 'so highly incensed against the arbetrary actions of the major generalls that they are greedy of any powers that will be ruled and limited by lawe'.[40]

Tensions between this 'kingship group' and the major-generals had been apparent from the early stages of the parliament. On 21 November 1656, James Berry had turned aggressively on John Bridges after the latter had intervened in a discussion he was having with another member on the subject of the succession. Berry had become so agitated that Desborough had been forced to restrain him physically.[41] In such a climate, the introduction of the militia bill proved a godsend for the kingship group, for by threatening permanent military rule it acted as a catalyst to the discussions about constitutional change and gave added urgency to their efforts to remove the major-generals. The kingship group both spoke in public against Desborough's bill and worked behind the scenes to coordinate resistance to it. For obvious reasons they have left no clear evidence of the exact nature of their activities, but it is nonetheless possible to obtain the occasional glimpse of their secret manoeuvres. On 7 January 1657, Thomas Burton was told by several of his fellow MPs that 'it was the distinguishing character of those that were against this bill that they were for hereditary rank.'[42] The private consultations involving the protector, St John and Pierrepont, which Gookin claimed had taken place throughout January, were clearly another important element of the campaign. The fact that the defeat of the militia bill was followed the next day by a substantial grant of general taxation suggests that those involved had not only discussed the offer of the crown, but assured Cromwell that, once the bill had fallen, alternative revenue sources would quickly be provided by parliament.[43]

The events of 19 January 1657, when the kingship question was openly discussed in the chamber for the first time, may also have been the result of the machinations of those who favoured a return to monarchy. Immediately after the House had been informed of the Sindercombe assassination plot against Cromwell, John Ashe, one of the members for Somerset, stood up to suggest that the protector should be urged to 'take upon him the government according to the ancient constitution; so that the hopes of our enemies plots would be at an end'. Predictably, the suggestion proved very contentious. While some members argued that it should be seriously considered, others objected strongly, and Desborough argued that the crown would be 'but a slender prop without taking care to secure his enemies'.[44]

Thomas Burton's remarks about the way this debate was concluded are particularly interesting. He was clearly very puzzled both by the abrupt ending of the discussions and by the fact that the issue was not taken up again over the next few days. He commented in his diary:

> the debate fell asleep, I know not how, but I believe it was by consent, (as I heard Mr. Nathaniel Bacon and others say, as they came out) and only started by way of probation. I have not seen so hot a debate vanish so strangely, like an *ignis fatuus*.[45]

These comments may indicate that, rather than being a spontaneous reaction to the news of the assassination attempt, Ashe's intervention was a premeditated ploy and that he may have deliberately floated the possibility of Cromwell taking the crown as a way of increasing the opposition within the House to the militia bill.[46] The fact that it was Ashe's son, James, who launched a furious attack on Desborough in the House just three days later on 22 January is perhaps further evidence that the bill's opponents were carefully planning their activities.[47]

In early March 1657, five weeks after the defeat of Desborough's bill, Cromwell met with the major-generals and some of their fellow army officers to explain to them his attitude to the question of the kingship. He began by defending himself against accusations that he had secretly conspired to gain the crown, and by claiming that the title of king was merely a 'feather in a hat', which 'he loved ... as little as they did'. He then reviewed the major political developments of the mid 1650s, arguing that throughout the past four years he had been the army officers' 'drudge' and had been forced by them first to dissolve the Rump, and then to summon two largely unproductive bodies: Barebone's Parliament and the 1654 parliament. As for the major-generals, after acknowledging that they had served him well, he went on to criticise them roundly both for advocating the calling of the 1656 parliament and for introducing the militia bill. At the end of the address he effectively drew down the curtain on their rule by declaring: 'it is time to come to a settlement and lay aside arbitrary proceedings, so unacceptable to the nation.'[48]

Despite this clear indication that Cromwell had by now bowed to the inevitable and decided to abandon the attempt to rule the provinces directly through the army, the major-generals continued to resent deeply their defeat and to argue fiercely against the re-introduction of the monarchy. In February 1657, all of them, with the sole exception of Charles Howard, voted against the motion that the House should take Packe's remonstrance into considera-tion.[49] Several days later, a delegation of their fellow army officers met with them at John Desborough's lodgings 'to acquaint them with the feares and jealousies that lay upon them in relation to the protector's alteracion of his title, and to desire the knowledge of the truth of things'. At a subsequent meeting, John Lambert assured them that the major-generals would keep them informed of developments and advised them to show moderation and patience and 'to wait upon the eye of providence therein'.[50]

In late March, it was reported that most of the major-generals were still 'much averse' to a return to monarchy.[51] On the 25th, William Boteler acted as one of the tellers for the noes when the House voted to offer Cromwell the crown in the document 'The Humble Petition and Advice', and two weeks later Desborough and Edward Whalley were again tellers for the noes when the House voted to repeat the offer after the protector had rejected it.[52] During April, however, some of them may have begun to change their minds. One report from this month claimed that Boteler, Whalley and Goffe were grudgingly coming to terms with the probable return of the monarchy, and Whalley admitted in parliament on 24 April that, rather than forego some of the good features of 'The Humble Petition and Advice', he could 'swallow that of the title'.[53] Some of the other major-generals, however, remained deeply opposed to the direction of political events, and one report stated that Desborough 'remained in sullen posture'.[54] That the government was still very concerned at this stage that one or more of these disgruntled major-generals might attempt to raise up sections of the army to prevent the move back to monarchy is suggested by that fact that Thurloe was intercepting some of their correspondence at this stage.[55]

By the beginning of May 1657, most observers believed Cromwell was about to accept the offer of the crown and that the rearguard action by some sections of the army against a rising tide of monarchism both inside and outside parliament was doomed to failure. On the 8th of that month, however, the protector announced to the surprised MPs that he felt compelled to decline their offer.[56] Historians have disagreed as to which considerations were most influential in producing this decision. Some, such as W. C. Abbott and Roger Hainsworth, have suggested that a last-minute intervention by Desborough, Charles Fleetwood and Lambert was crucial in persuading him to abandon his inclination to accept.[57] Others, such as Austin Woolrych, have argued that he had never intended to accept the crown and had all along manoeuvred to obtain an amended constitution without a change in his title.[58] For whatever reason, the major-generals had got their way and the kingship group which had masterminded their fall from power was, for the time being at least, thwarted in its ambition to restore the monarchy.

Once they had recovered from their collective shock at Cromwell's refusal of the offer of the crown, the MPs presented him with an amended version of 'The Humble Petition and Advice', which he accepted at the end of the month. This document made several important amendments to the constitution, including re-introducing a second chamber of parliament and allowing the protector to nominate his successor. As far as the major-generals were concerned the only other significant development prior to the prorogation of the parliament at the end of June was the passing of an act granting them and their commissioners for securing the peace of the commonwealth complete immunity from prosecution for their actions over the previous two years.

Following the presentation of an army petition, the House had set up a committee to consider the indemnity issue as early as November 1656. Little progress, however, had been made over the ensuing weeks and, as has been seen, the question surfaced again during the debates on the abortive militia bill in early January. On 20 March 1657, the attorney general was ordered to draw up an indemnity bill, and a few days later his draft was presented to the House for the first time and referred to a committee which included John Desborough. Again, little progress was made over the next two months and on 15 June Edward Whalley urged the House to turn its attention to the bill as a matter of urgency. A week later, several amendments were accepted and the bill subsequently passed the House on 23 June. On 26 June, the final day of the session, Cromwell gave his assent to the 'Act for Indempnifying of such Persons as have acted for the Service of the Publique'. While this legislation did not specifically mention the office of major-general or commissioner for securing the peace of the commonwealth, it stated that the uprisings in the spring of 1655 had forced the government to appoint people to ensure the safety of the regime and that 'their endeavours tended onely to the security and advantage of the publique and reformation of these nations without any sinister respects of their own'. It went on to declare that the government was obliged in 'honour and justice' to ensure that 'they be protected and acquitted from any suit action, prosecution or molestation for or in respect of such service'.[59]

While the defeat of Desborough's militia bill brought an end to the rule of the major-generals in its fully fledged form, it is important to note that the system did not disappear overnight. In the weeks that followed the defeat of the militia bill, the council continued to refer routine matters to the major-generals almost as if nothing had happened. During February 1657, for example, Tobias Bridge was asked to find a governor for a hospital in Chester, Robert Lilburne was directed to intervene in a dispute concerning some lands in Yorkshire belonging to the Mauleverer family, and William Goffe was told to discuss the activities of the Quakers in Sussex with John Desborough and Sir Gilbert Pickering.[60] In March, the council referred a petition to Lilburne, and at the end of April they ordered him to send up one of his prisoners to London.[61]

Most of the major-generals in fact remained very much in evidence in their associations for some time after the defeat of the militia bill. Sir John Barkstead, Rowland Dawkins, Charles Howard, Thomas Kelsey, Robert Lilburne and John Nicholas all continued to exercise authority in their associations during 1657 and 1658 as governors of important garrison towns within them. Some of their fellow major-generals, such as William Boteler in Northamptonshire and Hezekiah Haynes in Essex, also remained active within part of their old areas as justices of the peace.[62] On occasions, too, Cromwell still gathered them together in London to consult them about security issues; according to one report, for example, in April 1658 he 'spent much tyme in private debate with the majour generalls, to the further security of the nations'.[63] But, if the major-generals were still much in evidence, their status was now ambiguous. In August 1657, for example, the council acknowledged the confusion over Lilburne's position by writing both to him and to the sheriff of Durham to ask them to investigate an alleged breach of the sabbath in that county.[64]

Despite the substantial arrears of pay they were owed and the disappearance after January 1657 of any real prospect of regular ongoing funding, a number of the county militia troops also remained in existence. In February 1657, Cromwell wrote to all the militia captains to inform them that he had received intelligence of an imminent popish insurrection at home and an invasion on behalf of Charles Stuart from abroad. After directing them to prepare their troops for action, he told them they would receive more detailed orders from their major-generals 'with whome wee have spoken more at large and to whome we referre you'.[65] A year later, in February 1658, he wrote to his friend, Alban Cox, who was still acting as the captain of the Hertfordshire militia troop, to ask him to be vigilant against a possible uprising. In the letter, he expressed his regret at the government's failure to pay the troops and promised he would do his utmost to rectify this.[66] The militia troops in some other parts of the country, including Hampshire and the west country, also continued in existence during 1658 and 1659.[67] Thus, while the rule of the major-generals had been effectively killed off in early 1657, a not insubstantial ghostly remnant of it lingered on until Cromwell's death eighteen months later.

This detailed consideration of the complex series of events which occurred at Whitehall and Westminster during the midwinter months of 1656–57 has suggested that the story of the fall of the major-generals is a 'whodunit' in which all the suspects bear some degree of guilt. To a degree, the major-generals were undoubtedly the authors of their own misfortune, for by the autumn of 1656 their rule had given rise to widespread resentment in the nation and this was reflected in the hostility exhibited towards them both during the election campaign and subsequently at Westminster. It is also difficult not to conclude that Desborough's decision to ask parliament to confirm the decimation tax was both unnecessary and ill-conceived, as it provided the House with the perfect opportunity to attack the major-generals' rule and, by raising the spectre of a permanent military state, persuaded many of the more moderate MPs to fall into line behind the kingship group's plan to bring about a return to monarchy. Ivan Roots's remark that 'the major-generals were not politically murdered, they almost but not quite committed suicide' is thus broadly accurate, for while Desborough clearly did not set out to bring down his colleagues, his tactical error did a great deal to ensure their demise.[68]

Cromwell for his part was almost certainly not a devious Machiavellian intriguer who deliberately betrayed his army colleagues by secretly conspiring with their opponents. He did, however, react to the crisis with his characteristic dithering and evasiveness and conspicuously failed to provide the major-generals with the firm public backing that might have done much to bolster their threatened authority. He was certainly, therefore, guilty of sins of omission, if not commission, against them. Finally, a large share of the blame – or credit – for the fall of the major-generals must be laid at the feet of the group of MPs around Lord Broghill who wished to see the soldiers removed to make way for the return of the monarchy. Seizing the opportunity which Desborough presented them with on Christmas Day 1656, they went on to conduct a highly organised campaign and to engineer the fall of the major-generals as a first step towards their ultimate aim of securing the accession of King Oliver I. Their ultimate failure to achieve this end was to a large extent a product of Oliver Cromwell's chronic indecisiveness. It should also be seen, however, as the revenge of the ousted major-generals, who even after they had fallen from power continued to be numbered amongst the protectors's closest and most respected colleagues.

NOTES

1   Abbott, *Writings and Speeches of Cromwell*, vol. 4, pp. 260–79.

2   Bod. Lib., Rawlinson MSS, A 41, fols 698–9, 860–1.

3   *Ibid.*, A35, fol. 4.

4   Rutt, *Diary of Thomas Burton*, vol. 1, pp. 24–170.

5   Bod. Lib., Carte MSS, 228, fol. 81.

6   Buckinghamshire Record Office, M11/14, Denton to Verney, 29 Dec. 1656. The phrase translates as 'when the gentry were feasting'.

7   For the petition see BL, 669.f.20.44; the response is given in Rutt, *Diary of Thomas Burton*, vol. 1, pp. 208–9.

8   Rutt, *Diary of Thomas Burton*, vol. 1, pp. 313, 316–17.

9   J. Kenyon (ed.), *The Stuart Constitution* (Cambridge, 1966), pp. 342–8; Bod. Lib., Tanner MSS, 52, fol. 149.

10 *Calendar of State Papers Domestic, 1656–7*, pp. xxi, 202, 208–10, 211–12, 214–15; Rutt, *Diary of Thomas Burton*, vol. 1, p. 384.

11 For the debate on 25 Dec., see Rutt, *Diary of Thomas Burton*, vol. 1, pp. 230–43.

12 According to Burton, Bampfield cited chapter 21 of the first book of Samuel as his biblical reference. The story is in fact told in chapter 21 of the second book of Samuel. For the trickery involved in the original treaty see Joshua, 9: 4–27.

13 Rutt, *Diary of Thomas Burton*, vol. 1, p. 312.

14 BL, E. 884.2, *A Letter from a True and Lawfull Member of Parliament*, (London, 1656). For the October declaration, see chapter 2.

15 Buckinghamshire RO, M11/14, Denton to Verney, 29 Dec. 1656.

16 For the debate on 7 Jan., see Rutt, *Diary of Thomas Burton*, vol. 1, pp. 310–21; an abstract of Broghill's speech can be found in Bod. Lib., Tanner MSS, 52, fol. 186.

17 C. H. Firth (ed.), *The Memoirs of Edmund Ludlow* (2 vols, Oxford, 1894), vol. 2, p. 20; see also C. H. Firth, *The Last Years of The Protectorate* (2 vols, London, 1909), vol. 1, pp. 110–11; and David Watson Rannie, 'Cromwell's Major-Generals', *English Historical Review*, 10 (1895), 504–5.

18 C. H. Firth (ed.), *The Clarke Papers*, vol. III, Camden Soc. Publs, new series, 61 (1899), 87–8.

19 Bod. Lib., Clarendon MSS, 53, fol. 244.

20 Rutt, *Diary of Thomas Burton*, vol. 1, p. 369; Birch, *State Papers of John Thurloe*, vol. 6, pp. 19–21.

21 Bod. Lib. Rawlinson MSS, A 30, fols 371–8.

22 Buckinghamshire RO, M11/14, Denton to Verney, 29 Jan. 1657; *Clarke Papers*, vol. III, p. 88.

23 Birch, *State Papers of John Thurloe*, vol. 6, p. 38.

24 *Ibid.*, vol. 6, pp. 37–8.

25 *Ibid.*, vol. 6, pp. 37–8.

26 Firth, *Memoirs of Edmund Ludlow*, vol. 2, pp. 19–20.

27 *Calendar of State Papers Venetian, 1657–9*, pp. 5, 12, 15.

28 Birch, *State Papers of John Thurloe*, vol. 6, pp. 19–21.

29 *Ibid.*, vol 6, p. 37.

30 *Ibid.*, vol. 6, pp. 19–21.

31 Bod. Lib., Carte MSS, 73, fol. 18.

32 Abbott, *Writings and Speeches of Cromwell*, vol. 4, p. 396; the italics are mine.

33 *Ibid.*, vol. 4, p. 414.

34 Rutt, *Diary of Thomas Burton Diary*, vol. 1, p. 382; Abbott, *Writings and Speeches of Cromwell*, vol. 4, pp. 418–19.

35 Quoted by C. H. Firth in 'Cromwell and the Crown, Part II', *English Historical Review*, 18 (1903), 78.

36 Carol S. Egloff, 'Settlement and Kingship: The Army, the Gentry, and the Offer of the Crown to Oliver Cromwell' (Unpub. Ph.D. thesis, Yale University, 1990), pp. 172–261.

37 Abbott, *Writings and Speeches of Cromwell*, vol. 4, pp. 493–4.

38 For more details see Egloff, 'Settlement and Kingship', pp. 289–397.

39 Birch, *State Papers of John Thurloe*, vol. 6, p. 84.

40 Firth, *Clarke Papers*, vol. III, pp. 90–1.

41 Firth, *Last Years of the Protectorate*, vol. 1, p. 60; C. H. Firth, 'Cromwell and the Crown, Part I', *English Historical Review*, 17 (1902), 438–9.

42 Rutt, *Diary of Thomas Burton*, vol. 1, p. 321.

43 *Calendar of State Papers Venetian, 1657–9*, p. 2; Birch, *State Papers of John Thurloe*, vol. 6, p. 37.

44 Rutt, *Diary of Thomas Burton*, vol. 1, pp. 362–5.

45 *Ibid.*, vol. 1, pp. 365–6; an *ignis fatuus* is a will-o-the-wisp, or optical illusion.

46 Whether Ashe's intervention had been approved by Broghill is not clear. Egloff has argued that he was acting on his own initiative and had not consulted the kingship cabal, who declined to support him, believing his move was premature; see Egloff, 'Settlement and Kingship', pp. 311–13. Once again, however, there is insufficient evidence to sustain her analysis.

47 Rutt, *Diary of Thomas Burton*, vol. 1, p. 369.

48 *Ibid.*, vol. 1, pp. 383–4.

49 Firth, *Clarke Papers*, vol. III, pp. 91–2.

50 *Ibid.*, pp. 91–2.

51 Abbott, *Writings and Speeches of Cromwell*, vol. 4, pp. 434–5.

52 Rutt, *Diary of Thomas Burton*, vol. 1, pp. 393, 420–1.

53 Abbott, *Writings and Speeches of Cromwell*, vol. 4, pp. 434–5; Firth 'Cromwell and the Crown, II', p. 67; Rutt, *Diary of Thomas Burton*, vol. 2, p. 43.

54 Abbott, *Writings and Speeches of Cromwell*, vol. 4, pp. 434–5; Firth 'Cromwell and the Crown, II', p. 67.

55 Thurloe's state papers contain a copy of an intercepted letter dated 19 May 1657 from Robert Lilburne to one of his commissioners in Yorkshire, Luke Robinson. It is likely that Thurloe had been reading Lilburne's earlier letters and probably also those of some of his fellow major-generals. See Bod. Lib., Rawlinson MSS, A 50, fols 195–6.

56 Abbott, *Writings and Speeches of Cromwell*, vol. 4, pp. 512–14.

57 *Ibid.*, vol. 4, pp. 508–12; Roger Hainsworth, *The Swordsmen in Power: War and Politics under the English Republic* (Stroud, 1997), p. 235.

58 Austin Woolrych, 'The Cromwellian Protectorate: A Military Dictatorship?', *History*, 75 (1990), 225–7. I am grateful to Prof. Woolrych and Dr Peter Gaunt for sharing with me their views on this complex issue.

59 *Commons Journal*, vol. 7, pp. 452, 509, 514, 516, 563, 570, 577; Rutt, *Diary of Thomas Burton*, vol. 2, pp. 253–5, 257–8, 283; Firth and Rait, *Acts and Ordinances*, vol. 2, pp. 1180–2.

60 *Calendar of State Papers Domestic, 1656–7*, pp. 264, 276, 278.

61 *Ibid.*, pp. 298, 357.

62 Barkstead was lieutenant of the Tower of London; Dawkins, governor of Camarthen; Howard, of Carlisle; Kelsey, of Dover; Lilburne, of York; and Nicholas, of Chepstow. For Boteler and Haynes, see Joan Wake (ed.), *Quarter Sessions Records of the County of Northants, 1630, 1657, 1657–8*, Northants Records Soc. Publs, 1 (1924), 153, 205; D. H. Allen (ed.), *Essex Quarter Sessions Order Book 1652–1661* (Chelmsford, 1974). pp. 107, 114, 122, 126.

63 Firth, *Clarke Papers*, vol. III, pp. 145–7; Abbott, *Writings and Speeches of Cromwell*, vol. 4, pp. 777.

64 PRO, SP.25.77, pp. 981–2.

65 PRO, SP.18.153.125.

66 Abbott, *Writings and Speeches of Cromwell*, vol. 4, p. 735.

67 Andrew Coleby, *Central Government and the Localities: Hampshire 1649–1689* (Cambridge, 1987), p. 38; Richard Williams, 'County and Municipal Government in Cornwall, Devon, Dorset and Somerset, 1649–60' (Unpub. Ph.D. thesis, University of Bristol, 1981), pp. 179–80. See also J. G. I. Ive, 'The Local Dimension of Defence: The Standing Army and Militia in Norfolk, Suffolk and Essex, 1649–1660' (Unpub. Ph.D. thesis, University of Cambridge, 1986).

68 Ivan Roots, 'Lawmaking in the Second Protectorate Parliament', in H. Hearder and H. R. Loyn (eds), *British Government and Administration: Studies Presented to S. B. Chrimes* (Cardiff, 1974), p. 133.

Chapter 11

Conclusion

The major-generals were sent into the English and Welsh provinces in the autumn of 1655 with the dual task of creating a more godly society and enhancing the security of the Cromwellian regime. With regard to the first of these objectives, they failed unequivocally. As was seen in chapter 8, although most of them were utterly committed to the attempt to improve the morality of the English and Welsh peoples, they were unable to prevent large numbers of them from continuing to offend their religious values by frequenting alehouses, attending traditional sports and festivities, or indulging in illicit sexual activity. They also had little success in reducing the large numbers of the idle poor who roamed the English and Welsh countryside. To a large degree, their failure in this area stemmed from their inability to forge a sufficiently close partnership with the county magistracy and parochial ministry and thus to create a large enough godly presence at the grassroots level to regulate popular behaviour and punish transgressors. As was seen in chapters 6 and 9, they also failed as collectors of the decimation tax and as local electoral managers.

The one area where they can perhaps be regarded as having at least partly achieved their aim was that of security. As was shown in chapter 7, the measures they enforced against royalists, including disarming them, imposing upon them heavy security bonds, and closely monitoring their movements through the London register office, clearly made it much more difficult for regime's enemies to conspire against it. Even here, however, the achievement was not unalloyed. Their new county militia troops were rendered far less effective than they might have been had adequate funds for their payment been made available. Moreover, it is also arguable that following the failure of the risings of the spring of 1655 the royalist underground was already on its knees, and that in setting up the rule of the major-generals Cromwell had overreacted and employed what proved to be a highly unpopular sledgehammer to crack an already seriously weakened nut.

Whether this is a correct assessment, or whether conversely but for the major-generals the active royalist opposition would have recovered much more quickly from the disasters of March 1655, must remain a matter of conjecture. But the view that the major-generals' experiment had been a big mistake was certainly being voiced in some influential circles within a few months of its abandonment. In June 1658, Cromwell's son, Henry, wrote to Thurloe from Ireland to give his verdict on the short-lived experiment. He argued that it would have been better either to have left the royalist community alone or to have utterly destroyed them, rather than to have inaugurated a system which left them with the bulk of their property intact and provided them with further grounds for maintaining their quarrel with the government. He told Thurloe:

> I like well your comprehensive principle to do good, justice, and right to all; but I think such as would lay a burden promiscuously upon all the old cavalieer party, do not own that rule; and I wonder those who can dispense with it, do not rather advise by a total ruin to secure that party, then [to] provoke and necessitate to a perpetuall enmity such in whose hand you leave power enough to destroy you, when you have made their cause just.[1]

The primary reasons for the major-generals' failure to achieve more of their objectives were that they had been given far too ambitious a brief, far too little support from their masters in London and, as it turned out, far too little time in which to do their work. All of them were expected to perform a wide range of tasks, each of which was sufficiently onerous in its own right to keep them more than busy. As a result, their letters to Thurloe were peppered with complaints about their tiredness and sense of overwork. In January 1656, John Desborough told Thurloe that there was enough work in the west country for two major-generals, and the same month Edward Whalley exclaimed in another letter: 'Truly Sir, the worke his highness and the councill have put us upon is very great. I wish there had bin more maior generalls.'[2] Hezekiah Haynes's serious illness in 1657 was probably not unconnected to his service as major-general, and Charles Worsley almost certainly worked himself into a premature grave by his superhuman efforts in the north-west.

Severely overstretched as they were, the major-generals could not even rely on central government to provide them with the firm and prompt support which was so vital if they were to make any real progress. As was seen in chapter 5, the council did respond positively to their demands for the appointment of new justices of the peace, and did also take steps to remove the disincentives which were making it so difficult to find suitable men willing to serve as sheriffs. In a number of other crucial areas, however, the major-generals were badly let down by their masters in London. The government had failed to think through sufficiently carefully the idea of the decimation tax, and when the major-generals reported that the new levy would not produce enough money to pay their militia troops, it vetoed their proposal to lower the thresholds without producing any alternative remedy of its own. It also failed to organise the transportation out of the country of the beggars and vagabonds who had been imprisoned by some of the major-generals, and, as was seen in chapter 9, it gave them little meaningful help during the election campaign of August 1656.

It is possible to argue that if Cromwell had possessed the human and financial resources which would have allowed him to appoint a major-general for each of the English and Welsh counties, if these fifty or so hypothetical major-generals had been given the full and uninterrupted attention of the government in London, and if they been allowed a minimum of five years in which to accomplish their work, their rate of success might have been considerably higher. Even given such an unlikely scenario, however, one could still not argue with confidence that they would have made much progress with their central aim of improving the moral calibre of the nation. Many governments both before and since the 1650s have failed in this endeavour, which, if it is attainable at all, can only be achieved through the exercise of a level of surveillance and oppression which was far beyond the capability of any early-modern state.

The fact that Cromwell's major-generals failed does not, however, mean that they were, or are, unimportant. In constitutional terms, they were a radical innovation with no real antecedents in earlier English history. While superficially they resembled the old pre-war lord-lieutenants, as Victor Slater has pointed out, they in fact differed from them radically both in 'form and function'.[3] The lord-lieutenants had been pre-eminent socially in the areas they controlled, had been given responsibility for only one county, and had restricted themselves to purely military concerns. As we have seen, the major-generals by contrast were for the most part socially obscure, presided over large regional groupings of counties, and involved themselves in a much wider range of both military and non-military duties.

The significance of the major-generals is further attested by the degree of opprobrium they evoked while in office and the strength and persistence of the black legend which grew up around them after their demise. To some extent, this hostility can be attributed to the fact that they were agents of centralisation, for they had been sent into the provinces by the national government and throughout their period of office remained directly responsible to it. To a rather greater degree, it stemmed from the fact that they were soldiers. As Henry Reece has pointed out, there had, of course, been a very visible military presence in England for some years before their appointment and would be for some time after their fall.[4] Further, as was seen in chapters 6 and 7, the lack of sufficient money to pay the militia forces raised in 1655 meant that in many parts of the country their new militia troops were only mustered very infrequently. Despite these facts, for many contemporaries and later commentators the rule of the 'swordmen and decimators' nonetheless became a convenient and powerful symbol of the military nature of the unpopular Interregnum state.

Two additional, and probably more potent, reasons for the unpopularity of the rule of the major-generals, were its lack of constitutional legitimacy and its overtly godly nature. Undoubtedly, many of the major-generals' contemporaries objected to the arbitrary and unconstitutional nature of their rule. Evidence of the widespread disquiet this evoked is not difficult to find. At the end of 1656, William Prynne argued they were guilty of 'usurping all the civil as well as military power and jurisdiction into their own hands', and several months later in the debates in parliament on Desborough's militia bill, John Trevor claimed that the effect of their rule had been to 'prostitute our laws and civil peace, to a power that never was set up in any nation without dangerous consequences'.[5] In 1659, one of the MPs in Richard Cromwell's parliament, Sir John Stephens, declared: 'the little finger of the Major-Generals have I found heavier than the loins of the greatest tyrant kings that went before.' The phrase referred to the words of the biblical King Rehoboam, but Stephens may also have been implying that the major-generals had behaved as autocratically as Charles I's hated minister, Thomas Wentworth, earl of Strafford, who had been accused at his trial of having declared in the 1630s that the king's little finger was heavier than the loins of the law.[6]

Closely linked to the unconstitutionality of the major-generals' rule was its profoundly godly character. The major-generals had been prepared to ride roughshod over the English constitution because they believed that the end of establishing the godly state more than justified the means of their unparliamentary, and arguably illegal, jurisdiction. Thomas Kelsey had nicely summed up their collective outlook when he baldly told John Thurloe in August 1656 that 'the interests of God's people' had to be preserved 'before a thousand parliaments'.[7] The major-generals arrived in the localities as the self-conscious champions of the godly cause and their subsequent administration empowered small and deeply unpopular cliques of often socially insignificant local puritans and encouraged them to lord it over their neighbours and to seek to impose upon them their alien and unpopular moral and cultural values. In many parts of the country, these dedicated assistants of the major-generals, who rather than being imported from beyond the county boundaries had emerged from relative obscurity within them, spent much of 1656 re-opening the wounds which had been inflicted upon local society in the 1640s and had just begun to heal. In this sense, the rule of the major-generals did not so much attack the traditional autonomy of the provincial communities of seventeenth-century England and Wales, as distort their internal political structures by allowing them to be dominated by what the bulk of their inhabitants regarded as highly unrepresentative elements from within.

These godly minorities within the English and Welsh counties remained devoted to the major-generals throughout their period in power. The great enthusiasm with which they had greeted them on their arrival has been described in chapter 4. The fact that some of them reacted to their departure with an equal measure of regret and sadness can be seen from the remonstrance which the pastors of a number of gathered churches in Gloucestershire sent to Cromwell, probably in early 1657, to express their concern at the course of events and the behaviour of their enemies since the recent recall of the major-generals. They declared to the protector:

> We cannot but lay before you to what a height the malignant and persecuting spirrit is of late risen in this nation, how they openly boast of laying levell the Lord's blessed work among his poore people and what affronts and violence they meet withall from that party, especially upon the rumour of the major-generalls being voted down, under whom the Lord's people had comfortable protection.[8]

Such comments make clear that, while the major-generals had fallen far short of their original aims, they had done enough during their short time in power to bring comfort to their religious friends and create anxiety amongst their religious foes, and to give both these groups ample notice that they were intent on building the kind of godly commonwealth which the former so fervently desired and the latter so vehemently rejected. The fact that they had not got very far with this work by September 1656 was little consolation to their opponents, who objected to them less for what they had so far done than for what they threatened to do and for what they epitomised: strident godly fundamentalism. The quintessential feature of the rule of the major-generals was not that it was army rule, nor that it was London rule, but rather that it was godly rule, and it was as such that it was decisively rejected by the great majority of the English and Welsh people.

NOTES

1 Birch, *State Papers of John Thurloe*, vol. 7, pp. 217–18.

2 Bod. Lib., Rawlinson MSS, A 34, fols 561–4, 899–902.

3 Victor L. Slater, *Noble Government: The Stuart Lord Lieutenancy and the Transformation of English Politics* (Athens, Georgia, and London, 1994), pp. 69-70.

4 H. M. Reece, 'The Military Presence in England, 1649-1660' (Unpub. D.Phil. thesis, University of Oxford, 1981), *passim*.

5 BL, E.892.3, William Prynne, *A Summary Collection of the Principal Fundamental Rights,*

Liberties, Proprieties of all English Freemen ... (London, 1656), pp. 34–5; Rutt, *Diary of Thomas Burton*, vol. 1, p. 315.

6 Rutt, *Diary of Thomas Burton*, vol. 4, p. 11; J. P. Kenyon, *The Stuart Constitution* (Cambridge, 1966), p. 207. For the biblical allusion, see 1 Kings, 12:10 and 2 Chronicles, 10:10.

7 PRO, SP.18.129.156.

8 J. Nickolls (ed.), *Original Letters and Papers of State Addressed to Oliver Cromwell* (London, 1743), p. 140.

Postscript

The major-generals' later careers

What became of the major-generals after their fall from power in 1657? Charles Worsley was already dead, and the subsequent career of James Berry's deputy in Monmouthshire, John Nicholas, is unclear. The fates of the other fourteen active generals were very mixed. One was executed for treason after the Restoration, several others were imprisoned for lengthy periods, and two ended up living in a cave in New England. Others, by contrast, escaped serious punishment, and one even became a privy councillor for the restored king and was granted an earldom.[1]

Sir John Barkstead was named to Cromwell's Other House in late 1657 and sat in Richard Cromwell's parliament, where, as was seen in chapter 3, he came under fierce attack for his behaviour as lieutenant of the Tower of London. In June 1659, the recalled Rump dismissed him from this post. At the Restoration he escaped to Germany, but in 1661 travelled to Holland where, along with John Okey and Miles Corbet, he was arrested by the English ambassador, Sir George Downing, and sent back to England. Following a brief trial, he was hung, drawn and quartered for treason on 19 April 1662. He died still professing his belief in the rightness of his actions and his commitment to congregationalism. His scaffold speeches were later published as *The Speeches, Discourses and Prayers of John Barkstead, John Okey and Miles Corbet.*[2]

James Berry may have joined his regiment in Scotland after the prorogation of parliament in June 1657, and at the end of that year he was named to the Other House. In 1659, he supported the army in its quarrel with Richard Cromwell and he is reported to have declared later that the new protector should have hanged him. After Cromwell's resignation he was closely associated with John Lambert in the power struggle which developed with the restored Rump. By mid 1659, he was sharing command of the army with Lambert and Desborough and in the autumn he was named as a member of the council of state and regularly attended its sessions. George Monck, who engineered

Charles II's return in 1660, distrusted Berry deeply, believing that both he and many of his regiment were Quaker sympathisers. Following the readmission of the secluded members to the Rump Parliament in early 1660, he was imprisoned for refusing to take an engagement to live peaceably. After the Restoration, he was held as a prisoner at Scarborough Castle, where for a while in the mid 1660s he shared a cell with George Fox. In 1667 he refused an offer of release in exchange for an admission of guilt. He was eventually released, probably in the early 1670s, and settled at Stoke Newington in Middlesex, where Charles Fleetwood was lord of the manor and John Owen, Cromwell's former chaplain, was minister. He died there in 1691.[3]

In early 1658, William Boteler replaced his fellow major-general, William Packer, as commander of Cromwell's regiment of horse on the latter's dismissal for suspected subversion. He sat in Richard Cromwell's parliament in 1659 where, despite the 1657 indemnity act, he came under fierce attack from his fellow MPs for his behaviour as major-general and was subsequently dismissed from the Northamptonshire bench. At the Restoration, he narrowly avoided being exempted from the general pardon but in the event escaped serious punishment. In 1665, he was arrested and held in the Tower of London for suspected involvement in a conspiracy against Charles II, and in 1670 he was again arrested for attending a conventicle. The date of his death is unknown.[4]

John Desborough sat in the Other House in 1658. After Oliver Cromwell's death, he backed the army against Richard Cromwell and in 1659 he sat on the council of state. Following the Restoration, he was held for a brief period in the Tower of London and afterwards travelled to Holland to liaise with other exiled republicans there. In the mid 1660s, he returned to England after Charles II's government had warned him that if he did not he would be declared a traitor. After being held and interrogated for a time, he was released and retired to Hackney. He took no further part in public life and died there in 1680.[5]

The extraordinary subsequent careers of William Goffe and his father-in-law, Edward Whalley, were closely intertwined. Both were named to Cromwell's Other House in late 1657 and remained staunch allies of Oliver Cromwell until his death. Unlike a number of their fellow major-generals, they were both also strong supporters of Richard Cromwell and in early 1659 advised him to resist the army by force. They were officially relieved of their commands by the restored Rump in the spring of 1659, and in November of that year they were part of a delegation sent to Scotland to outline to Monck the reasons for Lambert's closure of the Rump. Their intervention failed, however, to bring about a reconciliation between Monck and the New Model regiments stationed in England which might have prevented the return of Charles Stuart.

At the Restoration, they were both excluded from the general pardon as regicides, but managed to escape to New England. They arrived at Boston in July 1660 and lived initially in Cambridge, where they attended religious services and were described as 'grave, serious, and devout'. They moved to New Haven in 1661, where tradition has it they lived in a cave in the woods outside the town for three years to avoid discovery by the agents sent from England to capture them. In 1664, they moved on to Hadley where they remained until their deaths. All efforts to arrest them proved fruitless as the colonists were generally sympathetic to them and refused to reveal their whereabouts. One report declared that they were held in 'exceeding great esteem for their piety and parts' and that they 'held meetings where they preached and prayed, and were looked upon as men dropped down from heaven'. Another stated that they were feasted in every place they visited and provided with horses and guides.

In 1675, Hadley came under attack from native Americans and, according to local tradition, Goffe emerged from his hiding place to rally the settlers and save them from defeat. As was seen in chapter 3, Goffe wrote a number of letters to his wife from America, the contents of which make clear that his religious convictions remained unshaken by the failure of the puritan revolution and that he still confidently expected the imminent rule of Christ's saints. By 1674, Whalley was in very poor health and Goffe wrote to his wife that her father was 'scarce capable of any rational discourse, his understanding, memory and speech doth so much fail him and [he] seems not to take much notice of anything that is either done or said, but patiently bears all things'. He seems to have died soon afterwards. Goffe himself probably died in 1679. They were buried along side each other at Hadley in unmarked graves. Their story later passed into legend and was incorporated by Sir Walter Scott into his novel, *Peveril of the Peak*.[6]

George Fleetwood was named to Cromwell's Other House in late 1657. In August 1659, the restored Rump authorised him to raise a troop of 'well affected volunteers' to resist Sir George Booth's rising in Cheshire. He subsequently threw in his lot with Monck, who put him in command of a regiment in February 1660. Although he proclaimed Charles II at York in early May 1660, following the Restoration he was exempted from pardon as a regicide, put on trial and sentenced to death. He petitioned parliament for a reprieve on the grounds that he had been appointed a commissioner for Charles I's trial without his knowledge and had only signed Charles I's death warrant as a result of Cromwell's threats and intimidation. He also produced testimony from Monck and Lord Ashley that he had helped to bring about the king's return and asked to be 'represented to his majesty as a fit object of his royal clemency and mercy'. In the event, his death sentence was commuted but he remained in prison and his Buckinghamshire estates were confiscated and given to James, duke of York. In 1664 a warrant was issued for his transportation to Tangier. Whether he was actually sent to North Africa is unclear; some authorities claim he died there in 1672, but others that the plan was abandoned after representations from his wife and that he was subsequently released from the Tower of London and allowed to emigrate to America.

Following Oliver Cromwell's death, Hezekiah Haynes joined his commanding officer, Charles Fleetwood, in opposing Richard Cromwell and calling for the return of the Rump. In 1659, he backed Fleetwood and Lambert in their struggle with the parliament and supported its forcible closure by the army in October. Following the Rump's re-assembly in December, he lost his commission and was ordered to return home to Essex. He remained there during the summer months, but in November 1660 was arrested on suspicion of involvement in subversive activities and held in the Tower of London for the next eighteen months. He was released in April 1662, after signing a bond of £5,000 for his future good behaviour. Following his release, he lived quietly at Copford Hall until 1684, when he made the property over to his son and moved to Coggeshall. He died there in 1693.[7]

Charles Howard was named to the Other House in late 1657. Following Cromwell's death he supported his son, Richard, and after his resignation the recalled Rump removed Howard from command of his regiment. The only major-general who had supported the idea that Oliver Cromwell should accept the crown, Howard seems never to have shared the anti-monarchical views of his fellow major-generals and after 1660 he quickly accommodated himself to the restored king. He was soon appointed to Charles II's privy council, and in 1661 was raised to the peerage as the first earl of Carlisle. He remained an active soldier during much of Charles II's reign, and during the 1670s and early 1680s served as governor of Jamaica. According to Stephen Saunders Webb, when he drew up the orders for the colonial governor-generals as a member of the privy council's plantations committee, he based them substantially on the instructions he had received as major-general. He died in 1685.[8]

Thomas Kelsey continued to serve in the army until October 1659, when he was deprived of his commission by the Rump for his involvement in the drawing up of a petition calling for the army to be freed from civilian control. He subsequently helped Lambert to close the Rump, but on its return at the end of 1659 was deprived of office. He fled to Holland at the Restoration and returned in 1666, perhaps to become a brewer.[9] Robert Lilburne was named to Cromwell's Other House in late 1657, and in 1659 supported Lambert against the restored Rump. Following the Restoration, he was tried for treason as a regicide in October 1660, found guilty and sentenced to death. His sentence was subsequently commuted and he was imprisoned on St Nicholas Island in Plymouth Sound, where he died in 1665.[10]

William Packer was cashiered from the army by Cromwell in 1658 on the grounds of disaffection. He subsequently expressed his deep sense of betrayal by his erstwhile commander in a speech in Richard Cromwell's parliament in 1659. After Richard's resignation, he supported John Lambert in his power struggle with the restored Rump. At the Restoration, he lost the crown land at Theobalds in Hertfordshire he had purchased in the early 1650s. While he avoided long-term imprisonment, he was arrested and held in the Gatehouse for some time in 1661. His subsequent career is unknown. Tobias Bridge was made governor of Dunkirk in 1659 and supported Monck in the lead-up to the Restoration. He retained his commission after Charles II's return and subsequently served at Tangier and Barbados, whose capital, Bridgetown, was probably named after him. Rowland Dawkins escaped serious punishment at the Restoration and subsequently joined a dissenting community in his native Gower. In 1677, he was described as 'one who had raised his fortune in the late time' and was reputed to be worth £250 per annum. By the 1680s he was serving again as a justice of the peace in Glamorgan, but during Monmouth's rising in 1685 he was imprisoned for a time in Chepstow Castle. He died in 1691.[11]

NOTES

1 As in chapter 3, unless otherwise stated, the subsequent biographical material is taken from references to individual generals in *DNB*; C. H. Firth and G. Davies, *A Regimental History of Cromwell's Army* (2 vols, Oxford, 1940); R. L. Greaves and R. Zaller (eds), *A Biographical Dictionary of British Radicals in the Seventeenth Century* (3 vols, Brighton, 1982); Maurice Ashley, *Cromwell's Generals* (London, 1954); and Anthony Fletcher, 'The Religious Motivation of Cromwell's Major-Generals', in D. Baker (ed.), *Religious Motivation: Biographical and Social Problems for the Church Historian*, Studies in Church History, 15 (1978), 259–66. Other references are noted below.

2 *The Speeches ... and Prayers of John Barkstead, John Okey, and Miles Corbet* (London, 1662).

3 J. Berry and S. G. Lee, *A Cromwellian Major-General: The Career of Colonel James Berry* (Oxford, 1938), pp. 203–71.

4 Paul H. Hardacre, 'William Boteler: A Cromwellian Oligarch', *Huntington Library Quarterly*, XI (1947), 1–11. For the attack on him in parliament in 1659, see Rutt, *Diary of Thomas Burton*, vol. 4, pp. 403–12.

5 A. R. Williams, 'John Desborough: Gloucestershire's Major-General', *Transactions of the Bristol and Gloucestershire Archaeological Society*, 89 (1970), 123–9.

6 *Calendar of State Papers Colonial, America and West Indies, 1661–8*, pp. 15–16, 26, 27–8, 33–4, 53–4, 345, 420; Thomas Hutchinson, *The History of Massachusetts* (2 vols, Boston, 1795). vol. I, pp. 197–201; *Collections of the Massachusetts Historical Society*, 3rd series, I (1865), 60–2, and 4th series, 8 (1868), 122–5.

7 W. L. F. Nuttall, 'Hezekiah Haynes: Oliver Cromwell's Major-General for the Eastern Counties', *Transactions of the Essex Archaeological Society*, 3rd series, I (1964), 196–209.

8 Stephen Saunders Webb, *The Governors-General: The English Army and the Defence of Empire, 1569–1681* (Chapel Hill, 1979), pp. 69–79. For a collection of his personal papers dating from the reign of Charles II, see BL, Sloane MSS, 2723–4.

9 *Commons Journal*, vol. 7, pp. 669, 723, 749, 796, 806, 812.

10 Roger Howell, 'The Army and the English Revolution: the Case of Robert Lilburne', *Archaeologia Aeliana*, 5th series 9 (1981), 299–315.

11 I am grateful to Stephen Roberts, the author of Dawkins's entry in the *New DNB*, for allowing me to see his entry prior to publication. See also, Geraint H. Jenkins, *The Foundations of Modern Wales* (Oxford, 1987), pp. 127–8.

Select bibliography

PRIMARY SOURCES

MANUSCRIPT SOURCES

BEDFORDSHIRE RECORD OFFICE

QSM1: Quarter Sessions Information and Indictments Book, 1650s

BODLEIAN LIBRARY, OXFORD

Carte MSS, 73, fols 9,10, 12,15; 74, fols 31, 39: Letters to Edward Montague

Carte MSS, 131, fols 179–80, 183–5, 189–90: Intelligence letters

Carte MSS, 228, fols 83, 86–8: Letters of Thomas Burton

Clarendon MSS, 53, fols 244, 262–3: Letters to Edward Hyde

Rawlinson MSS, A 29–48: State Papers of John Thurloe

Rawlinson MSS, C 182, fols 101–2: Sir John Glynne's charge to the grand jury at the Worcestershire assizes, July 1656

Tanner MSS, 52, fol. 96: Josias Berners to John Hobart, 21 Nov. 1655

Tanner MSS, 52, fol. 97: William Sancroft to Thomas Sancroft, 19 Nov. 1655

Tanner MSS, 52, fol. 149: 'Grounds of John Hobart's dissatisfaction with the Protector's Proceedings', September 1656

Tanner MSS, 52 fol. 186: 'Heads of Lord Broghills Speech against the Bill of Decimating the Cavaleers'

Top Cheshire MSS, e 3 fols 20–1: Henry Bradshaw's account of Cheshire poll of 1656

BRITISH LIBRARY, LONDON

Additional MSS, 4196, fol. 24: Warrant to Thomas Kelsey

Additional MSS, 6689, fol. 320: Petition of Sir Charles Egerton to Protector

Additional MSS, 19516, 34011–16: Records of Thomas Dunn's London register office

Additional MSS, 28003: Oxinden Correspondence

Additional MSS, 44058, fols 40–2: Cromwell to Gen. Lisburne and Sir John Copplestone, 29 Jan. 1656

Additional MSS, 44846: Thomas Peyton's Letter Book

Egerton MSS, 2986, fol. 279: Boteler to Edward Heath, 18 Jan. 1656

Sloane MSS, 2723–4: Papers of Charles Howard, earl of Carlisle

BUCKINGHAMSHIRE RECORD OFFICE

M11/13–15: Microfilms of Claydon House letters relating to Verney family

CENTRE FOR KENTISH STUDIES, MAIDSTONE

Q/SB 6–7: Kent Quarter Sessions Papers, 1650s
Q/SO W2, E1: East and West Kent Quarter Sessions Order Books, 1650s
U2341: Minute Book of Kentish Commissioners, 1655–56 [missing]

CHESHIRE RECORD OFFICE

DDX 384/1: Sir Thomas Mainwaring's Diary
QJB 2/7: Indictments and Presentments Book, 1656 (microfilm 200/5)
QJF 84, 1–4, Quarter Sessions files, 1656 (microfilm, 212/113–14)

DR WILLIAMS'S LIBRARY, LONDON

Baxter Treatises, vol. 20, no. 352; manuscript text of sermon 'The Power of Magistrates in
    Religion'

ESSEX RECORD OFFICE

Q/SO1: Quarter Sessions Order Book, 1652–61
QSBa2/91–97: Quarter Session Depositions and Petitions, 1655–56

HAMPSHIRE RECORD OFFICE

Q1/3: Quarter Sessions Order Book, 1649–58
Q4/1: Quarter Sessions Indictments Book, 1640–60
19M61: Kingsmill Papers

LANCASHIRE RECORD OFFICE

QDV/29: Papers concerning alehouses in Lancashire 1655–56
QSO 28–9: Quarter Sessions Order Books, 1655–56
QSP 130- 156: Quarter Sessions Petitions, 1655–57

MANCHESTER LOCAL STUDIES ARCHIVE SERVICE

M35: Carill-Worsley Papers

NORTHAMPTONSHIRE RECORD OFFICE

IC: Isham Correspondence

OXFORDSHIRE RECORD OFFICE

C/FC/1/A1/03: Council Act Book, 1629–63
C/FC/1/A2/03: Council Minute Book, 1635–57

Select bibliography

PUBLIC RECORD OFFICE, LONDON

C.231.6: Chancery Crown Office Docquet Book, 1650s

SP.18: Interregnum State Papers

SP.23: Records of Committee for Compounding

SP.25, 75, 76, 76A, 77: Interregnum State Papers, Council Order Books

SP.28: Commonwealth Exchequer Papers

SP.46, 47, 48: Miscellaneous Interregnum State Papers

STAFFORDSHIRE RECORD OFFICE

Q/SO6: Quarter Sessions Order Book, 1650s

D260/M/F/1/6: Persehowse Papers

D793: Bowers papers (xerox copies)

D593/P/8/1: Leveson Civil War and Interregnum Papers

D868: Leveson Correspondence

WEST YORKSHIRE ARCHIVE SERVICE, WAKEFIELD

QS 4/4, 5: West Riding of Yorkshire Quarter Sessions Indictments Books, 1650s

QS 10/3: West Riding of Yorkshire Quarter Sessions Order Book, 1650s

WILTSHIRE RECORD OFFICE

A1/150/11, A1/160/2: Quarter Sessions Records, 1650s

WORCESTERSHIRE RECORD OFFICE

110/BA/90–93: Quarter Sessions Indictments, 1650s

BA4657(i): Sir John Packington's suffering for adhering to King Charles I

PRINTED PRIMARY SOURCES

Abbott, W. C., *The Writings and Speeches of Oliver Cromwell* (4 vols, Cambridge, Mass., 1937–47)

Allen, D. H. (ed.), *Essex Quarter Sessions Order Book 1652–1661* (Chelmsford, 1974)

Allen, William, *A Memorial of the Remarkable Meeting of Many Officers of the Army in England at Windsor Castle in the Year 1648* (London, 1659)

Atkinson, J. C. (ed.) *North Riding Quarter Sessions Records*, North Riding Records Soc. Publs, 5 (1887)

Bates-Harbin, E. H. (ed.), *Quarter Sessions Records for the County of Somerset*, Somerset Records Soc. Publs, vol. III, 28 (1912)

Baxter, Richard, *Reliquiae Baxterianae* (London, 1696)

Baxter, Richard, 'Directions to Justices of the Peace especially in Corporations for the discharge of their Duties to God', in Richard Baxter, *The Practical Works of the Late Reverend and Pious Mr Richard Baxter* (4 vols, London, 1707)

Bennett, J. H. E. and Dewhurst, J. C. (eds), *Quarter Sessions Records ... For the County Palatine of Chester, 1559–1760*, Records Soc. of Lancashire and Cheshire Publs, 94 (1940)

Birch, Thomas (ed.), *A Collection of the State Papers of John Thurloe Esq* (7 vols, London, 1742)

Bushnell, Walter, *A Narrative of the Proceedings of the Commissioners appointed by Oliver Cromwell for the Ejecting of Scandalous and Ignorant Ministers in the Case of Walter Bushnell, Clerk* (London, 1660)

Calendar of Committee for Compounding

Calendar of State Papers Colonial, America and West Indies (1660–70)

Calendar State Papers Domestic (1660–70)

Calendar State Papers Venetian (1655–59)

Calendar of Wynn (of Gwydir) Papers, 1515–1690 (Aberystwyth, 1926)

Carte, Thomas (ed.), *A Collection of Original Letters and Papers Concerning the Affairs of England from the year 1641 to 1660* (2 vols, London, 1739)

Certain Passages of Everyday Intelligence

Chambers, Humphrey, *An Answer of Humphrey Chambers, Rector of Pewsey ... to the Charges of Walter Bushnal* (London, 1660)

Charles, B. G. (ed.), *Calendar of the Records of the Borough of Haverfordwest, 1539–1660* (Cardiff, 1967)

Cockburn, S. (ed.), *Somerset Assizes Orders, 1640–59*, Somerset Records Soc. Publs, 71 (1971)

Coke, Roger, *A Detection of the Court and State of England during the Last Four Reigns and Interregnum* (2 vols, London, 1694)

Commons Journal (1650–60)

Copnall, H. H. (ed.), *Nottingham County Records* (Nottingham, 1915)

Cunnington, B. H., *Some Annals of the Borough of Devizes* (Devizes, 1925)

Daemonium Meridianum (London, 1655)

A Declaration of His Highness by the Advice of his Council, 31 October 1655 (London, 1655)

Dodds, M. H. (ed.), *Extracts from the Newcastle-upon-Tyne Council Minute Book, 1639–1656*, Newcastle-upon-Tyne Records Committee, 1 (1920)

Davies, Godfrey (ed.), *Memoirs of the Family of Guise*, Camden Soc. Publs, 3rd series, 28 (1917)

John Evelyn, *The Diary of John Evelyn*, ed. E. S. de Beer (6 vols, Oxford, 1950)

The Faithful Scout (1655–56)

Firth, C. H. (ed.), *The Memoirs of Edmund Ludlow* (2 vols, Oxford, 1894)

Firth, C. H. (ed.), *The Clarke Papers*, Camden Soc. Publs, vol. III, new series, 60 (1899)

Firth, C. H. and Rait, R. S. (eds), *Acts and Ordinances of the Interregnum* (3 vols, London, 1911)

Fishwick, Henry (ed.), *The Notebook of the Reverend Thomas Jolley*, Chetham Soc. Publs, new series, 33 (1895)

Select bibliography

The Fourth Paper presented by Maj. Butler to the Honorable Committee of Parliament for the Propagation of the Gospel of Christ Jesus (London, 1652)

Fox, George, *The Journal of George Fox*, ed. John L. Nickalls (London, 1952)

Fox, L. (ed.), 'The Diary of Robert Beake, mayor of Coventry, 1655–6', *Dugdale Miscellany Volume I*, Dugdale Soc. Publs, 31 (1977)

Gauden, John, *A Petitionary Remonstrance Presented to Oliver Cromwell, 4th February 1656* (London, 1659)

Goad, Christopher, *Refreshing Drops and Scorching Vials* (London, 1653)

Grantham, Thomas, *A Complaint to the Lord Protector* (London, 1656)

Gurnall, William, *The Magistrates Pourtraiture* (London, 1656)

HMC, *Fifth Report*, Duke of Sutherland MSS

HMC, *Sixth Report, Appendix*, MSS of Ffarington of Worden Hall

HMC, *11th Report, Appendix 3*, Southampton Corporation MSS

HMC, *11th Report, Appendix 7*, Reading Corporation MSS

HMC, *14th Report, Appendix 8*, Lincoln Corporation MSS

HMC, *Bath MSS*, vols 2 and 4

HMC, *Portland MSS*, vols 2 and 3

HMC, *Rutland MSS*

HMC, *Various MSS*, vol. 2, MSS of Miss Buxton

Howell James, D. E. (ed.), *Norfolk Quarter Sessions Order Book*, Norfolk Records Soc. Publs, 26 (1955)

Howells, B. E. (ed.), *A Calendar of Letters Relating to North Wales 1533 – circa 1700* (Cardiff, 1967)

Hutchinson, Lucy, *Memoirs of the Life of Colonel Hutchinson*, ed. John Sutherland (Oxford 1973)

'Hutchinson Papers', *Collections of the Massachusetts Historical Society*, 3rd series, 1 (1865)

Hyde, Edward, earl of Clarendon, *The History of the Rebellion and Civil Wars in England*, ed. W. Dunn Macray (6 vols, Oxford, 1888)

Invisible John Made Visible ... (London, 1659)

Jeaffreson, J. C. (ed.), *Middlesex County Records*, Old Series, vol. 3, (London, 1974)

Le Hardy, W. (ed.), *Calendar to Sessions Books and Sessions Minute Books, 1619–1657*, Hertfordshire County Records, 5 (1928)

A Letter from a True and Lawfull Member of Parliament (London, 1656)

'Letters and Papers relating to the Regicides', *Collections of the Massachusetts Historical Society*, 4th series, 8 (1868)

Macfarlane, Alan (ed.), *The Diary of Ralph Josselin, 1616–1683* (London, 1976)

'Manuscript List of the Norfolk Poll, 1656', *Norfolk Archaeology*, 1 (1847)

Mercurius Politicus (1655–56)

Nickolls, J. (ed.), *Original Letters and Papers of State Addressed to Oliver Cromwell* (London, 1743).

An Order and Declaration of Oliver Cromwell and the Council, 5th November 1655 (London, 1655)

An Order by the Justices of the Peace of London and Westminster, 10th March 1656 (London, 1656)

Parsloe, Guy (ed.), *The Minute Book of Bedford Corporation, 1647–1664,* Bedfordshire Historical Records Soc. Publs, 26 (1949)

Penney, N. (ed.), *The First Publishers of Truth* (London, 1907)

A Perfect Account (1655–57)

The Perfect Diurnall (1655–57)

Perfect Proceedings of State Affairs (1655–57)

Prynne, William, *A Summary Collection of the Principal Fundamental Rights, Liberties, Proprieties of all English Freemen* ... (London, 1656)

The Public Intelligencer (1655–57)

Ratcliff, S. C. and Johnson, H. C. (eds), *Warwick County Records III* (Warwick, 1937)

Records of the Borough of Nottingham, vol. 5 (1900)

Roberts, Michael (ed.), *Swedish Diplomats at Cromwell's Court, 1655–1656,* Camden Soc. Publs, 4th series, 36 (1988)

Rutt, J. T. (ed.), *The Diary of Thomas Burton Esq.* (4 vols, London, 1828)

Scandal on the Corporation: Royalists and Puritans in Mid Seventeenth Century Kingston from the Kingston Borough Archives (Kingston, 1982)

The Speeches ... and Prayers of John Barkstead, John Okey, and Miles Corbet (London, 1662).

Stocks, H. (ed.), *Records of the Borough of Leicester, 1603–1688* (Cambridge, 1923)

A True and Perfect Relation of the Manner and Proceeding held by the Sheriff of the County of Berks ... (London 1656)

Wake, Joan (ed.), *Quarter Sessions Records of the County of Northants, 1630, 1657, 1657–8,* Northants Records Soc. Publs, 1 (1924)

Wakeman, O. and Kenyon, R. L. (eds), *Orders of the Shropshire Quarter Sessions, Volume 1, 1638–1708,* Shropshire County Records, 11–12 (1908)

Warner, George F. (ed.), *The Nicholas Papers: Correspondence of Sir Edward Nicholas, Secretary of State,* Camden Soc. Publs, vol. 2, new series 50 (1842), vol. 3 new series, 57 (1897)

The Weekly Intelligencer (1655–56)

The Weekly Post (1655–56)

Willis Bund, J. W. (ed.), *The Diary of Henry Townshend of Elmley Lovett 1640–1663,* Worcestershire Historical Soc. Publs, 31, part 1 (1920)

Woodhouse, A. S. P., *Puritanism and Liberty* (London, 1951)

SECONDARY SOURCES

BOOKS AND PAMPHLETS

Ashley, Maurice, *Cromwell's Generals* (London, 1954)

Ashley, Maurice, *Financial and Commercial Policy under the Cromwellian Protectorate* (London, 1962 edn)

Aylmer, G. E., *The State's Servants: The Civil Service of the English Republic, 1649–1660* (London, 1973)

Berry J. and Lee, S. G., *A Cromwellian Major-General: The Career of Colonel James Berry* (Oxford, 1938)

Brenner, Robert, *Merchants and Revolution: Commercial Change, Political Conflict and London's Overseas Traders, 1550–1653* (Cambridge, 1993)

Capp, Bernard, *The Fifth Monarchy Men* (London, 1972)

Coate, Mary, *Cornwall in the Great Civil War and Interregnum, 1642–1660* (Oxford, 1933)

Coleby, Andrew, *Central Government and the Localities: Hampshire 1649–1689* (Cambridge, 1987)

Coward, Barry, *Oliver Cromwell* (London, 1991)

Dawson, W. H., *Cromwell's Understudy: The Life and Times of Colonel John Lambert* (London, 1938)

Dictionary of National Biography

Dow, Frances, *Cromwellian Scotland* (Edinburgh, 1979)

Durston, Christopher, *The Family in the English Revolution* (Oxford, 1989)

Evans, John T., *Seventeenth Century Norwich: Politics, Religion and Government, 1620–1690* (Oxford, 1979)

Everitt, Alan, *The Community of Kent and the Great Rebellion* (Leicester, 1966)

Firth, C. H., *The Last Years of the Protectorate*, (2 vols, London, 1909)

Firth, C. H. and Davies, G., *A Regimental History of Cromwell's Army* (2 vols, Oxford, 1940)

Fletcher, A. J., *A County Community in Peace and War: Sussex 1600–1660* (London, 1975)

Fletcher, Anthony, *Reform in the Provinces: The Government of Stuart England* (New Haven and London, 1986)

Gardiner, Samuel Rawson, *The History of the Commonwealth and Protectorate, 1649–1656* (4 vols, New York, 1965 edn)

Gaunt, Peter, *Oliver Cromwell* (Oxford, 1996)

Gentles, Ian, *The New Model Army in England, Ireland and Scotland,1645–1653* (Oxford, 1992)

Godwin, William, *The History of the Commonwealth of England* (4 vols, London, 1828)

Goodwin, Tim, *Dorset in the Civil War, 1625–1665* (Tiverton, 1996)

Greaves R. L. and Zaller, R. (eds), *A Biographical Dictionary of British Radicals in the Seventeenth Century* (3 vols, Brighton, 1982)

Hainsworth, Roger, *The Swordsmen in Power: War and Politics under the English Republic* (Stroud, 1997)

Halliday, Paul D., *Dismembering the Body Politic: Partisan Politics in England's Towns* (Cambridge, 1998)

Hamilton, A. H. A., *Quarter Sessions from Queen Elizabeth to Queen Anne* (London, 1878)

Hardacre, Paul H., *The Royalists During the Puritan Revolution* (The Hague, 1956)

Holmes, Clive, *Seventeenth Century Lincolnshire* (Lincoln, 1980)

Hughes, Ann, *Politics, Society and Civil War in Warwickshire, 1620–1660* (Cambridge, 1987)

Hutchinson, Thomas, *The History of Massachusetts* (2 vols, Boston, Mass., 1795)

Jenkins, Philip, *The Making of a Ruling Class: The Glamorgan Gentry, 1640–1790* (Cambridge, 1983)

Kingston, A., *Hertfordshire during the Great Civil War* (London and Hertford, 1894)

Kishlansky, Mark, *Parliamentary Selection: Social and Political Choice in Early Modern England* (Cambridge, 1986)

Lindley, Keith, *Popular Politics and Religion in Civil War London* (Aldershot, 1997)

Matthews, A. G., *Walker Revised* (Oxford, 1948)

Matthews, Nancy L., *William Sheppard: Cromwell's Law Reformer* (Cambridge, 1984)

Morrill, J. S., *Cheshire 1630–1660: County Government and Society during the English Revolution* (Oxford, 1974)

Reay, Barry, *The Quakers in the English Revolution* (London, 1985)

Roberts, Stephen, *Recovery and Restoration in an English County: Devon Local Administration, 1646–1670* (Exeter, 1985)

Shaw, William A., *A History of the English Church during the Civil Wars and under the Commonwealth 1640–1660* (2 vols, London, 1900)

Slater, Victor L., *Noble Government: The Stuart Lord Lieutenancy and the Transformation of English Politics* (Athens, Georgia, and London, 1994)

Smith, Harold, *The Ecclesiastical History of Essex under the Long Parliament and Commonwealth* (Colchester, 1933)

Tatham, G. B., *The Puritans in Power: a Study in the History of the English Church from 1640 to 1660* (Cambridge, 1913)

Tolmie, Murray, *The Triumph of the Saints: The Separate Churches of London, 1616–1649* (Cambridge, 1977)

Underdown, David, *Royalist Conspiracy in England 1649–1660* (New Haven, 1960)

Underdown, David, *Somerset in the Civil War and Interregnum* (Newton Abbot, 1973)

Underdown, David, *Revel, Riot and Rebellion: Popular Politics and Culture in England, 1603–1660* (Oxford, 1985)

Verney, M. M., *Memoirs of the Verney Family* (4 vols, London, 1894)

Waters, S. H., *Wakefield in the Seventeenth Century from 1550–1710* (Wakefield, 1933)

Webb, Stephen Saunders, *The Governors-General: The English Army and the Definition of the Empire* (Chapel Hill, 1979)

Wood, A. C., *Nottinghamshire in the Civil War* (Oxford, 1937)

Woolrych, A. H., *Penruddock's Rising 1655* (London, 1955)

Woolrych, Austin, *Commonwealth to Protectorate* (Oxford, 1982)

Select bibliography

ARTICLES AND ESSAYS

Beier, A. L., 'Poor Relief in Warwickshire, 1630–1660', *Past and Present*, 35 (1966)

Bloomfield, Peter, 'The Cromwellian Commission in Kent, 1655–57', in Alec Detsicas and Nigel Yates (eds), *Studies in Modern Kentish History* (Maidstone, 1983)

Booker, John, *A History of the Ancient Chapel of Birch in Manchester Parish*, Chetham Soc. Publs, 47 (1859)

Button, Andrea E., 'Penruddock's Rising, 1655', *Southern History*, 19 (1997)

Cliffe, J. T., 'The Cromwellian Decimation Tax of 1655: The Assessment Lists', *Camden Miscellany*, Camden Soc. Publs, 5th series, 7 (1996)

Coleby, Andrew, 'Military-Civilian Relations on the Solent', *Historical Journal*, 29 (1986)

Durston, Christopher, 'Puritan Rule and the Failure of Cultural Revolution', in Christopher Durston and Jacqueline Eales (eds), *The Culture of English Puritanism, 1560–1700* (Basingstoke, 1996)

Durston, Christopher, 'The Fall of Cromwell's Major-Generals', *English Historical Review*, 113 (1998)

Durston, Christopher, '"Settling the Hearts and Quieting the Minds of All Good People": The Major-Generals and the Puritan Minorities of Interregnum England', *History*, 85 (2000)

Egloff, Carol S., 'John Hobart of Norwich and the Politics of the Cromwellian Protectorate', *Norfolk Archaeology*, 42 (1994)

Egloff, Carol S., 'The Search for a Cromwellian Settlement: Exclusions from the Second Protectorate Parliament, Parts 1 and 2', *Parliamentary History*, 17 (1998)

Firth, C. H., 'Cromwell and the Crown', *English Historical Review*, 17, 18 (1902, 1903)

Fletcher, Anthony, 'The Religious Motivation of Cromwell's Major-Generals', in D. Baker (ed.), *Religious Motivation: Biographical and and Social Problems for the Church Historian*, Studies in Church History, 15 (1978)

Fletcher, Anthony, 'Oliver Cromwell and the Localities; The Problem of Consent', in Colin Jones, Malyn Newitt and Stephen Roberts (eds), *Politics and People in Revolutionary England* (Oxford, 1986)

Fletcher, Anthony, 'Oliver Cromwell and the Godly Nation', in John Morrill (ed.), *Oliver Cromwell and the English Revolution* (London, 1990)

Forster, G. C. F., 'County Government in Yorkshire during the Interregnum', *Northern History*, 12 (1976)

Gilbert, C. D., 'Magistracy and Ministry in Cromwellian England: The Case of King's Norton, Worcestershire', *Midland History*, 23 (1998)

Green, Ian, 'The Persecution of "Scandalous" and "Maligant" Parish Clergy during the Civil War', *English Historical Review*, 94 (1979)

Hardacre, Paul H., 'William Boteler: A Cromwellian Oligarch', *Huntington Library Quarterly*, 11 (1947)

Henderson, B. L. K., 'The Commonwealth Charters', *Transactions of the Royal Historical Society*, 3rd series, 6 (1912)

Hirst, Derek, 'The Failure of Godly Rule in the English Republic', *Past and Present*, 132 (1991)

Howell, Roger, 'The Army and the English Revolution: the Case of Robert Lilburne', *Archaeologia Aeliana*, 5th series, 9 (1981)

Jenkins, Philip, '"The Old Leaven": The Welsh Roundheads after 1660', *Historical Journal*, 24 (1981)

Jones, J. Gwynfor, 'Caernarvonshire Administration: Activities of the Justices of the Peace, 1603–1660', *Welsh History Review*, 5 (1970–1)

Massarella, Derek, 'The Politics of the Army and the Quest for Settlement', in Ivan Roots (ed.), *Into Another Mould: Aspects of the Interregnum* (Exeter, 1981)

Mather, Jean, 'The Moral Code of the English Civil War and Interregnum', *The Historian*, 44 (1982)

Morrill, John, 'Postlude: Between War and Peace, 1651–1662', in John Kenyon and Jane Ohlmeyer (eds), *The Civil Wars: A Military History of England, Scotland and Ireland, 1638–1660* (Oxford, 1998)

Nuttall, W. L. F., 'Hezekiah Haynes: Oliver Cromwell's Major-General for the Eastern Counties', *Transactions of the Essex Archaeological Society*, 3rd series, 1 (1964)

Parsloe, C. G., 'The Corporation of Bedford, 1647–1664', *Transactions of the Royal Historical Society*, 4th series, 29 (1947)

Pinckney, Paul J., 'The Cheshire Election of 1656', *Bulletin of John Rylands Library*, 49 (1967)

Pinckney, Paul, 'The Suffolk Elections to the Protectorate Parliaments', in Colin Jones, Malyn Newitt and Stephen Roberts (eds), *Politics and People in Revolutionary England* (Oxford, 1986)

Rannie, David Watson, 'Cromwell's Major-Generals', *English Historical Review*, 10 (1895)

Roberts, Stephen, 'Local Government Reform in England and Wales during the Interregnum', in Ivan Roots (ed.), *Into Another Mould: Aspects of the Interregnum* (Exeter, 1981)

Roberts, Stephen K., 'Initiative and Control: The Devon Quarter Sessions Grand Jury, 1640–1670, *Bulletin of the Institute of Historical Research*, 57 (1984)

Roberts, S. K., 'Public or Private?: Revenge and Recovery at the Restoration of Charles II', *Bulletin of the Institute of Historical Research*, 59 (1986)

Roots, Ivan, 'Swordsmen and Decimators: Cromwell's Major-Generals', in R. H. Parry (ed.), *The English Civil War and After, 1642–1658* (London 1970)

Roots, Ivan, 'Lawmaking in the Second Protectorate Parliament', in H. Hearder and H. R. Loyn (eds), *British Government and Administration: Studies Presented to S. B. Chrimes* (Cardiff, 1974)

Round, J. H., 'Colchester during the Commonwealth', *English Historical Review*, 15 (1900)

Seddon, P. R., 'The Nottinghamshire Elections to the Protectorate Parliaments of 1654 and 1656', *Transactions of the Thoroton Society of Nottinghamshire*, 102 (1998)

Snow, Vernon F., 'Parliamentary Reapportionment Proposals in the Puritan Revolution', *English Historical Review*, 74 (1959)

Sutton, John, 'Cromwell's Commissioners for preserving the peace of the commonwealth: a Staffordshire case study', in Ian Gentles, John Morrill and Blair Worden (eds), *Soldiers, Writers and Statesmen in the English Revolution* (Cambridge, 1998)

Underdown, David, 'Settlement in the Counties', in G. E. Aylmer, *The Interregnum: The Quest for Settlement* (London, 1972)

Select bibliography

Williams, A. R., 'John Desborough: Gloucestershire's Major-General', *Transactions of the Bristol and Gloucestershire Archaeological Society*, 89 (1970)

Woolrych, Austin, 'The Cromwellian Protectorate: A Military Dictatorship?', *History*, 75 (1990)

UNPUBLISHED THESES

Bennett, Ronan A. H., 'Enforcing the Law in Revolutionary England: Yorkshire *c.* 1640–*c.* 1660' (Ph.D. thesis, University of London, 1988)

Egloff, Carol. S., 'Settlement and Kingship: The Army, the Gentry and the offer of the Crown to Oliver Cromwell' (Ph.D. thesis, University of Yale, 1990)

Farr, David, 'The Military and Political Career of John Lambert, 1619–1657 (Ph.D. thesis, University of Cambridge, 1996)

Gentles, Ian, 'The Debentures Market and the Military Purchases of Crown Lands, 1649–1660' (Ph.D. thesis, University of London, 1969)

Ive, J. G. I., 'The Local Dimension of Defence: The Standing Army and Militia in Norfolk, Suffolk and Essex, 1649–1660' (Ph.D. thesis, University of Cambridge, 1986)

Jaggar, G., 'The Fortunes of the Whalley Family of Screveton, Notts: a study of some of its members *c.* 1540–1690, with special reference to Major-General Edward Whalley' (M.Phil. thesis, University of Southampton, 1973)

Mildon, W. H., 'Puritanism in Hampshire and the Isle of Wight from the Reign of Elizabeth to the Restoration' (Ph.D. thesis, University of London, 1934)

Pinckney, Paul, 'A Cromwellian Parliament: The Elections and Personnel of 1656' (Ph.D. thesis, University of Vanderbilt, 1962)

Reece, H. M., 'The Military Presence in England, 1649–1660' (D.Phil. thesis, University of Oxford, 1981)

Schilling, William A. H., 'The Central Government and the Municipal Corporations in England, 1642–1663' (Ph.D. thesis, University of Vanderbilt, 1970)

Williams, Richard, 'County and Municipal Goverment in Cornwall, Devon, Dorset and Somerset, 1649–60' (Ph.D. thesis, University of Bristol, 1981)

Index

Note: 'n' after a page reference indicates the number of the note on that page.

Act of Oblivion (1652) 4, 32, 108, 211, 212, 213

adultery, *see* Adultery Act (1650); sexual offences

Adultery Act (1650) 156

alehouse regulation 79, 85–6, 90, 171–8, 179; *see also* drunkards and drunkenness

Altham (Lancashire) 155

Anglesey (Wales) 107, 159

Arundel (Sussex) 61

Ashe, James 214, 220

Ashe, John 220, 226n.46

assizes courts and judges 73, 77, 80, 82–3, 170, 174, 177

Aylesbury (Buckinghamshire) 111

Bagot, Sir Hervey 67, 110, 123n.66

Bampfield, Thomas 211

Barkstead, Sir John (major-general) 18, 26, 28, 29, 30, 31, 38, 39–43, 51, 59, 76, 79, 91, 118, 133, 135, 137, 141, 142, 149n.20, 152n.74, 156, 157, 158, 175, 181n.28, 191, 195, 196, 200, 204n.43, 223, 227n.62, 234

Barnardiston, Sir Thomas 196

Baxter, Richard 41, 43, 48, 80, 177–8

Beake, Robert 67, 74, 77, 89, 162, 167

bear-baiting 22, 157

beargarden, in Bankside 157

Bedford 88, 91

Bedfordshire 22, 27, 31, 76, 81, 116, 136, 167, 212

 commissioners for securing peace in 68, 70n.2, 105, 155

 decimation tax in 114, 122n.49, 123n.62

 militia troops in 142

beggars *see* vagrants and vagabonds

Berkshire 20, 22, 24, 27, 31, 53, 76, 82, 109

 commissioners for securing peace in 59, 70n.2

 decimation tax in 114, 123n.62

 ejection of ministers in 158–9, 181n.29, 182n.43

 elections of 1656 in 191, 195

 militia troop in 139, 145, 152n.92

Berry, James (major-general) 22, 26, 27, 28, 29, 30, 31, 35, 39–43, 43–4, 55n.18, 59, 65, 67, 73, 75, 76, 80, 81, 86, 89, 90, 92n.5, 106, 109, 111, 116, 135, 138, 142, 145, 147, 149n.20, 151n.74, 155, 159, 167, 173, 177, 181n.28, 189, 191, 195, 200, 204n.43, 219, 234–5

Bertie, Montague, earl of Lindsey 116

Birch, John 138

Blackburn (Lancashire) 175

Boatman, John 194

Booth, Sir George 193, 214, 236

Boteler, William (major-general) 8, 22, 27, 29, 30, 31, 35, 39–43, 45–6, 65–6, 68, 76, 81, 82, 84, 88, 100, 105, 112, 116, 118, 120n.4, 129, 132, 139, 142, 143, 145, 147, 149n.20, 152n.74, 155, 167, 181n.28, 191, 195, 200, 204n.43, 208, 214, 216, 217, 221, 223, 227n.62, 235

Box (Wiltshire) 160, 162, 164

Boyle, Richard, earl of Clare 109

Boyle, Roger, Lord Broghill 109, 212, 213, 217, 219, 224

Bradshaw, John 4, 83, 193, 195

Brecon (Wales) 159

Brentford (Middlesex) 195

Brereton, Sir William 195

Bridge, Tobias (major-general) 27, 28, 30, 31, 39–43, 52, 90, 137, 158, 163, 189, 191, 193, 200, 204n.43, 208, 223, 238

Bridges, John 219

Bridport (Dorset) 67
Bristol 18, 45, 47, 77, 88, 91
  commissioners for securing peace in
    59, 60, 64, 65, 70n.2
  ejection of ministers in 159, 163, 163–4
Broghill, Lord *see* Boyle, Roger
brothels 156
Buckinghamshire 19, 22, 27, 28, 31, 35, 77,
    78, 81, 236
  commissioners for securing peace in
    59, 69, 70n.2, 110–11, 155
  ejection of ministers in 181n.28,
    182n.43
  militia troops in 141, 144, 152n.92
Burgoyne, Sir Roger 101, 129
Burton, Thomas 40, 208, 213, 214, 218,
    219, 220
Bury St Edmunds (Suffolk) 132, 139
Busbridge, John 61, 65, 82, 144
Bushnell, Walter 160–1, 162, 164, 182n.47

Caernarvonshire
  alehouse regulation in 173
Caerphilly (Monmouthshire) 157
Camarthen 29, 42, 227n.62
Camarthenshire 31, 59
  commissioners for securing peace in
    59, 70n.2
  elections of 1656 in 204n.43
  militia troops in 141
Cambridge 68
Cambridgeshire 18, 22, 27, 31, 76, 103
  commissioners for securing peace in 107
  decimation tax in 114, 122n.49, 123n.62
  ejection of ministers in 182n.43
  militia troops in 141, 152n.92
Cardiganshire 31
  militia troops in 141
Carlisle (Cumberland) 29, 42, 90, 227n.62
Cavendish, William, earl of Devonshire 111,
    116, 147
Chadwick, James 59, 66
charters, town 87–8; *see also* municipal
    government
Chelmsford (Essex) 165
Chepstow (Monmouthshire) 29, 42,
    227n.62, 238
Cheshire 17, 18, 22, 27, 31, 76, 81, 83, 86,
    94n.46, 110, 113, 129, 130, 178,
    236

alehouse regulation in 176
commissioners for securing peace in
    60–1, 64, 69, 70n.2, 103, 193
ejection of ministers in 160, 161,
    182n.43, 183n.55
elections of 1656 in 193, 195
militia troops in 142
Chester 18, 83, 193, 223
  alehouse regulation in 176
Chichester (Sussex) 61, 62, 68, 90
Chipping Wycombe (Buckinghamshire) *see*
    High Wycombe
Christchurch (Hampshire) 108
Claypole, Elizabeth 40–1
Claypole, Lord John 144, 192, 213
Cleveland, John 129
cock-fighting 22
Colchester (Essex) 89–90, 91, 194–5
commissioners for securing the peace of
    the commonwealth 23, 24, 25,
    26, 28, 36n.26, 59–70 *passim*,
    70n.2, 98, 106, 158, 189; *see also*
    under individual counties
committee for compounding 103–4
Compton, James, earl of Northampton 46,
    122n.49, 130, 132
constables 73, 85–7, 168, 172, 174, 175,
    175–6
Coppin, Richard 139
Cornwall 21, 27, 31, 77, 81
  commissioners for securing peace in
    60, 62, 70n.2
  ejection of ministers in 182n.43, 183n.55
  elections of 1656 in 189, 192
  militia troops in 141, 144
corporations *see* municipal government
Coventry (Warwickshire) 73, 74, 75, 77, 89,
    167
  alehouse regulation in 172
Cox, Alban 142, 223–4
Cromwell
  Henry (Oliver's son) 20, 21, 147, 188,
    189, 214, 216, 218, 229
  Henry (Oliver's second cousin) 214, 216
  Richard (Oliver's son) 46, 50, 62, 73,
    191, 234, 235, 237, 238
Cumberland 22, 27, 31, 59
  commissioners for securing peace in
    70n.2
  decimation tax in 114, 123n.62

ejection of ministers in 181n.28,
182n.43, 183n.55
elections of 1656 in 204n.43
militia troops in 141

Dartford (Kent) 140
Dawkins, Roland (deputy major-general)
28, 29, 30, 31, 39–43, 52, 53, 76,
90, 157, 167, 178, 181n.28, 195,
204n.43, 223, 227n.62, 238
Deal (Kent) 135, 136
decimation tax 19, 23, 25, 26, 32, 66, 75, 91,
97–120 *passim*, 137, 144–5, 146,
165, 179, 188, 206, 207, 224,
228, 230
account books for 114–15
exemptions and suspensions from 108–
13
number of royalists assessed for 107
parliamentary debate on 1656–57 *see*
militia bill
Denbighshire 103, 109
Denne, Henry 47
Denton, William 101, 209, 212, 214
Derby 66
Derbyshire 22, 26, 27, 31, 111
commissioners for securing peace in
59, 65, 66, 70n.2, 103
decimation tax in 114, 115, 122n.49,
123n.62
ejection of ministers in 181n.28, 181n.31,
182n.43
Desborough, John (major-general) 18, 21,
24, 27, 28, 29, 30, 31, 35, 39–43,
47, 62, 65, 66, 73, 76, 77, 82, 83–
4, 87, 88, 102, 107, 112, 113, 117,
118, 130, 142, 143, 144, 145,
149n.20, 151n.74, 156, 161, 163,
163–4, 181n.28, 188, 189, 191,
192, 196, 200, 204n.43, 208,
209, 210, 212, 213, 215, 218, 219,
220, 221, 222, 223, 224, 231, 234,
235
Devizes (Wiltshire) 73
Devon 17, 21, 27, 31, 76, 77, 81, 84, 156
commissioners for securing peace in 62
ejection of ministers in 181n.28,
182n.43
militia troops in 141, 144
Dorchester (Dorset) 73

Dorset 17, 18, 19, 21, 27, 31, 76, 77, 82, 109
commissioners for securing peace in
62, 67, 70n.2, 107
ejection of ministers in 181n.31, 182n.43
Dover (Kent) 29, 42, 61, 135, 136, 227n.62
elections of 1656 in 204n.43
drunkards and drunkenness 154, 155, 157,
158, 167, 171–8; *see also* alehouse
regulation
Dugdale, William 7, 130
Dunn, Thomas 133–7 *passim*, 140, 150n.40;
see also register office, in London
Durham (city) 140
Durham (county) 18, 22, 27, 31, 99, 130,
223
commissioners for securing peace in
70n.2, 99
ejection of ministers in 163, 181n.28,
182n.43, 183n.55
elections of 1656 in 193

ejected clergy 25, 32, 154, 158, 159, 164,
165–6, 183n.59, 183n.62
ejection of ministers *see* ejected clergy;
scandalous and insufficient
ministers and schoolmasters
ejectors 23, 64, 158, 163, 181n.28
elections, to 1656 parliament 187–202
passim
Eltisley (Cambridgeshire) 47
enclosure 48, 170–1
Essex 18, 22, 27, 31, 49, 76, 78, 81, 102, 110,
160, 164, 223, 237
alehouse regulation in 172–3
commissioners for securing peace in
69, 70n.2, 78–9, 105
decimation tax in 114, 121n.18, 122n.49,
123n.62, 123n.65
ejection of ministers in 164–5, 181n.28,
182n.43
elections of 1656 in 196, 204n.43
militia troops in 141, 142
Eure, Lord George 141, 209
Evelyn, John 165
Evesham (Worcestershire) 43
Exeter (Devon) 128, 211

fairs *see* markets and fairs
festivities *see* sports and festivities
Fifth Monarchists 4, 43, 49, 137–9, 155, 194

Fleetwood, Charles (major-general) 22, 27, 28, 29, 31, 38, 54n.2, 55n.11, 89, 90, 123n.63, 141, 160, 196, 222, 235, 237
Fleetwood, George (deputy major-general) 28, 30, 31, 39–43, 141, 144, 181n.28, 191, 195, 196, 200, 207, 236–7
Flintshire 79–80
fornication *see* sexual offences
Fox, George 45, 46, 47, 50, 52, 139, 235; *see also* Quakers
Freeman, William 144
Frescheville, John 111, 122n.49

Gauden, John 165
Glamorgan 31, 178
   commissioners for securing peace in 167
   militia troops in 141
Gloucester 19, 88, 192
Gloucestershire 21, 27, 31, 76, 77, 81, 112, 159, 162, 232
   commissioners for securing peace in 65, 66, 70n.2, 192
   ejection of ministers in 163, 182n.43, 183n.55
   elections of 1656 in 192
   militia troops in 141
Glynne, Sir John 210, 219
godly reformation 7, 154–79 *passim*, 228
Goffe, William (major-general) 20, 21, 22, 23, 24, 27, 29, 30, 31, 35, 39–43, 44–5, 47, 53, 61, 62, 65, 68, 73, 76, 77, 79, 82, 85, 90, 100, 101, 104, 105, 106, 109, 113, 117, 118, 138, 139, 140, 141, 142, 144, 145, 146–7, 147, 149n.20, 151n.74, 158, 174, 175, 177, 181n.28, 188, 189, 191–2, 196, 197, 198, 200, 204n.43, 207, 208, 221, 223, 235–6
Goldsmiths Hall committee *see* committee for compounding
Gookin, Vincent 214, 215, 216, 219
Grantham, Thomas 160
Gravesend (Kent) 135
Great Yarmouth (Norfolk) *see* Yarmouth
Grove, Thomas 65
Guise, Christopher 66, 192

Gurnall, William 190
Gwydir (Denbighshire) 103

Haberdashers Hall committee *see* committee for compounding
Hale, Matthew 48, 82, 83, 170
Hampshire 11, 20, 22, 27, 31, 73, 76, 82, 85, 100, 103, 108, 140, 150n.26, 207
   alehouse regulation in 174–5, 177
   commissioners for securing peace in 24, 59, 60, 62, 65, 70n.2, 100, 104, 192, 197
   decimation tax in 114, 123n.62
   ejection of ministers in 182n.43
   elections of 1656 in 191–2, 192, 197, 204n.43
   militia troops in 141, 145, 147, 152n.92, 192, 207, 224
Harley, Edward 195
Haselrig, Sir Arthur 4, 193, 197
Hatsell, Henry 156
Haverfordwest (Pembrokeshire) 90
Haynes, Hezekiah (deputy major-general) 27, 29, 30, 31, 35, 39–43, 49–50, 53, 68, 75, 76, 77, 78, 81, 83, 85, 89, 96n.102, 103, 106, 112, 113, 114, 116, 118, 129, 138, 139, 142, 143, 145, 146, 147, 149n.20, 151n.74, 172, 181n.28, 189, 190, 194, 196, 197, 198, 200, 204n.43, 208, 223, 227n.62, 229, 237
help-ales 174–5
Hereford 138
Herefordshire 22, 27, 31, 76, 81, 85, 88
   commissioners for securing peace in 67–8
   ejection of ministers in 182n.43, 183n.55
   elections of 1656 in 195
   militia troops in 142
Hertfordshire 18, 19, 22, 27, 28, 31, 35, 77, 78, 103, 168, 181n.28, 238
   alehouse regulation in 173
   commissioners for securing peace in 70n.2
   decimation tax in 114, 122n.49, 123n.62
   ejection of ministers in 182n.43
   militia troops in 142, 152n.92, 223–4
Hessay Moor (Yorkshire) 17, 128
High Wycombe (Buckinghamshire) 27, 90
   elections of 1656 in 204n.43

Hobart, John 194, 196, 198, 209
horse races 18, 22, 157, 158, 178; *see also*
    sports and festivities
Horsham (Sussex) 139
Howard, Charles (deputy major-general)
    27, 29, 30, 31, 35, 39–43, 51–2, 53,
    90, 92n.5, 118, 142, 149n.20,
    152n.74, 154, 181n.28, 191, 195,
    200, 201, 204n.43, 208, 214, 221,
    223, 227n.62, 237
Hull (Yorkshire) 90, 183n.55
Huntingdonshire 18, 22, 27, 31, 76, 167
    commissioners for securing peace in
    70n.2, 155
    decimation tax in 114, 122n.49, 123n.62
    ejection of ministers in 182n.43
    militia troops in 143, 152n.92
Hutchinson, Col. John 193
Hutchinson, Lucy 34, 40, 66
Hyde, Edward, earl of Clarendon 8, 32,
    37n.48, 40, 102, 212

Indemnity Act (1657) *see* major-generals,
    indemnity for
Instrument of Government (1653) 2–3, 16,
    28, 187, 189, 209–10
Isle of Ely 18, 22, 27, 31, 76
    militia troops in 141
    elections of 1656 in 194
Isle of Wight 100, 135

Jones Edmund, 109
Jones, Philip 28, 108, 219
Josselin, Ralph 49, 50, 164–5, 196, 201
juries and jurors 73, 79–80, 83–5, 129, 170,
    172, 174, 191
justices of the peace 19, 73, 74–80 *passim*,
    82, 168, 172–7, 229; *see also*
    quarter sessions courts

Kelsey, Thomas (major-general) 22, 27, 29,
    30, 31, 35, 39–43, 52, 53–4, 68,
    69, 77, 90, 107, 112, 116, 118, 130,
    132, 139, 140, 142, 145, 147,
    149n.20, 152n.74, 152n.102, 157,
    181n.28, 191, 195, 197, 198–9,
    200, 204n.43, 208, 212, 214, 223,
    227n.62, 231, 237
Kent 22, 27, 31, 53, 77, 78, 81, 94n.46, 102,
    132, 148

alehouse regulation in 174
commissioners for securing peace in
    60, 61, 65, 67, 68, 69, 70n.2,
    107, 112, 132, 157, 199
decimation tax in 114, 115, 116, 118,
    122n.49, 123n.62, 123n.65
ejection of ministers in 181n.28,
    182n.43, 183n.55
elections of 1656 in 198–9, 204n.43
militia troops in 141, 142
Kidderminster (Worcestershire) 177
kingship, offer of to Oliver Cromwell 217,
    219–22, 224
King's Norton (Worcestershire) 177
Kingsmill, Sir William 104
Kingston (Surrey) 90, 107, 132

Lambert, John (major-general) 3, 21, 22, 23,
    24, 26, 27, 28, 31, 32, 33–4, 38,
    42, 54n.2, 55n.11, 82, 88, 123n.63,
    142, 163, 212, 216, 221, 222, 234,
    235, 237, 238
Lancashire 18, 19, 22, 26, 27, 31, 42, 86,
    106, 130
    alehouse regulation in 175–6, 176–7
    commissioners for securing peace in
    68, 70n.2
    ejection of ministers in 160, 161, 162,
    163, 181n.28, 182n.43, 183n.55
    elections of 1656 in 193, 194
Launceston (Cornwall) 47
Lavenham (Suffolk) 190
Leicester 73, 74, 170
Leicestershire 18, 19, 22, 27, 31, 136, 171
    commissioners for securing peace in
    70n.2, 112
    decimation tax in 121n.18
    ejection of ministers in 159, 160,
    181n.31, 182n.43
Lenthall, William 211
Leominster (Herefordshire) 88
Lewes (Sussex) 119
Lilburne, Robert (deputy major-general) 27,
    29, 30, 31, 35, 39–43, 51, 76, 81,
    84, 90, 99, 106, 112, 113, 117, 118,
    128, 130, 136, 140, 142, 149n.20,
    151n.74, 157, 158, 163, 174, 189,
    191, 193, 200, 204n.43, 213, 223,
    227n.55, 227n.62, 237
Lincoln 43, 48, 89, 92n.5, 159

Index

Lincolnshire 22, 27, 31, 77, 138, 160
    commissioners for securing peace in
        59, 70n.2, 75, 100, 103, 105, 106,
        107, 160
    ejection of ministers in 159, 160,
        181n.28, 181n.31, 182n.43
    elections of 1656 in 192, 204n.44
    militia troops in 141
Lloyd, Sir Edward 109
London 18, 22, 26, 27, 28, 29, 31, 35, 42,
    49, 50, 51, 52, 90–1, 110, 130, 132,
    133, 143, 156–7, 158, 178, 193, 223,
    227n.62
    alehouse regulation in 175
    commissioners for securing peace in
        29, 59, 60, 64, 70n.2
    ejection of ministers in 159
    register office in *see* register office, in
        London
    vagrancy in 168
Long, George 164
Ludlow, Edmund 4, 8, 189, 213, 215, 216

magistrates *see* justices of the peace
Maidstone (Kent) 61, 68, 199
majors-generals
    ages of 39
    associations of 26–8, 30, 31
    commissioners *see* commissioners for
        securing the peace of the
        commonwealth
    commissions to 27
    declaration by Cromwell justifying
        appointment 29–30, 32, 98, 108
    ejections of ministers by 158–66,
        181n.28
    electioneering by 187–202 *passim*, 228
    indemnity for 213, 222–3
    land purchases by 41–2
    military careers of 42
    millenarianism of 44, 49
    political experience of 43
    religious beliefs of 53–4, 154–5
    reputation of 5–12, 230–2
    salaries of 119, 142
    security work of 127–48 *passim*
    social origins of 39–41
    see also militia, major-generals'
markets and fairs 48, 155, 157, 170
Meux, Sir John 100

Middlesex 18, 22, 26, 28, 29, 31, 76, 79, 157
    alehouse regulation in 175
    commissioners for securing peace in
        70n.2, 113
    ejection of ministers in 181n.28,
        182n.43
    elections of 1656 in 195, 204n.43
    militia troops in 118, 141
militia
    major-generals' 20, 140–7, 223–4, 228,
        231
        officers of 142, 196, 197
        pay of 141, 144–7
        raised in 1650 35n.7, 140
        raised in spring of 1655 18
militia bill (1656–57) 5, 40, 119, 208–20
    passim, 221, 223
Mohun, Warwick Lord 116
Monck, George 28, 43, 50, 234–5, 235, 236,
    238
Monmouth 75, 90
    alehouse regulation in 173
Monmouthshire 18, 28, 31, 109
    ejection of ministers in 181n.28,
        182n.43
    elections of 1656 in 204n.43
    militia troops in 141, 142
Monson, Sir John 107
Montgomeryshire 109
Moore, John 170
moral reformation *see* godly reformation
Morley, Sir William 106
Morpeth (Northumberland) 17, 128
municipal government 73, 87–91

Nantwich (Cheshire) 175, 193
Nayler, James 45, 46, 47, 48, 50, 51, 52,
    208; *see also* Quakers
Neville, Henry 193, 195
Newcastle (Northumberland) 17, 42, 92n.5
Nicholas, John (deputy major-general) 28,
    29, 30, 31, 39–43, 52, 181n.28,
    195, 204n.43, 223, 227n.62, 234
Norfolk 22, 27, 31, 78, 81, 106, 113, 138
    alehouse regulation in 173
    commissioners for securing peace in
        68, 70n.2, 99, 103, 112–13, 198
    ejection of ministers in 181n.28,
        182n.43
    elections of 1656 in 194, 196, 198

militia troops in 141, 152n.92
Northampton 66, 139, 195
Northamptonshire 18, 22, 27, 31, 46, 76,
    81, 139, 167, 223, 235
  commissioners for securing peace in
    66, 70n.2, 99
  decimation tax in 114, 122n.49, 123n.62
  ejection of ministers in 181n.28,
    182n.43
  elections of 1656 in 195, 204n.43
  militia troops in 139, 141, 143–4, 144
Northumberland 22, 27, 31
  commissioners for securing peace in
    70n.2
  ejection of ministers in 181n.28,
    182n.43, 183n.55
  elections of 1656 in 193
Norwich (Norfolk) 20, 89, 194, 198
  militia troops in 141
Nottingham 66, 92n.5, 193
Nottinghamshire 5, 22, 27, 31, 34, 77, 111,
    167, 168
  alehouse regulation in 172
  commissioners for securing peace in
    40, 59, 66, 69, 70n.2, 103, 106,
    114, 117
  decimation tax in 114, 117, 123n.62
  ejection of ministers in 160, 181n.28,
    181n.31, 182n.43
  elections of 1656 in 204n.43

Oundle (Northamptonshire) 45
Owen, John 45, 46, 48, 235
Oxford 42, 90, 92n.5
  elections of 1656 in 196
Oxfordshire 19, 22, 27, 28, 31, 35, 81, 109,
    160
  commissioners for securing peace in
    70n.2
  ejection of ministers in 159, 182n.43
  elections of 1656 in 204n.43
  militia troops in 152n.92
Oxinden, Henry 148

Packe, Sir Christopher 217, 219, 221
Packer, William (deputy major-general) 8,
    28, 29, 30, 31, 39–43, 50–1, 53,
    77, 87, 90, 92n.5, 142, 149n.20,
    152n.74, 158, 181n.28, 191, 195,
    196, 200, 204n.43, 208, 235, 238

parliaments
  Barebone's (1653) 2, 15, 43, 52, 170, 221
  first protectorate (1654) 3, 5, 15–16, 43,
    221
  Rump (1649–53) 2, 44, 87, 88, 211, 221
  second protectorate (1656) 5, 119, 148,
    171, 178, 187, 206–24 *passim*
    elections to 187–202 *passim*
    exclusions from 197–8, 198, 199–201
    individuals returned to 197
Paulet, John, marquis of Winchester 100
Pembrokeshire 31
  militia troops in 141
Penruddock, Col. John 17, 83; *see also*
    royalists, uprisings of March 1655
    by
petty sessions, by justices of the peace 175
Pickering, Sir Gilbert 21, 123n.63, 195, 212,
    223
Pierrepont, William 216, 219
Plymouth (Devon) 135
Poole (Dorset) 67
poor relief *see* poverty and the poor
Pordage, John 181n.29
Portland (Dorset) 67
ports, deputy-registers in 135–6
Portsmouth (Hampshire) 62, 153n.102
posts 139–40
poverty and the poor 79, 166–71, 228
Powell, Vavasour 43, 138, 155
Pride, Thomas 28–9, 157
prostitutes 91, 156; *see also* brothels
Prynne, William 5–6, 7, 8, 78, 231

Quakers 4, 43, 45, 46, 49, 51, 52, 137–9,
    144, 164, 192, 208, 223, 235; *see
    also* Fox, George; Nayler, James
quarter sessions courts 75, 76, 79, 80, 84,
    162, 168, 180n.12
  alehouse regulation by 172–7
  prosecutions for immorality at 79, 157

Reading (Berkshire) 42, 139, 195
  elections of 1656 in 196
reformation of manners *see* godly
    reformation
register office, in London 26, 133–7, 148,
    150n.40, 228; *see also* Dunn,
    Thomas; ports, deputy-registers
    in

Robinson, Luke 119, 120, 209, 212, 227n.55
Rochester (Kent) 139
Roman Catholics 22, 101, 129
royalists 147–8, 148
  appearances at London register office by
    134–5
  disarming of 129, 228
  security bonds taken from 26, 27, 46,
    129–33, 149n.20, 228
  uprisings of March 1655 by 8, 15, 16–17,
    19, 20, 25, 83, 127–8, 161, 228–9
Rufford Abbey (Nottinghamshire) 17, 128
Rutland 18, 22, 27, 31, 76, 167
  decimation tax in 114, 120n.4, 123n.62
  ejection of ministers in 181n.31, 182n.43
  militia troops in 141, 152n.92
Rye (Sussex) 68, 135, 136

sabbath, profanation of 91, 155, 156–7, 158,
  161, 174, 175, 176, 223
St John, Oliver 216, 219
Salford (Lancashire) 175, 176–7
Salisbury (Wiltshire) 174, 192
Sancroft, William 147, 160
scandalous and insufficient ministers and
  schoolmasters
  ejection of by major-generals 158–66,
    179
  ordinance for ejection of (1654) 23, 154,
    155, 158, 162, 163
  see also ejected clergy; ejectors
security bonds *see* royalists
sexual offences 156, 158, 161, 176, 180n.13
Shaftesbury (Dorset) 140
Sheffield, Edmund, earl of Mulgrave
  123n.63
Sheppard, William 88
sheriffs 29, 73, 80–2, 229
Shrewsbury (Shropshire) 17, 73, 81, 86,
  167, 177
Shropshire 17, 22, 27, 31, 76, 81, 177
  alehouse regulation in 173
  commissioners for securing peace in
    70n.2, 129
  ejection of ministers in 182n.43
Sidney, Philip, viscount Lisle 123n.63
Simpson, John 50, 52
Sindercombe Plot 220
Skippon, Philip (major-general) 18, 22, 27,
  28, 31, 54n.2

Slingsby, Sir Henry 128
Somerset 17, 19, 21, 27, 31, 76, 77, 168, 188,
  220
  alehouse regulation in 174
  commissioners for securing peace in
    62, 105
  ejection of ministers in 181n.28, 181n.31,
    182n.43
  elections of 1656 in 204n.43
  militia troops in 141, 144
Southampton (Hampshire) 62, 140, 192
South Molton (Devon) 17
sports and festivities 156–8, 174, 175, 178;
  see also horse races
Stafford 63
Staffordshire 18, 22, 26, 27, 31, 76, 79, 110,
  113, 130
  alehouse regulation in 175
  commissioners for securing peace in
    60, 62–4, 67, 70n.2, 79
  ejection of ministers in 160, 161,
    181n.31, 182n.43, 183n.55
  elections of 1656 in 193, 194
Stamford (Lincolnshire) 158, 192
Stepney (Middlesex) 156, 157
Stowmarket (Suffolk) 190
Strickland, Walter 108
Sturgeon, John 138–9
Suffolk 18, 19, 22, 27, 31, 76, 77, 78, 85, 132,
  138
  commissioners for securing peace in
    68–9, 70n.2, 132, 196
  decimation tax in 114, 118, 123n.62
  ejection of ministers in 182n.43
  elections of 1656 in 190, 194, 196
  militia troops in 141, 142, 152n.92, 194
Surrey 22, 27, 29, 31, 78
  commissioners for securing peace in
    107, 132
  ejection of ministers in 181n.31,
    182n.43, 183n.55
  militia troops in 142
Sussex 20, 22, 27, 31, 45, 76, 77, 79, 82,
  102, 106, 108, 113, 119, 139, 223
  commissioners for securing peace in
    23–4, 60, 61–2, 68, 70n.2, 104,
    105
  decimation tax in 104, 114, 122n.49,
    123n.62
  ejection of ministers in 182n.43

elections of 1656 in 192, 197–8
militia troops in 141, 144, 145, 152n.92
Sutton, Robert, Lord Lexington 111
swearing and swearers 154, 155, 158, 176

Tenby (Pembrokeshire) 42
Tewkesbury (Gloucestershire) 88
Tiverton (Devon) 88
towns *see* municipal government
Trevor, John 119, 120, 213, 231
Triers 25, 44, 50, 158

Ussher, James, archbishop of Armagh 165–6

vagrants and vagabonds 166–9, 179, 230
Vane, Sir Henry (the younger) 192, 193,
    196, 204n.44
Verney, Sir Ralph 49, 101, 110–11, 129, 131,
    132, 209, 214

Wakefield (Yorkshire) 157
Warwick 67
Warwickshire 22, 27, 31, 129, 168
    alehouse regulation in 172
    commissioners for securing peace in
        67, 74, 101, 102
    ejection of ministers in 160, 162,
        182n.43
    poor relief in 171
Wales 18, 22, 26, 27, 28, 29, 31, 35, 43, 44,
    76, 103, 106, 159, 181n.28
    commissioners for securing peace in
        59, 65, 70n.2, 107, 109
    decimation tax in 116–17, 118
    militia troops in 141
    see also under individual counties
Weaver, John 192, 197
weights and measures, regulation of 170
Wellingborough (Northamptonshire) 167
Western Design 15, 21, 33
Westminster 18, 26, 28, 29, 31, 45, 130, 168
    alehouse regulation in 175
    elections of 1656 in 195
Westmorland 22, 27, 31, 59
    commissioners for securing peace in
        70n.2
    decimation tax in 114, 123n.62
    ejection of ministers in 181n.28,
        182n.43, 183n.55
    militia troops in 141

Whalley (Lancashire) 175
Whalley, Edward (major-general) 22, 26,
    27, 29, 30, 31, 35, 39–43, 47–8,
    53, 66, 73, 74, 75, 76, 77, 82, 83,
    87, 88, 89, 92n.5, 100, 101, 102,
    103, 104, 105, 111, 113, 117, 118,
    128, 129, 131, 138, 142, 149n.20,
    151n.74, 155, 158, 159, 167, 169,
    170–1, 172, 178, 179, 181n.28,
    189, 191, 192, 197, 200, 204n.43,
    207, 208, 221, 222, 229, 235–6
Whitelocke, Bulstrode 210, 213
Widdrington, Sir Thomas 109, 209–10
Wiltshire 17, 21, 24, 27, 31, 76, 109, 112,
    168
    alehouse regulation in 174
    commissioners for securing peace in
        65, 70n.2, 112
    decimation tax in 117
    ejection of ministers in 160–1, 162, 164,
        181n.31, 182n.43
    militia troops in 141
Winchester (Hampshire) 17, 45, 62, 175,
    197, 207
Wolseley, Sir Charles 110, 123n.63, 219
Woodstock (Oxfordshire) 196
    elections of 1656 in 204n.43
Worcester 138
Worcestershire 22, 26, 27, 31, 43, 76, 80,
    110, 168
    alehouse regulation in 173–4
    commissioners for securing peace in
        70n.2, 106
    ejection of ministers in 182n.43,
        182n.46
    elections of 1656 in 204n.43
    militia troops in 142
Worsley, Charles (major-general) 22, 26,
    27, 28, 29, 30, 31, 35, 39–43, 48–
    9, 53, 75, 76, 79, 81, 83, 84, 86,
    87, 90, 103, 105, 106, 113, 117,
    129, 130, 131, 140, 142, 143, 145,
    149n.20, 152n.74, 155, 157, 159,
    160, 162, 163, 166, 167, 175–7,
    178, 179, 181n.28, 188, 193, 229,
    234
Wriothesley, Thomas, earl of Southampton
    107, 132, 150n.26
Wynn, Sir Owen 102–3

Yarmouth (Norfolk) 42, 132, 173
York 17, 18, 29, 51, 90, 236
Yorkshire 18, 19, 22, 27, 31, 34, 35, 51, 76,
        81, 84, 85, 106, 128, 130, 131, 156,
        157, 162, 183n.63, 209
    alehouse regulation in 174
    commissioners for securing peace in
        70n.2, 86, 117
    decimation tax in 117
    ejection of ministers in 158–9, 163,
        182n.43, 183n.55
    elections of 1656 in 193, 204n.43
    militia troops in 141, 142
    sexual offences in 180n.13

9368